SHAKESPEARE
STUDIES

All editorial correspondence concerning *Shakespeare Studies* should be addressed to the Editorial Office, *Shakespeare Studies*, Department of English, University of Maryland (Baltimore County), Catonsville, Maryland 21228. Send two copies of submitted articles and return postage. Correspondence concerning orders and subscriptions should be addressed to: Associated University Presses, 440 Forsgate Drive, Cranbury, New Jersey 08512.

SHAKESPEARE STUDIES VOLUME XXI

EDITOR
Leeds Barroll

ASSOCIATE EDITOR
Barry Gaines

Rutherford ● Madison ● Teaneck
Fairleigh Dickinson University Press
London and Toronto: Associated University Presses

Associated University Presses
440 Forsgate Drive
Cranbury, NJ 08512

Associated University Presses
25 Sicilian Avenue
London WC1A 2QH, England

Associated University Presses
P.O. Box 338, Port Credit
Mississauga, Ontario
Canada L5G 4L8

The paper used in this publication meets the requirements of the American National Standard for Permanence of Paper for Printed Library Materials Z39.48-1984.

International Standard Book Number 0-8386-3520-2 (vol. xxi)
International Standard Serial Number 0582-9399

PRINTED IN THE UNITED STATES OF AMERICA

Contents

Contributors

James P. Bednarz
Associate Professor of English, Long Island University (C. W. Post Campus)

Maurice Charney
Professor of English, Rutgers University

Derek Cohen
Associate Professor of English, Bethune College, York University

A. Stuart Daley
Professor Emeritus of English, Drake University

Charles Forker
Professor Emeritus of English, Indiana University

Henk K. Gras
Lecturer in Theatre Studies, University of Utrecht

Donna B. Hamilton
Professor of English, University of Maryland (College Park)

Nancy Elizabeth Hodge
Executive Secretary, Shakespeare Association of America

Joan Ozark Holmer
Professor of English, Georgetown University

Henry E. Jacobs
Late of University of Alabama

Janel Mueller
Professor of English and Humanities, University of Chicago

Contributors

JAMES L. O'ROURKE
Assistant Professor of English, Florida State University

REMINGTON P. PATTERSON
Professor of English, Barnard College

JEANNE ADDISON ROBERTS
Professor of Literature, American University

MARVIN ROSENBERG
Professor Emeritus of Dramatic Art, University of California, Berkeley

PETER L. RUDNYTSKY
Associate professor of English, University of Florida

GRACE C. TIFFANY
Assistant professor of English, University of New Orleans

MATTHEW H. WIKANDER
Associate Professor of English, Toledo University

W. B. WORTHEN
Professor of English and Theatre, Northwestern University

SHAKESPEARE STUDIES

Miles Mosse's *The Arraignment and Conviction of Vsurie* (1595): A New Source for *The Merchant of Venice*

Joan Ozark Holmer

Shylock's biblical defense of usury in his confrontation with Antonio in the third scene of *The Merchant of Venice* has been variously interpreted, but what truly puzzles us is why, with all the explicit passages on usury in the Bible to choose from, Shylock would use as his defense the Jacob-Laban story from chapter thirty of Genesis, which seems totally unrelated to usury. Indeed, what does this story about gaining wealth by breeding sheep have to do with usury as "a way to thrive" (1.3.84)? The biblical allusion does not appear in any of Shakespeare's narrative sources for his play. Moreover, Shakespeare *adds* the important element of usury to his main source for the flesh-bond story, Ser Giovanni Fiorentino's *Il Pecorone*, in which neither the Jew figure nor the merchant figure is associated with usury, whether for or against it; however, in the criticism on the play, usury is probably the most underestimated, or even misunderstood, element.

John Russell Brown speaks for most critics of the play in claiming that the Jacob-Laban story "has not been found in any sixteenth-century book on usury."[1] However, Miles Mosse's *The Arraignment and Conviction of Vsurie* not only specifically refers twice to the Jacob-Laban story at prominent points in the text (the preface and the conclusion), but also this "trial" of usury seems to have influenced Shakespeare's play in a variety of other significant ways. I propose that it is a new source for *The Merchant of Venice*.[2] This essay, however, does not intend to present an all-encompassing interpretation of the entire play or even of such complex characters as Shylock and Antonio. Rather, it seeks to validate a new source, to explain the significance of usury in the play in light of that source, and to show how artfully Shakespeare adapts it to his own ends. Why might the problem of usury be so pertinent for Shakespeare's audience, how might usury be defined, and why might usury be condemned as violating God's law, charity, friendship, nature, and even commutative justice? How and why did Shakespeare incorporate usury into *The Merchant of Venice*?

I

In 1595, a time corresponding to scholars' best estimates for the composition date of *The Merchant of Venice*,[3] Miles Mosse published an important treatise on usury: *The Arraignment and Conviction of Vsurie. That is. The iniquitie, and vnlawfulnes of vsurie, displayed in sixe Sermons, preached at Saint Edmunds Burie in Suffolke, vpon Prouerb. 28.8.*[4] Mosse swells the ranks of a group of traditionalist writers at the end of the sixteenth century who fulminated against the growing practice of usury in Elizabethan England and who accurately argued that the Act Against Usury of 1571, tolerating (but not approving) a 10 percent rate of return in England, was chiefly intended to curtail usury.[5] R. H. Tawney describes Mosse as the writer who, following Thomas Wilson, "produced the most elaborate discussion of usury in the latter part of the century," and Richard Greaves finds Mosse's treatise "to be the most learned work by an Elizabethan Puritan on usury."[6] Mosse's dedicatory epistle, preface, list of authorities, and organizational format suggest Mosse intended his treatise to be a major statement on the subject. His title page bears a Latin inscription from St. Ambrose denouncing usury. It proclaims that Mosse is a "Minister of the worde, and Bacheler of Diuinitie,"[7] that his book has been "seene and allowed by authoritie," and that the reader should "reade all, or censure none." His governing scriptural text of Prov. 28:8 reads: *"He that increaseth his riches by vsurie and interest, gathereth them for him that will be mercifull to the poore"* (sig. C1). The book is 171 pages long, excluding 18 pages of prefatory material that comprises the dedicatory epistle, the preface "To the Christian Reader," and an alphabetical list of *"the names of the speciall Authors vsed in this treatise: besides the bookes of the holie and Canonicall Scriptures."* The list of no fewer than 157 names (additional authors are cited in his marginalia) includes a wide variety of authors—classical (e.g., Aristotle, Cicero, Plato, Virgil), "the Fathers" (e.g., Ambrose, Augustine, Chrysostom), "the schoolemen" (e.g., Thomas Aquinas, Peter Lombard, Dionysius Carthusianus, Gabriel Biel), and "the late writers" (e.g., Luther, Musculus, Hemmingsen, Viguerius; see p. 114). Mosse protests that he is publishing the list not out of vainglory, but because someone had misused in print these "*names of* [his] *mouth . . . farre otherwise then they were deliuered by* [him], *or they are in themselues*" (sig. C2).

The dedicatory epistle is addressed to the archbishop of Canterbury, John Whitgift, to whom only three other books were dedicated in 1595. Mosse has chosen "Iohn Archbishop of Canturburie" as his dedicatee for three reasons: the debate about usury needs a wise "arbitrer of much reading, experience, and moderation" because usury is "being controuerted in these dayes among manie (and those verie learned) diuines"; the archbishop has a reputation for neither lending nor taking upon usury, and because he is guiltless of this sin, he may the more freely judge the ungodliness of it; and the archbishop's position grants him a special role in maintaining the laws of the Church of England which prohibit the practice of usury (sigs. A4–A4v). In his preface to the Christian reader, Mosse acknowledges that others in various places, such as Cambridge, have written cogently against usury, and even in London, men like Wilson, Smith, Caesar, and Turnbull have inveighed against this ungodly practice. But Mosse promotes his book for a London audience because usury is "not hetherto thorowly conuicted in the consciences of the people, much lesse put to death and executed as it should" be (sig. B4). The typographical format and careful organization of the text further indicate the seriousness of Mosse's intent to educate his London readers. He provides an outline of major points at the beginning of the text and more specialized outlines at the beginning of each sermon. He uses summary captions at the head of each page, and he includes documentary marginalia. The four principal points his treatise seeks to address are: (1) the description and definition of usury; (2) the condemnation of usury on the basis of Scripture and various other arguments; (3) the refutation of any defenses for usury (especially those attempting to use Scripture); and (4) the examination of why usury should not be practiced by a Christian (especially an English Christian)—"*no not though it could be proued, that it is not simplie forbidden in the Scriptures*" (sig. C2v).

Mosse's treatise consists of six sermons, the first preached in March of 1592 and the next five preached between April and July of 1593. In his first sermon, crucial for the Elizabethan controversy over usury, he explains why he has chosen Prov. 28:8 for his text and why his argument is so important for his present audience (pp. 2–9). He presents various definitions of usury and its sundry kinds and branches, some of which are developed further in his subsequent sermons. For the modern reader this sermon can be quite confusing, despite Mosse's pains to be organized and lucid, but its ultimate aim is to define by evaluating received opinions what precisely constitutes usury that is condemned by the word of God. In what appears to be an etymologically based discussion of the term usury, Mosse explores what is in this word to conclude, as do other authorities such as Bullinger, that usury has a proper and an improper signification (use versus abuse). Usury properly signifies the use of a thing, and therefore this kind of usury is not generally unlawful, because of necessity no man can live without the use of many things (pp. 10–11, 32). What Mosse argues is "condemned by the word of God" is "the sinne or fault of vsurie" (pp. 31–32)—not "the name of vsurie" but "the abuse of vsurie" (p. 11). Consequently, Mosse reviews various old and new definitions of usury, progressively limiting the scope of definition so that he aligns himself basically with the more recent restrictive stance that not all usury is sinful, a stance espoused by Calvin, Bucer, Beza, and Bullinger. Because Mosse is vehemently opposed to sinful usury, he carefully describes these authors as "godly writers who have large tolerations (that I may not say approbations) of some kind of vsurie" (p. 20). For example, Mosse sees natural, spiritual, and voluntary ("liberall") usury as lawful kinds (pp. 12–15, 17–18), but he sees as sinful two branches of civil usury, namely "Outward or Actuall" usury (with its "Open" and "Cloaked" kinds of compacting usury) and "mentall vsurie," focusing on these latter kinds of usury because they "fall into controuersie and question in these daies" (pp. 16, 19).

Mosse is primarily concerned to educate his audience about what constitutes sinful usury because he sees enlightenment as the best means for reforming misinformed opinion, whereby men mistakenly judge according to what is right in their own eyes and what is gainful to their own purse, rather than judging by God's word (pp. 170–71). The word of God, repeatedly upheld throughout the treatise, is Mosse's yardstick for all final judgments. Therefore, the climax of the first sermon is Mosse's definition of "Open, Outward, and Actuall vsurie," which he takes "to be forbidden by the word of God" (p. 31) and which he will discuss further in his next two sermons. Revealing the fundamental importance of this matter of definition, Mosse presents three different rephrasings of his definition (pp. 31–32). Then, as if to avoid any possible confusion, he proceeds to spell out the four "thinges" ("whereupon dependeth the waight and substance of this controuersie") that must "concur" for the sin of usury to occur: (1) lending; (2) lending for gain; (3) compacting for gain; and (4) not risking the principal (p. 32). Unless otherwise specified, I will use the term usury in its sinful sense, as Mosse himself does with the exception of his first sermon.

II

The contemporary controversy over usury that prompted Mosse to publish his sermons in 1595 found dramatic voice in Shakespeare's *The Merchant of Venice*, especially regarding the more intensely discussed kinds of usury (covert usury and mental usury), rendering this play far more timely for Shakespeare's audience than has usually been recognized. Let us begin by considering the significance of Mosse's two original Jacob-Laban references. In his preface "*To the Christian* Reader" Mosse uses Laban's harassment of Jacob as an analogy for his own harassment by the raging usurers whom he has sought to serve spiritually through enlightened argument. Mosse complains that since he began preaching about the evils of usury, he has incurred much ill will, even from those who professed to be interested in hearing the cause debated. Other writers on usury, such as Thomas Wilson, use the genre of dialogue to present their case. Because Parliament was not actively debating usury at this time, Mosse's emphasis on debate may be the most likely source for Shakespeare's decision to stage a debate between Shylock and Antonio to present the case for and against usury in *The Merchant of Venice*. Mosse complains that for debating usury he has been slandered behind his back and insulted to his face—he has been "bitten and backbitten": "*The best and most temperate men / of that trade [usury], though before they seemed desirous to heare the cause [of usury] debated: yet since that time they haue dealt with me, as Laban dealt with Iacob, when he sawe how God had blessed him;*[n] *their countenance hath not been towards me*" (sigs. B3–B3v). Mosse's marginal gloss refers his reader to Gen. 31:2, which explains Laban's hostility toward Jacob as due to the fact that Jacob so successfully increased his flocks by the wand device described at the end of the preceding chapter (Gen. 30:30–43); Shylock refers to this in his defense of usury (1.3.66–85). Mosse, like Jacob, has been so blessed by God (albeit not by increased wealth) that he may rejoice in his freedom from the sin of usury and in his thriving as a preacher. Mosse's successes have inflamed defenders of usury who "so raged and stormed . . . [that he] had almost waxed proude with conceit that [he] had spoken much against them" (sig. B3). Mosse's reference to pride may find a parallel in *The Merchant of Venice* in the play's reference to the proud posture of Antonio; his posture infuriates Shylock, who refers to Antonio as "so smug upon the mart" (3.1.41; cf. 1.3.102–3). Moreover, in this Jacob-Laban reference, Mosse equates himself with Jacob and London's usurers with Laban. As we shall discover, Shylock's spiritual affinity is with Laban rather than Jacob, though he wishes to identify with the latter.

The context in which Mosse's first reference to the Jacob-Laban story appears is at least as important for Shakespeare's play as the reference itself is. Mosse's preface to the Christian reader precedes his list of principal points to be argued. One of those points is to prove that Scripture provides no justification for usury. This cardinal point surfaces surprisingly early in Mosse's preface. It immediately precedes the Jacob-Laban reference. Mosse fumes that the worst kind of usurers ("*the worst in nature, and in the highest degree of sinne*") and "*those of whom* [he has] *most cause to complaine*" are those who ignore or misuse Scripture in order to practice usury: "*There is no Vsurer about vs (that I knowe) so simple and ignorant, but he can relate what is sayd against*" vsurie "*in the word. And on the other side, there is none so well learned about vs, (I dare auouch) that is able to iustifie and defend it by the word*" (sig. B3).

Mosse's concern with the abuse of Scripture by the worst kind of usurers, juxtaposed with his explicit reference to the Jacob-Laban story, strikingly anticipates Shakespeare's selection of that very biblical story as Shylock's defense for usury, a scriptural defense which necessarily fosters Antonio's contrary exegesis and his "education" of Bassanio through his reprimand of Shylock: "Mark you this Bassanio, / The devil can cite Scripture for his purpose" (1.3.92–93). Although the notion that the devil can cite Scripture is biblical in origin (see Matt. 4:5 and Luke 4:10), Shakespeare is further inspired in his characterization of Shylock as a usurer by Mosse's conviction that the worst usurers cite Scripture in their defense. Such a similar association of idea and exact biblical allusion, not found in any other known sixteenth-century sources, cannot be mere coincidence.

Later in his treatise Mosse further excoriates the corruption of his age. Not only do usurers cloak their sin with a pretense of righteousness, "but some haue so farre forgotten themselues, as that they runne on openly to defend it" (p. 6). In explaining how it is that the word of God is used to defend usury, Mosse proclaims in the opening sentence of his fifth sermon: "There is no Scripture so euident, but it hath been, or may be misconstrued: neither is there any trueth, so cleare and bright, whereupon the inuention of man may not cast some cloudie darkenes" (p. 112). The most abused scriptural passages, Mosse contends, concern usury. Shakespeare's decision to have Antonio biblically refute Shylock's attempt to defend usury by Scripture therefore probably derives from Mosse. Shakespeare also forgoes whatever historical reasons he might have Shylock offer in defense of his usury to stress instead that Shylock's defense is based on personal preference and misinterpretation of Scripture, thereby underlining Shylock's need for enlightenment about the evil of usury.

Mosse condemns all sinful or unlawful usury on the page preceding his condemnation of the worst usurers as abusers of the Word. Although he is writing not for a Jewish but rather for a Christian— specifically London—audience, his rigor in attacking the immorality of usury permits no excuse for anyone—infidel or Christian—to practice it: "*Those that be ignorant for want of the word, are without question much to be pitied: and yet is their want that way, the iust punishment of sinne*" (sigs. B2–B2v). Later he makes the connection that is at the center of *The Merchant of Venice* between the Jews and usury by calling it "this unchristian, this heathenish, this Jewish kinde of practise," whereby usurious Christians become heathens or Jews in terms of their behavior. Usury is the main bone of contention between Antonio and Shylock. Shylock tells us that he hates Antonio because he is a Christian and even more because he lends money freely (1.3.37–40). Antonio hates Shylock because he practices usury and therefore violates human friendship (1.3.125–32) and makes victims moan. Antonio underestimates Shylock's hatred of his Christianity (3.3.21–24) as Shylock overestimates Antonio's hatred of his Judaism (3.1.52). Both men can disrespect and misperceive the other. For example, if Shylock is absolutely right that his being a Jew is the main reason Antonio hates him, how can we explain Antonio's approval of Shylock as soon as Shylock appears to forgo a usurious loan, yet still remains a Jew by faith (1.3.134–74)? How also can we explain why Antonio bears no personal animosity toward Tubal, another Venetian Jew and Shylock's friend?

However, Mosse's designation of usury as an unchristian or Jewish practice indicates that, for Elizabethans, matters of money and faith are integrally related. Shylock resents Antonio's calling him a "usurer" (3.1.43), and he sees free lending as a specifically "Christian cur'sy" (3.1.44) and a foolish one at that (1.3.38; 3.3.2). Perhaps responding to Shylock's clue that he thinks "mercy" and lending "money gratis" sheer folly (3.3.1–2), Antonio finally concludes that Shylock hates him because he has often delivered from Shylock's forfeitures those who have appealed to him for financial assistance (3.3.21–24). By the time of the trial, Antonio, resigned to Shylock's obduracy, no longer addresses Shylock by his personal name but rather by his religious epithet, "the Jew," declaring nothing is harder than "his Jewish heart" (4.1.79–80). With controlled contempt, Shylock shrewdly refuses to tell the court his real reasons for hating "the Christian" (4.1.314) that he has shared with us and with Tubal: "So can I give no reason, nor I will not, / More than a lodg'd hate and a certain loathing / I bear Antonio . . . " (4.1.59–61). As I have written elsewhere, Antonio's participation in Shylock's judgment is Shakespeare's own complex innovation, fusing financial and religious concerns, but at least one probable, and often overlooked, motive for Antonio's conversion stipulation is an attempt to curtail Shylock's usury. The genuine success of any such attempt, as the Elizabethans would be the first to acknowledge, depends on Shylock's inner self, his true will and intent.

But unlike our typically modern divorce between issues of wealth and faith, the Elizabethans would be inclined to argue that how one views and uses wealth depends on one's faith and whether or not one rightly understands that faith and enacts its principles or betrays them. Shylock and Antonio, like the mis-choosers Morocco and Arragon, deserve our sympathy because they, like us, often choose wrongly when they are passionately convinced that they choose rightly. Shylock believes he is right to practice usury as he does, and Antonio just as strongly believes he is right to ridicule Shylock for the same practice. Each will be weighed in the balance and found wanting; legitimate disgreement should not degenerate to hateful persecution. True changes in outward human behavior derive chiefly from inward changes in beliefs or attitudes.

Hence, Mosse's treatise attempts to educate his audience, an emphasis which Shakespeare also adapts for his theatrical medium, wherein we are invited to entertain new ways of seeing and perhaps end up judging ourselves as well.

Material relevant to *The Merchant of Venice* literally frames Mosse's first Jacob-Laban allusion. Prefaced with a condemnation of the worst usurers, the allusion is concluded with the opposite motif of praise for the man guiltless of usury. In Mosse's gratitude for God's blessing of his spiritual thriving, he confides to the reader: "*I may say without boasting, as did the Prophet* [Jeremiah; marginal gloss refers to Jer. 15:10], *I haue neither lent nor taken vpon vsurie . . .* " (sig. B3v).Shakespeare emphasizes that his Christian merchant neither lends nor takes usury (1.3.56, 65). This surprising point is not found in any of Shakespeare's narrative sources, but it is noteworthy in Mosse's book and is particularly important, because Christian merchants in both Elizabethan society and literature were the most notorious merchants; however, Shakespeare's "royal merchant" (4.1.29) anticipates the merchant-prince figure of civic heroism that begins to gain literary dominance in the 1590's over the old, despicable usurer-merchant figure.[8] Just as Shylock is the only Jewish usurer Antonio attacks, so also only Antonio, of all the Christian merchants in Shakespeare's Venice, is singled out by Shylock as dangerous because he lends freely and "brings down / The rate of usance here with us in Venice" (1.3.39–40). Later, in the midst of his discussion of what constitutes "gain," Mosse disgresses to emphasize the rarity of contemporary Christian men who lend freely: "And certainelie that free lending in these dayes is so scante, and that all lending is almost turned into vsurie, is no small argument that true Christians, righteous & mercifull men, begin to growe rare & geason [sic] in the world" (p. 45).[9]

In his dedicatory epistle, Mosse extols Archbishop Whitgift for never committing the sin of usury, and the way in which Mosse praises the archbishop's purity is especially suggestive for how Shakespeare presents Antonio:

> . . . your *Grace* is reported to bee one, who neither lendeth, nor taketh vpon *vsurie*, which is not in this age euery such mans commendation. And therefore being free from the guiltines of this sinne, you may the more freelie giue sentence vpon the vngodlines thereof. [Mosse now quotes and translates Ambrose's sentiments on this idea of just judg-

ment.] "Let him iudge of an other mans default, who hath not the same fault to condemne in himselfe: Let him iudge of another, who committeth not the same things which hee deemeth worthie the punishing in another." (Sigs. A4–A4v).

In act 1, scene 3, Shakespeare enriches this motif of fair judgment by complicating it through irony and dilemma. He improves on Mosse's idea of the guiltless, praiseworthy Christian by portraying Antonio not just as an avoider of usury, but also as a champion who actively combats usury by lending out "money gratis" (1.3.39) and who often delivers from Shylock's forfeitures "many that have at times made moan to [him]" (3.3.21–24). Antonio thus fits the description in Prov. 28:8 of a man who "will be merciful to the poore." Here we encounter a significant paradox. Antonio's decision to make an exception ("break a custom," 1.3.59) and engage in a usurious bond with Shylock "to supply the ripe wants of [his] friend" (1.3.58) ironically renders him guilty of that for which he condemns Shylock. Antonio seems oblivious to how his superficially good reasons for engaging in usury on his friend's behalf violate a fundamental Christian principle, a principle used by writers like Mosse to condemn usury even when the cause is a good one, such as relieving orphans or redeeming Christians from the Turks: *"We must not doe euill that good may come thereof"* (Mosse, p. 160; cf. Rom. 3:8). This same principle underlies Bassanio's plea to the disguised Portia in the trial scene when Bassanio begs, "Wrest once the law to your authority,— / To do a great right, do a little wrong" (4.1 211–12). Shakespeare, then, crafts for Antonio a highly charged dilemma, fraught with ironic implications, involving the employment of usury to do good. Mosse's treatise provides a helpful moral perspective for interpreting Antonio's dilemma, and, as I have suggested elsewhere, Shakespeare molds this dilemma to rouse further the audience's curiosity about the character of the mysteriously melancholic Antonio as well as to involve the audience in another of the play's many difficult choices.

Mosse's second reference to the Jacob-Laban story appears prominently in the final moments of what he terms the "conclusion of this whole treatise" (p. 166). It clinches his thesis about the importance of Prov. 28:8 for the fate of usurers. The context for this reference in Mosse's sixth and final sermon is likewise important, because Mosse reveals his profound spiritual concern about usury and its consequences in his urgent exhortation to the usurer to repent and be saved from the "vtter darkenes" (p. 167) of Hell:

And because the nature of worldly men is such, that the losse of their goodes will rende their hearts in peices, when the feare of the losse of heauen will not once stirre their affections: therefore let mee end my speech to them, with that sentence of *Salomon*, wherewith I began this treatise: [Mosse's marginal gloss refers to Prov. 28:8] *He that increaseth his riches by vsurie and interest, gathereth them for him that will be mercifull to the poore.* If God be true and this be the word of God, let them feare, that as God tooke the goods [Mosse's marginal gloss refers to Gen. 31:9] of couetous *Laban*, and gaue them to holy *Iacob*: so he will take the riches which they haue vnlawfully gathered, from them, and from their house, and from their children: and will bestow them vpon others, who shall shew themselues better imployers and disposers of his blessinges. (Pp. 167–68)[10]

Mosse's reference here is to Gen. 31:9, which refers back to the conclusion of the preceding chapter in the Bible (Gen. 30:30–43), as does Mosse's first Jacob-Laban reference. Like Shylock's verses, this reference describes what Jacob did with the wands to gain Laban's sheep. The point of the passage is that God has rewarded Jacob with Laban's "substance," and the gloss in the Geneva Bible (1560) further emphasizes that Jacob's thriving was done according to God's commandment and was not achieved through "deceite." The explanation that Jacob, divinely inspired in a dream (Gen. 31:9–12), obeyed the will of God in the means he used to increase his wealth parallels Antonio's refutation of Shylock's justification of usury: "This was a venture . . . / A thing not in his power to bring to pass, / But sway'd and fashion'd by the hand of heaven" (1.3.86–80). The reference to avoiding deceitful means recalls Shylock's line, "And thrift is blessing if men *steal* it not" (1.3.85; my italics). One of the most common criticisms of usury equates it with theft or describes it as worse than theft, and "thrift" could be used as a euphemism for usury.[11]

Shakespeare's financial judgment in the trial scene, as I have argued elsewhere, is also deeply influenced by Prov. 28:8, which is dramatically enacted, though not specifically cited, when Antonio is granted the power to participate in the judgment passed on Shylock's wealth. Since this proverb, like Mosse's unique Jacob-Laban allusions, does not receive significant emphasis elsewhere in sixteenth-century English literature on usury,[12] Shakespeare's most likely source is Mosse. Moreover, the context of Mosse's reference is also important for Shakespeare, as was the context of the Jacob-Laban reference in Mosse's introduction. In the present case, the context includes a constellation of concerns that are reflected in Shakespeare's play: the preoccupation with God's providence, the consequences attendant upon a usurer's wealth, the issue of inheritance, and the salvation of the usurer's soul through repentance.

Mosse's concentrated focus on the importance of the usurer's wealth and what becomes of it seems to have made a deep impression on Shakespeare, because he adds this dimension to his narrative sources for the play. Mosse's observation that the threat of loss of salvation does not move the natures of worldly usurers but that the fear of losing "their goodes will rende their hearts in peices" anticipates Portia's admonition to Shylock that "in the course of justice, none of us / Should see salvation" (4.1.195–96) and Shylock's adamant refusal: "My deeds upon my head! I crave the law, / The penalty and forfeit of my bond" (4.1.202–3). It is precisely Shylock's fear of losing his goods that first deters him from taking his bond (4.1.302–15) and to which he voices his only objection (4.1.370–73) during the final judgment passed on him. But Shakespeare's creative genius modulates his use of Mosse, and if anything, Shakespeare appears far more merciful than even the kindly, good-natured Mosse, who tends to forgive his own enemies (see sig. B4v). Like Mosse, Shakespeare is not only concerned with the fact of the disposition of the usurer's wealth, granted by God to a man who will be merciful to the poor, but also is interested in the usurer's children. Although it was common in the literature of the moralists and dramatists to suggest that the temporal punishments for usurers included lost heirs and ungrateful children or unthrifty heirs,[13] Mosse, in his exegesis of Prov. 28:8 (based on Ludwig Lavater's commentary on this proverb), departs from this idea when he suggests that one can hope that a usurer will have a good heir, one who is mercifully inclined and who will fulfill the import of the proverb. Ultimately, however, he concludes that the chance of a usurer having a good heir is low. A good heir is as unlikely as a "blacke Swan" (p. 4).

Shakespeare becomes involved in his own way in this issue of familial inheritance and blessing by creating for Shylock a daughter as well as a Christian son-in-law, family figures who do not appear in his main source, Il Pecorone, but who may be suggested by several other sources—Christopher Marlowe's The Jew of Malta (Barabbas's daughter, Abigail, and her Christian lover, Don Mathias), Anthony Munday's Zelauto (Brisana and Rodolfo, the daughter and son-in-law, respectively, of the Christian usurer Truculento) and, of course, what is considered the main source for the Jessica-Lorenzo subplot, Masuccio Salernitano's *Il Novellino* (Carmosina and Giuffredi Saccano, the daughter and son-in-law, respectively, of the wealthy miser). The subject of Jessica and Lorenzo deserves more analysis than I can afford here, but if considered from the perspective of Mosse's treatise, at least one possible aspect of their role in the play is that of offspring who may potentially thwart the curse of barrenness appropriate to the usurer (whose own trade was considered barren breeding). Such a daughter and son-in-law might be seen as a mixed blessing for Shylock, and Antonio will seek to reunite Shylock with them through the disposition of Shylock's wealth and the request for conversion.

Arresting imagery bonds this family, prompting suggestive comparisons. Shylock as a usurer is a thief for greed who celebrates thrift ("thrift is blessing if men steal it not," 1.3.85), while Lorenzo and Jessica are thieves for love whose unthrifty, liberal natures contrast with Shylock's niggardliness—"in such a night / Did Jessica steal from the wealthy Jew, / And with an unthrift love did run from Venice" (5.1.14–16; cf. 2.6.23, 4.1.381, 5.1.19). Jessica and Lorenzo may serve as a temporary punishment for Shylock; a rough justice guides Jessica's stealing jewels and ducats from her father (perhaps as a self-appointed dowry) and Lorenzo's stealing his bride from his father-in-law, since the usurious thief now has done unto him what he has done unto others, a justice that complements the spirit of Prov. 28:8. As Jessica realizes, "manners" have a higher value in human relationships than "blood" (2.3.28–29). The statement "It is a wise father that knows his own child" (2.2.73–74) and the Gobbo parody of blind Isaac's mistaken recognition and blessing of Jacob (2.2.70–95)[14] comically suggest the lesser identification by flesh and blood—"I'll be sworn if thou be Launcelot, thou art mine own flesh and blood" (2.2.87–88)—as well as the child's desire for the blind father's blessing (2.2.80–82). Likewise, Shylock echoes that phrase of physical identification for Jessica—"My own flesh and blood to rebel! . . . I say my daughter is my flesh and my blood" (3.1.51, 33). But although Shylock as a father is not literally blind, like the sand-blind Old Gobbo, he is blind to his child's unhappiness while she and Launcelot see Shylock's house as "hell" (2.3.2). Shylock is blind to her guilt for being ashamed of her father's behavior (2.3.16–19) and blind to her repudiation of his blessing (2.5.55–56). However, the conversion of Jessica's rebellion to a possible reconciliation with her father, whose requested conversion in the trial scene is intended to effect a change in "manners," is hinted by Antonio's attempted "bonding" of Jessica and Lorenzo with Shylock through both shared wealth and faith. What is most compelling, however, is how the lowly dramatist Shakespeare improves upon Mosse's interpretation of Prov. 28:8 for his own far more *merciful* ends: to minister to the *financial* needs of the usurer and his family and not, as Mosse would desire, to defeat them. Condemn the deed, but help the man.

Mosse carefully considers "how and by what meanes God conuerteth the vsurers wealth to the relieuing of the needie" (p. 3) by reviewing the comments on Prov. 28:8 by authorities such as Joannes Mercerus, Ludwig Lavater, Franciscus Vatablus, and Conrad Pellicanus (pp. 3–4). He concludes finally that God's means are infinite, and "God hating the vsurer and condemning his course, doth one way or other defeate him and his of their expectation, and the goods which he gathereth by oppressing of the poore . . . one way or other, sooner or later, the Lorde by his prouidence will defeate the vsurer of them [his riches]: and conuey them into the hands of those, which of charitie will imploy them to the benefite of the poore" (pp. 4–5). Mosse continues to emphasize "the miserable effect which shall betide such riches" when he reasons that the very purpose men have in gathering riches is that "they may abide to themselves, and to their posteritie" (p. 5), but the significance of Prov. 28:8 is that this natural course of behavior will be thwarted in the usurer's case when God takes from him, as well as perhaps "from all that are his," the wealth gained through usury and casts it into "the lappe of one that will be mercifull to the poore" (p. 5).[15]

Shakespeare reflects Mosse's exegesis of the proverb by allowing Antonio in the trial scene to participate in the financial judgment of Shylock. Usury is involved indirectly because Shylock, as an alien, attempts to take the life of a Venetian citizen by means of a bond that is indeed usurious, as we shall explain later, in exacting the "excess" of a pound of flesh to be taken nearest the victim's heart. Mosse cites Cato to show why usury and murder are interdependent: "Cato sayd, *Foenerari est hominem occidere*, To lend to vsurie was to kill a man" (p. 96). Although the quotation is fairly commonplace in usury literature, Shakespeare found it clearly articulated by Mosse, and he adapted the concept to include both Shylock's "direct, or indirect attempts" (4.1.346, 355) on Antonio. A usurer is a murderer chiefly because he destroys, to borrow Shylock's words,, "the means whereby I live" (4.1.373), and the interrelationship between what Antonio terms "life and living" (5.1.286), which both Antonio and Shylock well appreciate, is implicit in Cato's warning. It is echoed in Shakespeare's compound judgment against Shylock, who is threatened first with loss of wealth and then loss of life (4.1.328, 343–59).

Shakespeare's originality in adding Shylock's risk of wealth in the execution of his bond (4.1.306–8) and in his emphasis on the Venetian legal penalty against an alien seeking the life of a Venetian citizen (4.1.343–59), elements not found in any of his narrative sources, also might have been suggested in part by Mosse's consideration of Mercerus's interpretation of Prov. 28:8 (based on "one of the Rabbins," p. 3). Mercerus suggests that the way in which God converts the usurer's wealth to relieve the poor is through "the confiscation of the vsurers goods vnto the Magistrate . . . [because] God often suffereth men which by euill meanes haue gathered their riches, to fall into the danger of politique penall lawes and so to forfeite their goods to the crowne . . ." (p. 3).[16] Shakespeare follows Mercerus's suggestion in the threatened confiscation of Shylock's wealth by the state according to "the laws of Venice" (4.1.307). In his treatment of the Venetian legal penalty he innovatively combines Mercerus's suggestion with Mosse's interpretation of the devolution of a usurer's wealth by devising the law's other "hold" (4.1.343) on Shylock, so that half of his wealth will go to "the state" (4.1.350) and the other half to "the party 'gainst the which [Shylock] doth contrive" (4.1.348), in this case a man of merciful inclinations.

Above all, Shakespeare droppeth the gentle rain of mercy on Mosse's rigorous financial deprivation of the usurer and his heirs by having Antonio request that the court remit Shylock's fine and restore to Shylock half his wealth. While the other half is to be rendered to Lorenzo at Shylock's death, during Shylock's lifetime it will be administered as a trust by Antonio, with the profits accruing to Shylock. Antonio thus ministers to Shylock's children—his only heirs, his daughter and new son-in-law—who emphasize their need for Shylock's "special deed of gift" or "manna" for "starved people" (5.1.291–95). At Shylock's death his wealth will pass on to Jessica and Lorenzo as it naturally should, just as Mosse has stipulated that the reason for financial thriving is to benefit oneself and one's offspring (pp. 5, 168).

Although Shakespeare does not specifically refer to the Jacob-

Laban story in his trial scene, he does recall in Antonio's financial provision for Jessica and Lorenzo why Jacob used the wand device to increase his flocks, namely to provide for his own family: "The ordre of nature requireth that euerie one prouide for his owne familie" (Gen. 30.30, gloss). That Shylock does not demur (even in an aside) regarding the disposition of his wealth to his children, Jessica and Lorenzo, speaks well for him and his prospects for moral change. As Bishop Gervase Babington declares in his commentary on Jacob's query to Laban about providing for his own family, "For *he that prouideth not for his family* (saith the Apostle) [the marginal gloss refers to 1 Tim. 5] *hath denied the faith, and is worse then an infidell.*"[17] Even Shylock's rage at Jessica seems to have abated slightly. During the trial he comments: "I have a daughter—/ Would any of the stock of Barrabas / Had been her husband, rather than a Christian" (4.1.291–93). Although this attitude is extremely harsh, it is milder than his last reflection, in which he wished her dead with his ducats in her coffin (3.1.80–83). Perhaps there is more truth than appears at first blush in Lorenzo's claim, "If e'er the Jew her father come to heaven, / It will be for his gentle daughter's sake" (2.4.33–34). While Lorenzo sees Shylock here as "a faithless Jew" (2.4.37), he also sees him as part of his family—"my father Jew" (2.6.25).

The other emphasis found in Mosse's conclusion that seems to influence Shakespeare is concern for saving the usurer's soul from damnation. Most anti-usury writers stress the themes of punishment and damnation for usurers.[18] Instead Mosse emphasizes repentance and salvation. Shakespeare's context obviously differs from Mosse's (in which the usurers attacked are Christians), but the interest in ultimate spiritual consequences is strikingly similar. Mosse's linkage of worldly wealth and spiritual salvation probably contributed to Shakespeare's creative union of complementary judgments upon Shylock's wealth and soul—the financial and conversion stipulations proposed by Antonio—because neither appears in Shakespeare's main source for the play, *Il Pecorone*. The conversion stipulation in *The Merchant of Venice*, then, may be seen not just as an attempt to save a Jew's soul, but a Jewish usurer's soul. In light of Mosse's treatise, such a conversion cannot guarantee, but should promote, the avoidance of usury. Hence Shylock's moaning victims (3.3.23) will be relieved. From the Christian perspective, if Shylock does not repent and eschew usury, he cannot be saved. Moral law traditionally condemns the usurer because his sin fundamentally violates the commandment of love: it overthrows "the rule of charitie, doe as thou wouldest be done vnto" (p. 114), and *"vsurie cutteth the throat of mercy"* (p. 83), wherein we may remember that Antonio has called Shylock "misbeliever, cut-throat dog" (1.3.106). Mosse treats the repentance and salvation of a Christian usurer. Shakespeare treats the conversion and possible repentance and salvation of a Jewish usurer.

Mosse creates the connection between the Jacob-Laban story and usury through his exegesis of Prov. 28:8. He seems to be the only sixteenth-century English writer on usury who explores, let alone even mentions, the significance of Jacob's increase of wealth, and Laban's loss of it, through Jacob's divinely inspired wand device, although Mosse doesn't explicitly treat the device itself but rather its purpose. Shakespeare shares Mosse's interest in the usurer's wealth, and with the unerring sense of the dramatist, he provides Shylock with a lively description of the wand device (1.3.66–85). Shakespeare discovered in Mosse's treatise the pertinence of the Jacob-Laban story as an argument against usury, and he adapted it to exploit the irony of his Jewish usurer's identification with Jacob.[19]

Reading Mosse would also have encouraged Shakespeare to look more deeply into the way the Bible was interpreted, and especially into interpretations of the Jacob-Laban story. The Christian accusation that Jews misread the Bible was certainly common enough in this era of religious intolerance. Shakespeare takes pains to characterize Shylock as a literalist, thus swelling his play's thematic exploration of literal and spiritual perception. In giving Shylock the Jacob-Laban story as a scriptural defense of usury, while Mosse interprets it as an attack on usury, Shakespeare stresses Shylock's spiritual blindness and his unwitting self-condemnation. Mosse's marginal glosses directing the reader to the relevant passages in Genesis and his unique use of this story would have prompted Shakespeare to study it anew in the Bishops' Bible and Geneva Bible, so that, as Richmond Noble suggests,[20] the whole narrative about Jacob in Genesis becomes a source for Shakespeare, especially the juxtaposed and thematically related passages at the end of chapter 30 and the beginning of chapter 31.

Shakespeare found that the nonusury story of Jacob and Laban and the anti-usury arguments held in common the important ideas of theft, deceit, covetousness, and venture. Usury, regularly seen as theft involving deceit, is an onus Shylock seeks to avoid (1.3.85), but Jacob's thriving was seen as "a venture" (cf. 1.3.85) subject to God's providence, unlike the ventureless, certain gain of usury which is reliant not on God but on human cunning. Therefore, Jacob's venture was not "theft" (see Gen. 30:33) nor was it accomplished through "deceite" (Gen. 31:9, gloss). Jacob's strategy for the natural increase of his wealth was inspired by God through a dream (see Gen. 31:9–12), whereas Shylock's only dream parodies Jacob's godly one in its mundane superstition, and its reference to money bags symbolizes the unnatural increase of usury: "There is some ill a-brewing toward my rest, / For I did dream of money-bags to-night" (2.5.17–18). The significance of the gloss on Jacob's thriving in the Bishops' Bible (1568) for Shylock's reference to this biblical story has already been noted by Christian David Ginsburg. The gloss reads: "It is not lawefull by fraude to seke recompence of iniurie: therfore Moyses sheweth afterwarde that God thus instructed Jacob,"[21] and "afterwarde" refers to the explanation in Gen. 31:9 which Mosse cites in his second allusion to Jacob and Laban. What seems to have escaped Ginsburg's consideration is Shakespeare's parallel between the Antonio-Shylock relationship and the unhappy Jacob-Laban relationship (underscored by the use of fraud to "recompence" injury), in which personal relationships feed personal injury. Indeed, Shakespeare's play, unlike its narrative sources, establishes a history of personal enmity between the merchant and usurer before they seek to contract a bond. Shakespeare, of course, stresses the need for charity and reconciliation. In this he again may follow Mosse, who twice emphasizes the need to love one's enemies (pp. 45, 114). Moreover, in his further reading of Genesis, Shakespeare would have found Jacob presented as even an anti-revenge figure in how he responds to the rape of his only daughter, Dinah, compared to the deceitful cruelty of his sons, Simeon and Levi (see Gen. 34.5–31 and glosses in the Geneva Bible and especially the Bishops' Bible).

Shakespeare's reading of Mosse would have led him to other biblical passages suggesting dramatic ironies. The Bishops' Bible (1568) describes Jacob as "very ryche" (Gen. 30, chapter heading 43) and states that his wealth "increased exceedingly" (Gen. 30:43). Shylock identifies with Jacob for these reasons, but ironically "the rich Jew" (5.1.292) is more like "couetous Laban," who respects only "his owne gayne" (Gen. 30:31, gloss, Bishops' Bible), who was guilty of fraud in depriving Jacob of his wages (Gen. 31:7), and who, according to Mosse's interpretation of Prov. 28:8 and Genesis's depiction of Laban (see Gen. 31.1–2), is going to lose his wealth. Unlike his patriarch Solomon, the author of the Book of Proverbs, Shylock does not choose the wealth of wisdom over the wealth of gold and silver (Wis. 7.7–15). In "breeding" gold and silver and defending the deceitful theft of usury, Shylock thus deceives himself by ignoring the fate explained in Scripture for the covetous and the usurious.

Mosse's preoccupation with the idea of inheritance may be reflected as early in Shakespeare's play as Shylock's use of the word "possessor" when he identifies Jacob as "the third possessor" (1.3.69), Abram being the original possessor of God's promise (see Gen. 15). Like Barabbas in Marlowe's *The Jew of Malta*, Shylock mentions his descent from Jacob with "pride and satisfaction,"[22] but also like Barabbas, he focuses carnally on the blessings of this earth that God has promised Abram: "I am the Lord, that broght thee out of Vr of the Caldees, to giue thee this land to inherit it" (Gen. 15:7). The cheif blessing, however, which was to be the Israelites' inheritance is spiritual, namely God himself: "Feare not, Abram, I am thy buckler, *and* thine exceeding great rewarde" (Gen. 15:1). Indeed, the real treasure promised to the family of Abraham is the spiritual blessing of the Messiah, and although sixteenth-century Christians intolerantly considered it "subversive" for Jews to claim the patriarchs as their own,[23] Shylock's promise to convert enables him, from that Christian perspective, to identify truly with his favored patriarch Jacob and to inherit rightly the blessings promised to Abraham. Shakespeare clearly begins early in the play to adumbrate the interwoven concerns of physical and spiritual possessions, of wealth and love's wealth, of financial and spiritual reward, that for Shylock, at least, culminate in the trial scene.[24]

III

In addition to Mosse's specific use of the Jacob-Laban references, their contexts, and the pertinence of Prov. 28:8, Shakespeare especially responds to Mosse's ideas and diction in his section on the definition of usury and the kinds of usury. Shakespeare seems to have been especially impressed by Mosse's discussion of the different kinds of usury mentioned by various learned authors, especially the kinds termed spiritual, mental, and natural usury.

For his characterization of Antonio, Shakespeare responded to

Mosse's presentation of spiritual usury and especially mental usury. Mosse explains that "liberalitie towards the poore and needie" is one "sorte" of spiritual usury that is virtuous (p. 13), and Shakespeare departs from all his literary sources in portraying his merchant as a man who has a reputation for charity among his fellow Christians, especially regarding usury, because he relieves Shylock's victims through his free lending.[25] Mosse also maintains that the spiritual usurer will be rewarded by God "with a most liberall increase, *as it were with a threefolde* vsurie."[26] And the reward motif happily suits Mosse's main thesis about the "mercifull" man of Prov. 28:8 to whom the usurer's wealth will be given so that the poor may benefit. Shakespeare rewards Antonio at the play's end with "life and living" (5.1.286). Perhaps the return of "three" (5.1.276) of Antonio's argosies (not all six, ventured forth originally to Tripolis, Mexico, England, Lisbon, Barbary, and India—3.2.267–68) reflects Mosse's reference to "threefold" increase, whereas Shylock is denied a threefold increase on his principal when he seeks it (4.1.314–18). The use of "threefold" is atypical in usury literature because "foure folde" always constitutes the penalty of restitution that the usurer is obliged to make.[27] Interestingly, neither Mosse nor Shakespeare concern themselves with the recurrent theme of restitution, let alone fourfold restitution, of the usurer's goods to the injured parties. In light of this consideration, Antonio's financial settlement for Shylock appears all the more generous by keeping Shylock's wealth within his own family. Antonio and Shylock, however, both discover the hazards of what they had misperceived as riskless choices, and both exit the play with roughly half their original wealth in hand.

Mosse is uniquely important for presenting the most developed discussion of mental usury in sixteenth-century English literature on the subject, and Shakespeare creatively responds to Mosse's treatment, subtly adapting the idea for his portrayal of Antonio's love for Bassanio. By far the longest sustained section in Mosse's book is his definition of what constitutes civil usury and his identification of its "parts and branches" (p. 75), such as mental usury and covert usury. He justifies his thoroughness here partly because he finds "that *few* writers haue *largely,* and *thoroughly* laboured in this point" (p. 75; my italics). Mosse seems to be particularly intrigued by the concept of mental usury, presenting just its traditional definition in his first sermon but returning later in his third sermon to discuss it more fully in a personal way that Shakespeare found especially provocative. Mosse's text chiefly examines "ciuill, or politique vsurie," that is, the "gaine an increase . . . raised from the use of worldly goods, which are things belonging to the ciuil and politique estates of men" (p. 16). Mosse tells us that "learned writers" (p. 71) commonly distinguish between two kinds of civil usury—"Actual or Outward, when by acte & outward deede, increase is made by the use of a thing . . . [and] Mental or Inward, which consisteth onely in the hope and purpose, and expectation of the man" (p. 16). Mosse declares mental usury sinful, and citing Ioannes Viguerius, he further defines it as "the hope of gaine without any couenant" (p. 19).

The traditional sense of "gain," in the writings of the Fathers, such as Augustine, Ambrose, and Jerome, is broadly interpreted as *anything* taken above the principal, not necessarily money.[28] Thomas Wilson, for example, cites St. Augustine's explanation that "an usurer is then said to be, when he doth demaund more money or *any other thing els* then he hath delivered . . . bee yt corne, wyne, oyle, or *anye thinge els whatsoever.* . . ." His quotation from St. Ambrose is particularly haunting in view of Shylock's demand for a pound of flesh, albeit a man's flesh: "Thou shalt not take usurye of meates, nor yet of *anye other thinge whatsoever*, for *flesh is usurye*, apparel is usury, and *what-soever* is taken above the principal is usury, *whatsoever name* you geve unto it."[29] Mosse also cites Ambrose ("whatsoeuer is aboue the principall, that is vsurie") and Jerome (". . . to receiue giftes, or rewardes of another kinde . . . is called vsurie and increase, if they receiue any thing more then that which they deliuered") who argue that usury does not involve only money, citing a variety of things which qualify as usurious gain, such as cattle, land, food, and apparel (see pp. 21, 47–48). But Shakespeare would have found in Mosse, who prefers to follow the nominalist position of the late medieval theologian Gabriel Biel, a marked financial emphasis, so that Mosse tends to limit (in a more "modern" manner), as the more traditional approach does not, the concept of usurious gain to money or "that which can bee measured and valued by money" (p. 45). The progressiveness of this concept is indicated by the time lapse of nearly two centuries before words like "moneylender" and "moneylending" become common in the English language.

Mosse acknowledges the traditional line of argument about mental usury that also appears in Thomas Wilson's few, brief sentences on the subject: *"Mentalis usura"* is "an usurie of the mynde, when one hopeth for gayne although no contracte be made" so that in return for a loan a man hopes "to have some thankfull recompence" because the borrower "is a man able to do him good dyvers wayes . . . [e.g.,] to get an office [for him] . . . [to] speke a good word for him, or do hym a certayne pleasure."[30] For Mosse, a mental usurer is "one that committeth vsurie *onely inwardly with himselfe* and with his owne minde . . . if his purpose, and desire, and expectation be, that the borrower should not bring his goods weeping home, but that he should tender him *consideration* for the vse of his goods . . ." (p. 19; my italics). Mosse's definition of mental usury seems to be the proverbvial exception that proves the rule, because it technically lacks his third essential point of covenanting, although Mosse may intend a figurative sense of one covenanting silently with oneself. Mosse therfore carefully explains the doctrine for indicting mental usury as a sinful kind of usury. When Mosse later returns in his text to the subject of mental usury, he highlights the basic principle underlying its condemnation: "All the Schoolemen and Canonistes . . . do agree with one consent, and mutual harmonie in this point: namely that the only intent, & sole expectation of gaine in lending, maketh a man an vsurer" (p. 72). As I have written elsewhere, Shakespeare employs the concept of mental usury in his complex characterization of Antonio, when Antonio faces adversity in act 3 and begins to seek an overplus of love from Bassanio, in order to educate Antonio, as well as the audience, in a better understanding of wise love by the play's end.

Mosse also adds features to the subject of mental usury which appear to interest Shakespeare greatly. He devotes several pages to the importance of intention, the legitimate expectation of love, and the need for moderation. Mosse's concern with discerning a man's real intentions and their pivotal relation to the morality of his outward actions would not only be appealing to a dramatic artist like Shakespeare, who can tantalize his audience about what motivates his characters, but would also be fundamentally germane to the problem of recognizing mental usury, as opposed to outward and actual compacting usury (whether in its open or cloaked forms).

Prefaced with this discussion of intention, Mosse's examination of mental usury elaborates on the subject of lending in Luke's gospel—"*Lend looking for nothing againe*" (p. 74)—to explain that, according to Rainerus de Pisis, the lender may indeed justly "hope or expect three things of the borower": the lender may expect the exact repayment or value of the loan, the lender "may haue his action in law against the borower, if his owne be not repayed," and the lender may expect the borrower to relieve him when his need arises (p. 74). But Mosse's apparently unique emphasis on a legitimate fourth expectation dazzles us: "Unto which three, I may also adde the fourth particular, and that is, the lender may lawfully expect the loue and good will of the borower. For that he hath iustly deserued by his kindnesse: and besides loue is not a thing which can be valued for money: and therefore hee that expecteth loue cannot bee sayd to expect gaine from lending" (p. 74; my italics).[31] If one read no further in Mosse, it would be hard to fault Antonio for mental usury, because whatever gainful expectations Antonio might be conjectured to have are not measurable in monetary terms. Shakespeare's reference to this very expectation of love, so clearly enunciated in Antonio's letter to recall Bassanio to Venice, a letter that is wholly Shakespeare's addition to his narrative sources, would give us no pause: *if your love do not persuade you to come, let not my letter"* (3.2.319–20). But Mosse continues his own line of argument that "the lender may expect loue: and no further" (p. 75) in a passage that I think Shakespeare found particularly stimulating for developing his own sophisticated portrayal of Antonio's mental usury: "But otherwise, if a man without an *ouerreaching* head, doe onely expecte in lending, the *procuring of the fauour,* and *friendship* of the borrower: this hope can make him no vsurer, for the reason before expressed" (p. 75; my italics). Ay, there's the rub. Although Antonio perhaps might be seeking to ensure Bassanio's love through his exceptional negotiation with Shylock (1.3.56–60, 127–32), Antonio need not *procure* Bassanio's favor and friendship through his free lending because Bassanio is already Antonio's best friend; this very friendship is Shakespeare's major change in the relationship between the Antonio and Bassanio counterparts found in his main source, *Il Pecorone.*

Once adversity strikes and the bond is forfeit, Antonio ultimately strains too far, "overreaching" in his desire to have Bassanio emotionally indebted to him. His increasing demands on Bassanio's love finally culminate in the ring episode. But Shakespeare makes Antonio's "overreaching" emotional rather than financial. In exempting love as legitimate repayment, Mosse warns the lender against seeking beyond love with "too farre a reach" to "some gaine, or commoditie" that may be obtained through "the good wil" of the borrower (p. 75). While Mosse advises the lender to be moderate in seeking the love of the borrower so that his expectations do not exceed to financial rewards, he excuses gaining "exceedinglie" in a spiritual sense (e.g.; any nonfinancial gain, such as God's rewards) precisely because such purpose and gain do not constitute financial increase. In *The Merchant of Venice* Shakespeare obviously differs from Mosse. He stresses the need for moderation even in love (see, e.g., 3.2.11–14). Shakespeare's creative genius recasts Mosse's treatment of mental usury, with its exemption of love as legitimate return, to support the traditionally broader view of mental usury as the hope of any gain beyond the principal without covenanting, including excessive love. He expands Mosse's dichotomy between love and usury to include the Elizabethan poetic paradox of love as usury that has been described by Brown,[32] although Antonio manifests a negative rather than a positive version of this trope until its harmonious resolution in his soul bond with Portia for Bassanio's fidelity (5.1.251–53).

With his discussion of natural usury, Mosse continues to hold Shakespeare's interest in specific kinds of usury. Although the Aristotelian notion that usury is unnatural because inanimate money cannot beget itself or "breed" (1.3.90; cf. Mosse, p. 110) was commonplace in Shakespeare's time, Mosse provides a new twist to this notion by distinguishing between unnatural usury and natural usury, claiming that husbandry is "naturall vsurie" (p. 12). Even though Mosse seems to limit the idea of husbandry to agriculture and does not refer again at this point in his text to the Jacob-Laban story, the concept of husbandry in the sixteenth century could also include the raising of livestock.[33] Shakespeare appears to make the logical connection between the story of Jacob's thriving through the increase of his sheep and Mosse's contrast between the story of Jacob's thriving through the increase of his sheep and Mosse's contrast between the natural usury of husbandry and the unnatural usury of money. Shylock's attempt to justify usury by blurring the distinction between natural and unnatural breeding is refuted by Antonio's insistence on that very distinction: "Was this [the Jacob-Laban story] inserted to make interest good? / Or is your gold and silver ewes and rams?" (1.3.89–90). Perhaps Shakespeare's clever use of "well-won thrift" (1.3.45) as a euphemism for usurious theft ("And thrift is blessing if men steal it not," 1.3.85) derives from associated wordplay on the natural usury of "husbandry" (a synonym for "thrift"), but it is more likely that Shylock's witty juggling of terms derives from a less commonly known equation of usury and thrift. For example, the anonymous author of *The Death of*

Vsury argues that the usurer lends to the rich to augment his own gains, and "such thrift is a braunch of theft by the opinion of *D. P. Martyr* vpon the 2. Rom. and all his mony will but turne to his own misery."[34]

IV

Shakespeare creates the most innovative and timely example of covert usury in Elizabethan drama, adapting the latest strategies in theory and practice, especially the lenders' elaboration of contracts to *appear* nonusurious in order to avoid the legal repercussion of the Act Against Usury of 1571. Shylock's sophisticated articulation of his merry bond as "kind" (1.3.138), and therefore not usurious, echoes a configuration of ideas and words marshaled within roughly the first half of Mosse's important third sermon, a sermon which examines covert usury, mental usury, and the scriptural writings that condemn usury. The arguments that surface in Shylock's deceptive dialogue involve the ideas of covert usury and its "innumerable deuices" (p. 68), the importance of intention in determining the good or evil nature of a man's actions, the expectation of gain as essential to usury, the interpretation of gain in terms of "moneys worth" (pp. 71), and the expectation of love as a lawful return. Just how Shylock's apparently nonusurious bond is in fact usurious has not been fully appreciated in the play's criticism. Herein Mosse's treatise affords much illumination.

Early in his treatise Mosse defines usury by compact, which is a branch of outward and actual usury. It occurs "when he that lendeth Couenanteth with the borrower to receiue againe not onely his owne, and his principal, but also increase and aduantage." Mosse finds two types: "*Vsura explicata,* manifest or vnfoulded vsurie" and "*Vsura palliata,* cloaked, or couert vsurie." The latter is not "cleare, and maifest: but . . . is cloaked or couered with the title of honestie" (p. 18). In his third sermon Mosse returns to explicate more fully the dangers of this covert usury that lends for gain "vnder the colour of some lawfull contracte" (p. 61) and uses a variety of pretenses, including the pretenses of befriending the borrower, doing him a "pleasure," and freely lending to him (pp. 64–66). Mosse bewails the protean disguises too numerous to specify that usurers adopt to cloak the fact of their usury: "For as their shiftes are infinite on the one side, so are they exceeding subtile and craftie on the other" (p. 59). Mosse's treatise is noteworthy for its lengthy exposure of usurers' schemes, and Shakespeare's London audience would have been very interested in this contemporary problem and presumably more appreciative than a modern audience might be of Shylock's skill in formulating his scheme. Although the deceitfulness of usurers was commonly derided in Elizabethan England, Mosse's description of "couert and cloaked vsurie . . . and how it seazeth vpon lawfull contractes" (p. 58) directly characterizes Shylock's formulation of a lawful bond that is *apparently* nonusurious, but in fact is usurious, as we shall explain.

Mosse's discussion of the importance of intention links his explanation of covert usury by compact to his examination of mental usury which, as we have discovered, represents a more hidden form of usury—"a serpent in the bosome" (p. 69)—because it "inward and mentall" form (p. 73) lacks the telltale sign of compact. Complementing Shakespeare's preoccupation in *The Merchant of Venice* with distinguishing appearances from realities is Mosse's own powerful emphasis on the importance of intention as determining the good or evil nature of a man's outward deeds. Mosse wants the usurer to recognize the futility of his hypocrisy; he says that no matter how the usurer's deeds may deceive others or appear to conform to man's laws, God sees "the wils, purposes, and intents of men . . . which doe set [them] on worke, & prouoke [them], to the doing of any thing" (p. 72). Although Antonio and Bassanio are mere men who must acknowledge that "there's no art / To find the mind's construction in the face,"[35] Shakespeare's audience is privileged to play God when it discerns Shylock's general intention for Antonio in his initial aside: "If I can catch him once upon the hip, / I will feed fat the ancient grudge I bear him" (1.3.41–42). Regarding this issue of intent, Shylock's best defense later becomes offense: "O father Abram, what these Christians are, / Whose own hard dealing teaches them suspect / The *thoughts* of others!" (1.3.156–58; my italics). We might recollect here Mosse's relation between law and intention: "mens lawes can onely restraine the outward deedes, committed . . . but the lawes of God restraine the euill *thoughts*, and conceipts, and intentions of the heart" (p. 69; my italics).

Usurers were known to sweeten their bait by feigning friendliness to their would-be debtors,[36] and Shylock also cloaks his ulterior motive by emphasizing his desire to have Antonio's "*love*" (1.3.134; my italics): he says that "to *buy* his *favour*" he extends "this *friendship*" (1.3.164; my italics). This recalls Mosse's explanation of what a lender may righfully expect, namely the gratitude of the borrower (pp. 21, 23), "the *loue* and good will of the borower" (p. 74; my italics). A lender is no usurer if he "onely expecte in lending, the procuring of the *favour*, and *friendship* of the borrower" (p.75; my italics). In his important section on the definition of "gain," Mosse anticipates these remarks on the legitimate return of love and echoes Shylock's idiom of "buying" love and favor: "A man may lend to *purchase* the *loue* and liking of another" (p. 46; my italics). when Mosse returns to this subject, he quotes and translates an example of mental usury from Gabriel Biel, using the phrase "to *purchase* their *fauour*" (p. 75). The verbal parallels between Mosse and Shakespeare speak for themselves. Mosse also contends that the lender deserves the borrower's love "by his *kindnesse*" (p. 74; my italics). Shakespeare plays upon the same term three times within eleven lines (1.3.139–49). It is spoken by each of the three characters in the scene—Bassanio, Shylock, and Antonio—in responding to Shylock's proposal. The variant "kind"— in the double sense of "natural" and "benevolent"—appears twice (1.3.138, 174). Shylock's civil duplicity (1.3.134–69) outwits Antonio's rude honesty (1.3.125–32). Shylock's language and logic in offering his shrewdly deceitful formulation of a "kind" bond (1.3.138) clearly owes much to Mosse. Because Shylock pretends to be lending in order to gain only the love and favor of the borrower, he does not appear to be usurious. He thus cleverly tailors his argument to suit Antonio's belief in friendship and to counter his earlier espousal of enmity (1.3.130).

As we have already observed, the expectation or hope of gain by itself makes a man a usurer (pp. 72–73), and traditionally "gain" is broadly interpreted as *anything* taken above the principal, not necessarily money, so that Shylock's pound of flesh technically constitutes overplus, his gain in addition to his principal of three thousand ducats. But Mosse, following chiefly Gabriel Biel, personally prefers to limit "gaine" to "money" or "moneys worth" (pp. 47–48, 71), and this definition receives at least a double emphasis; it is adumbrated in his treatment of mental usury, as well as earlier in the passage where he flatly states, "lending for any thing which is not money or monies worth, is not lending for gaine, and therefore no vsurie" (p. 48).

The typical usurious expectation of financial gain is rejected by Shylock when he proposes his "kind" bond, for he will "take no doit / Of usance for [his] moneys" (1.3.136–37), and Bassanio quickly affirms the kindness of Shylock's offer (1.3.139). But as Brown points out, "[Shylock's] short line [1.3.138] and Bassanio's interjection suggest Antonio hesitates—so Shylock proceeds."[37] Shakespeare must have Antonio hesitate so that Shylock can add his "pound of flesh" condition, but Antonio also hesitates momentarily out of sheer surprise at Shylock's offer. To the surprise of the audience, after Shylock in "merry sport" (1.3.141) adds his pound of flesh condition, Antonio accepts the bond, genuinely affirming, as Bassanio now does not, that the bond shows "much kindness in the Jew" (1.3.149). In a positive response to Shylock's apparent change of heart, Antonio expresses a change of heart toward Shylock because the primary basis for his antagonism against Shylock has been redressed (or so he thinks) by Shylock's "kind"—that is, nonusurious—lending. Later that night Antonio will help in Shylock's search for Jessica (2.7.4–11), and three months later when Antonio faces bankruptcy, he will even plead with "good Shylock" as if he expects Shylock might yet be capable of a "kind" response toward him, only to conclude ultimately that Shylock hates him for his free lending (3.3.3–24).

How can Antonio be so deceived about "this merry bond" (1.3.166)? It cannot be argued that Antonio is ironic in his remark about Shylock's kindness, because his best friend takes that remark at face value and attempts to dissuade Antonio from believing the Jew "grows kind" (1.3.174): "You shall not seal to such a bond for me, / I'll rather dwell in my necessity" (1.3.150–51). In addition to Antonio's faulty self-reliance and avoidance of risk here, [38] it would appear that Mosse's definition of gain in terms of money's worth immediately occurs to the merchant, while Shylock has to spell out the implications of his offer for the merchant's gentleman friend. Mosse's definition informs Shylock's carefully worded rhetorical question to the now fearful Bassanio:

> . . . Pray you tell me this,—
> If he should break his day what should I *gain*
> By the exaction of the forfeiture?
> A pound of man's flesh taken from a man,
> Is not so *estimable*, *profitable* neither
> As flesh of muttons, beefs, or goats,—I say
> To buy his favour, I extend this friendship,—
> If he will take it, so,—if not, adieu,
> And for my love I pray you wrong me not. (1.3.158–66; my italics).

In keeping with Mosse's description of the deviousness of usurers, Shylock has cloaked his usury by compact; he first suggests a genuinely nonusurious proposal (1.3.134–38), only to qualify it craftily in his next utterance (1.3.139–47) so that it *appears* nonusurious or "kind."

But Shylock's pound of flesh does indeed constitute "gain" because, as Mosse reminds us, God discerns usurious intent even "though the factes doe differ before men, and the hope of gaine cannot be discerned by men" (p. 72). Shylock's intent is evil, and he hopes for the gain of deadly revenge. The pound of flesh also qualifies as "excess" (1.3.57) or something taken above the principal so that "Vsurie taketh two recompenses for one thing" (p. 92, heading). For Shylock, the "monies worth" of Antonio's flesh exceeds an almost unimaginable sum (4.1.85–87) until Shylock decides to forgo the pound of flesh and gain instead thrice his original bond (4.1.314)—a "profitable, estimable" threefold increase on his principal. But because Shylock has denied this legal tender in open court, he cannot now legally gain it. Moreover, Shylock intends his pound of flesh to yield financial gain—gain in terms of "monies worth"—for he tells Tubal: "I will have the heart of [Antonio] if he forfeit, for were he out of Venice I can make what merchandise I will" (3.1.116–18). Given this idea of monetary worth, perhaps an English audience would even hear in the pound of flesh a pun on the English "pound." In Shakespeare's narrative sources the pound of flesh also generates possibilities for great financial gain for the lender (large sums of money are offered to release the bond), but Shakespeare's version surpasses in sophisticated complexity anything found in those sources.

By maintaining that all he expects in return is love—an expectation to which Antonio is most susceptible—Shylock disarms his borrowers. As Mosse explains, "loue is not a thing which can be valued for money: and therefore hee that expecteth loue cannot bee sayd to expect *gaine* from lending" (p. 74; my italics). Now we can better understand why Bassanio is palliated somewhat and shifts his stance from outrage—"You shall not seal to such a bond for me, / I'll rather dwell in my necessity" (1.3.150–51)—to concession. Shylock offers "fair terms," albeit Bassanio distrusts what he suspects is "a villain's mind" (1.3.175). In lamenting the usurer's crafty villainy, Mosse provides some excuse for Antonio's entrapment: "I doe not thinke (saith Aretius,) that any man knoweth throughlie the artes of vsurie, but onely those which are dailie conuersant in the *practice* of the same" (p. 60; my italics; cf. p. 68). We realize that Antonio, who neither gives nor takes usury, lacks this conversance.

Antonio's blindness to his own violation of Christian principles (loving one's enemy and avoiding evil to do good) as well as his blindness from his own overconfidence (1.3.152–55; 176–77) aptly parallel his misperception of how dangerous Shylock's merry bond really is: "Content in faith, I'll seal to such a bond, / And say there is much kindness in the Jew" (1.3.148–49) and "Hie thee gentle Jew. / The Hebrew will turn Christian, he grows kind" (1.3.173–74). We know Shylock does not intend to be kind, because his initial aside alerts us. Later in the trial we discover that when the bond was formulated, Shylock specifically requested that Antonio's pound of flesh was to be taken from his breast, cut off "'nearest his heart'" (4.1.248–50); clearly, Shylock intends to murder Antonio. It may be objected that Shylock as a Jew could lawfully take usury from a stranger like Antonio according to Deut. 23:20: "Vnto a stranger thou maiest lend vpon vsurie, but thou shalt not lend vpon vsurie vnto thy brother. . . ." Shakespeare does not provide Shylock with this classic defense; rather, this passage seems to underlie Antonio's counterattack in condemning Shylock's treatment of others as strangers or enemies instead of as brothers or friends (1.3.127–32). But Deut. 23:20 cannot be used to excuse Shylock's bond from a Jewish perspective. Shylock's murderous intent and attempt to enact that intent violate the kind spirit of the Old Testament (see Exod. 22:21; Lev. 19:33–34; Deut. 15:3–4) as well as the letter of its law in the sixth of the Ten Commandments (Exod. 20:13). When Cromwell planned to resettle Jews in England, Rabbi Menasseh ben Israel (1604–57) offered an official explanation of the Deuteronomic text that condemned "biting and exorbitant" usury, insisting that in Judaic law "it is a greater sinne to rob or defraud a stranger, than if I did it to one of my owne profession; because a Jew is bound to shew his charity to all men."[39]

Shylock has adroitly succeeded in adapting anti-usury arguments to his own ends in creating a bond that appears not to be usurious, a bond that thus contributes to the play's theme of wisely discerning between appearances and realities. Mosse illuminates many of the economic issues that confound recent critics.[40] Mosse's criteria for the "sinne or fault of vsurie," which is the "lending for gaine, by compact, not aduenturing the principall," inform Shylock's merry bond: Shylock is "lending for Gaine," "Compacting for gaine" (the sealing of a "single bond" witnessed by "a notary,"

(1.3.140–47), and "not aduenturing of the principall" (pp. 31–32). Regarding the latter, Mosse carefully explains how all men have no choice but to adventure their goods "as touching the issue" (p. 56), because no man has omnipotent control and "the ouerruling prouidence of God will worke when it pleaseth" (p. 56). But the usurer does not adventure his goods "as touching the meanes" (p. 56), because he ensures again with "bandes and pawnes" (p. 57) and only lends "vpon all *sufficient* securitie" (p. 56; my italics; cf. p. 55), never taking usury of "a man that is not very *sufficient* for to pay" (p. 57; my italics). Mosse's diction here parallels Shylock's concern with Antonio's being "sufficient" (1.3.14, 23). Although "sufficient" is a relatively common term in usury literature, as one would expect, these particular pages of Mosse's treatise caught Shakespeare's eye since, in addition to "sufficient," Mosse's use of "aduenturing" (pp. 54–56) appears to influence Shakespeare's singular use of that term, and the parallel usage of "mine owne" also seems pertinent, as we shall see.

V

Let us examine some of the other possible verbal parallels and similar imagery for Shakespeare and Mosse. Shakespeare's use of the specific verbal substantive "adventuring" (1.1.143) appears only once in his canon, and it is in this play. Bassanio introduces by way of analogy his hopes for fruitful "adventuring" of Antonio's "hazard" (1.1.151).[41] The *OED* cites only one example of "adventuring" as a verbal substantive that predates *The Merchant of Venice:* an example from Baret's *Alvearie* (1580). The only other use of "adventuring" I have found predates this *OED* example and casually appears once in Wilson's long treatise on usury (p. 246).[42] Mosse favors this specific word, using it along with "hazard" in his text to convey the idea that usury wrongfully lacks adventuring or hazard. Of the two terms Shakespeare prefers "hazard"—used in the leaden casket motto and repeated no less than eleven times in the play. The word crops up in his plays dated before and after *The Merchant of Venice.* Although the lack of risk is a very important criticism of usury, Mosse sees himself as fairly unique in emphasizing this concept, as well as the term "aduenturing"; he climaxes his first sermon with his definition of sinful usury by adding this point to the other three points (lending for gain by compact) basic to the definitions given by many of his contemporaries: "And this fourth point ['not aduenturing of the principall'] *I* take vp and adioyne to the former out of the Councell of Laterane. . . . This is the proper interpretation of vsurie, (say the Fathers assembled in that Council) when men labour to get gaine and increase from the vse of a thing which groweth or increaseth not: and that with no labour, with no cost, with no danger, or aduenturing" (p. 31; my italics). The contrast between the certain gain of usury and the risk inherent in braving "merchant-marring rocks" (3.2.270) is often underscored in the play, as in Shylock's awareness that "ships are but boards, sailors but men .. and there is the peril of waters, winds, and rocks" (1.3.19–23). Shakespeare ingeniously inter-weaves his Venice and Belmont plots with the necessity for adven-turing in business and in love. The leaden casket choice, with its emphasis on adventuring and giving, symbolizes a concept of love that counters usury and the "gain" and "get" orientation of the gold and silver caskets.

Another possible verbal parallel is "mine owne," which refers to the usurer's defense that he merely uses what is rightfully his own, as in Shylock's complaint that Antonio has abused him: "And all for use of that which is *mine owne*" (1.3.108; my italics). Mosse attacks the usurer's false complaint—"I may be defeated of *mine owne*" (p. 55; my italics). The accusation that usury makes use of another's goods or that which is "none of his owne" (p. 90) and therefore "demandeth consideration for that which is none of the vsurers owne" (p. 89) is commonplace,[43] but this idea receives re-current emphasis in Mosse's treatise, especially at points in his text that we've seen caught Shakespeare's attention. For example, Mosse's first presentation of the idea of lending for gain defined in terms of financial worth (pp. 46–48) uses the precise diction that Shylock uses—"mine owne" (pp. 46–47)—three times to argue that the usurer can't lend to gain more than his own. The phrase "mine owne" reappears later (p. 55) on the same page where "aduentur-ing" appears in the heading and "sufficient" in the text; the next two pages feature Mosse's further use of "sufficient." Obviously, the clustering of the verbal parallels is significant. Mosse also uses "mine owne" later (pp. 67, 91), while "owne" is used in various other constructions (pp. 57, 66, 74, 89–92), all related to this anti-usury argument.

Perhaps the most intriguing verbal echo concerns the much-dis-cussed use of "publican" in Shylock's opening aside when he contemplates Antonio: "How like a fawning publican he looks!" (1.3.36).[44] Brown, endorsing Frederick T. Wood's note, is probably right to suggest that "it was appropriate for Shylock to call Antonio a *publican*, i.e., a servant of Gentile oppressors who robbed the Jews of lawful gains." But Shylock's line may be fraught with irony if considered in light of Mosse's historical description of the publicans as usurers, a description that appears to be unique in sixteenth-century English usury literature:

> Plutarch saith that the Publicane was a most infamous person, euen among the heathen: and so much also the Scriptures doe witnesse vnto vs. The Pharisies noted it as a contemptible thing in our Sauiour Christ, that he did eate and drinke with Publicanes. Now, *foeneratores Publicanos agunt* (saith Plutarch:) the vsurers play the Publicanes. And so they do indeed. For the Publicanes were ... such as gathered tols or customes, or tributes, or taskes, or subsidies of the people. And the vsurers will haue their custome penny, a man must pay their taske or he cannot escape their hands, he must pay deepe tribut that is subiect to their dominion. And as for their conditions, the Publicanes were such as ... by their rauenousness & gripplenes, did sucke vp, & soake dry the poore people of the Prouinces vnder their iurisdiction. Wherein they were a liuely patterne of the greediness & couetousnesse of the vsurer: whereby he casteth into an irrecouerable consumption, all those which for their disease seeke phisicke at his hands. Wel then, the Publicane was an infamous person: and the vsurer playeth the Publicane: and therefore no maruaile though he be of bad report among men." (Pp. 148–49)

While seeing Antonio in the primary sense of "publican" designated above, Shylock remains ironically blind to how his term of contempt could apply to himself as a usurer. The irony doubles with Shylock's expectation that Antonio will be "fawning," since the "royal merchant" (4.1.29) seeks Shylock's service. But Antonio does not beg. Instead he openly confronts (1.3.56–60), criticizes (1.3.86–90, 92–97), and storms (1.3.125–32). It is Shylock who feigns the strategy of fawning: "I would be friends with you, and have your love, / Forget the shames that you have stain'd me with, / Supply your present wants, and take no doit / Of usance for my moneys;. . . ." (1.3.134–37). With brilliant dramaturgy Shakespeare juxtaposes ironic inversions of expectations: Shylock does not get the fawning he expects, nor does Antonio expect the merry bond Shylock proposes.

Several other points arise from Mosse's passage on publicans. Christ's social intercourse with publicans is condemned by the

Pharisees, and this Pharisaic posture might be said to characterize Shylock. He refuses to socialize with Christians when Bassanio invites him to dinner to arrange a meeting with Antonio: ". . . I will buy with you, sell with you, talk with you, walk with you, and so following: but I will not eat with you, drink with you, nor pray with you" (1.3.30–33). Since Antonio enters the scene at this precise moment, the need for such a businesslike dinner meeting is canceled, but curiously enough Bassanio reissues his invitation, presumably for social reasons since business has been concluded, and Launcelot Gobbo is "to bid [his] old master the Jew to sup tonight with [his] new master the Christian" (2.4.16–17). Perhaps the wordplay here upon the Old and New Law takes some of its resonance from Christ's example of eating and drinking with publicans. Shylock does not think he has been invited out of love but rather out of flattery (2.5.12). Yet he was wrong once before when he thought Antonio would fawn on him. Whatever the case, Shylock turns the social festivity inside-out when he goes not to dine with but to "feed upon / The prodigal Christian" (2.5.14–15). Although Shylock intends his usurious pound of flesh to be the means by which he will "feed fat the ancient grudge" against Antonio (1.3.43), such blood lust is metaphorical, not literally cannibalistic. But an Elizabethan audience attuned to the Bible might see Shylock's appetitive desire as missing the spiritual intent behind the Judaic law against the literal feeding upon bloody flesh, such flesh being reserved for the altar and sacrifices of atonement for souls. Shylock's diction and desire once again reveal his unenlightened awareness of his own faith, and it is doubly ironic that Shylock omits the word "blood" in his flesh bond and his intent to "cut off" (4.1.298, 320) the flesh nearest Antonio's heart: "For the life of all flesh is his blood, it is *ioyned* with his life: therefore I said vnto the children of Israel, Ye shal eat the blood of no flesh: for the life of all flesh is the blood thereof: whosoeuer eateth it, shal be cut of" (Lev. 17:14).

Mosse also may have encouraged Shakespeare's emphasis on dog imagery,[45] though the significance of this image for depicting a usurer has not yet been fully explained. Richmond Noble was intrigued by this imagery, noting that despite Shakespeare's use of "dog" elsewhere in his plays as a term of abuse, the insult seems to have the most scathing effect on Shylock. In pondering this, Noble suggests that Shakespeare was influenced by the biblical significance of "dog" as a term of "absolute contempt" that would be "specifically odious to a Jew like Shylock."[46] As helpful as this is, the appropriateness of "dog" imagery for a usurer remains neglected. Although Shylock's name has been glossed as possibly signifying "cormorant" from the Hebrew word *shallach*, and Wilson's treatise on usury images usurers as "cormorant wolfes,"[47] which suits the idea of usury as bestial in its carnivorous devouring of a man's means to live and hence the man himself, why does Shakespeare choose the specific image of a dog for portraying Shylock as a usurer? Why not choose some other animal of prey?

First let us note that a dog would be a familiar, not exotic, image for the usurers who daily plagued Shakespeare's London. The image of a dog concretizes the idea of "biting," which underlies the gruesome metaphor of Shylock's appetite for revenge, his feeding his ancient grudge with Antonio's flesh (3.1.48). But "biting" is also the common, metaphorical term for exorbitant usury, because "byting" usury "carieth with it a deuouring and oppressing of an other."[48] Although Shakespeare employs this idea of "biting" in Shylock's threat—"since I am a dog, beware my fangs" (3.3.7)—in the motif of "feeding" (e.g., 1.3.42; 2.5.14–15; 3.1.47–48; 4.1.137–38), and in the image of Antonio's being "bated" or having little flesh to spare (e.g., 3.3.32–33; 4.1.265–67), Shakespeare never uses the explicit term "biting," just as he does not explicitly use the term "cormorant" in this play, although both terms appear elsewhere in his works. At any rate, in Mosse's etymological explication of usury, "dog" is one of the two specific images presented to convey the meaning of usury as "biting" from the Hebrew word· *Naeshaech* which "signifieth properly *Morsus*, a biting or gnawing of a thing." Mosse notes the divided judgment of authorities on the word's derivation: "And it is a worde borrowed as some thinke, from the biting or stinging of a serpent: as others have iudged from the gnawing, or tyring [sic] of a dogge vpon a bone. So that, vnlesse vsurie bee *Naeshaech*, biting, vnlesse by it a man sting his neighbour, as a serpent, or pray vpon him as a dogge vpon a carrion: some holde opinion that it is not forbidden in the worde of God" (p. 133). Although this etymological information is by no means unique to Mosse, Shakespeare would have found it presented fully and clearly in Mosse.

Mosse himself opted to favor dog imagery in his preface to the reader when he exulted over the success God had granted him in stinging the consciences of usurers through his sermons so that now they storm against him: "*For, as it is the nature of the greater*

and stronger beasts [usurers], *to despise the barking whelpe*
[Mosse], *and then only to turne againe, when they feele themselues
bitten and touched indeede: so I began to conceiue of these Vsurers, that because now they stormed, therefore they were stung"* (sig.
B3). Mosse condemns all sinful usury as biting—"vsurie hath the
name of biting: for it doth secretly bite, gnawe, and consume a man"
(p. 135), and Shakespeare masterfully coalesces the idea of the
inner consumption of Antonio's flesh and life due to biting usury
with the idea of literally cutting off the same flesh and life due to
sharp-edged revenge. Both usury and revenge interrelate through
their opposition to charity. There is no need to list all the possible
verbal echoes from Mosse, but these considered seem to be especially important ones.

Almost all one can imagine Shakespeare would need to know
about usury he could find in Mosse's book—the basic arguments,
such as usury being condemned by the Scriptures because it overthrows lending and charity (p. 84), as well as the more personal
emphases: the misuse of Scripture by the worst usurers, the legitimate expectation of the return of love, the focus on gain in terms
of money or money's worth, and the description of publicans as
usurers. In addition to the significant verbal parallels, of chief importance are Mosse's exceptionally full treatment of the concepts
of mental usury and covert usury by compact and his unique use
of the Jacob-Laban story and Prov. 28:8 regarding the usurer's
wealth. But Shakespeare probaby read other works on usury and
used his own knowledge of commerce and law in London. Thomas
Wilson's *A Discourse upon Usury,* for example, seems to me to have
influenced Shakespeare, but that is matter for another essay. We
can be certain, however, that Shakespeare knew Mosse's book and
was strongly influenced by it. Two recent historical studies of usury
concur that usury does not receive sympathetic treatment in *The
Merchant of Venice.* Norman Jones affirms that "Shylock was the
usurer in the flesh to many English people, both educated and
uneducated," and Joseph Shatzmiller argues that although Shylock
the character might evoke sympathy, "it is difficult to find any sympathy in the play for the profession of moneylending" because the
play "fits comfortably within a long European anti-usury tradition."[49] But how usury is invested in the play's ideas, language, and
above all, characters, Antonio and Shylock, reveals that Shakespeare's multifarious use of source material, like Mosse's treatise,
demonstrates once again his extraordinary talent for *imitatio* as he

commands his sources to "suffer a sea change / Into something rich and strange"[50]—in this case, an artistic vision as profoundly complex as that of *The Merchant of Venice*.

Notes

1. All references to this play are to John Russell Brown, ed., *The Merchant of Venice* New Arden edition (London: Methuen, 1955); see p. 26, n. on 11.72–85. The Variorum quotes Ambrose Eccles, who also ponders why Shakespeare uses the Jacob-Laban story: "In Shylock's defense of usury, drawn from the example of Jacob's conduct, there seems to be little appositeness or ingenuity; indeed, it is not easy to discover in what the parallelism of the two cases consists. . . ." See H. H. Furness, ed., *The Merchant of Venice* (Philadelphia: J. B. Lippincott, 1888), p. 44. Unless specified otherwise, all biblical references are to the Geneva version of the Bible (Geneva, 1560). For some helpful studies of usury, see Arthur B. Stonex, "The Usurer in Elizabethan Drama," *PLMA* 31 (1916): 190-210 Stonex, "Money Lending and Money-Lenders in England During the 16th and 17th Centuries," in *Schelling Anniversary Papers* (New York: Russell & Russell, 1923), pp. 263–85 (see esp. pp. 263–64, 278); R. H. Tawney, *Religion and the Rise of Capitalism: A Historical Study*, Holland Memorial Lectures, 1922 (1926; rpt. London: John Murray, 1948); Celeste Turner Wright, "Some Conventions Regarding the Usurer in Elizabethan Literature," *SP* 31 (1934): 176–97; Wright, "The Usurer's Sin in Elizabethan Literature," *SP* 35 (1938): 178–94; J. W. Draper, "Usury in The Merchant of Venice, *MP* 33 (1935): 37–47; E. C. Pettet, "*The Merchant of Venice* and the Problem of Usury," *Essays and Studies* 31 (1945): 19–33; John T. Noonan, Jr., *The Scholastic Analysis of Usury* (Cambridge: Harvard Univ. Press, 1957), esp. "mental usury," pp. 32–33; Benjamin Nelson, *The Idea of Usury: From Tribal Brotherhood to Universal Otherhood*, 2d ed. (Chicago: Univ. of Chicago Press, 1969), esp. pp. 86–87, 141–47; E. Pearlman, "Shakespeare, Freud, and the Two Usuries, or Money's a Meddler," *ELR* 2 (1972): 217–36; and Laura Caroline Stevenson, *Praise and Pradox: Merchants and Craftsmen in Elizabethan Popular Literature* (Cambridge: Cambrdige Univ. Press, 1984), pp. 92–106. Although it appeared too late for the composition of my essay, but fortunately prior to its publication, Norman Jones's exceptionally helpful study of usury, *God and the Moneylenders: Usury and Law in Early Modern England* (Oxford: Basil Blackwell Ltd., 1989), must be noted here. In light of Jones's careful explanation of relevant usury statutes in sixteenth-century England, I suspect that Shakespeare's particular articulation of the judgment passed on Shylock (4.1) might reflect some aspect of these English laws, which Shakespeare adapts to his own purposes: see, e.g., the conjunction of financial and spiritual judgments (cf. the legality of "double jeopardy" in usury, Jones, p. 116); the halving of a financial penalty (cf. Jones, p. 92); and perhaps the language of "direct or indirect attempts" (4.1.346) viewed as unlawful (cf. the clarification of the intent of the 1571 statue, Jones, p. 64; cf. pp. 118–44 for attempts to evade this law by taking interest indirectly). See my review of Jones's book in *Shakespeare Quarterly* 42 (1991): 506–9.

2. See also my note, "When Jacob Graz'd His Uncle Laban's Sheep: A New Source for *The Merchant of Venice*," *SQ* 36 (1985): 64–65. Some ideas in my essay here necessarily refer to arguments in my other two essays on the *Merchant*. See "Loving Wisely and the Casket Test: Symbolic and Structural Unity in *The Merchant of Venice*," *ShakS* 11 (1978): esp. 63–66, and "The Education of the Mer-

chant of Venice," *SEL* 25 (1985): esp. 312–13, 319–21, 324–31, regarding Antonio in relation to the concept of risk, the financial judgment of Shylock, Prov. 28.8, and mental usury.

3. See Brown, pp. xxii–xxvii.

4. All subsequent references to Mosse will be documented parenthetically in my text. Mosse's quarto text was printed in London by the Widow Orwin for Thomas Man in 1595; the date of entry in the Stationers' Register is 18 February 1594/5. The preface to the reader is dated 6 February 1594, and the dedicatory epistle is dated 1 January 1595. The type in Mosse's treatise varies. Mosse's own prose is primarily textura, but he also employs roman for translations of quotations and emphasis as well as italics chiefly for Latin quotations, marginalia, and initial statement of each sermon's contents. Unless otherwise indicated, I have rendered the textura and roman as roman and have used italics to indicate Mosse's italics.

5. See Nelson, pp. 84–85, esp. n. 33 regarding the well-documented religious opposition to the Bill of 1571. Nelson, however, merely mentions Mosse's work in passing, overlooking its unique use of the Jacob-Laban story as well as Prov. 28:8. Mosse rightly interprets Queen Elizabeth's statute as financially punitive, whether one takes ten in the hundred or above or under that rate (see pp. 159–60). Regarding that statute, see Lawrence Stone, *The Crisis of the Aristocracy, 1558–1641* (Oxford: Clarendon Press, 1965), p. 530; see Stonex, "Money Lending," 264, on confused interpretation of this statute; and for a thorough analysis, see Jones, pp. 45–144. Jones notes that "the Queen was the only person in the realm who could legally borrow at interest" (p. 52), and although the intent of the statute was clearly *against* usury, its effect over time was to create a *de facto* acceptance of 10 percent interest (p. 64).

6. Thomas Wilson, *A Discourse upon Usury* [1572], ed. Tawney (New York: Harcourt Brace & Co., 1925), p. 114; Greaves, *Society and Religion in Elizabethan England* (Minneapolis: Univ. of Minnesota Press, 1981), p. 606.

7. Miles Mosse was educated at Cambridge University and proceeded D.D. between 1595 and 1603. He became a minister at Norwich around 1580 and sometime later pastor of Combes, Suffolk. Besides his tract on usury, he published a catechism (1590) and two other sermons (1603 and 1613). See *DNB* 13, 1081–82.

8. The idea that it is unchristian for individuals to give or take usury was held by many theologians; see Nelson, p. 37n and Jones, pp. 6–46. But Antonio's exemplification of that attitude seems to derive from Mosse's praise of particular individuals, such as his dedicatee Archbishop Whitgift and himself, whose own lives have borne witness to that belief, despite the current trend to succumb to usury. The importance of how carefully Shakespeare developed the usury motif for his merchant is evident, for example, by contrast with its lack of emphasis in the newly discovered fourteenth-century French analogue, *Le Miracle de un marchant et un juif*, where the merchant's generosity operates independently of usury, as is also the case in Shakespeare's main source for the flesh-bond plot, *Il Pecorone*. See J. Madison Davis and Sylvie L. F. Richards, "The Merchant and the Jew: A Fourteenth-Century French Analogue to *The Merchant of Venice*," *SQ* 36 (1985): 60–62. Regarding usury and merchants, see Stevenson, pp. 92–106, p. 108 n. 2; Stonex, "The Usurer," 90–210; Stonex, "Money Lending," 265–69, 275–79. The usurer in Thomas Wilson's *A Discourse uppon Usurye* (1572) is a merchant.

9. Other writers corroborate Mosse's view of the widespread growth of usury, so that Richard Porder asserts, "No nation [is] free from vsurie at this time" (f. 88). See Porder, *A Sermon of gods fearefull threatenings for Idolatrye . . . : with a Treatise against Usurie* (London: Henry Denham, 1570), fol. 88–88v, fols. 72v–73,

sig. A5. Cf. Wolfgang Musculus, *Common Places of Christian Religion. Hereunto are added two other treatises . . . one of Othes, and an other of Usury,* trans. John Man (London: Henry Bynneman, 1578), pp. 29, 42. Other writers attest to the appalling dominance of usury in England, with Archbishop Edwin Sandys bemoaning how usury "hath corrupted all England" so that "it is become the chief chaffer and merchandize of England." See Sandys, *The Sermons of Edwin Sandys, D.D.,* ed. Rev. John Ayre, vol. 41 (Cambridge, England: The University Press, 1841), p. 50. Cf. also Phillip Stubbes, *The Anatomie of Abuses: Contayning A Discoverie . . . of such Notable Vices . . . in a verie famous Ilande called Ailgna . . .* (London: Richard Jones, 1583), sig. K5–K5v; Richard Turnbull, *An Exposition Vpon the Canonicall Epistle of Saint James . . . Sainte Jude . . . An Exposition Vpon the XV. Psalme, Devided Into Foure Sermons* (London: John Windet, 1592), fol. 47v.

10. In this quotation I italicize Mosse's proper names, which stand out in roman against textura in his text.

11. See Mosse, p. 143. See also Bishop John Jewel, *An Exposition vpon the two Epistles of the Apostle Sainct Paule to the Thessalonians* (London: R. Newberie, 1583), pp. 114, 117–19; Stubbes, sig. K8v; Turnbull, fol. 46; and Porder, fols. 68–69. Philippus Caesar quotes St. Bernard on the legal theft of usury: "*Vsurie is a legal theefe, foretellyng aforewhat he doth mynde afterward to steale:* (f. 6). Cf. also Brown, p. 26 n. 85; Nelson, pp. 9–10.

12. This proverb does not even appear in Nelson's Index to Scriptural Passages (see p. 310). After extensive reading, I can find only one sixteenth-century English author, Henry Smith, who writes against usury and even cites Prov. 28:8, but his own thesis for his two sermons is based on Ps. 15, verses 1 and 5. See *The Examination of Vsury, in Two Sermons* (London: R. Field, 1591). Although Mosse doesn't name Smith in his prefatory list of authors, we know that Mosse read Smith because he documents four references to him in his marginalia (sig. B4, p. 6, p. 30, p. 60), all of which, however, refer to Smith's first sermon and not his second, where the reference to Prov. 28:8 appears (pp. 34–37). Smith's development of Prov. 28:8, however, is very brief and generalized compared to Mosse's, and even differs importantly in the precise wording of the proverb. One might suspect that Mosse derived from Smith the germ for his idea to examine Prov. 28:8. But it is also likely that Mosse's interest in Prov. 28:8 is essentially his own. Note how carefully he uses biblical commentators on that proverb, such as Mercerus, Vatablus, Lavater, and Pellicanus (see pp. 3–5), to analyze its meaning. Most importantly, there is no evidence in Smith's two sermons to suggest that Shakespeare knew them.

13. See Niels Hemmingsen, *A Godlie Treatise Concerning The lawfull vse of ritches,* so entitled and adapted (from Hemmingsen's *Commentary on the Epistle of James*) by Thomas Rogers and annexed to Philippus Caesar, *A General Discovrse Against the damnable sect of Vsurers,* trans. Thomas Rogers (London: John Kyngston, 1578), p. 18. Cf. Mosse, p. 168; Smith, pp. 35–37; and Wright, "The Usurer's Sin in Elizabethan Literature," 191–92. Stonex identifies similar dramatic devices in Elizabethan and Jacobean plays, where the usurer is frequently punished by his offspring (male and female); Stonex especially notes the motif of the usurer's rebellious daughter who takes some wealth when she elopes. But he also notes the familial reconciliation (and sometimes even the usurer's conversion to virtue) that often concludes the comedies that postdate Shakespeare's play. See "The Usurer in Elizabethan Drama," 197–209.

14. Regarding the parallels and significance of the Gobbo business (2.2) in terms of the Jacob-Isaac-Esau story, see Dorothy C. Hockey, "The Patch Is Kind Enough," *SQ* 10 (1959): 448–50; René E. Fortin, "Launcelot Gobbo and the Uses of Allegory

in *The Merchant of Venice*," *SEL* 14 (1974): 265–68; and Lawrence Danson, *The Harmonies of "The Merchant of Venice"* (New Haven and London: Yale Univ. Press, 1978), pp. 72–76.

15. Regarding this important issue of inheritance, Mosse warns the reader not to take Prov. 28:8 as "a friuolous surmise" by giving examples from Niels Hemmingsen of usurers whose children fell into poverty (pp. 167–68). See Pearlman, pp. 227, 231, and 233, where he insightfully puzzles over the question of the two usuries—moneylending and propagation—and why children and money are interlinked, but overlooks the critical issue of inheritance as one fundamental reason why parents labor for wealth for their heirs. If we note with Brown (pp. xxi, 168) that the germ for the idea of giving the usurer's wealth to his daughter and new son-in-law may derive from Anthony Munday's *Zelauto*, we must also observe that in *Zelauto* the Christian usurer himself, not the judge, makes this decision (p. 168, Brown's edition). Hence, *Zelauto* does not parallel Shakespeare's *Merchant* as closely as Mosse's treatise does, because there is no idea in *Zelauto* of *legally* taking the usurer's wealth from him and giving it to another who then is merciful to the poor.

16. Mosse later reviews laws under former English monarchs that financially penalize usurers; see pp. 156–60, esp. p. 159 where Mosse notes that the 1571 statute against usury penalizes loans over the rate of 10 percent by a "treble forfeiture of the principall." Shakespeare's formulation of the financial penalty in the trial scene might be colored by the legal realities of the Act Against Usury of 1571. Shylock loses both his principal and Bassanio's offer for treble the principal. As Jones explains, the Elizabethan statute declared contracts in excess of 10 percent to be void and punishable with treble forfeiture; loans at under 10 percent were punished by forfeiture of the interest (p. 92). Wilson focuses chiefly on the confiscation of wealth only at the time of the unrepentant usurer's death and the disinheritance of the usurer's heir (pp. 183–84, 268, 376–77, 379); he also wishes a death penalty were mandated (p. 232). Of the various temporal punishments that could be inflicted on usurers, one of the most interesting descriptions, for our purposes here, appears in William Harrys's translation of *The market or fayre of Usurers* (London: Steuen Mierdman, 1550) (photostat facsimile reproduced from the copy of STC 17330 in the Henry E. Huntington Library): usurers have worthily deserved "at the hands of the temporall magistrates the punyshement of losyng both honour body and goodes with other corrections" (sig. L7).

17. Babington, *Certaine Plaine, Briefe, and Comfortable Notes vpon euerie Chapter of Genesis* (London: A. Jeffes and P. Short, 1592), sig. O8.

18. See, e.g., Thomas Lodge, *An Alarum against Vsurers* [1584], in *The Complete Works of Thomas Lodge*, vol. 1 (New York: Russell & Russell, 1963), sig. F4; Sandys, p. 204; Caesar, fols. 5, 6v, 7v; Jewel, pp. 124, 128–29, 192; and Porder, fols. 87v–88, 100v, 104–04v, 105v, 107v–08v.

19. Regarding the problematic patriarch Jacob, cf. also Arnold Williams, *The Common Expositor: An Account of the Commentaries on Genesis 1527–1633* (Chapel Hill: Univ. of North Carolina Press, 1948), pp. 169–71; John S. Coolidge, "Law and Love in *The Merchant of Venice*," *SQ* 27 (1976): 246–50. For an argument that supports my reading, see Norman Nathan, "Shylock, Jacob, and God's Judgment," *SQ* 1 (1950): 257–58, 259 n. 6. For a different argument about identifying the Shylock-Antonio relation in terms of the relation between Jacob and Laban, as well as the possible identifications of Shylock with Jacob, Laban, and Esau, see Lars Engle, "'Thrift is Blessing': Exchange and Explanation in *The Merchant of Venice*," *SQ* 37 (1986): 29–32.

20. See Noble, *Shakespeare's Biblical Knowledge and Use of the Book of Common Prayer* (1935; rpt. New York: Octagon Books, 1970), p. 161. Noble finds it

"interesting" that Shylock's speech (1.3.66–85) proves Shakespeare used the Genevan Bible, but Antonio's protest (1.3.86–88) suggests the influence of the Bishops', and "on points, [he thinks] the Bishops' has the better of it" (p. 61). An overlooked example of just how closely Shakespeare is using the Bible, in this case the Genevan version, appears in Shylock's designation of the time of year ("In end of autumn," 1.3.76) for the generation of Jacob's sheep. This information corresponds to the gloss in the Geneva Bible—"As they which toke the ram about September, & brought forthe about marche . . ." (Gen. 30:41)—and such specific information about the time of year does not appear in the Bishops' Bible.

21. See Ginsburg, cited in Brown, pp. 26–27, n. on 11.87–88. All references in my text to the Bishops' Bible are to the 1568 edition (London: Richard Jugge).

22. See Brown, p. 25, n. on 11.67–69. Another overlooked but possible parallel between Shylock's and Barabas's spiritual obtuseness may be the obsession of each with the wealth of a patriarch. Just as Shylock is fascinated by Jacob's "thriving," so Barabas recalls only Job's wealth when his fellow Jews attempt to mitigate his financial loss by counseling him to "remember Job" (1.2.181)—intending, of course, for Barabas to be inspired by Job's patience in the midst of adversity. But Barabas remains blind to the spiritual example of Job's life. Lamenting that his brothers' advice is valueless since he had far greater wealth than Job, he says that he, not Job, deserves to curse (1.2.182–92). References to Marlowe's *The Jew of Malta* are from *The Complete Plays of Christopher Marlowe*, ed. Irving Ribner (New York, 1963).

23. See G. K. Hunter, "The Theology of Marlowe's *The Jew of Malta*," *JWCI* 17 (1964): 216–17, who cites Gal. 3:3–16, 29.

24. It is not inconceivable that Shakespeare pursued his interest in the Jacob-Laban story by reading commentaries on Genesis. If he did or even if he didn't, one such commentary that provides particularly "comfortable notes" for the modern reader is by Bishop Babington, who reveals how negatively the greed, deceit, and foolishness of "a subtill worldling" (sig. O7v) like Laban could be viewed and how positively the "faith and truth" of a good servant like Jacob could be admired (sig. R1v). Herein he develops more fully the spirit of the glosses in both the Geneva and Bishops' Bibles. Although wrestling imagery is not unusual in Jacob's history (see esp. Gen. 30:8 and 32.24–28) and Shylock's desire to catch Antonio "upon the hip" (1.3.41) refers to a proverbial phrase derived from wrestling, it is nonetheless very interesting to note that Babington depicts Laban as a cunning wrestler who, like Shylock, seeks to catch his opponent "on the hip": "yet is hee [Laban] glad to haue *Iacob* on the hip for a bad bargaine as hee hoped, and thinking hereby to gaine *Iacobs* seruice for little or nothing, *would God* saith he, this bargaine might stand" (sig. R). Brown suggests that Shylock's line might allude to Jacob's wrestling with the angel (see p. 24, n. 41), but in both the Geneva and Bishops' Bibles the word "thigh," not "hip," is used. Gratiano echoes this phrase when the tables are turned on Shylock: "Now infidel I have you on the hip" (4.1.330).

25. See 1.3.38–40, 3.1.116–17, 3.2.291–95, and 3.3.21–24.

26. Mosse, p. 13. I use italics in this quotation to signify the words which stand out in textura against the roman print of Mosse's translation of Mercerus.

27. See Jewel, p. 117. Cf. Turnbull, fols. 49v, 52; Caesar, fols. 15, 32; and *The ruinate fall of the Pope Vsury, deriued from the Pope Idolatrie / reueled by a Saxon of antiquitie* (London: Iohn Allde, c. 1580) (photostate facsimile reproduced from the copy of STC 24558b in the Henry E. Huntington Library), sig. A7.

28. This concept appears in almost every sixteenth-century treatise on usury. See, e.g., Nicolas Sander, *A Brief Treatise of Vsurie* (Lovanii: Ioannem Foulerum, 1568), in *English Recusant Literature 1558–1640*, ed. D. M. Rogers, vol. 97 (Mens-

ton, England: Scolar Press, 1972), sigs. A7, E6, F1, G8; Musculus, p. 22; Harrys, sig. E8; Smith, pp. 5, 18; Hemmingsen, pp. 11–12; and the anonymous *The Death of Vsury, or, The Disgrace of Vsurers* (Cambridge, England: Iohn Legatt, 1594), pp. 3–5). *The Death of Vsury* is the work that Mosse refers to in his preface as having plagiarized from him to his "discredit" (sigs. B4–B4v). Compared to the pithiness that *Death* boasts of on its title page, Mosse is much more scholarly and thorough, citing well over twice as many authorities and presenting over four times as many pages of substantive text. Moreover, all of Mosse's sermons, preached in 1592–93, antedate the 1594 appearance of the anonymous author's work. Although the two works are similar, both authors can reveal their own idiosyncratic biases; for example, they differ regarding the 1571 statute's allowance of usury for the relief of orphans: the author of *Death* approves, but Mosse disapproves, suggesting by analogous argument that the spirit of God's law is violated when we do evil to do good (p. 160).

29. Wilson, pp. 218–19; my italics.

30. Wilson, p. 292. Cf. Where Wilson does not specifically mention the term "mental usury," but does briefly articulate the concept when he declares as forbidden "the very hope also to loke for a good turne agayne, or any thynge els over and above the principal. . . ." (p. 350). Cf. other authors who very briefly refer to mental usury: Sander, sigs. A4v, and Lv (and for the concept but not the term, see sigs. F1, H6v–H7, H8v); *The Death of Usury*, p. 3; Thomas Bell, *The Speculation of Vsurie* (London: V. Symmes, 1596), sigs. B1, C2v–C3. To the best of my knowledge, the Catholic writer Nicolas Sander is the first to use the term "mental vsurie" in English usury literature.

31. Mosse cites only one author, Bartholomus Fumus, for a definition of mental usury which is more limited than the traditional view just discussed, but which suits Mosse's penchant for defining "gain" in terms of financial worth: "Mental vsurie is committed without couenant, when a man lendeth with hope of receiuing somewhat that is moneys worth, aboue or besides the principall" (p. 71). Gabriel Biel also defines gain this way.

32. Brown, pp. liv–lvi.

33. See, e.g., John Fitzherbert, *The Boke of Husbandrye* (London: Thomas Petyt, c. 1540), fols. xix–xxiv.

34. See *Death of Vsury*, p. 33. I have been unable to locate the author's reference, as cited, in Pietro Martire Vermigli, *Most learned and fruitfull Commentaries of D. Peter Martir Vermilius . . . vpon the Epistle of S. Paul to the Romanes*, trans. Henry Billingsley (London: Iohn Daye, 1568). Cf. also Lodge, *Alarum*, sig. F3, where he mentions "thriftinesse" as one euphemism for usury.

35. *Macbeth*, 1.4.12. All quotations from Shakespeare's plays will be to the Riverside edition, gen. ed. G. Blakemore Evans (Boston: Houghton Mifflin, 1974). In common opinion "good intent" becomes increasingly important in the determination of usury. See, e.g., the attempted defense of the rich Jacobean usurer, Thomas Sutton, on the grounds of "good intentions," cited in Jones, pp. 179–80.

36. See Mosse, pp. 64–66. Cf. Harrys, sigs. B6v, K2, L3v, L4v; Porder, fol. 92; Turnbull, fols. 53–53v; and Thomas Lodge, *Wits Miserie, and the Worlds Madnesse: Discouering the Deuils Incarnat of this Age* [1596], in *The Complete Works of Thomas Lodge*, vol. 4 (New York: Russell & Russell, 1963), sig. E4v; Lodge, *Alarum*, sig. B2v. See also Brown, p. 29, n. 134.

37. Brown, p. 29, n. 138.

38. On the moral necessity for risk or uncertainty in business dealings and the concomitant trust in God's providence, see Mosse, pp. 31, 54–57. Cf. Jewel, p. 142. Turnbull, fol. 46; Porder, fols. 78v–79; *Death of Vsury*, p. 27; and Jones, pp. 4, 11.

39. Rabbi Menasseh ben Israel's instructive remarks are cited in Nelson, pp.

98–99. His remarks reflect the new ideology regarding the legalization of moderate usury recorded in England's 1624 Usury Act; by the mid-seventeenth century most men seem to concur that moderate usury (6 to 8 percent) "stands in good reason" for Jews and Christians alike (p. 99). He concludes that if Jews do not charitably "they do it not as Iewes simply, but as wicked Iewes . . ." (p. 100). But cf. also Mosse, pp. 121–27, where he discusses at length the interpretation of Deut. 23:20: from a Christian perspective, the Jews were permitted to take usury from strangers because of the hardness of their hearts, but this exemption was only supposed to be a temporary one, and not meant to be directed against Christians. See the glosses on Deut. 23:20 in both the Geneva Bible and the Bishops' Bible, and cf. Sander, sig. A6v, Vermigli, *Commonplaces*, pt. 2, fol. 330a, fol. 536b; and Porder, fols. 105v–6. See Nelson (pp. 86–89, esp. n. 36), who suggests Shakespeare counters Deut. 23:19–20 in 1.3.127–32 with Luke 6:35 in 4.1.17–34.

40. For example, W. H. Auden believes Shylock as a usurer acts unprofessionally because "he refuses to charge Antonio interest." See *The Dyer's Hand and Other Essays* (New York: Random House, 1962), p. 227. Marc Shell argues Shylock's pound of flesh is not "use" but only "a conditional security." See "The Wether and the Ewe: Verbal Usury in *The Merchant of Venice*," *The Kenyon Review*, n.s. 1, no. 4 (Fall 1979): 70, 89. René Girard sees Shylock as demanding "no interest for his money, no positive guarantees in case of default . . ." See "'To Entrap the Wisest': A Reading of *The Merchant of Venice*," in *Literature and Society*, ed. Edward W. Said, Selected Papers from the English Institute, 1978, n.s. 3 (Baltimore and London: Johns Hopkins Univ. Press, 1980), pp. 103–4. David Bady also misses how Shylock's bond with Antonio is indeed usurious, constituting not "an equivalent value" but rather "excess." See "The Sum of Something: Arithmetic in *The Merchant of Venice*," *SQ* 36 (1985): 27; however, Bady offers some valuable comments on "the theology of the devil's overcharge" (pp. 28–29) which amplify the common association of the devil with usury. Engle sees Shylock's merry bond "as unbusinesslike a proposition as one could find" (p. 27), and his too-laudatory view of how Shylock as a Jacob figure "'blesses'" (p. 31) the Christians' financial ventures erroneously maintains that scene 3 of the play also depicts "the diabolism forced on Shylock by Antonio's near-hysterical resistance" to usurious exchange (p. 32). Walter Cohen claims that Shakespeare deviates from the anti-usury tracts and that Shylock genuinely refuses to take usury but instead takes legitimate interest. See "*The Merchant of Venice* and the Possibilities of Historical Criticism," *ELH* 49 (1982): 768–69. Unfortunately, Cohen misunderstands what constitutes legitimate interest and misreads Mosse's careful definition of it (see Mosse, p. 27). "Interest" could be used negatively as a synonym for usury (Antonio's use of "interest" in this sense—see 1.3.46, 70–71, 89—particularly offends Shylock, who himself prefers the term "usance"—see 1.3.40, 103, 137; "usance" is one of the "finer phrase[s]" (p. 108) Mosse says usurers adopt to salve their guilty consciences). "Interest" could also refer not to usury but positively to the concept of just compensation for damages suffered by the lender, specified as due "from the appointed day of payment forward" (see Mosse, p. 27)—a usage which, for whatever reasons, Shakespeare does not employ in this play. "Interest" in this latter sense cannot be applied to Shylock's pound of flesh, because Shylock's stipulation satisfies the sixteenth-century definition of usury, as has been explained, and violates the principles governing legitimate interest: he has suffered no true damages nor has any gain been hindered (Bassanio offers far more in return than Shylock's principal), and the pound of flesh was stipulated in the bond on the day of borrowing and not added afterwards as a compensation on the due date of the bond. Other authors support Mosse's interpretation of interest; see, e.g., Jewel, p. 135; Wilson, pp. 319–20; Caesar, fols. 25–27; and John Blaxton,

ed., *The English Vsurer; or, Vsury Condemned. By The most learned . . . Diuines of the Church of England . . .* (London: Iohn Norton, 1634), pp. 9–10, where other conditions are added that even further deny any claim of legitimate interest for Shylock's pound of flesh. Cf. also Noonan, pp. 105–6; Jones, pp. 5, 10 for "interest" and pp. 22–23, 199, 201–2 for adherence to the rule of charity and virtuous intent necessary for a positive view of moneylending in sixteenth-century England.

41. Pope and Dyce emended "adventuring" to "ventring" and "venturing" respectively. See Brown, p. 13, textual notes.

42. Wilson's spelling ("adventuringe") differs from Mosse's spelling ("aduenturing," see p. 54–56), but Mosse's spelling concurs with that found in the first quarto and first folio texts for Shakespeare's play.

43. While this criticism and its language probably derive from the lending principle of *mutuum* (see Wilson, p. 276; Sander, sig. B7), the typical phrasing is "his own," "her own," or "their own" (see, e.g., Jewel, p. 118; Wilson, pp. 372–73; Sander, sig. B6v). The precise phrase, "mine owne," is atypical, but three instances appear in Wilson's lengthy treatise (pp. 236, 248, 276) and one in Sander, sig. C1v.

44. See Brown's summary of some of the commentary on this line, pp. 23–24, n. 36.

45. Shakespeare uses "cur" or its variants ("currish") four times and "dog" at least seven times in the play: see 1.3.113, 1.3.117, 3.3.18, 4.1.289; 1.1.106, 1.3.116, 1.3.123, 2.8.14, 3.3.6, 3.3.7, 4.1.128.

46. Noble, p. 97.

47. See Brown, pp. xxiv, 3, 160.

48. Mosse, p. 133. Cf. also, Henry Ainsworth, *Annotations. Upon the Fifth Book of Moses Called Deuteronomie* (Amsterdam: G. Thorp, 1619), sig. V2; Wilson, pp. 218, 241, 275, 285; Lodge, *Alarum*, sig. B3v; Sandys, p. 50; and Smith, p. 8 ("vsurers are byters").

49. See Jones, p. 29; Shatzmiller, *Shylock Reconsidered: Jews, Moneylending, and Medieval Society* (Berkeley: Univ. of California Press, 1990), p. 71. Shatzmiller studies a different type of historical and benign Jewish moneylender—one named Bondavid—in medieval Marseilles, as a contrast to the malevolent image of the Jewish moneylender popularized by the fictitious Shylock.

50. *The Tempest*, 1.2.401–2. Shakespeare's use of usury and the flesh bond will be further explored in my forthcoming book, *Choice, Hazard, and Consequence in "The Merchant of Venice,"* to be published by The Macmillan Press Ltd.

The Culture of Violence in *2 Henry IV*

Derek Cohen

I

THE SCHISM BETWEEN prose and verse plots in *2 Henry IV* is an index of the political dimension of the play's manifestation as an instrument of the patriarchal system which produced it. In recognizing the function of the differentiation between these plots we come closer to understanding one of the ways in which the concept of ideology is deployed by tracing the "cultural connections between signification and legitimation."[1] Wittingly or not and ambiguously or not, by its very existence the play is a piece of direct propaganda that serves the interests of the dominant class of the social formation from which it issues. Its use in the centuries since it was first written and produced testifies to the overwhelming capacity of the societies it has served to incorporate, absorb, and appropriate the results of the individual and collective labors of their members. The distinction within the play between its disparate worlds of comedy and court has usually been made to support the patriarchal value systems of the societies in which it is produced and taught. David Margolies notes that the force of the hegemonic use of Shakespeare lies "in the use of the plays as a whole, in how they have been 'naturalised' into the dominant ideology."[2] While it is true that some of the most adversarial and critical political points are made in the vernacular by ordinary characters, it is also true, as Margot Heinemann asserts, that the ruling class maintains its commercial and ideological hold on the play in production by routinely presenting these "low" characters "as gross, stupid and barely human—rogues, sluts and varlets with straw in their hair, whose antics the audience can laugh at but whose comments it can't be expected to take seriously. Indeed, the combination of Loamshire dialect and dated jokes often makes the comments unintelligible anyway."[3]

The political and dramatic value of Eastcheap is an established
feature of the criticism of the play. Eastcheap travesties Westminster; it inverts it and thus provides one of the potential displace-
ments of that dominant political world. It fleshes out the England
of the play and shows that England's ordinary people, like its high
people, have hearts, souls, and minds. Eastcheap, however, is not
only a funny place, a locus of irresponsibility and mirth: it is also
an ugly place of violence and poverty and corruption. And it is
these aspects of the play which I wish to address. I believe that
most discussions of the "low" comedy of the play are presented
and analyzed conservatively. That is, the dominant responses to
the "low" comedy of the play have been largely determined by what
Greenblatt has called the "monological" approach of scholarship,
which is itself an example of the readings it has recovered from the
play.[4] The "low" comedy of 2 Henry IV has been used both on
stage and in criticism to support the hierarchical and patriarchal
structures that produced the play and which criticism avers domi-
nates it. The most influential such analysis is, probably, Dover Wilson's The Fortunes of Falstaff,[5] whose exculpation of Prince Hal
still forms the basis of most such arguments. It is widely accepted
that the scenes of prose comedy provide an alternative action to
the court scenes. That is, the prose comic scenes are directly linked,
by parody and symbiosis, to those verse scenes of high seriousness.
Neither world exists independently of the other. The comedy needs
the court to give itself something to parody. These mutual needs,
however, go deeper than those of mere theatricality. Power structures always exist in vertical relationships. The court, in other
words, needs the comedy so that it can be the court. Comedy—
virtually synonymous with poverty in the play—needs the court
so that it can exist as comedy.

In 2 Henry IV the links between the court and the tavern are far
less a part of the author's design of a unified world than much
traditional reading has taught us to believe. The essential point
about the comedy of this play is that it represents a world which
is incompatible with and separate from the world of political
power. The agents of political power are violence and repression;
these are the instruments by which power contains the disaffection
of the poor and their impulses of subversion within a vertical structure of material well-being in which they are at the bottom. The
deeper we get into that comic world—the more complex and intricate its relationships seem, the more solid its traditions, lore, and

mysteries—the more complete we discover its separateness from the "serious" world to be. This is not to discount or challenge the critical notion of the interrelatedness of the various plots. Rather, I wish to propose that the relationship of the plots in the play is as tentative and contingent as the "low" characters perceive their relationship to the world of power to be, and that the severance of the worlds of poverty and power is deliberately maintained and encouraged by the world of power. Power has manipulated poverty into intensifying the separateness by creating conditions in the world of poverty which demand the development of social and political practices ultimately under its (power's) own control.

II

Notwithstanding its complexity, the prose of 2 *Henry IV* is an evident means of deepening the division between power and poverty. Brian Vickers has demonstrated that the prose has the effect of "conveying information about particular characters who are below the dignity and norm of verse."[6] The worlds of prose and verse meet rarely in the play, but when they do meet, as in the rejection scene, for example, the meeting is a violent collision in which prose is discomfited. A revealing encounter of this kind is, for example, the occasion in Part 1 at Shrewsbury when Falstaff dares to interject during the hard and charged verse dialogue between Worcester and the king:

> WORCESTER. Hear me my liege.
>   For mine own part, I could be well content
>   To entertain the lag-end of my life
>   With quiet hours, for I protest
>   I have not sought the day of this dislike.
> KING.   You have not sought it? How comes it then?
> FALSTAFF.   Rebellion lay in his way, and he found it.
> PRINCE.   Peace, chewet, peace! (5.1, 22–29)

Falstaff's interruption and Hal's reaction introduce a social complication. The smoothly functioning dialogue is disrupted by an intrusive sarcasm that wittily calls into question the entire structure of authority implied in the exchange. Falstaff interrupts the king; interposing himself between Worcester and Henry, he supplies an impudent answer for Worcester and, in so doing, mocks both the rebellion and the monarchy by subverting the high solemnity of the moment. Hal's reaction, embarrassed or angry, is designed to put an end to the disruption, to enable monarchy and support established authority. And, of course, it succeeds. Falstaff doesn't open his mouth again until the king and Worcester are gone.

The comedy of Part 2 begins with Falstaff trying to penetrate the ranks of power. His cynicism and open avarice, expressed most notoriously in his determination to "turn diseases into commodity" (1.1.250), have been the delight of some critics who have recognized a virtue in his frankness—a contrast, they say, to the hypocrisy of the court. The celebration of Falstaff's candor has itself served the forces of established order under the terms of that celebration. That order has developed sufficient resilience over the centuries to be able to absorb an amount of self-criticism (and even subversion) as long as it is not endangered. The criticism that can valorize Falstaff can do so only in forms that are themselves absorbable by the social order. Falstaff is, after all, defeated; his ambitions are alternatively constructable as delusions. For all its subversive possibilities, the narrative impulses of the play destroy him and the political, judicial, social, psychological, and economic upheaval adumbrated in his potential triumph. It seems to me erroneous to argue, however, that the play offers the vision of Falstaff's rule in its alternatively depicted actions or in Falstaff's megalomaniacal fantasies. When he proposes to ennoble Shallow or to take any man's horses, or when he declares that the laws of England are at his commandment, he only proposes one vision of his rule. But it is at moments like these that the drama becomes an overtly political instrument; Falstaff's declarations grossly reify the established order. His dramatic function becomes circumscribed by being contained within the limits of an antithesis already well-established in the play—his own, for example, to the Lord Chief Justice. Some may laugh at the idea of the reign of Falstaff, some may be horrified by it. Some may argue that the idea offers a world that is very little different from that which presently exists. The point is that what is offered by way of alternative—and alternatives do abound, not least in the king's proleptic description of chaos—is always partial, and always produced in the play in terms of static and hierarchical values. By way of egregious example: no one in the play puts into words the idea that the monarchy may be overthrown and replaced by a nonhierarchical communism. That alternative is imaginable, perhaps, but it has no perceptible touchstones within the dialogue of the play, nor are these appropriate historical referents to give it imaginative reality. As an option it could exist only in the minds of certain readers.

The much-quoted alternative to the rule of order is the speech of the king to Hal in 4.5:

> Harry the fifth is crown'd! Up vanity!
> Down, royal state! All you sage counsellors, hence!
> And to the English court assemble now
> From every region, apes of idleness!
> Now, neighbour confines, purge you of your scum!
> Have you a ruffian that will swear, drink, dance,
> Revel the night, rob, murder, and commit
> The oldest sins the newest kind of ways?
> Be happy, he will trouble you no more.
> England shall double gild his treble guilt,
> England shall give him office, honour, might:
> For the fifth Harry from curb'd license plucks
> The muzzle of restraint, and the wild dog
> Shall flesh his tooth on every innocent. (120–32)

The rule of Hal promises to be different from the present rule, and it is clear that he will have to make the choice of following in his father's footsteps or creating a new direction for the nation. But the construction of disorder is merely one of the play's many images of moral chaos designed to serve the entrenched structure of authority. For its images are all contingent on the rule of crime and criminals, on a vision of the nation as a wilderness of savage dogs, riot, sin, foreign scum, and ruffians dancing and drinking in the street. This notion of a nation governed by moral madmen is political and rhetorical, though it refers to a frequently expressed fear by "those in charge of Elizabethan and Jacobean England that disaffection might escalate into organized resistance."[7] It really proposes government by the poor as they are represented in the play. Henry's view of the tavern is a characteristic demonization, within the echelons of the privileged, of the forces of potential subversion. It is a typical example of the ideological displacement of the disorder generated by his rule onto those who are least politially powerful in his kingdom and therefore most vulnerable to such displacement. C. L. Barber has made the point that such inversions as the linguistic, in which Carnival is put on trial, are malign demonstrations of the potential destruction of society.[8] The king warns the prince against the people with whom he has been associating, and does so in terms designed to represent their worthlessness. If this vision has validity, then where does it leave Eastcheap? And what is Eastcheap?

The prince, of course, makes his choice to support monarchy and the traditions of his father in words that make plain his commitment to the conservative political values of patriarchy and order. In his most ceremonially solemn moments in the play he alludes directly to the tradition, to the values of his father, and to his determination to continue them:

> Not Amurath an Amurath succeeds,
> But Harry Harry. (5.2. 48–49)

And to the Lord Chief Justice:

> And I do wish your honours may increase
> Till you do live to see a son of mine
> Offend you and obey you, as I did.
> So shall I live to speak my father's words. (105–8)

III

Hal's words are a repudiation of Eastcheap and Eastcheap values. And if audiences and readers have been relieved at his recovery it is no wonder. For the play has made havoc of its own underworld. Notwithstanding its occasional subversive celebration of the mirth and pleasure in the stews, it is unambiguous about the calamitous political morality that obtains there. It is simply not a viable alternative to the rule of Henry. The rebels, on the other hand, with their political and military power, are a real threat to the king's position. But the threat is contemplated without horror. The potential rule of the rebels is not a rule of chaos, of nightmarish inversion. It is clearly understood by Henry's party that the rule of the rebels would be a substitutive rule. As Elliot Krieger has noted with regard to Part 1, "The rebel forces . . . oppose the state (not just as represented by King Henry; they want to divide the kingdom itself among themselves) without opposing the principle of authority."[9] Speaking the same language as the present monarchy, their rule promises to maintain the structure of hierarchical values already in place. The classes, under the rebels, would remain divided—prose and verse divisions ensure that. The threat of East-cheap, however, is a threat to the entire system of class-ification.

Now the king, the prophet of national doom, never sees East-cheap. In common, I believe, with most of the audiences and readers of Shakespeare in the last two or three centuries, his view of tavern life and poverty is largely imaginary and literary. The separation from that world is important. This is not to say that he is wrong—or right—about that world. Rather it is to recall that his separation from it releases him from the responsibility entailed in knowing; it releases his imagination. Eastcheap is indeed another "world," and not just in the dramatic sense. And its different language is merely one of the features of that otherness. In his discussion of *Measure for Measure*, Jonathan Goldberg makes the point that everyone in that play arrives in the prison "so that it reconstitutes the world and erases the margin between the world outside the prison walls."[10] Prince Hal is often thought of as the means of linking the two worlds of *Henry IV*, or erasing the margins between them. However, there really is no such erasure in *2 Henry IV*, no such intermingling in the play. Prince Hal's command of tavern language—in Part 1 he boasts, "I can drink with any tinker in his own language" (2.4.20)—powerfully maintains the structure of separation necessary to the relation of power and powerlessness.

The first scene to be specifically set in Eastcheap begins with Hostess Quickly, Fang and Snare employed to arrest Falstaff for debt. Snare is afraid of Falstaff, "for he will stab" (2.1.11). The fear gives rise to one of the play's better-known *double entendres* as the Hostess declares:

> Alas the day, take heed of him—he stabbed me in mine own house, most beastly in good faith. A cares not what mischief he does, if his weapon be out; he will foin like any devil, he will spare neither man, woman, nor child. (2.1.13–27)

Aside from the fact of this speech being in prose, there are elements of it that mark the class of its speaker and the world from which it issues. While it is certainly true that some of the most glowing Shakespearean heroines engage in bawdy talk without damaging their reputations or losing their status, there remains a significant difference between the present example of bawdiness and those others. First of all, on the level of sheer conciousness: when Desdemona, Rosalind, or Portia use bawdy conversation, they do so with wit and full awareness of the meaning of what they are saying. The

notable—and funny—thing about Hostess Quickly's speech is that
she seems not to understand what she is saying. As far as I know
there is no way of knowing what she knows except under the manipulation of an actor or director. Can it be that she thinks that
Snare's fear of Falstaff is sexual? If so, the implications of her
speech become outrageous and illogical. If, on the other hand, she
understands Snare as we understand him—that Falstaff's propen-
sity to stab people with knives and swords frightens him—then her
speech becomes outrageous in another way. She says that he
stabbed her in her own house, and she means, if she is confirming
Snare's reasonable fear of being knifed, that he stuck a knife or
dagger into her flesh. And we laugh. Naturally, we have to laugh
because the text is formally made funny at that moment by the
palpable use of sexual equivocation.

The equivocation, however, is subtextual. It depends on external
recognition. And it has been put there by a very clever man. For
the equivocation lends an enormous authority to the laughers.
Their (our) laughter is a declaration of the willingness to accept
the fusion of violence with sexuality and stupidity in the world of
Eastcheap. The laughter depends upon a subtextual, shared recognition within the audience or among readers. The hostess's words,
we are made to see, contradict themselves in a curious way. We
note the contradiction and we laugh at her, in part, because she
does not note it. But nor do Fang or Snare note the contradiction.
They, after all, are part of this world of lawlessness and fear. The
subtlety of the joke, the dependency on the recognition of wit by
those outside the play, and the failure of such recognition by those
within it, who—unlike us—are too stupid to understand it, have
the simple effect of deepening the division between the two worlds
within the play and of placing the audience in an alliance with the
mirthless world of the court and power.

The humor is given shape as Falstaff enters and a violent altercation occurs. Falstaff's fearsome rage and violent threats—"Draw
Bardolph! Cut me off the villain's head! Throw the quean into the
channel!" (45–46)—have the wild farcical force of comic cartoons.
They, and the actions that surround them—noisy, confused, chaotic—propose the possibility of violence without making it a likely
outcome. The risibility of this episode, unlike that of the passage
of *double entendre*, comes from the fact that a harmless outcome
stands as one of its immediate and initial conditions. This is
achieved by the use of outrageous exaggeration of implied gesture

and language, and reasonable audience expectation of the shape of the future.

It is interesting, nevertheless, to note how the violence is put to an end and order is restored. The Lord Chief Justice and his men intrude into the scene of violence. The forces of order and power arrive and demonstrate, once again, their capacity to contain riot and murder. However, the effect of this recovery has at least two significant social by-products. One is to reassert the value of patriarchy and hierarchy—society needs to have the instruments of physical suppression at its command. The other by-product of the intervention at this threatening moment is to contain poverty. Eastcheap, bursting with potential violence and the threat, therefore, of serious social disruption, needs to be accessible to authority. It is a fact that the prince and the Lord Chief Justice can enter Eastcheap at will; but the inhabitants of this ghetto are utterly excluded from the world of authority. We have seen, for example, one instance in which Falstaff—who occupies an ambiguous lower-middle ground between Eastcheap and the court—is chastised for not following the rules of court. The rejection scene makes even clearer the need to follow the rules.

The court's existence is contingent. It needs military power to maintain its existence and it needs to maintain the illusion of its own social necessity. The people need to believe that it is mighty and necessary for their own sakes. The existence of Eastcheap is contingent under entirely other conditions. But the overriding condition of its continued existence is that it be ultimately subject to the court. What happens in Eastcheap, we note, is of little concern to the court except insofar as it concerns the prince. The talk of violence, dishonesty and deception is personal, casual and everyday. These are conditions of life in the world of the poor. And, for the most part, they go on until they interrupt the workings of the state—in this case by involving the prince. The condition of visibility is crucial. Eastcheap needs to be identifiable to authority so that its power structures can be contained. In the play that visibility is maintained by a multiplicity of systems and social and psychological structures.

One psychological structure is the motive of social formation, the urge to be part of a structure. That is, the material conditions of the divided worlds of wealth and poverty compel community. It is unnecessarily paranoic to regard this spontaneous community of poverty as part of a conspiracy of power over poverty, but we ought not overlook the way in which this tendency to form groups is made to serve the system of power. The important question of why, and under what conditions, differentiated collectivities of people come to be organized in terms of one ideology rather than another is produced by the powerful/powerless dichotomy of the play and represented by its clearly marked patterns of differentiation such as its linguistic and discursive forms. Power tends to surround, locate, and determine powerlessness. We might note that in *2 Henry IV* authority can invade, defeat, and contain Eastcheap at will. The ease with which this can be managed is shown in the effect of the Lord Chief Justice's intrusion. He brings order and submission back to Eastcheap, and, notwithstanding Falstaff's verbal fencing with him in this scene, the Lord Chief Justice's last words—"Now the Lord lighten thee, thou art a great fool" (190)—make very clear his authority over this world to which he doesn't quite belong.

IV

Language and place help to isolate poverty—they make it recognizable and they keep it contained. Language, as I have proposed, functions in part to make poverty comic. It also has the power to make physical violence comic. The farcical momentum of violence in the first Eastcheap scene acquires new impetus in the major tavern scene of the play—act 2, scene 4. As a whole this play has an overriding political force which is designed not just to marginalize Falstaff, but to contain and separate the whole of Eastcheap. The value of separation as an instrument of political control is largely contingent on the presentation of physical violence in Eastcheap. Greenblatt's argument and demonstration that in Renaissance culture "contemporary authorities tried to contain or, when containment seemed impossible, to destroy" subversion is validated by the representations of the relations between authority and Eastcheap.[11] In this scene the effects of violence, from the point of view of the narrative, remain farcical largely by the ironically neutralizing use of sexual innuendo. While physical harm is really possible on one level, on another that possibility is effaced by the deflection of that threat. If a sword or dagger is equally a phallus, and if rape is a tavern joke (it is *never* a court joke), the idea of an attack with a sword is automatically split into two possibilities—one harmful and one harmless, one serious and one comic. The immediate and automatic association of the contradictory possibilities vitiates or neutralizes the danger.

Pistol, whose entrance arouses passionate responses, is the source of much violent language in this scene. His offer to "charge" (119) Doll Tearsheet elicits a vicious harangue and Doll's warning: "I'll thrust my knife in your mouldy chaps and you play the saucy cuttle with me" (126–27). This sentence, in the middle of a speech of comic invective, is unequivocal and therefore unfunny. It alerts us to the habit of violence in Eastcheap and to its real potential for social harm.

Eastcheap has two languages of violence. The equivocal language of violence in which violent bodily harm is made equivalent to and synonymous with the sexual act is one kind of language; its real potential for harm and danger is neutralized by a sexual meaning. Then there is the direct language of violence, unambiguous, deliberate, precise. "I'll thrust my knife in your mouldy chaps" is uncomic largely because of its use of detail and precision. It is the kind of language that uses some of the devices of realism—especially local specificity—for its effect. It operates without subtextual or comic meaning and thus makes the threat it proposes seem the more real.

Hal and Poins eavesdrop on Falstaff boasting to Doll Tearsheet. Their asides to each other, as they allow Falstaff to continue bragging, exemplify this kind of direct and undisguised language of violence found in Eastcheap:

PRINCE. Would not this nave of wheel have his ears cut off?
POINS. Let's beat him before his whore. (253–55)

Hal's threat is somewhat abstract and speculative, expressive of nothing so much as his anger and a quasi-comic wish for an extravagant punishment for the treacherous old villain. Poins, however, has a real and available resolution: to beat Falstaff and then to compound the "humiliation" of the beating by doing it before "his whore." The conjunction of the two punishments argues a structure of violence that is almost ritualized by repetition. Poins proposes to inflict physical suffering and public shame as a way of teaching Falstaff a lesson. It is as though he is arguing the social efficacy of this form of violence. The precision of the violence of such lines, which occur only in the prose scenes of the play, is what makes them seem real and more horrible than the grandiosity of the violent language in the court scenes. When, in Part 1, for example, Hal promises to kill Hotspur, he tells the king that he will wear a garment all of blood, that he will stain his favors in a bloody mask. He tells Hotspur at the moment of encounter not that he intends to shove a sword into his guts, but, rather, that he will crop Hotspur's honors to wear as a garland. The difference between Poins and Hal, indicated by their remarks as they eavesdrop, signifies a difference in their classes, in the worlds to which they really belong. Hal's words denote control through hyperbole—no one thinks he intends to cut off Falstaff's ears. Poins, on the other hand, speaks of a violent retribution that has real potential expression in the context of the scene. His threat, in a way, is almost reasonable and precedented. He belongs to this world of vice and prose, and his knowledge of such punishments as beating Falstaff before his whore brings the ugliness of the prospect unpleasantly close.[12]

In Part 2, the notorious threat of violence in the verse scenes of the play is evident in Northumberland's invocation of a spirit of universal bloodshed:

> Let order die!
> And let this world no longer be a stage to feed
> contention in a ling'ring act;
> But let one spirit of the first-born Cain
> Reign in all bosoms, that, each heart being set
> On bloody courses, the rude scene may end,
> And darkness be the burier of the dead! (1.1.154–60)

There is no question about the passion for violence and vengeance expressed in these words. Northumberland is revealing his capability, even his desire, to stick knives and swords into other people's bodies, to cut off their heads and throw them into the channel. But such details as these are not provided at times like these or in places like these. This is the world of the court, of real power, of potential monarchy, and the illusion of government and self-government must be maintained. Grim though Northumberland's vision of violent retribution may be, more sickening is the idea of Tearsheet's knife in Pistol's chaps. The antithesis of order in Northumberland's construction is freedom to commit murder. Order, that is, stands as political control.

It is going too far to suggest that the violence of the court is presented in a sanitized form, though it is normally justified in terms of its political and social value. Thus when Northumberland's friends protest at his "strained passion" (1.1.161), they are protesting at the way his call for destruction robs their enterprise of social and political value and validity. Northumberland's world of destruction greatly resembles the king's vision of the rule of ruffianism. All verse speakers agree—with the temporary exception of the grieving father, Northumberland—that the tavern and its inhabitants, the poor of the play, must be kept separate from the court. The distinctions of class must be maintained for the world to be governable. The poor must contained and controlled. Even a rebel government would be preferable to a social revolution. The ideology of order espoused by the rebels shows their desire to continue the hierarchical and patriarchal political practice already in place. The only true opposition to this order is in the riotous and violent tavern. The rural poor that we see are disunited and utterly obedient to authority, to the very point of approving its function, as Feeble's famous patriotic utterance eloquently shows.

V

Murder, obliquely referred to in Northumberland's summons of the spirit of Cain, truly exists only in the tavern. In act 5, scene 4, the beadles have come to arrest Doll Tearsheet and Hostess Quickly for murder. The First Beadle mentions the murder in the same breath as a joke about false pregnancy:

> HOSTESS. O the Lord, that Sir John were come! He would make this a bloody day to somebody. But I pray God the fruit of her womb miscarry!
> FIRST BEADLE. If it do, you shall have a dozen of cushions again; you have but eleven now. Come I charge you both, go with me, for the man is dead that you and Pistol beat amongst you. (12–18)

This is chilling. These characters we have been prepared to laugh at have really meant what they have been saying all along. They really do kill people. Stabbing and cutting off heads have ceased to be the jocose hyperbole of the early scenes, and the need to contain poverty and its ugly consequences is made more urgent. This murdering by beating touches us more nearly than the large mythologies encompassed in the Northumberland curse: a man has been beaten to death by two characters who possess more humanity, ordinariness, and recognizable frailty than all the kings, princes and earls of the cycle.[13]

The need for the containment of this potential violence at our doorsteps is fulfilled theatrically. From this world of murder and crime we are removed to a world of stability and certainty. Ritual and order are restored with the entrance of grooms announcing the time of day and accompanied by the sounds of ceremony. Trumpets blare, and the new king passes over the stage. His appearance is a reminder of the power he embodies. His train includes those characters who determine the directions of the nation, enforce its laws, hold its security in their hands: the Lord Chief Justice is with him, so is his brother John. The presence of the latter and his ready embrace by Hal confirms Greenblatt's claim that the moral authority of monarchical power in England "rests upon a hypocrisy so deep that the hypocrites themselves believe it."[14]

King Henry V passes over the stage surrounded by the agents of political control. The stage is then given to Falstaff, the very man Hostess Quickly is relying on to rescue her from a charge of murder which she hasn't even bothered to deny. As King Hal returns, Falstaff, who seems virtually to have exploded onto this scene breathing excitement and anticipation, tells Pistol that he, Falstaff, will "deliver her" from the charge of murder. It is, as Dover Wilson quite reasonably describes it, a kind of madness[15]—hubris in search of nemesis.

VI

The hypocrisy of King Hal—a necessary condition of power maintaining its moral dominance over poverty—is palpable even to Falstaff. But Falstaff, whose life of deceit has blinded him to the power of deceit, cannot recognize that Hal's hypocrisy is a permanent condition of his power. He knows that Hal's rejection is "but a colour" (5.5.84); why should he not know it? He is a man of good instincts and intelligence. But he has devoted a great deal of his life to breaking down the separation of power and poverty and calculates that this public declaration is the moment at which it all must happen. This is the risk of Falstaff's life as he claims the king as his own: "my royal Hal!" (41), "my sweet boy!" (42), "My King! My Jove! I speak to thee, my heart!" (46). In this public place, in the presence of the nation itself, its power and might contrasting with the ill-dressed rag tag of the tavern, Falstaff calls on the king to make his choice, to declare before the nation what its fate shall be.

That the rejection speech is a piece of blatant hypocrisy is certainly evident to Falstaff. His first words after Hal's speech indicate defeat: "Master Shallow, I owe you a thousand pound."(73) The quick cover-up of "I shall be sent for in private"(77) does little to take away the effect of the first recognition of rejection which has been validated theatrically and politically by previous events to which the audience or reader has been privy. It is in that reference to his debt to Shallow that Falstaff makes acknowledgment of the ultimate triumph of the patriarchal polity and of his exclusion from it. What he owes Shallow must come, after all, not from the public coffers but from his own pocket. Falstaff has been separated from those institutions which maintain power. He is relegated to his place ten miles from the person of the king; poverty and violence, having been authoritatively *named*, are restored to their safer places where they can be seen from a distance.

The public repudiation of Falstaff and those others whom Hal pleases to call his "misleaders" is eloquent political discourse. To describe it as hypocrisy—which it surely is—is to neglect its brilliant efficacy as an example of the discourse of political order. It is part of a performance designed for a public panting for order. It is part of Hal's genius to have made them pant. He has generated among his subjects a fear of revolution, a fear of the conflation or the inversion of prose and verse and the worlds they separately stand for. The rejection speech and its charged emblematic background entirely dispel that fear. Power is retained by the king. The rule of hypocrisy which has become synonymous with the rule of order is reentrenched. Hal's speech is a masterly example of the act of containment and separation. "I have long dreamt of such a kind of man"(49) is an act of separation of illusion and reality. It reconstructs the "real" as it separates the king's selves into a real one and an illusory one. As he has become king, the speech proclaims, Hal has been restored to the world of reality where poverty and patriarchy are separate and ought to be separate. "I do despise my dream"(51) he states, reinforcing the notion of his former self as an unreal ephemeral self. *This* is now, this is the real me. And, of course, he goes further, makes the point explicit. "Presume not that I am the thing I was"(56) is a declaration for one audience only— that audience onstage who have not been given repeated assurances of the underlying hypocrisy of Prince Hal. And it is that audience which requires the assurance that power has not changed purpose, that its interest is the same as those interests which have helped maintain it to this point. The moral issues of deception, friendship, loyalty are made subservient to the large issue addressed in the drama, the issue of power's ability to identify and contain subversion and violence and to perpetuate itself and fortify its own institutions in the process. In its identification of the threat of violent subversion, authority in this play succeeds—as the ending eloquently shows—in displacing its own violent impulses and failures upon those least able to reply.

Notes

1. Jonathan Dollimore, "Introduction: Shakespeare, Cultural Materialism and the New Historicism," *Political Shakespeare* (Ithaca and London: Cornell University Press, 1985), p. 5.
2. "Teaching the Handsaw to Fly: Shakespeare as a Hegemonic Instrument," *The Shakespeare Myth*, ed. Graham Holderness (Manchester: Manchester University Press, 1988), p. 52.
3. Margot Heinemann, "How Brecht Read Shakespeare," *Political Shakespeare: New Essays in Cultural Materialism,* edited by Jonathan Dollimore and Alan Sinfield (Ithaca: Cornell University Press, 1985), p. 225.
4. Stephen Greenblatt, ed., *The Power of Forms in the English Renaissance* (Norman, Okla.: Pilgrim Books, 1982), p. 5.
5. J. Dover Wilson, *The Fortunes of Falstaff* (Cambridge: Cambridge University Press, 1964).
6. Brian Vickers, *The Artistry of Shakespeare's Prose* (London: Methuen, 1979), p. 6.
7. Jonathan Dollimore, "Transgression and Surveillance in *Measure for Measure*" *Political Shakespeare*, p. 77.
8. C. L. Barber, *Shakespeare's Festive Comedy* (Princeton: Princeton University Press, 1972), p. 214.
9. Elliot Krieger, *A Marxist Study of Shakespeare's Comedies* (London: Macmillan, 1979), p. 133. I am in less confident agreement with Krieger's notion of Falstaff as an opponent of the images and institutions of authority, having perfect faith in his Machiavellian instincts for power, which he employs misguidedly in selecting the subtle prince as his means for acquiring power.
10. Jonathan Goldberg, *James I and the Politics of Literature: Jonson, Shakespeare, Donne and Their Contemporaries* (Baltimore: Johns Hopkins University Press, 1983), p. 236.
11. Stephen Greenblatt, "Invisible Bullets: Renaissance Authority and its Subversion, *Henry IV* and *Henry V,*" in *The Power of Forms*, p. 28.
12. In Part 1 after the Gad's Hill episode, Falstaff suggests that Hal and Poins are cowards. Hal pretends not to understand the reference; Poins takes a more immediate, spontaneous kind of umbrage, as though in the midst of this joke there are some things that cannot be joked about, and threatens Falstaff with slightly

alarming realism: "'Zounds, ye fat paunch, and ye call me coward by the Lord I'll stab thee" (2.4.141–42).

13. This is of course an assertion that accepts the notion that in Shakespeare's plays the prose is produced as being more "realistic" than verse—that it is more imitative of ordinary English speech than is verse.

14. Greenblatt, "Invisible Bullets," p. 41.

15. Wilson, The Fortunes of Falstaff, p. 118.

The Idea of Hunting in *As You Like It*

A. Stuart Daley

D R. SAMUEL JOHNSON counsels us that, "He who will understand Shakespeare must not be content to study him in the closet, he must look for his meaning sometimes among the sports of the field."[1] This good counsel certainly applies to studying *As You Like It*, which is in some respects a hunter's play. We learn in the opening scene that the banished duke has taken refuge in the Forest of Arden, and in Elizabethan parlance forest means a spacious habitat for game. Almost immediately thereafter we learn that the hapless duke and his fellow outlaws live like old Robin Hood of England, that is to say by shooting deer for venison. In keeping with this role they will come on wearing, like Robin Hood, the forester's standard summer coat of camouflage green. We are prepared to see why, "in these woods," the exiles must "go and kill us venison" (2.1.21), and hear them talk at some length about a stag "that from the hunter's aim had ta'en a hurt," and come "to languish" at a sylvan brookside (34–35).[2] Subsequently, the topic appears in three more scenes, culminating in the ancient motif of the princely hero who pits his strength and skill against the royal beast, a lioness. Elsewhere, too, the diction and action of venery supplies symbols, metaphors, and similes for lovers, the jester's shaft of wit, and so on.[3]

The pervasiveness and centrality of the theme can be indicated by the extent to which it attaches to the core character, Rosalind, when she plans to escape to the forest disguised as a boy, no less a one than "Jove's own page," Ganymed. It merits attention here since nothing has been made of its significance. For the long, dangerous tramp to the Forest of Arden, Rosalind dresses like a stripling soldier (many then going to the Irish war) or a boyish hunter. Lodge armed his Rosalynde with only a gentlemanly rapier, but Shakespeare gives Rosalind the formidable armament of a "curtle-ax upon my thigh / A boar spear in my hand" (1.3.117–18). The boar spear introduces a fitting symbolism as a traditional weapon for a champion of virtue against intemperance and, more specifically, lust, both being vices represented sometimes by a boar or sanglier.[4] Rosalind's boar spear, then, betokens her temperance and chastity, qualities she shares with a "goodlie Ladie clad in hunter's weed," Spenser's Belphoebe, of whom he declares that "in her hand a sharpe bore-speare she held" (*Faerie Queene* 2.1.21.7 and 29.1). Spenser's chaste and noble Britomart also yields a puissant spear. Moreover, classical symbolism assigns a spear to the goddess of wisdom and sometimes the virgin goddess of hunting, Diana. On the stage, a trident would have especially suggested the "chaste eyed, thrice-crowned queen of night," later invoked by Orlando when he rightly identifies "the fair, the chaste, the unexpressive" Rosalind as a huntress of Diana,[5] because Rosalind's role, like Belphoebe's, is Dianan as well as Venerean.

In a pleasantly allusive manner, royal Rosalind's hunting spear also relates her to her new namesake, for Ganymed, the puer regius, as readers of *Aeneid* V. 251–57 (Loeb Classics edition, pp. 462/463) would recall, was pursuing fleet stags with a javelin in his hand when Jove's eagle swooped to abduct him. Rosalind herself has recourse to the hart-heart pun, and she understands the figurative meaning of hunting the hare, the medieval hunt of Venus (4.3.18).[6] Then, too, in the forest context, with a slyly lewd rhyme and pun (on hind and lined), the Clown likens Rosalind to an estrous hind and hound bitch (2.2.101–2; 105–6). Altogether, this mélange of allusions and symbols drawn from classical and contemporary venery corresponds to the complexities of Rosalind's character and its dramatic tensions with her predicament, making her both the hunted and the huntress, pursued and pursuer, and a Renaissance Venerean-Dianan figure harmonizing in herself virtues both masculine and feminine.

Merely to notice Shakespeare's allusions to hunting, however, no longer assures our understanding of the sixteenth-century facts he designates by them, because to us, the words convey little exact meaning. A production of *A Midsummer Night's Dream* 4.1 that turned the royal couple into bird shooters illustrates the problem. The Amazon Queen came on, fowling piece at the ready, looking like, say, a painting of the Electress of Bavaria in Hunting Costume. She, Duke Theseus, and loaders have pushed into the woods, like Puck, through bog, bush, brake, and brier before sunup on May Day, shooting en route the pheasants draped on their aide. Haply, the shooting has not startled awake the charmed sleepers, like russet-pated choughs "rising and cawing at the gun's report" (3.2.21–22). They need to be aroused by a blast of a deer hunter's horn! The date, time (first light), and place of this astonishing pheasant hunt left the audience unperturbed.

Nor did the audience seem puzzled, much less bewildered, by the totally incongruous conviction of Duke Theseus that he was in the woods to set up a stag hunt. The presence of himself, with his forester, huntsmen and a pack of deerhounds in the woods at daybreak means that they have been harbouring, i.e. searching for, a warrantable stag in the covert. (A "palace wood" [1.2.101] is a deer park.) Duke Theseus wants the report without delay so that the chase can be started, as was usually done, in the "vaward of the day" (4.1.105): "Dispatch, I say, and find the forester" (108). The dialogue reports routine preliminaries of a deer chase. The bird-shoot innovators believed, or expected us to believe, that the Duke's pack of basset hounds had been brought along in couples to track down, with tunable thunder, the nesting pheasants.[7] In the woods! With hunting horn calls! As Theseus says in another connection, "Such tricks have strong imagination" (5.1.18). But the lesson is that in this arena actions now speak louder than words; for the audience, the Duke simply uttered high-sounding phatic patter. For both audience and players, the startling, even hilarious, contradiction between what was seen and what was spoken did not exist.

This passage uses technical details (103–11, 182–83) to account plausibly for the presence of Theseus and Hippolyta in the woods before the lovers awake at sunrise. They are keeping the hunt assembly at which the woodmen will describe the harbouring of the deer so that one may be selected. In short, their "observation is perform'd" (104) apparently for the game and for the rites of May simultaneously, and the Duke now sends impatiently for the forester (103, 108, and cf. 3.2.390–93) to come and report the tokens. Meanwhile, the huntsmen with their horns (138) and the coupled deer hounds (107) with their handlers stand by at wood's edge ready to begin "Our purpos'd hunting" (183). The only birds of note are the lark (94), signalling approaching sunrise, and the still sleeping "wood-birds" (140), whose discovery delays the preliminaries of the intended chase beyond resumption.[8]

I think it useful, therefore, to discriminate among the usual kinds of Elizabethan deer hunting so that the means of capture can be recognized and, in consequence, their implications about the conditions, purpose, and mood of the participants clarified. These findings can help to solve several interpretive and critical problems. In *As You Like It*, for example, are the refugees fleeting the time in careless idyllic escape, or eking out their existence in fairly straitened circumstances? Are they killing deer as a noble pastime sport, or are they hunting for survival? Is the Duke the comfortable old humbug invented by Shaw's untutored fancy, or a competent, compassionate, and indeed, ideal figure of the Renaissance governor? Is the hunting an arbitrarily imposed piece of humanistic propaganda against blood sports, or is it, on the contrary, an element artistically organic to the meaning of the play? What is there about the shot the Duke mentions that "irks" him? These and other matters in *As You Like It*, may be elucidated by reviewing the pertinent Elizabethan hunting practice and terminology.[9]

Broadly speaking, the Elizabethans pursued or sought for deer (their only big game) either on horseback or on foot, and killed their prey with, respectively, an arme blanche or a missile weapon. For the pursuit on horseback, the two common methods were coursing with greyhounds or chasing with scent-tracking hounds. The present-day British restriction of the word hunt to the use of horses with hounds came in later, but is anticipated as in Beaumont and Fletcher's *Philaster* (1608–10), 4.2, where one woodman declares that the princess will shoot and his fellow denies it, saying, "No, she'll hunt."[10] Both kinds of mounted pursuit may be called the chase, as was also a private game preserve large enough for enjoying them. Only the landed well-to-do could afford the many servants, horses, scores of hounds, hundreds of deer, appertaining facilities, and the extensive hunting rights required by this royal sport. The Queen spent far more on her hunting establishment than on her Office of Revels.

Coursing was the less complicated kind of horse and hound hunting. One or more dog varlets on foot accompanied the courser, each leading a brace or leash of greyhounds, swift, keen-sighted dogs. When a suitable hart or buck was located and started, they slipped the greyhounds, and the courser tried to be on hand to kill the animal when the greyhounds caught it. References to horses and the crossbow—or "bent" bow—indicate coursing. Since the courser usually shot the animal held by his greyhounds, he carried his crossbow "bent," i.e. with the string levered back against the powerful steel bow and cocked, ready to discharge the bolt. In contrast, the English longbow, which was bent only in the act of aiming and shooting, could not be effectively handled by a horseman.

A detail in Benozzo Gozzoli's "The Journey of the Magi to Jerusalem" shows a lance-carrying rider pursuing a large red-deer hind, seasonable at that time of year. The dog varlet has just slipped his leash of three greyhounds. Although it was painted about 1460, the detail gives us an easily looked-up picture of this sport if we imagine for the lance a more likely sword or crossbow.[11] In *As You Like It*, however, only the stag's tears "Cours'd one another down his innocent nose / In piteous chase" (2.1.39–40).

A stereotype of the criticism holds that, as R. P. Draper (1958) puts it, the play is concerned with "an ideally leisured existence which gives men and women the opportunity to enjoy life." Are we, then, to picture the refugees passing the days mindlessly chasing the deer? The commentators have given so little analysis to this question that the New Variorum Edition (1977) has no index entry for hunting. In recent years, Marco Mincoff has announced as if it were self-evident that "the picture develops rather on the background of the Elizabethan chase than on the Robin Hood ballads." Madeleine Doran assures us that Duke Senior's "companions find hunting and rough weather at least temporarily attractive," intimating a party of wealthy sportsmen roughing it in the backwoods. Speaking of Jaques' lament for the wounded deer, Claus Uhlig opines that "In *As You Like It* as a whole this characteristically Shakespearean assimilation of the humanistic *topos* investigated [the cruelty of hunting], serves, especially since hunting belongs to the trifling pastimes of courtiers, to accentuate strongly the criticism of courtly life which pervades the play and is explicitly formulated by the banished duke (2.1.1–8)."[12] For our present purpose, Judy Z. Kronenfeld excellently states this position and some of its interpretative consequences. Along the way, an uneasy sense of an ambiguity amounting to artistic incompatibility reveals itself.

> Outside a specifically pastoral setting, hunting is a way to turn a noble's "banishment" into holiday "liberty" (1.3.138). For this reason, the Duke's remarks about hunting, seen in a specifically pastoral context, seem to point to a discrepancy between the social idealism of pastoral (which opposes hunting) and the reality of privilege (which licenses it). It is true that Robin Hood, the hunter who champions the poor, becomes a pastoral figure in Renaissance literature, but his hunting is

surely in part a matter of *denying* noble privilege. In Arden hunting seems not clearly a necessity (in which case it might be excused), for fruit and wine are apparently available (2.6[7]. 98; 2.5.32). So it seems quite likely that Shakespeare is mildly questioning the Duke's position. And if this genuine questioning is muted by the self-indulgent sentimentality of Jaques' anti-hunting sentiments, it is still important to remember that hunting is a specifically non-pastoral activity—the prototype of the exploitation of man by man and of war, and unknown in the vegetarian and communal Golden Age. . . . Thus the Duke enters into an exploitative relation with the forest—a relation to which our attention is called—by engaging in the specifically noble leisure-time sport of hunting, which is traditionally opposed to the peaceful activities of shepherds who live in harmony with nature.[13]

This discourse poses the critical points to be examined here. To begin with, the "specifically noble leisure-time sport of hunting" has been understood for centuries as being above all the chase or hunt at force. This is the noble sport that Robert Langham praises for being "incomparable."[14] The author of *Turbervile's Booke of Hunting (1576)* announces that "I thinke meete likewise to instruct (according to my simple skill) the huntsmen on horseback how *to chase and hunte an Harte at force.*" (My emphasis.) He several times reminds his reader of this aim. Although a fallow deer (the species described in *As You Like It*) might be chased, it was, the author points out, "the hart, the whiche is the right chace to yeeld pleasure unto Kyngs and Princes."[15] By a hunt at force (French, *à force*; cf. Chaucer, slee with strengthe) Turberville's readers understood the pursuit of a deer by a party of horsemen and auxiliaries with as many as fifty or more scenting-hounds across, usually, miles of country open enough for their passage.

In his unfinished play, *The Sad Shepherd*, Ben Jonson has Robin Hood's woodmen put on (surprisingly) a hunt at force "to kill him venison" for a June feast. The interest to us here is the compression into the dialogue of Scenes 2 and 6 of Act 1 of an epitome—a useful cram—of the textbook stages and technical vocabulary of such a hunt, from the harboring and rousing of the stag to breaking it up and rewarding the hounds and raven. The game is not only a warrantable stag, a hart of ten, but a big wily one which runs for "five hours and more," a heroic hunt.

It is apparent that this sport partook of elements of a cavalry terrain exercise, and Elizabethans emphasized its value in providing the nobility and gentry with an exciting schooling in cavalry techniques. Indeed, the sport had been considered for centuries as a mimic war, hence a recreation of merit, a duty in fact, for princes and noblemen. Thus Thomas Dekker explains in some detail that "hunting is a noble, a manly, and a healthful exercise; it is a very true picture of warre, nay it is a war in itself."[16]

In 1599, the year that As You Like It was perhaps first presented, James VI of Scotland, advising his heir about suitable physical exercises, writes, "I cannot omit heere the hunting, namelye with running houndes; which is the moste honourable and noblest sorte thereof," and he deprecates the rival sport of hawking partly "because it neither resembleth the warres as neere as hunting dothe, in making a man hardy, and skilfully ridden in all groundes."[17] Near the end of the era, Henry Peacham cites the opinion of Eusebius "that wilde beasts were of purpose created by God, that men by chasing and encountring them, might be fitted and enabled for warlike exercises."[18] Not surprisingly it is the logical source of some of Shakespeare's metaphors for the exigencies of battle. His Forest of Arden was good country for the chase and the hunt at force.

In Poly-Olbion Michael Drayton describes a hunt at force as a representative feature of the Forest of Arden. He devotes seventy-five lines, "Song 13," 87–161, to a vigorous sketch of a "most princely chase" with its troop of huntsmen, horses, and hounds streaming across the Arden landscapes and raising a bedlam of shouts, horn blasts, and barking as they follow "the noble deer" over pasture and ploughland, through herds and hamlets. Such a hunt began by first light, as noted in the plays, when the lord of the hunt had singled out one of the warrantable stags located by the woodman. Once laid on, the hunt might run across country for many miles before it caught up with the deer; despite his ruses, the animal probably rarely escaped from the "piteous chase" unless night fall intervened. With his "legs then fayling him at length" (140), the beast tried in his simple, instinctive way to find a place favorable for defending himself with his antlers against "The cruell ravenous hounds and bloody hunters neere" (151), e.g., "Some banke or quick-set" (153) to back into, or a pond or river where deep water would hamper the hounds.[19]

"Such," marvels Turberville, "is the benefite of nature to give the dumbe beast understanding which way to help himself . . . and to save its selfe by all meanes possible."[20] As the stag took his forlorn stand "in such a desperate bay of death" (R3, 4.4.233), the "bloody hounds with heads of steel" (1H6, 4.2.51) closed in clamoring, and he was quickly "bay'd about with many enemies" (*JC*, 4.1.49). Then a hunter dismounted, crept upon the distracted creature and cut its throat, or stabbed it to the heart, the horns winding "the mort o' th' deer" (*WT*, 1.2.118). Beholding dead Caesar, Antony recalls such a scene: "Here wast thou bay'd, brave hart, / Here did thou fall, and here thy hunters stand, / Sign'd in thy spoil, and crimson'd in thy lethe" (*JC*, 3.1.204–6). After that they field-dressed the carcass and awarded the "fees" to hounds and hunters according to long-standing practice.[21]

If Shakespeare had intended the audience to blame Duke Senior's party for an excessive indulgence in the chase for no better excuse than their sport, he could have made it known easily and forcefully. On the contrary, he does nothing of the kind. The dialogue avoids mention of any of the unmistakable features of the chase. The beasts are fallow, not red deer. We hear nothing of huntsmen, horns, horses, or hounds. Terms of the chase such as emboss or bay, which Shakespeare uses elsewhere, appear in this play only in their respective medical and geographic senses. Above all, apart from the argument of silence, the sport is, or was, ruled out by its glaring implausibility.

In this connection, it is to be remembered that a great many Elizabethans from the Queen to the ploughman understood the facts of hunting and shooting. Participation in, not to mention observation of, hunting at force, coursing with greyhounds, and shooting driven deer from stands was common enough for a citizen of London, one like Thomas Lodge the son of a Lord Mayor, to enjoy all three pastimes. In *Letters Written by John Chamberlain During the Reign of Queen Elizabeth*, ed. Sarah Williams, Camden Society ser. 1, no. 79 (1861; rpt New York: Johnson Reprint, 1968), pp. 114 and 150, Chamberlain reports from Ascot, 13 August 1601, that at Beckley Park "we coursed, and killed, and carried nothing away," and at Woodstock "last weeke" had great sport bow shooting, presumably from a stand at driven deer. It must have been a real battue: he likens the volume of shooting to a soldiers' skirmish. Then, a year later, on 2 October, he mentions having been in at the chase of a huge stag "which we hunted at force" over two counties.

The many people familiar with the chase would hardly have imagined that a deposed duke hiding in the woods of a "desert inaccessible" with a few fellow exiles "whose lands and revenues enrich the new Duke" (1.1.102), fugitives who have left their "wealth and ease" (2.5.52) to play in "a woeful pageant" (2.7.138), could have got together the large number of expensive, delicate animals, a retinue of foresters and woodmen, grooms and farriers, stable boys and dog varlets, with carters, butchers, and others, and constructed for them necessary stables, kennels, courts, offices, and lodgings. One did not winter horses on picket lines or bed greyhounds and basset hounds in the rain and snow. In that connection, the Duke would need a number of kennels for the scores of dogs required to enjoy a holiday of several hunts a week, each kennel "a little house or lodge, with a spacious and large chimney in the same, wherein in the wintertime you shal allow fire, before which your dogs returned from hunting may stretch, pick, dry, and trim themselues."[22] The dog varlet lodged on the second floor of his charges' kennel. One does not seriously think that the noble proprietors would have returned from a wintry hunt to crouch in a cave, or that they "endur'd shrewd days and nights" (5.4.173) in woodland hovels. Surely their foresters or dog varlets would have taken them in.

On the grounds of silence and verisimilitude, we may dismiss the speculation of any specific leisure-time indulgence in the chase or hunt at force. The elimination of hunting on horseback now leaves deer shooting to be considered as the method.

Before the different ways of shooting deer are explained, it is useful to understand that they were not classed with the noble form of the chase or hunting at force. In Tudor opinion, the shooting methods had come to be tainted with crass utilitarianism. Elyot writes that, "Killing of deer with bows or greyhounds serveth well for the pot (as is the common saying), and there it must of necessity be sometimes used. But it containeth therein no commendable solace or exercise, in comparison to other forms of hunting, if it be diligently perceived."[23] Turberville simply ignores shooting. In the *Basilikon Doron*, James warns his heir that "it is a thievish forme of hunting to shoote with gunnes and bowes."[24] In Ben Jonson's *The Gipsies Metamorphosed*, Part I, lines 215–18, the Captain compliments James for being one who loves "a horse and a hound," and "hunt[s] the brave stag not so much for your food, / As for the weal of your body and the health of your blood." William Harrison had reported that the sale of venison by aristocrats excited strong popular disapproval, "infinite scoffes and mockes, euen of the poorest pezzants of the countrie, who thinke them as odious matters," being one of "such like affaires as belong not to men of honor."[25] Peacham, in turn, cites for his young gentleman reader the example of ancient kings who hunted "not to purchase Venison and purvey for the belly, but to maintain their strength, and preserve their health" (218).

One form of shooting, as will be seen, was certainly a pastime for princes and noble persons, but evidently not a noble pastime in the same sense as the chase. Today, Americans who kill deer for meat and by-products do not think of their activity as primarily a sport,[26] and apparently neither did the Elizabethans. The realization of this attitude toward pot hunting gives distinctive connotations to Duke Senior's command, "Come, shall we go and kill us venison?" (2.1.21), meanings that help us to understand the significance of the deer shooting in *As You Like It*. It is not a matter of noble sport; the Robin Hood type was not a sportsman but a survivor. He killed to eat.

For investigating the subject of shooting deer, two basic means remain to be considered. In one, stand-and-bow shooting, the shooter took a partially screened position ("stand") in or near a bush where he had unobstructed aim at any animal passing him at close range. The Elizabethans used this arrangement in two very different ways. One I shall explain later, the other provided a fashionable, even spectacular entertainment for grand personages, especially women of high rank and eminent men who had passed their physical prime. In such events, the host's woodmen drove selected deer along a killing ground in front of the stands. Since some of the animals would be wounded rather than killed outright, foresters with greyhounds, and sometimes bloodhounds, stood by to run down and dispatch them. In order to regulate the drive and supervise the shooting, stand-and-bow entertainments took place in a large park, which was by definition enclosed with a "pale" or fence designed to confine herds of deer kept for meat and recreation and managed by the estate forester. The identifying details of such an amusement, put on in a royal park for the visiting Princess of France, are carefully mentioned in *Love's Labors Lost*. An elaborate one had been given for Queen Elizabeth in August, 1591, by Lord Montacute in his park at Cowdray where refreshments were served to the spectators and musicians played while the Queen shot deer with a crossbow presented to her by a Nymph singing a ditty.[27]

Almost exactly one year later, two days of shooting were arranged for the heir to the Duchy of Württemberg, Count Frederick Mompelgard, at Windsor Castle, where, his secretary relates, "there are upwards of sixty parks . . . so contiguous that in order to have a glorious and royal sport the animals can be driven out of one enclosure into another, and so on; all which enclosures are encompassed by fences." While no such shooting occurs in *As You Like It*, it does illustrate matters of interest in the play. The secretary's narrative continues:

> And thus it happened: the huntsmen who had been ordered for the occasion, and who live in splendid separate lodges in these parks, made some capital sport for his Highness. In the first enclosure his Highness shot off the leg of a fallow-deer, and the dogs soon after caught the animal. In the second, they chased a stag for a long time backwards and forwards with particularly good hounds, over an extensive and delightful plain; at length his Highness shot him in front with an English cross-bow, and this deer the dogs finally worried and caught. In the third the greyhounds chased a deer, but much too soon [cf. *1H4*, 1.3. 178, "Before the game is afoot, Thou still let'st slip."] for they caught it directly. . . .
> [Two days later], August 21st, . . . his Highness shot two fallow deer, one with a gun, the other with an English cross-bow; the latter deer we were obliged to follow a very long while, until at length a stray track- or blood-hound, as they are called, by its wonderful and peculiar nature, singled out the deer from several hundred others and pursued it so long, till at last the wounded deer was found on one side of a brook [cf. *AYL*, 2.1. 33, 35, "To which place a poor sequest'red stag . . . Did come to languish"] and the dog quite exhausted on the other [cf. *Shr.*, Ind. 1.17, "(Brach Merriman, the poor cur, is emboss'd)"]; and the stag, which could go no further, was taken by the huntsmen, and the hound feasted with its blood.[28]

In passing one notes that this historical example suggests contemporary realities behind some of Shakespeare's hunting images. For example, when Talbot realizes that he and his troops have been trapped by superior French forces, the park hunt metaphor defines his predicament exactly: "How are we park'd and bounded in a pale, / A little herd of England's timorous deer, / Maz'd with a yelping kennel of French curs!" (*1H6*, 4.2.45–47). More particularly, perhaps, we can see what the Princess of France had in mind when, taking her shooting stand, she said, "But come, the bow: now mercy goes to kill . . . Not wounding, pity would not let me do it" (*LLL*, 4.1.24, 26).

More directly to our subject, these examples suggest some of the reasons why it irks the Duke that the deer of "this desert city / should in their own confines, with forked heads / Have their round haunches gored" (*AYL*, 2.1.23–25). First, his "native burghers" are not captive park deer, such as we have just seen, but free wild animals, the ferae naturae that live under God and the sovereign "In their assign'd and native dwelling place" (63) in keeping with the divine dispensation (a text for this concept was Job 39:1–8). Second, a quick, clean kill largely depended on the physical fitness and skill of the archer. The preferred target was, and is, the heart-region seen broadside, but the cervine's slim, narrow conformation makes this small target just behind the foreshoulder difficult to hit. The other vital areas, the neck and the upper part of the head, present a small and restless mark. These well-known facts lie behind shooting exploits in romance and ballad, as well as incidents in the plays. Thus Robyn makes the perfect shot when he and Gandelayn go to the wood to get them meat: "Robyn bent hys joly bowe; / Therein he set a flo [arrow]. / The fattest der of alle / The herte he clef a to." Again, the poacher-poet of the Prologue of *The Parliament of the Three Ages* (ca. 1350) illustrates the well-known fact that even a fatally wounded deer may still run for some distance before it falls, even though the shot had "the herte smote, / And happenyd that I hitt hym by hynde the lefte scholdire" (53–54), i.e., the preferred point of aim.[29]

In Lodge's romance, Rosalynde comforts Rosader with the thought that wounded game sometimes escapes, saying, "What newes Forrester? hast thou wounded some deere, and lost him in the falle? . . . 'Tis hunters lucke, to ayme faire and misse: and a woodmans fortune to strike and yet goe without the game."[30] The shot in the rump that Duke Senior speaks of, however, has not only that but other disturbing consequences. He would be further irked for reasons made clear by William F. Hollister, a wildlife biologist and bowhunter: "A rump or rear end shot is undoubtedly one of the worst that can be taken by an archer. Most modern bowhunters with any ethics and concern for the animal will pass up a rump shot. The likely effect on a deer hit with an arrow in [the] rump would more than likely result in a flesh wound in the 'hams'. If, however, the arrow passes through the 'hams' into the intestines and paunch the chances are that animal will die a lingering death."[31] (Cf. *AYL* 2.1.33–37).

In the dramatic situation, a bad hit resulting in the animal's escape (such as is reported by the First Lord), means the loss of a hundred pounds or more of food, and even if the carcass be recovered, the haunch, which was esteemed to be the choice cut, may be totally spoiled. In *As You Like It*, "to strike and yet goe without the game" means a calamity. Even though hunting for belly cheer may be demeaning and irksome to a nobleman, the refugees in the Forest of Arden face starvation, and therefore in the play's given circumstances hunting is as natural and needful as it had been for millenniums of human existence. Moreover, an attentive reading or auditing of the play, especially of Act 2, confutes the opinion that "alfresco meals are abundantly provided. . . . and there is no worse hardship than a salubrious winter wind,"[32] or, in the criticism quoted above, that "In Arden hunting seems not clearly a necessity (in which case it might be excused), for fruit and wine are apparently available (2.6.98; 2.5.32)." On the contrary, hardships crowd Act 2, including affliction by unsalubrious winds both winter and summer (2.1.7; 5.8; 6.15; 7.174). Shakespeare stresses afflictions in Act 2, but one above all, and that is hunger. Because of the persistent denial of these dark facts, it seems appropriate to state the record of hunger that colors Act 2.

2.1.21. Come, shall we go and kill us venison?

2.3.31. What, wouldst thou have me go and beg my food?

2.3.43–45. Take that, and He that doth the ravens feed, / Yea, providently caters for the sparrow, / Be comfort to my age! (Biblical allusions; Job 39.3 [Geneva; A.V., 38.41], Ps. 147.9, Matt. 10.29 and Luke 12.6, 24.)

2.4.64–66. . . . question yond man, / If he for gold will give us any food; / I faint almost to death. (This distress is Shakespeare's addition; in Lodge, they have food.)

2.4.73. Bring us where we may rest ourselves and feed.

2.4.80–83. My master is of churlish disposition, / And little reaks to find the way to heaven / By doing deeds of hospitality. (Allusions are seen to 1 Sam. 25, and, of course, to Matt. 25.31 ff.)

2.4.85–86. . . . there is nothing / That you will feed on; but what is, come see, . . .[33]

2.5.31–32. Sirs, cover the while; the Duke will drink under this tree.

2.5.39–41. [Who] loves to live i' th' sun, / Seeking the food he eats, / And pleas'd with what he gets. . . .[34]

2.5.62. And I'll go seek the Duke; his banket is prepar'd.

2.6.1–2. Dear master, I can go no further. O, I die for food!

2.6.16–18. . . . thou shalt not die for lack of a dinner if there live anything in this desert. (And more, but no thought of fruit!)

2.7.88, 89. Forbear, and eat no more . . . till necessity be serv'd.

2.7.105. I almost die for food, and let me have it.

2.7.128–29. Whiles, like a doe, I go to find my fawn, / And give it food.[35]

2.7.129, 132. There is an old poor man . . . / Oppress'd with two weak evils, age and hunger . . .

2.7.171. Welcome, fall to . . .

All but one, then, of the seven scenes of Act 2 feature hunger and food, a dramatic fact quite disregarded by the commentators. Yet, as the Duke makes clear at the outset, in the woods one lives not only in hardship, but also in peril. It may be morally commendable to take refuge there from ambition, but it is a risky place to seek one's food. The Duke's opinion has corroboration.

In a possible source, Anthony Munday's *The Downfall of Robert Earl of Huntington*, The Malone Society Reprints (1601; Oxford: Oxford Univ. Press, 1964), 1. 670, Prince John succinctly describes the outlawed earl as "The banisht, beggerd, bankrupt Huntington." When outlawed Fitzwater, "An aged man . . . Neere pin'd with hunger," happens upon Maid Marian in the forest, she gives him wine, venison, and "a manchet fine." He is welcomed like Adam (ll. 1517–27). Writing from experience, Spenser pictures the fate of the outcast Irish: "Out of every corner of the woods and glens they came creeping forth upon their hands, for their legs could not bear them; they looked like anatomies of death." When Spenser's vagrant Ape and Fox had "long straied . . . / Through everie field and forrest farre and nere," they too "almost sterv'd."[36] The Fox could hardly walk. In a famous scene, *2 Henry VI*, 4.10, Jack Cade too illustrates the fate of one who fled to the woods ("Fie on ambitions"), where he fruitlessly sought meat for five days, when, weak and desperate for food, rather like Orlando, he draws upon Alexander Iden, who kills him.

The great dearth of the late nineties would have made hunger of concern (the noted poor relief statute had passed Parliament in 1597). Furthermore, Elizabethans could respond to the subject with a considerable empirical knowledge of diet—Adam gives a brief example in scene 3. Jaques' simile of the "remainder biscuit" (2.7.39) and his jibe about the marriage "but for two months victuall'd" (5.4.183) were not lost on them. They understood that people living north of fifty degrees latitude like themselves need a high energy intake, and the civil and military authorities and the masters and mistresses of large households and holdings gave feeding frequent attention. The protein-rich field rations prescribed for the Queen's troops represent contemporary thinking.[37]

The commander of an isolated party forced to seek the food they eat would be eager to get protein-rich fresh venison, in Palamon's accurate phrase "lusty meat" (TNK, 3.3.27). Moreover, three literary analogues clarify for us the Duke's situation in these respects. In the source, Rosalynde, the exiled King of France and his outlaws, "frolikt it with store of wine and venison," with which they feed Rosader and old Adam. Later these two refresh Saladyne with "A peece of red Deere . . . and a bottle of wine. Tis Forresters fare brother, quoth Rosader: and so they sate downe and fell to their cates."[38] The analogue in the source behind Rosalynde, the romance of Gamelyn, comes closer when Gamelyn tells the outlaw king that he and Adam Spenser are seeking their food "under woode-shawes:"

> He moste needes walke in woode   that may not walke in toune.
> Sire, we walke not heer   noon harm for to do,
> But if we meete with a deer   to sheete thereto
> As men that been hungry   and mow no mete find
> And been harde bistad   under woode-linde. (Lines 672–76)

They are then bid to sit and eat of the outlaws' repast.[39] Third, Cymbeline, a later play (about 1610) yet one which resembles As You Like It with its deerhunting cave dwellers, who "are held as outlaws" (4.2.67, 138), a starving fugitive from the court and wilderness setting, presents a Shakespearean analogue with the deer hunting in Arden.

In straitened circumstances similar to those in the Forest of Arden, Belarius and the royal youths can kill deer in two ways only. One is the kind of stand-and-bow shooting that I have not yet described, often called still hunting nowadays, i.e., remaining quietly in concealment in a stand beside a deer run in order to ambush passing game. Sometimes a partner of the shooter tries to drive a deer to within range of the stand. An example occurs in 3 Henry VI, 3.1 where two keepers discuss the arrangements. The other way is stalking, i.e. working stealthily into close bowshot range without alarming the extremely wary beast; stalking is the demanding art of the "best woodman," the tribute awarded Guiderius. Even after the adoption of the long-range rifle for Highland stalking, a Victorian authority described the successful practitioner as a superior

type of man: "The *model* deer-stalker . . . should be of good proportions, moderately tall, narrow-hipped to give speed, and with powerful loins and well-developed chest for giving endurance and
wind . . . He . . . should care neither for fatigue, nor cold, nor
wet. . . . The bodily powers are not the only ones which should be
well developed, for the brain should be as active and energetic as
the body itself.[40] And somewhat more. A man who could fence,
wrestle, and pull the powerful long bow must have possessed similar physical qualities.

In any case, physical exertion gets attention in *Cymbeline*, which
excludes hunting on horseback and mentions no dog. They start
out at dawn (3.3.4, 7) when Belarius orders Guiderius and Arvira-
gus, "Now for our mountain sport: up to yond hill, / Your legs are
young" (10–11), and they return with their deer (75) "thoroughly
weary" and "weak with toil" (3.6.36–37) to cook their "meat" (38–
39), i.e. venison. Here, again, hunting means no trifling noble pastime, but an arduous pursuit of food, on foot with the bow and
arrow in the usual way of banished men, outlaws, poachers, and
others who "live i' th' sun."

With their assumptions of pothunting and feeding on venison,
all three analogues assume the hunters' charity. "If that he be
heende and come of gentil blood," Gamelyn asserts of the outlaw's
king, "He woll yeve us mete and drink and doon us some good"
(663–64). Moreover, being of "gentil blood," a true aristocrat, and
even more, a prince, was especially inclined to mercy because, unlike a churl, he was graced with a piteous heart, i.e. the capacity
for "sacred pity" (2.7.123) which the Duke exemplifies.[41]

A historical analogue occurs in a book that Shakespeare probably
had read, *The New Chronicles of England and France* by Robert
Fabyan where, in Capitulum Clxxii, Alfred ("Alured") the Great's
charity to an old religious man changes his fortunes. Several close
parallels between the circumstances of Alfred and Duke Senior are
seen.

Alured, being thus overset in multytude of enemyes, as affermeth Poli-
cronica and other, ladde an uncertayne lyfe, and uneasy, with fewe
folkes aboute hym, in the wode countree . . . and had ryght scante to
lyve with, but suche as he & his people myght purchase by huntynge
and fysshynge. [In whiche mysery, he thus by a certayne of tyme conty-
nuynge, . . . Upon a tyme when his company was from hym departed
and besyed in purchasynge of vytayle, . . . a pylgryme . . . requyred his
almes in Goddes name. . . Then the kynge anone called his servant, that

hadde but one lofe and a lytell whatte of wyne, and bad hym gyve the halfe thereof unto the poore man: ... Shortly after his company retourned to theyr maister, and brought with theym great plenty of fysshe that they hadde than taken. ...]

That night, in a vision, St. Cuthbert reveals himself as the pilgrim and promises Alfred victory over the Danes. "Than Alured, after this vysyon, was well comforted, & shewyd hym more at large. So y^t dayly resorted to hym men ... tyll y^t he was strongly companyed."[42]

The uncertain, uneasy life of King Alfred and his few followers in the wooded country gives a good idea of that of Duke Senior, for he too would have "ryght scante to lyue with, but suche as he & his people myght purchase by huntynge and fysshynge." Shakespeare makes abundantly clear in Acts 1 and 2 the impoverishment of the exiles and Orlando and Rosalind by the tyrants' confiscations and embezzlements (1.1.38–39, 102–4; 2.245–47; 3.65; 2.3.31; 5.52). Like the banished men and other fugitives in the sources and analogues examined here, the Duke's men suffer deprivation which forces them to seek their living in the sun like the outlaws idealized in "old Robin Hood of England." In consequence they give not out of superfluity but out of exiguity.

Presumably the scattered references in 2.7 to the "banket" bill of fare pointed to food-simulating properties to be seen on the stage by the audience. In any case, only fruit is named (98), probably indicating local bush berries. In the circumstances, however, it would be a mistake not to overlook its significance as an attribute of personified Misery, for "His food, for most, was wild fruits of the tree," Thomas Sackville tells us in The Induction of A Mirror for Magistrates (line 260).[43] Apart from fruit, the operative words are simply feed, food, and table. The dialogue supports two conclusions about the banket. First, food can hardly be abundant because the suppliant can only be offered "what help we have" (125), i.e., to the extent available to us. This implication is confirmed when the Duke assures Orlando, leaving to bring back Adam, "We will nothing waste till you return" (134). Second, while their food may be scanty, it must be substantial enough to revive the weak old man. "Let him feed," urges their host, and "fall to," expressions that suggest fare more substantial than, say, a bowl of berries. It seems logical that a cut of venison served as the expected pièce de résistance of the outlaws' woodland banket in the play as in the romances and Munday's Robin Hood plays.

We can conclude that they kill venison in As You Like It not for pastime but for food, and like woodmen or outlaws do so by shooting with the bow—probably the old-fashioned English longbow. Apart from Rosalind's "Love's keen arrows" (3.5.31), Celia mentions Orlando's bow and arrows (4.3.4) and Duke Senior speaks of wounding deer with the forked-head model (2.1.24). The deer that languishes by the brook has been shot, not chased. Moreover, Duke Senior has game shooting in mind when he remarks that Touchstone "uses his folly like a stalking-horse, and under the presentation of that he shoots his wit" (5.4.106–7). These outlaws shoot not for themselves alone, but for the common table of the band. Because for centuries hunters had shared their venison, they could typify on the stage one of the most distinctive human traits, the sharing of food.[44] The idea underlies Act 4, Scene 2, where the successful hunter's kill will be taken to the base camp to the Duke, who *has not been with the party at all!* Critics who accuse the Duke of indulgence in trifling pastime have not explained his absence from the deer kill.

The idea of hunting in *As You Like It* is to dramatize, first of all, the plight of the noble exiles. The particulars given us prevent our mistakenly supposing that they are carelessly passing the time in a happy, hunting holiday. In contrast, the introduction of the chase as their trifling pastime amidst an idyllic pastoral setting would be to trivialize and even falsify what began as a conflict of the virtuous and the loyal with the worldly unjust and capricious fortune. The first Act solidly establishes the reality of that evil and raises the issue of its remedy. To digress from this challenge into pastoral entertainments and anti-hunting topoi would be an artistically unjustifiable evasion of the dramatic issue that has been posed.

Presenting the deposed Duke and his loving lords as seeking their food with bows and arrows shows them reduced to means of survival that are both primitive and storied. Thus they identify with those outlaws in the analogues who "moste needes walke in woode that may not walke in toune," and so become "hard bistad under woode-linde." In the uncouth forest underneath the shade of melancholy boughs, they exist by their skill at pothunting. In addition to effecting this controlling circumstance, the idea of their hunting is to make clear the altruism of their sharing their scanty fare with Orlando and old Adam.

The idea of hunting makes other contributions to the play, of course, one being its rich allusiveness and symbolism.[45] But perhaps the essential idea flowers in Act 2, Scene 7 in the stage image of banished men, like outlaws and foresters, who, far from good men's feasts and where all things seem savage, welcome to their table two fellow players in this world's woeful pageant.

Notes

1. "Preface 1763," in *Johnson on Shakespeare*, ed. Arthur Sherbo, The Yale Edition of the Works of Samuel Johnson, vol. 7 (New Haven: Yale Univ. Press, 1968), 86.

2. My citations of Shakespeare are to *The Riverside Shakespeare*, gen. ed. G. Blakemore Evans (Boston: Houghton Mifflin, 1947).

3. I discuss the pattern of hunting language in 2.1 (which determines the time of year and the species of deer) in "The Midsummer Deer of *As You Like It*, 2.1," *Philological Quarterly*, 58 (1979), 103–7.

4. With reference to Rosalind's "martial outside," cf. *Faerie Queene*, 4.2.42.9, "But speare and curtaxe both used Priamond in field." Her weapons suggest a strong, tall girl. For the spear as an attribute see Adolf Katzenellenbogen, *Allegories of the Virtues and Vices in Medieval Art*, trans. Alan J. P. Crick (1939; rpt New York: W. W. Norton, 1964), 55. For boar and spear, James Hall, *Dictionary of Subjects and Symbols in Art* (New York: Harper & Row, 1974), 49, 247, 288; Guy de Tervarent, *Attributs et Symboles dans l'art profane 1450–1600* (Geneva: Libraire E. Droz, 1958): Minerva carries a *hallbarde*, col. 208, or a *javelot*, col. 224, as does Philosophy and, col. 225, Diana; also see *lance*, col. 230; and, col. 335, *Sanglier*, "Symbole ou Attribut de la Luxure." Cf. Spenser's Sir Sanglier, the "wild boar." Also, on boar symbolism, Beryl Rowland, *Animals with Human Faces* (Knoxville: Univ. of Tennessee, 1973), 38, and Marcelle Thiébaux, "The Mouth of the Boar as a Symbol in Medieval Literature," *Romance Philology*, 22 (1969), 296–98. Ovid's Salmacis, a type of narcissistic lethargy, takes no hunting spear nor does she vary her ease with the hardships of the hunt. Hunting found approval as an antidote to sinful idleness.

5. Furthermore, Diana has a proprietary connection with the Forest of Arden; she and Apollo were patron deities of Britain (cf. the oaths by Apollo, Lr. 1.1.160). As Diana Nemorensis, or surnamed Arden, the huntress goddess presides over the Forest of Arden, which is above all not a pastoral but a hunting ground. These associations duly appear in Michael Drayton's *Poly-Olbion*, where a nymph with a bow and arrows adorns the map of Warwickshire.

6. The *chace du connin* provided a classical hunting metaphor. Thus in the thirteenth century, with Ovid in mind, Jean de Meun speaks of his narrative as a "rabbit hunt" (ch. 81); see John V. Fleming, *The Roman de la Rose: A Study in Allegory and Iconography* (Princeton: Princeton Univ. Press, 1969), 186. D. W. Robertson, Jr., *A Preface to Chaucer* (Princeton: Princeton Univ. Press, 1970) explains this familiar medieval "hunt of Venus," 113, 263–64, and passim. Rosalind, in character, prefers the virtuous hunt of Diana. B. G. Koonce, *Chaucer and the Tradition of Fame* (Princeton: Princeton Univ. Press, 1966), 111, n. 46, cites references including the Ovidian source. Marta Powell Harley, "Rosalind, the Hare, and the Hyena in Shakespeare's *As You Like It*," *Shakespeare Quarterly*, 36 (1985), 335–37, arguing in part belief in the bisexuality of hares, relates the allusion to a latent "theme of homosexuality" (337) in the play. Actual hare hunting, coursing on horseback with greyhounds, was a popular upper-class recreation recommended for gentlewomen.

7. For the Duke's tracking hounds, slow goers with a true nose and a musical voice, see Henry L. Savage, "Hunting in the Middle Ages," *Speculum*, 8 (1933), 36 (the Old Southern Hound or an allied type); C. P. Onions, ed., *Shakespeare's England* (Oxford: Clarendon Press, 1917), II, 347 (bassets); Sacheverell Sitwell, *The Hunters and the Hunted* (New York: Macmillan, 1948), 74 (bassets); and D. H. Madden, *The Diary of Master William Silence*, new ed. (London: Longmans, Green, 1907), 47, 59, 78.

8. An early morning start adapts to the animal's habits; it often enabled the hunt to avoid the fatigues caused by the heat of the day. (Late hunts were shortened by being confined, as to a park.) The foresters first located one or more warrantable stags in their covert ("harbouring") and presented the "tokens" of the animals' age and size to the assembled hunt: then, one being selected, it was roused from cover, the scenting hounds loosed on its trail, and the hunt was off. *Turbervile's Booke of Hunting 1576*, Tudor & Stuart Library (Oxford: Clarendon Press, 1908) devotes much attention to these preliminaries. Also, *Shakespeare's England*, II, 335–36; Madden, ch. 2 and 3; Marcelle Thiébaux, *The Stag of Love: The Chase in Medieval Literature* (Ithaca: Cornell Univ. Press, 1974), 28–32. The early rising of foresters and hunters earned them admiring notice. On present-day practice, G. Kenneth Whitehead, *Hunting and Stalking Deer Throughout the World* (New York: St. Martin's Press, 1982), 16–17, reports that when deer are in open country and can be easily located, "the stalk and shot can be taken during the middle part of the day, even though most of the deer will probably be resting. In dense woodland habitat, however, the shot normally has to be taken when the deer are at feed or on the move, and this is only possible at dawn and dusk." Tudor bowmen would have followed much the same schedule, with a thought to saving daylight for the slow, arduous task of bringing in a heavy carcass unless they had a cart or pony for the purpose.

9. Michael Drayton gives an Elizabethan's impression of "that wondrous sport" of chasing the deer in the Forest of Arden in "Song 13" of his *Poly-Olbion*, and describes the occupation of a forester and the tools of his trade in *The Sixth Nymphal*. Edward, Second Duke of York, *The Master of Game*, ed. William A. and F. Baillie-Grohman (London: Chatto & Windus, 1909), apart from five original chapters, is York's translation (1406–1413) of Gaston de Foix, Comte de Foix, *Livre de Chasse* of which Savage says it "still remains unsuperseded in its knowledge of the habits of European game and its insight into the nature of hounds" (31). Much information about deer hunting ca. 1500 can be found in Margaret B. Freeman, *The Unicorn Tapestries* (New York: E. P. Dutton, 1976). Robert Langham (or Laneham) gives eye-witness accounts of the hunts put on for the Queen at the Kenilworth entertainments, 9–27 July 1575 in *A Letter*, ed. R. J. P. Kuin (Leiden: E. J. Brill, 1983). John Manwood, *A Treatise and Discourse of the Lawes of the Forrest* (London: Thomas Wight and Bonham Norton, 1598) deals with legal and managerial aspects contemporary with the play. T. R. Henn, *The Living Image* (London: Methuen, 1972) has useful background information, and G. Kenneth Whitehead surveys the subject in *Hunting and Stalking Deer in Britain Through the Ages* (London: B. T. Batsford, 1980). *Turbervile's Booke of Hunting 1576*, already cited, reprints the 1576 black-letter edition of George Turberville's *Noble Arte of Venerie or Hunting*. Although a study of German procedures, a valuable reference is David Dalby, *Lexicon of the Mediaeval German Hunt* (Berlin: Walter De Gruyter, 1965). Tudor writers emphasize the recreational and warlike benefits of pursuing deer with hounds and profess disdain for utilitarian pothunting—a distinction not always pragmatically evident.

10. Of modern usage Whitehead, *World*, 13, says, "In the United States of America and in many other countries, shooting—whether it be deer or birds—is

generally referred to as 'hunting.' In Great Britain, however, the word 'hunting' is reserved for any sport that entails the use of hounds." Sixteenth-century English usage was less restrictive, yet hunting with horses and hounds is virtually the only subject of the early treatises, with regard to deer.

11. Coursers are seen in the foreground of a painting of the great hunting estate of Nonesuch Palace by David Vinckboens in the Fitzwilliam Museum, Cambridge.

12. Draper, Mincoff, and Doran are quoted from extracts of their criticism in *A New Variorum Edition of Shakespeare: As You Like It*, ed. Richard Knowles (New York: The Modern Language Association of America, 1977), 523, 524, and 525 respectively. This edition is cited hereafter as The New Variorum. Uhlig, "'The Sobbing Deer': *As You Like It*, 2.1.21–66 and the Historical Context," *Renaissance Drama*, NS 3 (1970), 103.

13. Judy Z. Kronenfeld, "Social Rank and the Pastoral Ideals of *As You Like It*," *Shakespeare Quarterly*, 29, (1978), 338–39.

14. Robert Langham, 44–45, describes "the hunting of the Hart of fors," and asserts that "in mine opinion thear can be none [pastime] ony wey comparabl to this." For the Queen's ease that particular affair took place late in the day.

15. *Turbervile*, 109–10 and 9.

16. Thomas Dekker, *Lanthorne and Candlelight*, ch. 4, in *The Guls Hornbook and the Belman of London* (London: J. M. Dent & Sons, 1905), 209, and 210; the noblest hunters are those who chase the deer.

17. ΒΑΣΙΛΙΚΟΝ ΔΩΡΟΝ. or *His Majesties instructions to his Dearest Sonne, Henry the Prince* (1599; rpt. London, 1603), 121–22.

18. Henry Peacham, *Peacham's Compleat Gentleman 1634*, Tudor & Stuart Library (Oxford: Clarendon Press, 1906), 218.

19. Present-day versions of this sport exist in England and France. In his letter of 10 June 1986, Peter Atkinson, British Field Sports Society, informs me that, "Deer are still hunted with hounds in England as they have been for many centuries. There are three packs of staghounds all centred in and around Exmoor in the counties of Devon and Somerset, and they hunt the red deer. Bucks (male fallow) are hunted by the New Forest Buckhounds." He adds that, "The coursing of deer is no longer carried out in any form of organized way . . ." Whitehead, *World*, reports, "Hunting deer with horse and hound—*chasse á courre*—is still a very popular sport in France and more than eighty packs are actively hunting either stag or Roe buck—or both—throughout the country" (45).

20. The Tudor kill and that of the present-day English hunt seem to be significantly different. Atkinson states that, "The hunting of deer ends when the animal stands at bay. It is then shot either with a specifically adapted shotgun or a humane killer. The deer does not stand at bay when it is exhausted. It stands at bay when it discovers that [it cannot] escape the hounds. The hounds know that the deer is capable of putting up a robust defense and stand clear of it . . ." Drayton's huntsmen, however, run the animal to a standstill, when, like Actaeon's, their hounds lay "their cruell fangs on his harsh skin." Such an attack may be seen in sixteenth- and seventeenth-century paintings.

21. The ceremony of "breaking up" the deer and awarding customary portions to particular members of the hunting party, and the hounds, varied from place to place. *Turbervile*, 127ff, distinguishes between an English and a French procedure.

22. G[ervase] M[arkham], *Countrey Contentments* (1615), 14. Cf. *Shr.* Ind. I, 16, 28–29, where, after a severe run, the Lord gives orders for the recuperation of his pack—but the pack probably ought not to be run again "tomorrow."

23. Sir Thomas Elyot, *The Book Named the Governor*, ed. S. E. Lehmberg (London: Dent, 1962), 68.

24. The King's aversion (121) resembles that expressed by [Charles] Estienne

and [Jean] Liebault, *Maison Rustique, or, The Countrey Farme,* trans. Thomas Sur-flet (1600), 837, i.e., "The hunting of fower footed beasts . . . is performed princi-pally with dogs, horses, and strength of bodie," but the use of ropes, nets, and toils is "more fit for holidaie men, milke sops, and cowards, then for men of valour, which delight more in the taking of such beastes, in respecte of the exercise of their bodie and pleasure, then for the filling of the bellie."

25. *Holinshed's Chronicles* (1807–1808; rpt. New York: AMS Press, 1965), I, 344.

26. On this attitude, see *White-tailed Deer Ecology and Management,* ed. Lowell K. Halls (Harrisburg, PA: Stackpole Books, 1984), 710. The Tudor upper-class feeling that for a gentleman pothunting is unbecoming contrasts with their ances-tors' uninhibited slaughter of game for food, e.g. the drives cited in *Sir Gawain and the Green Knight* and *The Ballad of Chevy Chase.* In fact, the Elizabethans appear to have eaten the deer they killed, whatever the means. The nine hundred or so English game forests and parks had long been a major source of meat.

27. R. Warwick Bond, ed., *The Complete Works of John Lyly* (1902; rpt. Oxford: Vivien Ridler, 1967), I, 421–30. Also, E. K. Chambers, *The Elizabethan Stage* (Oxford: Clarendon Press, 1923), IV, 65. Madden somewhat digressively discusses the shooting from a stand, 226, 229–36. In Anthony Munday's *The Death of Robert Earl of Huntington,* the Queen Mother shoots "Mounted in a stand. / Six fallowe deere have dyed by her hand." See the Malone Society Reprint (Oxford: Univ. Press, 1965 [1967]), 11. 41–42. The men, with crossbows (13, 68–69), are coursing the stags and bucks.

28. Geoffrey Bullough, ed., *Narrative and Dramatic Sources of Shakespeare,* II, The Comedies 1597–1603 (London: Routledge and Kegan Paul, 1958), 47–48. The state of Württemberg had and continued to have good hunting; as late as 1914 grand-veneur was a Court post there as it still was in several royal households of Europe. Details in Lucas Cranach's painting, ca. 1529, "The Stag Hunt of the Elector Frederick the Wise" in the Kunsthistorisches Museum, Vienna, though on a lavish scale, might suggest typical features in the Count's hunting. The activities of the three potentates and their loaders, seen in the foreground, illustrate stand-and-bow shooting of the organized kind that Shakespeare presents in *LLL,* 4.1.

29. "Robyn and Gandelyn," *Middle English Literature,* ed. Charles W. Dunn and Edward T. Byrnes (New York: Harcourt, Brace, Jovanovich, 1973), 519, lines 20–23. Likewise, *The Parliament of the Three Ages,* 240.

30. *Rosalynde, Euphues Golden Legacie,* in Bullough, II, 200. Later, 215, Ro-sader shoots a deer "that but lightly hurt fled through the thicket." Also, in The New Variorum, 422, 437.

31. Principal Fish and Wildlife Biologist, Division of Fish & Wildlife, New York State Department of Environmental Conservation, letter to the author, 7 January 1986. In *Aeneid* 7, Ascanius looses exactly this "worse" shot, striking Silvia's pet stag through the paunch and the flank: perque uterum sonitu perque ilia venit harundo (499). The stricken deer flees and reaches its wonted shelter with fateful results. The Princess of France stresses the need to strike home, "Not wounding, pity would not let me do 't" (*LLL,* 4.1.27), and mutilated Lavinia, "Straying in the park, / Seeking to hide herself" is like "the deer / That hath receiv'd some unre-curing wound" (*Tit.* 3.1.88–90).

32. Harold Jenkins, "As You Like It," *Shakespeare Survey 8* (Cambridge: Univ. Press, 1968), 43. Since then, two editors who recognize the need to hunt food are Agnes Latham, *The Arden Shakespeare* (1975), lxix, and Roma Gill, *Oxford School Shakespeare* (1977). The latter observes that the duke "makes us aware that this life is not . . . the pastoral existence imagined by poets; in real life, men must eat meat, and they cannot do this without slaughtering the animals" (xvi). Whether

Stoic storm or Adam's penalty, wind and winter are ancient symbols of human afflictions; they teach us to know ourselves.

33. Caroline Spurgeon, *Shakespeare's Imagery* (1935; rpt. Cambridge: Univ. Press, 1965), 119, finds that, "The number of food and taste similes in *As You Like It* is remarkable." Corin's apology reminds the audience of the laborer's unpalatable diet of black bread, bacon, beans, and peas with milk or whey and cheese, a fact behind Orlando's sarcasm, "He lets me feed with his hinds" (1.1.19). In the hungry years from 1595 to about 1599, it could have been worse. See Andrew B. Appleby, *Famine in Tudor and Stuart England* (Stanford: Stanford Univ. Press, 1978), 5–7, and J. C. Drummond and Anne Wilbraham, *The Englishman's Food*, rev. ed. (1939; rpt. London: Jonathan Cape, 1957), 48–54 and passim. The use of fruit and vegetables was negligible; scorbutic ailments were common. The dramatic point is that Corin, the good shepherd, represents charity here ("I pity her"). In contrast, Corin's absent master ignores the Queen's order of 2 November 1596 "to stay all good householders in their countries, there in charitable sort to keep hospitality" for relief of the poor; see Paul L. Hughes and James F. Larkin, *Tudor Royal Proclamations*, III (New Haven: Yale Univ. Press, 1969), 172.

34. New Cambridge Shakespeare (1926), 180–81, interprets "to live i' th' sun" to mean "to live the life of an outlaw." The Arden (1975) editor aptly notes "a covert and paradoxical allusion to the distinction between living easily, under a roof, and living roughly exposed to all weather. Cf. the proverb 'Out of God's blessing into the warm sun'" (43–44). Unsurprisingly we are told at the end that they "have endur'd shrewd days and nights" (5.4.172). The New Variorum does not report these senses which also seem implicit in Amiens' concern that the "stanzo" will depress Jaques (10), and his own reluctance to sing it. Furthermore, Jaques already has his own "verse to this note," one which ridicules it. He who is "pleas'd with what he gets" makes a virtue of necessity.

35. The simile fits a period of a fortnight or so either side of Old Midsummer Day (5 July N.S.), and is consistent with Corin's "still handling our ewes" (2.2.53), the bucks being in velvet (1.1.50), and Jaques' charge that his companions "fright the animals" (2.1.62). Fawn habitat was supposed to be left undisturbed at this time, i.e. the "Fence Month."

36. As late as 1598, the Stratford district required relief from famine; see my, "The Dispraise of the Country in *As You Like It*," *Shakespeare Quarterly*, 36 (1985), 310, n.25. Shakespeare was required to report his holdings of corn and malt at New Place, 4 February 1598. The shortage of food cereals had seriously affected north Arden from 1596. According to V. H. T. Skipp's study of five parishes above Stratford, *Crisis and Development: An Ecological Case Study of the Forest of Arden* (Cambridge: Cambridge Univ. Press, 1978), 37, the crisis there was "characterized by a steady build-up in the number of pauper burials, while after two or three years the deaths of wanderers, strangers and beggars are recorded: unfortunate people whose lives had been unhinged by the severities of the times, leaving them no alternative but to take to the road and ultimately to die on it."

37. See C. G. Cruickshank, *Elizabeth's Army*, 2nd ed. (Oxford: Oxford Univ. Press, 1966), ch. 5, "Rations," esp. 82, and 88–89, where an issue of 1598 is given as a typical ration. Entries in the State Papers are numerous. On the necessity of adequate rations, Cruickshank points out that, "Although the bow weighed little, only a strong man could get the best out of it" (86), a fact relevant to the play. Also T. R. Henn, 78, 83. With respect to large households, even the minor landed gentry might feed a score or more of workers and dependents.

38. *Rosalynde*, 196 and 220 (New Variorum, 418, 441).

39. "Gamelyn," *Middle English Verse Romances,* ed. Donald B. Sands (New York: Holt, Rinehart and Winston, 1966), 174.

40. Stonehenge (John Henry Walsh), *British Rural Sports,* 13th ed. (London: Frederick Warne, 1877), 132. A diet of fruit and wine would soon render even this paragon of stalkers unfit.

41. Of interest here is J. D. Burnley, *Chaucer's Language and the Philosopher's Tradition* (Cambridge: D. S. Brewer, 1979), where the medieval concept of the association of *pitee* with *gentilesse* and the identification of the villain or churl with hardheartedness is explored. Traits of such psychological and moral types, including the tyrant, identify antagonists in the play.

42. Robert Fabyan, *The New Chronicles of England and France,* ed. Henry Ellis, rpt. from Pynson's ed. of 1516 (London, 1811), 167. The editions of 1542 and 1559 omitted the bracketed text for partisan reasons.

43. *Sackville's Induction, A Mirror for Magistrates,* ed. Lily B. Campbell (1938; rpt. New York: Barnes & Noble, 1960), 307, lines 260–62. Fruit sometimes suggests charity, and the angels brought fruit to Jesus in the wilderness (Hall, 134, 298). If Jaques' "reasons" (2.7.100) punningly (reasons = raisins) signifies grapes, as some believe, they might possibly recall Hosea 9.10: "I founde Israel like grapes in the wilderness."

44. Glynn Isaac, "The Food-Sharing Behavior of Protohuman Hominoids," *Scientific American,* 238:4 (April 1978), 90, writes, "Evidence for food-sharing by early manlike animals suggest it is the essence of being human," and, 92, "Among members of human social groupings of various sizes the active sharing of food is a characteristic form of behavior." In Elizabethan terms, sharing food obeys the natural law; in the play's opening scene the "unnatural" brother, Oliver, had denied Orlando a rightful place at his table. The green of the hunters' jackets visually signalled the play's appeal to love, hope, and regeneration, as well as the deer hunter's folklore-hero's role.

45. For some of the allusions and symbols, secular and religious, associated with stricken deer and the careless herd, see my, "To Moralize a Spectacle: *As You Like It,* Act 2, Scene 1," *Philological Quarterly,* 65 (1986), 147–70.

Shakespeare, Revenge Tragedy, and the Ideology of the *Memento Mori*

Henry E. Jacobs

THE SEVERED HAND, the skull beneath the skin, the blood-soaked handkerchief, and other such gruesome relics of human carnage show up repeatedly on the English stage between 1585 and 1640 in Renaissance revenge tragedy.[1] The *memento mori* of a revenger may be quite literal: Hieronimo keeps Horatio's rotting corpse, Hoffman preserves his father's skeleton, and Vendice clutches Gloriana's death's head.[2] These tableaux of the living and the dead are derived, at least in part, from well-established medieval traditions. In most cases, they represent a displacement of orthodox religious ideology and a superscription of the perverted and subversive religion of revenge over normative religious discourse. Shakespeare's use of the emblem and the tradition, however, is remarkable in its fidelity to medieval tradition and the orthodox discourse of the *memento mori*.

I

The God-centered orientation of the Middle Ages was expressed in a theoretical contempt for this world and a preference for the next. While both concerns emphasized the right way to live and to die, a notable aspect of the latter was an ever-growing fixation on the inevitability and horrors of death. The medieval fascination with death is well-documented; its pervasiveness in the early Middle Ages is illustrated in such texts as Notker's *Memento Mori* (c. 1060), Helinant's *Vers de la mort* (1194–97), and Pope Innocent III's *De contemptu mundi* (c.1200).

Throughout the Middle Ages, this fixation on death grew more focused and vivid, more emotional and realistic, and more pervasive. By the fifteenth century, English and Continental society were consumed with images and shows of death. In *The Waning of the Middle Ages,* J. Huizinga observes that "no other epoch . . . laid so much stress as the expiring Middle Ages on the thought of death" (124).[3] Similarly, Willard Farnham notes that "healthy people were writing *memento mori* and picturing the death's head over their fireplaces, on articles of daily use, wherever they would be likely to look while they were immersed in the business of living" (39).

In the late Middle Ages and early Renaissance, this fascination with death was expressed in three characteristic modes: the "genre" of the *Ars moriendi,* the Dance of Death, and the meditation on death. The *Ars moriendi,* in either textual or visual form, illustrates the temptation and ultimate salvation of the dying man. At the close of one of the shorter illustrated versions, we see the powers of salvation drive out the devils: "Moriens . . . used his free will responsibly, 'made a good death,' and found eternal salvation" (Beaty, 4). The Dance of Death presents a series of images in which "emperor and pope, empress and king, everyone down to the lowest peasant and child . . . is led away by dancing and grinning skeleton" (Spencer, 4). The symbolic iconography of the "dance" spread throughout England and the Continent in the form of frescoes, carvings, woodcuts, and even masques (Boase, 104). The third characteristic form—the meditation on the instant of death, the putrefaction of the body after death, or the death's head—is most germane to *Hamlet* and to revenge tragedy in general. In these meditative exercises, the same pattern is repeated over and over. Meditation on the moment of death and the decaying corpse leads to the contemplation of one's own sins, judgment after death, and ultimately, the Last Judgment and salvation.[4] "To think of death was to think of sin, and to think of sin was the only way to purify the soul" (Spencer, 6).

Taken in their totality and reduced to the common elements, the late medieval treatment of death establishes a series of orthodox religious doctrines that may be summarized as follows: (1) the inevitability of death; (2) the egalitarian universality of death; (3) the horror of the corpse and the grave; (4) the inexorable connection between sin and death; (5) the need to thrust aside worldly things; and (6) the movement beyond death and sin to judgment and salvation. The tradition thus creates a specific ideological matrix within which the literal *memento mori* can be seen. This discourse suggests that the *memento mori* should remind us of death, bring us to the contemplation of our own sins, detach us from the world, and move us beyond death to thoughts of God and redemption. Thus, the *memento mori* should re-present social and religious ideology that directs the contemplative individual into normative and codified patterns of meditation which spell out a logical and authorized progression from death to salvation.

II

This, however, is far from the case in most Renaissance revenge tragedies. Most revenge tragedians who employ death relics in their plays intentionally pervert the discourse of the tradition and obliterate the encoded orthodox religious ideology. In Kyd's *Spanish Tragedy* (c.1592), for example, we find two subverted forms of the *memento mori*. Although vengeance ostensibly begins with the appearance of the Ghost of Andrea and Revenge in the induction, the central revenge plot does not get underway until Horatio is hanged and stabbed in act 2. When Hieronimo discovers the body (2.5.), he immediately creates two remembrances of revenge, each of which we might term a *memento vindictae*. One of these is the handkerchief soaked in Horatio's blood that Hieronimo removes from the body: "See'st thou this handkercher besmeared with blood? / It shall not from me till I take revenge" (2.5.51–52).[5] The second and more gruesome *memento* is Horatio's body, which Hieronimo vows to keep unburied until he gains vengeance:

> See'st thou those wounds that yet bleed fresh?
> I'll not entomb them till I have revenged.
> Then will I joy amidst my discontent,
> Till then my sorrow never shall be spent. (2.5.53–56)

At the end of *The Spanish Tragedy*, Horatio's body appears once again. We must assume, I think, that Hieronimo has kept the corpse at home as a *memento vindictae* which goaded him, not toward the contemplation of mortality and salvation, but rather toward vengeance. Hieronimo's production of *Soliman and Persdeda* ends with the revelation that mimetic death has become the real thing, and the body is transformed into a sacred relic that justifies all:

> Behold the reason urging me to this: [*Shows his dead son.*]
> See here my show, look on this spectacle.

> . . . hope, heart, treasure, joy, and bliss
> All fled, failed, died, yea, all decayed with this. (4.4.88–95)

For Hieronimo, then, the *memento mori* becomes a visual and visceral encoding of the religion of revenge rather than a symbolic inscription of orthodox religious ideology. The blood-soaked handkerchief and the rotting corpse become the central relics in an inverted religion that displaces God with man and authorizes personal blood vengeance.

We find a similar perversion and subversion of religious discourse in Henry Chettle's *The Tragedy of Hoffman* (c. 1602). Here, the revenger walks on stage, commits himself to vengeance, and reveals his *memento vindictae* to the audience:

> Hence clouds of melancholy;
> I'll be no longer subject to your schisms.
> But thou, dear soul, whose nerves and arteries
> In dead resounding summon up revenge,
> And thou shall ha't; be but appeased sweet hearse,
> The dead remembrance of my living father,
> And with a heart as air, swift as thought,
> I'll execute justly in such a cause. (1.1.1–8)

While Clois Hoffman speaks these lines, he "*strikes open a curtain*" and reveals the bare "anatomy" or skeleton of his father hanging in a tree. The father was legally executed for piracy by having his brains burned out with a red-hot iron crown, having his flesh cut away, and being hanged in chains on the public gallows. The play never makes clear at quite which point in this process Hans Hoffman died. In any event, Clois has maintained his relic with all its symbolic attributes intact: the chains and the iron crown still adorn the skeleton.

The degree to which Hoffman cancels orthodox discourse and substitutes his own religion of vengeance is emphasized in his reaction to heavenly signs. During his first apostrophe to the skeleton, Hoffman hears "thunder and lightning." He reads into this celestial text divine authorization to strike swiftly:

> See, the powers of heaven in apparitions,
> And frightful aspects as incensed,
> That I thus tardy am to do an act
> Which justice and a father's death excites . . . (1.1.11–14)

Thus, Clois commits himself to a self-sanctioned course of ritual murders in which he will execute both the judges who condemned his father and their families.

Hoffman's first act of vengeance similarly reflects the extent to which the religion of vengeance has supplanted the orthodox discourse of the *memento mori*. His first victim, the son of the duke of Luningberg, is fortuitously shipwrecked on the coast of Prussia near Clois's cave. Hoffman captures Prince Otho, tells the history of his father's execution, and reveals the *memento vindictae* as a justification of the subsequent murder: "Look, Luningberg, 'tis done; / Behold a father hanged up by his son" (1.1.191–92). Hoffman then ritualistically duplicates his father's execution as he dispatches the prince of Luningberg; he burns out Otho's brains with a "burning crown" and strips off the flesh. Finally, he presents Otho's flayed corpse to the skeleton of his father and to the shrine of vengeance as a votive offering: "The first step to revenge, this scene is done; / Father, I offer thee thy murderer's son" (1.1.238–39).[6] Later, in the third scene, he actually hangs Otho's skeleton in chains next to his "long injured father's naked bones" (1.3.406), thus completing the ritual of duplication.

The perversion of the *memento mori* and the ideology it should represent reaches new heights (or depths) in Tourneur's *The Revenger's Tragedy* (1605–6). Vindice, like Hoffman, opens the play accompanied by his icon of death; he walks on stage holding the skull of Gloriana, his mistress, who was poisoned by the duke nine years earlier. Initially, Vindice plays the presenter; he introduces us to the nobles passing over the stage and to the skull. The opening monologue thus moves directly from a description of the corrupt courtiers to an apostrophe to the death's head:

> Thou sallow picture of my poison'd love,
> My study's ornament, thou shell of death,
> Once the bright face of my betrothed lady . . . (1.1.14–16)

This vision of Vindice clutching Gloriana's skull seems to carry all the symbolic inscriptions of orthodox religious ideology. Indeed, many scholars view it as an emblem of traditional medieval discourses. Peter Mullany, citing Theodore Spencer (238–41) and L. G. Salingar (402–22), asserts that Gloriana's skull "combines the themes of death, corruption, and judgment drawn from the medieval and Renaissance traditions of the Dance of Death, the *memento mori,* from homilitic and moral tradition, and from morality drama" (36). Parts of Vindice's first speech to the skull seem to support this interpretation. The skull has been the focus and the object of his contemplation for nine years: his "study's ornament." Such a perspective, however, fails to recognize the extent to which Vindice cancels or erases the very medieval discourses that the skull *should* encode. This "ornament" has not led him to contemplate his own sins, death, judgment, and salvation. Rather, it has become a *memento vindictae*, a sacred relic in Vindice's worship of revenge.

This displacement is hinted at in the three lines quoted above. Vindice calls the skull "thou shell of death." The near-homophonous pun on "shell" and "shall" converts Gloriana's skull from an object to a text that articulates the central commandment of the revenger's catechism; the phrase becomes the single "thou shall" of death. Cancellation and superscription are also evident in the parallel rhetorical and psychological movements of Vindice's opening speech. He moves directly from an apostrophe to the skull and meditation on Gloriana's beauty and death to an explicit commitment to revenge:

> Vengeance, thou murder's quit-rent, and whereby
> Thou show'st thyself tenant to Tragedy,
> O, keep thy day, hour, minute, I beseech,
> For those thou hast determined! (1.1.39–42)

This prayer to "Vengeance" is actually self-directed; as his name indicates, Vindice is both the spirit and the agent of revenge. The prayer thus displaces God, cancels the divine text of the *memento mori*, and replaces vengeance and Vindice at the center of a superscribed discourse of death. Like Hieronimo and Hoffman, Vindice turns the *memento mori* into the *memento vindictae*; his piece of dead flesh becomes the central relic in a perverted religious discourse that justifies his usurpation of God's place and authority.

But Vindice "out-Hieronimos" Hieronimo. His death's head—his *memento vindictae*—is more than simply a goad or a reminder. It moves beyond the symbolic encoding of the ideology of revenge to become the instrument of vengeance. Vindice, playing Piato the pander, arranges an assignation for the duke. He dresses out the skull, envenoms the teeth of the "bony lady," and leads his victim to a literal kiss of death. Before the deadly rendezvous begins, Vindice explains to his brother the ironic and perverse justice of his methods:

> I have not fashion'd this only for show
> And useless property; no, it shall bear a part
> E'en in its own revenge. This very skull,
> Whose mistress the duke poison'd, with this drug,
> The mortal curse of the earth, shall be reveng'd
> In the like strain, and kiss his lips to death. (3.5.100–105)

And it falls out just as planned: the duke kisses the lady with the "grave look" and is poisoned. As he dies, he is forced to face the death's head and acknowledge the consummation of revenge. Thus, we see the ultimate perversion of the *memento mori* and the orthodox discourse it encodes. No longer a key to meditation or a text that points toward the nexus of sin, death, and salvation, the skull becomes a relic of death and vengeance; the sign that saves becomes the kiss that kills.

IV

This pattern of cancellation and superscription is duplicated in many other revenge tragedies, including Marston's *Antonio's Revenge* (c. 1601), where Antonio creates a highly ritualized religion of vengeance centered on three crucial relics: the body, the coffin, and the tomb of his murdered father. The singular exception to this pattern, however, is Shakespeare's *Hamlet*, for the prince's contemplation of Yorick's skull remains consistent and conformative with the medieval traditions and the subtext of the *memento mori*.

We should note, at the outset, that there is a difference in kind as well as effect between Yorick's skull and the *memento mori* discussed in connection with other revenge tragedies. Unlike Horatio's corpse or Hoffman's skeleton, Yorick's skull is not a dead remnant of the once-living flesh that must be avenged. Nevertheless, the meditative tableau and the icon of the skull derive from the same late medieval tradition as the other gruesome relics, and they evoke the same contextual discourse of religious ideology. In addition, it is possible and reasonable to view Yorick's skull as an emblematic object that holds the place of two significant others. On the one hand, it simultaneously displaces on the stage and replaces in the audience's imagination the skull we really want to see—the relic of the dead father. This association between the present skull of Yorick and the absent skull of Old Hamlet is supported, at least in part, by Avi Erlich's assertion that "Shakespeare may have viewed Yorick as an ancestral figure in Hamlet's life. In fact, we know that Yorick must have substituted for the absent, wayfaring King Hamlet as a father to the Prince" (139). On the other hand, the skull is literally displaced to accommodate Ophelia's corpse.

The connection between Hamlet's contemplation of the skulls and the medieval traditions of meditation and *memento mori* has drawn significant critical comment, most notably by Louis Martz and Harold Jenkins. Martz's observations are seminal:

> The most striking aspect of all such meditations . . . is the full self-awareness of the vision: the eye of truth cuts aside all cant, looking with a grim, satirical humor upon all the follies of the world, seeing the worst of life and death with the poise of a detached, judicious intellect: the very poise of Hamlet in the gravediggers' scene. (137)

Similarly, Jenkins asserts that the "passage on *the skull* . . . is especially reminiscent of one in a popular book of meditation by Luis de Grenada" (551). And Theodore Lidz sees traces of the Dance of Death in Hamlet's musings: "as if viewing a painting of the Dance of Death, Hamlet sees the skeleton beneath the trappings, the pride, the pretense, the skin of Everyman" (98). The scene and the phenomenon warrant further consideration, however, in the context of the counter-tradition established in revenge tragedy.

The remarkable feature of Hamlet's reactions to the skulls is the degree to which the meditative Prince re-presents and reinscribes the orthodox religious ideology of the *memento mori* tradition. This fidelity is even more remarkable given the corruption and subversion that the conventions of revenge tragedy and the "School of Kyd" (Bowers, 101) seem to countenance. The first two skulls that are disinterred (5.1.73 s.d. and 95 s.d.) bring Hamlet to traditional and orthodox considerations of death's universality and the uselessness of earthly possessions. He suggests that the first skull may have been a politician, courtier, or "Lord Such-a-one" (5.1.83). He identifies the second skull as that of a "lawyer" or "great buyer of land" and goes on to contemplate the emptiness of worldly chattels:

> Hum, this fellow might be in's time a great buyer of land, with his statutes, his recognizances, his fines, his double vouchers, his recoveries. Is this the fine of his fines and the recovery of his recoveries, to have his fine pate full of fine dirt? (101–6)

The question, of course, is rhetorical; Hamlet clearly understands that this is the inevitable "fine" or end of earthly delights.

When the gravedigger identifies the skull of Yorick, Hamlet is led still farther along in the traditional meditative process. Similarly, his reflections further underscore the orthodox religious ideologies of the *memento mori*. At this point, Hamlet considers the horror of death and the corruption of the body: "He hath bore me on his back a thousand times, and now—how abhorred in my imagination it is. My gorge rises at it" (5.1.179–82). Again, he is led to consider the vanity of earthly existence: "Where be your gibes now, your gambols, your songs, your flashes of merriment, that were wont to set the table on a roar? Not one now to mock your own grinning?" (5.1.183–86). Finally, Hamlet moves on to contemplate the universal leveling power of death when he observes that Alexander and Caesar, like Yorick or any other corpse, are ultimately rendered dust, earth, and clay: "Imperious Caesar, dead and turn'd to clay, / Might stop a hole to keep the wind away" (5.1.206–7).

Beyond these immediate observations, Hamlet's meditation on Yorick's skull seems to have a traditional and ideologically normative impact on him. After the "gravedigger" scene, he is, at least in part, more prepared for death than for vengeance. This preparation is indicated symbolically in performance when Hamlet "leaps" into Ophelia's grave, grapples with Laertes, and calls for "Millions of acres" to be thrown on them (5.1.276). While the events may only indicate Hamlet's raging grief at Ophelia's death, the symbolism of leaping into the grave, an action justified by the stage direction in the First Quarto and centuries of performance practice, continues the linkage between Hamlet and death established in the meditation.

Hamlet's preparation for death, the authorized response to the ideology of the *memento mori*, is also conveyed in a subsequent conversation with Horatio. After Osric and an unnamed lord arrange the fencing match, Hamlet tells Horatio that he is ready:

> If it be now, 'tis not to come; if it be not to come,
> it will be now; if it be not now, yet it will come.
> The readiness is all. (5.2.216–18)

Harold Jenkins glosses the "it" in this set of parallel phrases as "death" (470n). The "readiness" that Hamlet prizes thus indicates his own preparation for death.

Hamlet's meditation on the *memento mori* does not conform in every respect to the authorized patterns of thought mandated by the tradition. He does not, for example, contemplate the connection between sin and death. Nor does he move to an explicit consideration of his own sins, death, judgment, and salvation, although other parts of the play suggest that these considerations are much in his thoughts. Most important, however, is the degree to which his articulated contemplations re-present and reinscribe the orthodox vision/version of the religious ideology encoded in the *memento mori*. Hamlet does not obliterate the authorized discourse; he does not deface the text of the skull, and he does not turn the *memento mori* into a *memento vindictae*.

V

We are left, at the end of this excursus, with two questions. First, how can we account for the perversion of the *memento mori* and the cancellation of its orthodox religious discourse in most English Renaissance revenge tragedy? And second, how can we account for Shakespeare's singular avoidance of this phenomenon? The answer to the first question is somewhat more accessible than the second. One solution to the general pattern is offered by Jonathan Dollimore, who argues that the plays themselves are subversive and that they "inscribe a subordinate viewpoint within a dominant one" (28). He goes on to assert that most Jacobean tragedy "subvert[s] providentialist ideology" (83) and "challenge[s] the basic premise of providentialism: . . . the idea of a teleologically encoded law governing the nature, identity, and interrelationship of all things" (107). Such a solution, while perhaps true in general, begs the question with reference to revenge tragedy. In these plays, the cancellation of orthodox religious doctrine stems from revenge itself rather than from a general subversive impulse in the drama. Revenge is the ultimate displacement of the God-centered discourse; it represents a personal usurpation of power that has already been appropriated explicitly by God *("Vindicta mihi,"* Rom. 12:19) and implicitly by the church and the state. Revenge itself is thus a subversive and dislocating process that obliterates God-centered texts and recenters man as god-revenger. The cancellation of the discourse normally associated with the *memento mori* and the superscription of the ideology of revenge thus re-presents the greater and more radical subversion embodied in vengeance itself. *Memento mori* becomes *memento vindictae* to illustrate the corruptive and subversive power of the impulse toward personal revenge. The ideological message is clear and providentialist: revenge disrupts authorized ideology, and religious discourse is one of its first victims. The *memento vindictae* thus became an emblem of the ideological subversion inherent in personal blood vengeance.

The answer to the second question has more to do with *Hamlet* and its revenger-protagonist than it does with ideology. Unlike Hieronimo, Hoffman, or Vindice, Hamlet never abandons religious orthodoxy and he never fully commits himself to vengeance. His adherence to doctrinal orthodoxy is reflected in both his eschewing of suicide and his careful evaluation of the Ghost's status. And while he affirms the need to eliminate Claudius after the Ghost's accusations are confirmed, his attitude throughout might best be described as ambivalent. This ambivalence even shapes the catastrophe of the play. Here, Shakespeare radically breaks with tradition and allows Claudius (the villain) rather than Hamlet (the revenger) to establish the shape of events. Thus, the fatal fencing match, the envenomed foil, and the poison wine are all Claudius's (or Laertes') inventions; Hamlet remains reactive to the end. It is this ambivalence, coupled with Hamlet's religious scruples and philosophical introspection, that accounts for the sustained orthodoxy of Hamlet's treatment of the *memento mori*. Hamlet never creates a religion of vengeance. Thus, he feels no need to cancel the orthodox ideology of the death's-head or transform it into a relic of vengeance.

Notes

1. The research for this essay was made possible by grant number 1231 of the Research Grants Committee of The University of Alabama.

2. Throughout this essay, the term *memento mori* is used in its most literal sense to refer to physical reminders of death. In this sense, it usually signifies some portion of (dead) human anatomy, ranging from a skull to a complete skeleton and even an entire corpse. Occasionally, however, the term refers to a type of late medieval text in which death is "remembered" through the contemplation of dying, human mortality, the corruption of the flesh, and the like. In all cases, context clarifies which usage is intended.

3. In *Death and Elizabethan Tragedy*, Theodore Spencer makes a similar observation, noting that "more than any other period in history, the late Middle Ages were preoccupied with the thought of death" (3).

4. This pattern of meditative and psychological progress from death, corrup-

tion, and the corpse to sin and then to judgment and salvation is evident in Renaissance texts that offer instruction in meditation. Frey Luis de Granada's *Book of Prayer and Meditation* (1554, translated 1582) instructs us to devote each Wednesday night to a meditation on every aspect of death and sin. The second part of this meditation focuses vividly on the corruption of the rotting body and the "loathsomeness of our grave" (191). Thursday night's meditation moves on to the contemplation of the Last Judgment and salvation. Similar meditative patterns are found in Gaspar Loarte's *The Exercise of a Christian Life* (1579) and Saint Francois de Sales's *Introduction to a Devout Life* (1609).

5. The handkerchief has a convoluted and interesting history as a symbolic object representing a series of sequential discourses. It begins as a favor of love that Bel-Imperia gave Don Andrea; she recognizes it and tells Horatio the beginning of its story:

> I know the scarf, would he had kept it still,
> For had he lived he would have kept it still,
> And worn it for his Bel-Imperia's sake:
> For 'twas my favor at his last depart. (1.4.44–47)

Horatio rescues the handkerchief from Don Andrea's corpse: "This scarf I plucked from off his lifeless arm, / And wear it in remembrance of my friend" (1.4.42–43). The transference thus cancels the amorous textuality of the handkerchief and turns it into a *memento mori*. Bel-Imperia, however, reinvests the scarf with some of its original significance when she awards it to Horatio: "But now wear thou it both for him and me, / For after him thou hast deserved it best" (1.4.48–49). At this point, the scarf bears a double encoding as a *memento mori* ("for him") and a *memento amoris* ("for me"). Almost immediately, however, Bel-Imperia begins to subvert these inscriptions and transform the handkerchief into a *memento vindictae* as she contemplates vengeance against Don Balthazar and asserts that "second love shall further my revenge" (1.4.66). This is the "handkercher" that Hieronimo removes from Horatio's corpse and transforms into his own *memento vindictae*.

6. The couplet illustrates the heavy-handed metadramatic devices that Chettle imposes at the beginning of the play. As we might expect, these lines actually signal the end of the play's first scene. One line earlier, Clois calls the murder of Otho "but the prologue to the'nsuing play" (1.1.237). It is, in fact, the first of five successful murders.

Works Cited

Beaty, Nancy Lee. *The Craft of Dying: A Study in the Literary Tradition of the "Ars Moriendi" in England.* New Haven and London: Yale University Press, 1970.

Boase, T. S. R. *Death in the Middle Ages: Mortality, Judgment, and Remembrance.* New York: McGraw-Hill, 1972.

Bowers, Fredson. *Elizabethan Revenge Tragedy: 1587–1642.* Princeton: Princeton University Press, 1940.

Chettle, Henry. *The Tragedy of Hoffman.* Malone Society reprints. Oxford: Oxford University Press, 1951.

Dollimore, Jonathan. *Radical Tragedy: Religion, Ideology and Power in the Drama of Shakespeare and his Contemporaries.* Brighton: Harvester Press, 1984.

Erlich, Avi. *Hamlet's Absent Father*. Princeton: Princeton University Press, 1977.

Farnham, Willard. *The Medieval Heritage of Elizabethan Tragedy*. Berkeley: University of California Press, 1936.

Huizinga, J. *The Waning of the Middle Ages: A Study of the Forms of Life, Thought, and Art in France and The Netherlands in the Fourteenth and Fifteenth Centuries*. London: Edward Arnold, 1924.

Jenkins, Harold, ed. *Hamlet*. The Arden Shakespeare. London and New York: Methuen, 1982.

Kyd, Thomas. *The Spanish Tragedy*. The New Mermaids. Ed. J. R. Mulryne. London and Tonbridge: Ernest Benn, 1970.

Lidz, Theodore. *Hamlet's Enemy: Madness and Myth in "Hamlet."* New York: Basic Books, 1975.

Luis de Granada, Frey. *Book of Prayer and Meditation*. Paris: Thomas Brumeau, 1582.

Martz, Louis L. *The Poetry of Meditation: A Study in English Religious Literature of the Seventeenth Century*. Revised edition. New Haven: Yale University Press, 1962.

Mullany, Peter F. *Religion and the Artifice of Jacobean and Caroline Drama*. Jacobean Drama Studies 41. Salzburg: Institut für Englische Sprache und Literatur, 1977.

Salingar, L. G. "*The Revenger's Tragedy* and the Morality Tradition." *Scrutiny* 6 (1938): 402–22.

Shakespeare, William. *Hamlet*. The Arden Shakespeare. Ed. Harold Jenkins. London and New York: Methuen, 1982.

Spencer, Theodore. *Death and Elizabethan Tragedy: A Study of Convention and Opinion in the Elizabethan Drama*. Cambridge: Harvard University Press, 1936.

Tourneur, Cyril. *The Revenger's Tragedy*. The Revels Plays. Ed. R. A. Foakes. Cambridge: Harvard University Press, 1966.

Direct Evidence and Audience Response to *Twelfth Night:* The Case of John Manningham of the Middle Temple

HENK K. GRAS

I

DURING THE LAST fifteen years or so, interest in communication in the theatre has grown and more attention has been paid to audience response. As regards the problem of methods in historical study, the importance of direct evidence for response has been emphasized, while the deduction of response from the dramatic text has become suspect.[1] Yet the historian of the Shakespearean stage cannot help being overwhelmed by feelings of despair, realizing how much information he lacks with which to tackle questions of audience response. The Elizabethans knew neither that special member of the audience known as the critic, nor the importance which producers today attach to documenting their views on their own art. This situation leads to a first basic remark on the nature of the direct evidence for response in the Elizabethan theatre: it was not meant to be criticism in the strict, modern sense. Any application of accounts of performances to answer our kind of questions about theatre response cannot take place without examining the kind of light these accounts throw on the performances referred to. Thus circumstantial evidence is needed to illuminate the context of the casual remarks which form the direct evidence.

*The author wishes to thank professor Andrew Gurr (Reading University) for his comments on drafts on this paper, which was presented at the Berlin Shakespeare Conference of 1986. I am also grateful to Frans Hijkoop, and, particularly, to Taco Kramers, for having corrected the English. Faults remaining are my responsibility.

Although it remains debatable whether the results of such proceedings are less unreliable than the traditional deductions of possible audience response from the dramatic texts, the principal case of study of historical response itself must not be distorted. For however unreliable, the aforementioned references are all we have to start with when arguing about concrete response. Their seeming inadequacy to cope with what today is perceived to be the deep and complex (innate) meaning of a dramatic text, reinforced by equally meaningful (innate) stage images, can be used to counterbalance too wild ideas on the original effect of drama in performance, and also form a starting point to study the function of drama and theatre in the Renaissance. If critical references appear to us to have been inadequate, it must be studied why they were and what impact of the performance on the spectator can still be deduced from the evidence. The consequent debates about the conclusions at least debate works of art in relation to their real original audiences, as contrasted to the hypothetical ideal ones.

The focus of this essay will be on Manningham's account of *Twelfth Night,* on fol. 12b of his diary, an account which is particularly interesting because it is one of the very few reports on a play containing sexual disguise. As the account is a private note, based on Manningham's memory of what apparently was a pleasant evening, it betrays "what was on the man's mind" in a more direct way than any more public kind of statement. The problem is that it is not easy to detect how that mind worked in the process of expressing itself in these words. Yet because Manningham did write just these things, they should not only be taken as important, genuine clues to a contemporary's attitude towards the theatre, but also as matters which somehow were of interest for him.

In order to get information about its content and form, the account will be related to the rest of his diary. For the account is itself part of the diary, also a text, having its own characteristics and aims. Any attempt to shed light on it may also provide some insight into the response to the play. Intertextuality between *Twelfth Night* and the diary, therefore, will be one of the focal points. Because of the play's sexual disguise plot and Manningham's main attention on the Malvolio plot, the erotic information in the diary will also receive special attention. The jokes in the diary will be used as a means to establish part of the mental frame with which Manningham approached *Twelfth Night.* Because jokes are part of a communication process, and Manningham always provides the narrator's name, they help us to understand part of the mental frame of his direct environment, thus of the way other Templars may have approached the play as well. The description of jokes will be based on the techniques Freud developed in his *Jokes and their Relationship to the Unconscious.*[2]

The life of John Manningham (ca. 1575–1622) has been written by the recent editor of his diary, R. Parker Sorlien.[3] Its demographic facts accord with Stone's description of the lives of late sixteenth-century gentlemen.[4] Manningham certainly belonged to the "privileged": he was not only his father's heir, but also the heir of his "cusin" from Kent, a wealthy former merchant and landowner who became his "father in love." In the Temple he was among the happy few (about 16 percent) to be called to the bar, and only his death in 1622 prevented him from becoming a Reader.[5] Manningham appears to have been acquainted with the central group in the Middle Temple, as described by P. J. Finkelpearl.[6] Manningham refers to Richard Martin, John Hoskyns, Benjamin Rudyerd, Thomas Overbury, John Davies, and others. But he does not appear to have been one of that central group himself.

Manningham's diary runs from Christmas 1601 to April 1603; the last account describes the final victory in the Irish war. Even though Manningham never states why he kept the notebook, nor why he kept it in that specific period, it is fairly certain that the book was for private use. "Private," however, was a relative notion in those days. That people had access to each other's notes is illustrated by the fact that Manningham gives "V.Ch. Davers booke" as the source of some information on fol. 44. There are also signs of self-censure, like the heavy canceling of names from an account about a love relationship (fol. 35b) and the sources of two more or less political jokes on fol. 59b.[7]

The account on *Twelfth Night,* which play Manningham saw on 2 February 1602 is, of course, very well-known:

febr. 1601.
2. At our feast wee had a play called [mid-cancelled] "Twelve night, or what you will"; much like the commedy of errores, or Menechmi in Plautus, but most like and neere to that in Italian called Inganni.

A good practise in it to make the steward beleeve his Lady widdowe was in Love with him, by counterfayting a letter, as from his Lady, in generall termes, telling him what she liked best in him, and prescribing

his gesture in smiling, his apparraile, etc., and then when he came to practise, making him beleeve they tooke him to be mad.

A superficial glance at the account yields elements of interest for historians. Manningham recalled the two names of *Twelfth Night*, and related the play to two plays whose titles are also mentioned. In fact, his report is one of the very few to relate a performance of one play to other plays, and this fact must be accounted for. We will try to explain his mentioning these plays' titles below.

Being well-informed about the titles, Manningham did not mention any names of characters within the play, nor of any actors playing them. (In his second account concerning the Chamberlain's Men, on fol. 29b, written some six weeks later he does use two names of actors.) He notices the characters as if they were living beings and more in terms of what they did than of what they said, more in terms of what they looked like, than of what they were.

As regards the characters, two things can be remarked: Manningham's manner of response is in line with the other references to *Twelfth Night* before 1642. Not one of them mentions actors featured in it. They do mention one character: Malvolio.[8] Secondly, Manningham takes Olivia to be a lady, not particularly responding to the fact that a boy played the part. Since he commented on a performance, not on a literary text, the theatrical illusion of reality worked for him. Again, his response accords with the scanty information on audience response to female characters, establishing the effectiveness of the boy actor on stage.[9] The apparent identification of actor and character is further suggested by the account on folio 29b, since that joke is based on the fact that Burbage had been asked to appear as the character he had acted.

Regarding the related plays mentioned, Manningham did not— as "structuralist" critics may wish he had—consider the play "in Italian called *Inganni*" as a derivative of Plautus' *Menechmi*. Their separation by "but" even suggests a perceived distinction. Critics may all too easily be inclined to consider the kind of plots deriving from *Calandria* and *Gl'Ingannati* to have been produced and deliberately received as variations on Plautus, to which the sexual disguise only gave an "extra" comic element. According to Manningham this was apparently not the case.[10] This should be a warning not to assume too quickly that similarities which are obvious to present-day views were also clear to audiences in the past. Again Manningham's response falls in with other evidence. The students of Gray's Inn in 1594 also likened *The Comedy of Errors* to *Menechmi*.

It is possible that Manningham did not even associate the title *Twelfth Night* with the feast of Epiphany. He first wrote "mid," then crossed it out and wrote "twelve." He may have thought of "mid night" being "twelve night." It may be that a particular epiphanic relation between the play's action and its title was not so obvious for an Elizabethan spectator, and there is evidence that the title *was* taken to mean "mid night."[11] For a first superficial survey, Manningham's account nonetheless reveals some substantial information.

Placing the scrap into context starts with looking to the sermon accounts, as sermons are the main body of the text of the diary. Forty-eight eyewitness reports of sermons are included, plus one deriving from another's notes and a handful of statements from sermons of uncertain origin. Actually, sermons literally took the form of literary criticism, starting with a few lines from the Bible and commenting on them. In addition to the Holy Writ, Manningham is also interested in verbal wit. Why did he busy himself with all this note-taking?

II

The reason why Manningham took notes on sermons can only be inferred indirectly. Explicit remarks can be distinguished from the contents of the notes themselves. Thus, in the first case, when Manningham himself uses the word "notes" for his sermon accounts, he uses it in the sense of (1) "account," or (2) "things noteworthy, to be kept for further reflection or remembrance." In relation to the sermons he uses "note" seven times, either in this specific form or in some derived form. Three instances suggest the second sense (fol. 27b: "noted by"; fol. 77: "[he] noted"; fol. 66b: "Note"). The instance referring (jokingly) to profane literature describes as a motive for note-taking the strangeness of the matter:

> One reading Horace happened upon that verse *Virtus est vitium fugere, et sapientia prima stultitia caruisse.* "Here is strange matter," said he. "Virtus est vitium." "Read on," said an other. "Nay first lett us examine this," and would not goe a word further. "Nay," said the other, "Yf you gather such notes I will finde an other as strange as that in the same verse: *Et sapientia prima stultitia.*" (T. Cranmer) (fol. 119)

He once remarks that a minister "taught" (fol. 54b). His irritation
in cases in which he had been unable to hear what was being said
can be ascribed to an eagerness to learn.[12] It accords with a witticism he quoted from Rudyerd, that those who only go to church
for the music come more for "fa" than "soul" (fol. 35b), and also
with Mr. Egerton's exhortation that "those which come to sermons
and goe away unreformed are like those which looke in a glas, spie
the spott in their face, but will not take the pains to wipe it off"
(fol. 77). Thus, the strangeness of the matter, combined with an
eagerness to learn may have motivated his note-taking.

How did Manningham take the notes? Traditionally "note-taking" is thought to have been written practice, both at plays and
at sermons. Jonson reports on "narrow-ey'd decipherers with their
writing tables" even in the theatres.[13] Against W. Fraser Mitchell,
who thought all notes to have been taken from memory, both Ramsey and Sorlien have claimed varying methods of note-taking. A
survey of the sermons does not lead to an unequivocal conclusion,
but Ramsey's and Sorlien's appears the most likely one.[14]

Although Manningham attended sermons for purposes of instruction, he proved to be no naïve supporter of everything said
there. Condemning one Mr. Richter, who "Reade muche but not
judicious" (fol. 13b), he himself shows some signs of an active,
judicial mind when attending to or describing the sermons mentioned. These signs can take the form of the use of the third person,
the creation of distance, criticism, or attentiveness.

The first two forms are a common element in Manningham's
notes. "The preacher said this or that" and its many variants create
a distance between the content of the sermon and accepting it naï-
vely as the truth. "It is told by him," is something different from
"it is." The notebook often uses phrases like "he collected" (fol.
44), "he defined," "he said this place in scripture is accounted the
hardest in all Paules epistles" (fol. 86), and "he interpreted the
words," "he expounded" (fol. 96b). There remains a loophole for
noncommitment.

Sometimes, Manningham openly criticizes some elements discussed during the sermons. The most clear examples describe the
position and pretensions of the ministers. Thus, when Mr. Barker
at Paul's Cross developed his argument into a rather hyperbolic
statement on the position of the minister, the notes break off, while
they indicate Manningham's intention to provide others. For, (a)
Manningham noticed three points to be developed, whereas the

minister had only reached his second point, and (b) there is a blank folio after the final note on fol. 25b. Manningham's phrasing may be felt to be slightly skeptical.

The ministers often managed to elaborate upon their own importance in relation to their economic need and social status (sermons on the fols. 20b–21, 25–25b, 27b–28, 40–43, 54b–55, 96), and in at least one case Manningham displays annoyance: when Dr. Dawson began to discuss this problem, after having already irritated Manningham by his bad rhetorical delivery, Manningham wrote: "here he stumbled into an invective against contempt of ministeres and impoverishing the Clergy" (fol. 65). And after having made notes on a sermon by Mr Layfeild, who preached, among other things, on "'Labour not for meat;' that is, make not meate the chiefest end of labour" (fol. 126), Manningham comments: "Mr. Hill told me that Mr. Layfeild married a rich wife, worth above 1,000 £. He speakes against covetousnes, but will exact the most of his dutyes in his parishe" (id.) He also quoted the following joke made by his chamber-fellow Curle: "Common preachers worse than common swearers, for thee doe abuse but Gods name, but they abuse Gods worde" (fol. 26b).

In a number of less transparent cases he seems to criticize or to refine the contents of the sermon. On folio 68b, the words "To peremptory to conclude before his premises," placed between the characteristically short lines, sound like a personal comment, because they have no bearing on the matter at hand (see also, more dubiously, fol. 27b, "he might have sayd," and fol. 46b, "the length of his text"). Dr. Overall invites the doubtful compliment that "He discoursed very scholastically" (fol. 128b). Although Manningham had strong anti-Catholic feelings and describes the Catholics (following the minister?) as "the common enimye" (fol. 71b); he criticizes "One at Paul's," because "his whole sermon was a strong continued invective against the Papistes and Jesuites. Not a notable villainous practise committed but a Pope, a cardinall, a bishop, a priest had a hand in it; they were still at the worst ende" (fol. 79b). His attentiveness, then, did not result in one-sidedness.

He criticizes Dr. Thomson for "laboured artificiall pronunciation; he regards that soe much that his speache hath no more matter than needes in it" (fol. 125b). This leads to what Manningham considered to be the elementary ingredients of a good sermon, which he found in Dr. Parry's: "it was right eloquent and full sound doctrine, grave exhortacions and heavenly meditacions" (fol. 38b).

He based his judgment, here, on a reading of Parry's text only, although the opening text "My God, my God, why hast thou forsaken me," is interestingly annotated with instructions for delivery: "*Vox horrentis*, forsaken; *Vox sperantis*, My God; *Vox admirantis*, Why hast thou etc." Parry proved as skilful in actual performance: "I was at the court at Richmond to hear Dr. Parry," "it was a very learned, eloquent, relligious, and moving sermon," and in his prayer "he left few eyes drye" (fol. 110). Admittedly, this happened on the eve of the queen's death. In addition to the qualities admired in Dr. Parry, there were those admired in that remarkable preacher at Paul's Wharf, Dr. Clapham, whom Manningham came to hear quite accidentally, but who became the most frequently quoted minister: "one Clapham, a blacke fellowe with a sour looke, but a good spirit, bold and sometymes bluntly witty" (fol. 80).

Comment on the delivery and habits of the ministers also formed a part of Manningham's critical attention. He not only noticed these things, but considered them important enough to be written down as well. What he wrote about Clapham reveals the two main points of attention: looks and habits. He describes Dr. Witheres as "a black man" (fol. 55b), and "one Barlowe" as "a beardlesse man of Pembrokes." He does not confine his descriptions to ministers. When he writes about a suit against Mr. Steven Beckingham, he provides the following portrait:

> A man of a hott collerick disposicion, a creaking loud voyce, a greasy whitish head, a ruddish beard, of long staring *mouchetons*; wore an outworne muff with two old gold laces, a playne falling band, his cuffs wrought with coloured silk and gold, a satten doublet, a wrought wastcoate, etc. *Ut facile quis cognoscat haud facile si cum aliis convenire posset, qui voce, facie, vestitu ita secum dissidet.* (Fol. 45b)

The description could have been a quote from literature, yet it is made from observation. Daily life is seen in terms of a book of characters; perception of the outer world corresponds with the images in literary texts.[15] Clapham's plain wit is also admired in others: "A good plain fellowe" preached at the Temple (fol. 66b). Manningham's admiration for plainness returns in social actions:

> When certaine schollers returning from Italy were at the Bishops of Canterbury, amongst other they came about my cosen Cranmer with their newfashioned salutacions belowe the knee. He, like a good plaine honest man, stoode still, and told them he had not learned to dissemble soe deepely. (Fol. 84)

And the same moral can be drawn from fol. 98b:

> Sir Christopher Hatton and another knight made challenge whoe
> should present the truest picture of hir Majestie to the Q[ueene]. One
> caused a flattering picture to be drawne; the other presented a glas,
> wherein the Q[ueene] sawe hir selfe, the truest picture that might be.
> (Reeves[?])

The second quotation is not only a plea for plainness, but also relates plainness to a view on art. The use of the mirror simile could have been an interesting point of reference for perception of the performance of *Twelfth Night*, with its natural perspective in tthe fifth act. Yet Manningham is silent on that aspect.

His interest in outward appearance can perhaps illuminate one point of his account on *Twelfth Night*—his reference to Olivia as a widow. Leaving aside the suggestion that the original play was different from the text we now possess,[16] two basic possibilities can be taken into account. The first is that Manningham referred to a widow because of the tradition of "widow-lore" which surrounded such plots containing stewards ("ste-wards") and unmarried mistresses; possibly he even thought about *Apolonius and Silla*, in which Julina indeed is a widow. The second is that Olivia, mourning, wore a widow-like costume. The first seems an improbable interpretation. Manningham does not refer to Riche's story when comparing the play with others, and the texts he mentions do not contain widows. (although there is no evidence he thought of the other plays as source-texts). His blunt way of looking at persons may very well support the idea already offered by Collier, that Manningham based his interpretation on Olivia's appearance. This might prove a form of face-value acceptance, a point to which we shall return.

Visual signs are related to comments on rhetorical delivery. Manningham expressed his annoyance with Dr. Dawson in the following manner: "All the while he prayed he kept on his velvet night cap untill he came to name the Queen, and then off went that to, when he had spoken before of and to God with it on his head" (fol. 65). Dawson was the man that "stumbled into an invective." "The plain plodding fellow" of fol. 76 did better, even compared to that "yong man" at Paules (fol. 99b), who "made a finicall boysterous exordium and rann him selfe out almost dry before he was halfe through." But Manningham must have suffered when seeing "At Paules, one with a long browne beard, a hanging looke, a gloting eye, and a tossing and learing jeasture" (fol. 79)—the same man who so un-justly attacked Catholics, who ran "over manie heresies," and re-peated, "take heede of them." It is understandable that Manningham preferred his "sour" Clapham, who could say, "An harlot is like a pantofle or a slipper at an Inne, which is ready to serve for every foote that comes" (fol. 81), or, "there are enough of Rahabs profession in every place; a man may finde a greate many moe then a goode sort. 'I would not give a penny for an 100 of them'" (fol. 80).

That Manningham was attentive to the text and did not simply like to "see" the service, as he said on fols. 54b–55, has been af-firmed independently by Sorlien and Ramsey. Ramsey discussed Wakeman's sermon on Jonah and the whale (fols. 27b–28; Ramsey pp. 324–25). It was printed in 1606 because "many copies of it, as they were taken by note, are scattered abroad in London and elsewhere," but "in unperfect form." Wakeman writes that he had the sermon printed as delivered, including the abridgments he had made as the result of a storm. Ramsey's conclusions indicate that Manningham's notes are a true outline of what is printed; it follows not only that Wakeman had the text printed as he indeed spoke it, but also that Manningham's notes were terse. Sorlien examined the sermon of Spenser at Paul's Cross, printed 1615, reported in the diary, folios 40ff. His conclusions generally correspond with Ramsey's.

Before getting irritated that Manningham's meticulousness did not display itself in the account on *Twelfth Night*, we should note that there is one phrase in it, which is remarkably detailed: "mak-ing him beleeve they tooke him to be mad." He could as well have written, "they tooke him to be mad." Manningham remained very well aware of the situation in its chaotic climax.

What did Manningham extract from the sermons? In addition to observations on their delivery, his notes show three types of digest-ing (or, "postprocessing") of the sermons' contents: the construc-tion of the argument (mostly with a paraphrase of its matter), disconnected notes, and notes on the method of interpreting texts.

Manningham appears to have been interested in the sermons' structure as such. Regarding the previously discussed sermon of Dr. Wakeman, he writes down, "His text 3 Jonah 4 et 5" and quotes it in full; next he describes the minister's division of the text. This is followed by a statement on the sermon's organization and notes on its content. In the same way he reports the following about a sermon of King: "The length of his text might make some tedious semblance of a long discourse, but the matter shortly cutt it self into two parts: example and rule" (fol. 46b). Sometimes a keen eye on structure seems to have been necessary because the ministers molded their sermons into true serial stories.[17]

When Manningham simply provides a number of unconnected notes, these bear sometimes on the matter of the sermon (as in his notes on fol. 5, which come close to a formally structured account, and in his notes on fol. 6). Often they are simply witticisms, mostly similes, which do not always display a very religious content and sometimes even border on satire and character-writing. It is no wonder that satirists became churchmen (like Hall, Donne, and Marston).[18] Dr. Mounforde's sermon apparently incorporated such interesting remarks that Manningham copied the notes from his friend Ch. Davers. Included were such statements as "Bacchus painted yonge because he makes men like children, unable to goe or to speake, naked because discovers all" (fol. 6b). Clapham's crudities have already been referred to. He was not the only one to frame edifying examples by dubious regard for women, as is shown by Mr. Philips who, among other things, taught that "pride is a theife and a whore too, for it robbes the maister of his wealth, and the mistress of hir honesty" (fol. 7b). The minister could use classical texts to support his examples, although there is only one clear reference to (classical) drama: "sin haunts us like the tragicall furies" (fol. 98; strikingly, this is one of the very few references to drama in the diary).

Benefiting from Chavers's account, Manningham extracted the following comment from Mr. Mounforde's sermon: "The malicious man is like the vultur, which passeth over manie sweete gardens and never rests but upon some carrion or garbage; so he never takes notice of anie thing but vices. Libellers are the Divels herauldes" (fol. 7). The image, interestingly, is quite similar to that used in *Hamlet*, 1.5.52–57, and 3.4.66–67. This kind of intertextuality can be detected in several places throughout the sermons. "Dissembled righteousness is like a smoake, which seemes to mount up to heaven, but never comes neare it" (fol. 8) could well be affirmed by King Claudius (3.3.97–98); "Ambitious men are like little children, which take great paynes in runninge up and downe to catch butterflyes, which are nothing but painted winges, and either perishe in takinge or flye away from them" (fol. 7b) could be affirmed by Coriolanus (1.3.57–65).[19]

Intertextuality can also be pointed out in relation to *Twelfth Night*. The imagery of the dove, olive branch, and song of peace in the sermon on fol. 27b is also used in 1.5.213. The pun on "to lie" in *Twelfth Night* (1.1.41) is also used in Donne's verse on the beggar on fol. 118. The clearest link between the diary and the text of *Twelfth Night* is the joke concerning Dr. Boleyn, who was forced to give the queen his dog and asked for it back again as a reward for giving it (fol. 112b). The joke appears in the play (5.1.1–6), yet Manningham quotes the joke from Curle without apparent awareness of having it heard before. A connection between the stage performance of *Twelfth Night* (2.3) and life in the Middle Temple occurs on fol. 57: "Barker told certaine gent[lemen] in the buttery that one of the benchers had sometime come downe for a lesse noyse."

Many examples in Manningham's notes illustrate his interest in the various techniques to interpret texts. He dutifully reports that:

> Speaches are either historicall, of a thing past; propheticall, of a thing to come; legall, of a thing to be done; or figurative, when one a thing is said and the other meant. [Of] figures there are in Scripture two almost peculiar—Typicall and Sacramentall: the one shewing one thing by an other, the other declaring what is conferred by another. (Fol. 18)

Spenser and King apparently used to lecture on hermeneutic techniques. They deserve to be quoted in full because of the obvious connection with poetics. They show distinct attitudes in the way of interpreting the text. Spenser's approach to the parables is allegorical, while King's emphasis on the function of example comes closer to Sidney's idea of rule and example.[20] Spenser says that human beings are so bad and so stupid

> that God is fayne to deale pollitikely with us, propounding our state unto us in parables as it were an others case, that thereby drawing man from conceit of himselfe which would make him partiall, he might draw an uncorrupt judgement of himself from himselfe.
>
> Parables are proportionable resemblances of thinges not well understoode; they be vayles indeed, which cover things, but being removed give a kind of light to the[m] which before was insensible, and makes them seeme as though they were sensible. (Fol. 40)

King says:

> Here is an acted performance, a demonstration, *to 'oti*, which are most forceable to persuade, being of all thinges saving the thinges them-

selves, neerest our apprehension, leading from the sense to the understanding, which is our certainest meane of acquiring knowledge, since
philosophie teacheth *quod nihil est intellectu, quod non prius fuit
sense; sicut audivimus, et fecerunt patres nostri.* Hystory and example
the strongest motives to imitation. Rules are but sleeping and seeming
admonitions [which is followed by the example of St. Thomas and the
wounds of Christ]. (Fol. 46b)

Although Manningham in various instances wrote about both
techniques of interpretation and the strong belief in "right reading"
of a text in such a way that it reveals a hidden meaning, the sense
must always be explained. Almost everything in the diary is explained, from the word of God to the silliest joke about a gentleman
and his "fescue." But within this frame of mono-interpretability,
poly-interpretability plays its part without attracting Manningham's conscious notice. Compare these two texts:

Our happiness is to be reunited to God, from which wee were fallen by
our first fathers synn; for as it is the perfection of a branche that is
broken of to be ingrafted againe that it may growe with the body, soe is
it the felicitie of man to be united to his Creator. And in this Union, as
well as God must be partaker of man, soe man be made partaker of God,
otherwise there can arise no Union. (Fol. 22b)

The branches are ingrafted; and as in planting all are tyed alike with
the outward bond, yet all prove not alike, soe all have the same profession and outward meanes, yet all growe not nor fructifie alike: but it is
the inward grace that maketh the true branche, as he is a Jewe that is
one within. (Rom. 2:28 et 29) (fol. 40b)

The same important image of the vine(yard) is interpreted to contain opposite messages. Thus while an attitude of symbolic interpretation exists, neither texts nor devices can be approached
through an unequivocal set of decoders. From the diary it appears
that the given meaning must be noticed carefully, because otherwise it gets lost. Authority and power of imagination (Manningham
would write "reason") decide about that meaning.

Manningham's favorite minister, Clapham, holds the literal text
in high esteem, commenting more than once on the stupid ways in
which "others" read and interpret texts. We will let him speak for
himself, in the way Manningham understood him:

Song of Salomon 4 ca.3v: Thy lips are like a thred of skarlett./ For the
exposition of his text he said he would not doe as many would after

the fancy of their owne braine, but according to the Scripture, expound it by some other place, and that was 2 of Joshua, where he findeth the same wordes, "a skarlet thred," v. 21 "Shee bound the skarlet threed in the windowe". He told a long story of Rahab before he came to the threed; and after almost all his sermon was an allusion to that story. (Fol. 80)

he said "Yf anie nowe after 44 years preaching and the Bible in English, were ignorant of that, it were a horrible shame. (Fol. 81)

It is a punishment for our synnes that wee cannot read right this age. They are unlearned malitious that read soe. (Fol. 88b)

The Revelacion might be better understood if men would better studye it. (Fol. 96b)

He noted that translators did very ill to foyst their inventions into the text and sett the originall in the margent. (Fol. 100)

Clapham, like Malvolio, is a man "not now to fool [him]self, to let imagination jade [him]; for every reason excites to this [meaning]" (*Twelfth Night* 2.5.157–58), and if we take note of his blackness and sour look, we only can wonder why Manningham did not see Malvolio in Paul's Wharf, or, vice versa, why he did not make more of the joke of the "counterfayted letter" when seeing the steward.

But we can also wonder why he did not connect Malvolio with Puritanism either. That Manningham did not like Puritans appears from his very first remark in the notebook, which claims that "A Puritan is a curious corrector of thinges indifferent," and also from fols. 31, 60, 70, 84 and 117b. Manningham also disregarded a link with Rainoldes, the Puritan critic related to *Twelfth Night* by Nancy Hayles.[21] Yet he knew Rainoldes and disliked him, for when he quotes his (very open-minded) cousin Cranmer, his criticism on Rainoldes is followed by the addition "Cran. and I" (fol. 66). The type of accident which befalls Malvolio, could also occur in reality and, again, could form a link with the plot line which Manningham did not establish:

It was told me by one of St. Johns Colledge that Dr. Playfare hath bin halfe frantike againe, and strangely doted for one Mrs. Hammond, a gent[lewoman] in Kent; is nowe well reclaimed, and hath reade some lectures since./ A mad reader for Divinity! *proh pudor, et dolor!* (Fol. 78b)

It may be that Manningham, among other things, used the sermons to study the practice of rhetoric, which as a lawyer he had to get used to.[22] The universities taught rhetoric, but there was no formal rhetorical training in the Inns, although it has been a topic of debate whether law students were interested in its theory and were well-trained in it.[23] There may have been several obvious reasons for Manningham's interest in sermons, other than interest in rhetoric. The ministers were scholars (Manningham almost always mentions the college that trained them), and were called "readers" (as in fol. 78b quoted above), like the readers in law who explained the statues of the realm in the Inns of Court during the holidays. Not only did both groups have the same social and intellectual background, but their very tasks themselves were also alike: textual interpretation.

The extreme juridicial interest on the part of ministers may be relevant here.[24] Important juridical explanations, similes and phrases can be found everywhere in the sermon notes, and they probably interested Manningham. This can be illustrated by some sermon notes that deal particularly with the comparison, such as:

> Fayth is the evidence of thinges not seene; as we hold our temporall inheritaunce by our writinges, which we call our evidence, soe wee clayme our eternall inheritaunce in the heavens by fayth, which is our evidence. (one King at Paules) (Fol. 103)

The juridical aspects of the sermons may have been of some use in the law courts. Among legal notes there is one which declares that a man who had set another man to manslaughter was like the actual killer condemned and executed (fol. 16). About six weeks later, Manningham wrote about the sermon of "one moore of baliol colledge in Oxford; his text: Amos 3:6: 'Shall there be evill in the City and the Lord hath not done it?'" (fol. 19b). Here the author of a sin is not necessarily a partaker of the sinful action. It includes a discussion of the common view that the meaning of a text is given by the listener, for, "Good meade is often tymes corrupted by a bad stommacke, and good doctrine of small effect with bad hearers." The sermon describes an attitude which should have led to a different legal treatment of "the author of the crime" as the crime's first cause but not its partaker.

Even setting aside these and similar relations (as on fols. 27, 58, 98), which prove the sermons to be useful in law, there remains the question whether the comparisons and reflections from the Holy Writ to legal matters affected the lawyer's view of his position in society. If Christ was an advocate or a judge, and if matters in heaven paralleled matters on earth, are we then dealing with that often presupposed Renaissance attitude—that earthly affairs reflect those in heaven? Does Manningham derive his earthly responsibility and even his very social position from the comparison with Christ? Were the sermons, reflecting on just behavior, examples to be adopted by the earthly advocates and judges? Unfortunately, the notebook does not explicitly comment upon this.

III

Having surveyed the sacred regions, it is now time to descend to profane matters: Manningham's response to literature and witticism. Manningham mentions many names: Spenser, Jonson, Shakespeare, Marston, and Montaigne, among lesser gods, but it is not easy to establish his precise interest in them or their work. In fact, authors praising Manningham for the "interesting range of reading and acquaintance" they find in the "young lawyer" (Ramsey, p. 329) overestimate him: we hardly know whether Manningham read or knew the authors he mentions. Spenser is only mentioned in a witty epitaph, probably copied from Mr. Holland (fol. 2), and as the alleged author of a rhyme composed to express his discontent with the queen's promised reward, which Manningham again took from someone else (Touse, fol. 31b). Marston is only mentioned in an anecdote (fol. 66b). The reference is to an evening of dancing at the revels that were concluded by the performance of *Twelfth Night*.[25] There is no hint that Manningham knew anything about their work, or was interested in the authors otherwise than for the sake of the noticed witticism. When writing about Jonson from Overbury (fol. 98b), he thinks it useful to add that he was a poet, even though there is some slight hint in the diary that he may have known *Every Man Out of his Humour*. He writes, "A covetous fellowe had hangd himselfe, and was angry with him that cutt the rope to save his lyfe" (fol. 118b), while on fol. 59 he comments on another joke about avarice as "sordid."[26] There is, however, no clue in Manningham's note either that he knew any of Jonson's works or Jonson's reasons for scorning the world. Montaigne is also referred to indirectly in a discussion with Mr. Girlingstone about men who "prefer a good hanging to prevent a bad marriage" (fol. 77b).

Manningham, then, only refers to Shakespeare in direct response to a work (on stage). Moreover, he reports an anecdote which shows that he is at least to some extent acquainted with other plays of his:

> Upon a tyme when Burbidge played Rich[ard] 3. there was a Citizen growe soe farr in liking with him, that before shee went from the play shee appointed him to come that night unto hir by the name of Ri[ch-ard] the 3. Shakespeare, overhearing their conclusion, went before, was intertained, and at his game ere Burbidge came. Then message being brought that Richard the 3d. was at the dore, Shakespeare caused re-turne to be made that William the Conqueror was before Rich[ard] the 3. Shakespeare's name William. (Mr. Touse) (fol. 29b)

From the phrasing it remains unclear to what extent he personally knew Burbage as an actor, although the joke assumes that Burbage and the play of *Richard III* did not need further explanation. How-ever, he must explain the joke by adding Shakespeare's Christian name, William, which is essential for the joke's impact, while it remains unclear whether or not he knew that Burbage's name was Richard. The name of his stage character was sufficient to under-stand the joke. Thus, although it is rather rash to claim that he had intimate knowledge of the Chamberlain's Men, it remains a fact that, of the authors who are today most highly estimated, Man-ningham devoted the largest number of words to Shakespeare. Yet the interest he took in Shakespeare, measured in words, is far less than the attention he devoted to other kinds of literature.

Counting the number of pages, political treatises in a more or less fictional style take up most of Manningham's writing. Their contents reflect Manningham's interest in the question of the aging of Elizabeth in a politically unstable situation and the succession by James.[27] As a type of literature they corroborate the juridical and sociopolitical apsects of the sermons.[28]

Most of the notes from such treatises are simply quotations from the texts he read. Only parts of the book describing the succession inspire exclamations like "a loggerheaded lye" (fol. 130b). Man-ningham expected judicious reading by others (fol. 13b), but he exhibits some remarkable examples of response himself. When he wrote down "Wee call an hippocrite a puritan, in briefe, as by an Ironized terme a good fellowe means a thiefe," he mentions *Albions England* as his source, but it turns out to be a very loose paraphrase of bk. 12, chap. 75, p. 311 (ed. 1602), in which no Puritan is men-tioned at all (fol. 54).

He wrote "pleasures are like sweete singing birds, which yf a man offer to take they fly awaye," (fol. 6b, from *The Picture of a Perfect Commonwealth*, chapter 36). In chapter 36 no comparison is made between pleasure and sweet singing birds, but in chapter 31 the third object of friendship, "pleasure," is said to be the pastime of youths and children who are comparable to "birds of the same feathers," that "do flocke and resort together," which kind of friendship is called ephemeral.[29] In this act of intertextual association a passage about birds sticking together in joyful unity of friendship is transformed into an account of physical separation and moral anxiety. The technique is one of condensation in the word "pleasure."[30] It leads Manningham's mind away from close intermale relationships.

An important part of Manningham's literary interest in the diary is directed towards the small poetic jokes and devices. The small poetic jokes emerge in the anagrams, epigrams, a fable, some paradoxes and mock epitaphs which the notebook abounds in; the devices are taken from Whitehall gallery, the mottoes of the lottery, and "poesies from rings." The jokes correspond to the witticisms of a less literary kind and can also be related to Manningham's interest in the nonreligious witticisms of the sermons; the designs can be related to the amount of interest shown in the sermons concerning similes and devices with a symbolic meaning.

The literature missing in the diary may also be of interest. Among the moral writers, the great Romans like Cicero and Seneca receive little attention. Plutarch is missing completely and neither do we find any reference to Ovid, nor to Ovidian poetry or to Elizabethan sonneteering. Romance is missing as well, including such a major work as Sidney's *Arcadia*. Besides the reference to the "feast" at which *Twelfth Night* was performed, and some use of the word "reveller" in jokes, Manningham never mentions revels, plays, or dancing in the Temple. Drama and theatre do not appear to have had the kind of attraction for him that they are usually taken to have had for the average Templar. In view of the literature not mentioned in the diary, we may even wonder whether Manningham can be considered as a representative Templar in the matter of judgment on literature and the theatre.

Apart from the reference to *Twelfth Night* there is no mention of attending any performances of plays, even though, as we will discuss below, Manningham probably did visit plays. Moreover, he only twice refers to other theatrical activities. He writes down a song from an unknown masque at court (fol. 1), and describes the entertainment of the queen at Cecil's house, including two masque-like shows. The debate by Davies between the widow, wife and virgin is among them, although Manningham shows no awareness of the parallels with Samuel Rowland's poem "It is Merry when Gossips Meete" (fol. 45), which itself is the only substantial literary poem included in the notebook.

Davies' device properly ended in pointing out the glory of virginity. This kind of allusion was generally understood to be allegorical at the time, probably also by Manningham: "Sundry devises; at hir entraunce, three women, a maid, a widdowe, and a wife, eache commending their owne states, but the virgin preferred" (fol. 75b). This may provide an example of a "mental set" in action. Manningham reads closely related texts using two different sorts of response: Davies' device as allegory and Rowland's poem as bawdry. It is, however, not at all clear whether or not he noticed their interdependence, or even whether his remark on Davies' masque can be taken as a sign of his consciousness of the allegory. Generally, Manningham does not consider any overt allegorical, thematic, or symbolic interpretation of literature, nor of drama in performance, e.g., *Twelfth Night*.[31] By describing coats of arms, or Davies' masque, or the lottery devices at court, let alone the "poesies" in rings, Manningham shows interest in emblematic devices, although he nowhere comments on them. It does not appear that these devices to him meant anything more than playfully conceived images created from a wide range of possibilities.

Of course, in his short notes on poetic wit Manningham was mostly recording materials which had not (yet) been published. But this cannot completely explain (or explain away) his interest, because the larger treatises he mentions, and the poem "It is Merry when Gossips Meete," were in print. What was the importance of being witty? We will briefly discuss joke techniques, before turning to the function of wit generally as it appears from the diary; then we will turn to the form and content of Manningham's remarks on love and friendship. It may be helpful to keep in mind that no case is made for the originality of any of the jokes. Most of the jokes reached Manningham through other men.

Although there is much display of wit in the diary, the range of joke techniques is rather limited. Predominant are simile; double meaning in its three forms (meaning as a name and as a thing, metaphorical and literal meaning, and double meaning proper—in terms of rhetorical figures of speech: *asteismus, antanaclasis* and *syllepsis*); and multiple use of the same material in a different order, which type actually appears in the form of a figure of speech (*antimetabole*).

Witty similes can be noticed quite often.[32] They may take the form of character writing, as Overbury's "Sniges nose loked downe to see howe many of his teeth were lost, and could never get up againe" (fol. 39b), and as such can be related to epigrams, like the one on fol. 2, on the splendor of Tom Horton's nose, with its dubious compliment to the sovereign:

> The radiant *splendor* of Tom Hortons nose
> Amates the ruby and puts down the rose.
> Had I a jewell of soe rich a hewe
> I would present it to some monarchs viewe.
> Subjects ought not to weare such gemms as those
> Therefore our prince shall have Tom Hortons nose.

They sometimes border on a more or less allegorical description, like those on fol. 30b or fol. 36b. The latter:

> Covetous man rides in a coache which runnes upon 4 wheeles: the 1. Pusillanimity. 2. Inhumanity. 3. Contempt of God. 4. Forgetfulnes of death (*Dr. Chamberlayne*); it is drawne with two horses: 1. *Rapacitas.* 2. *Tenacitas.* The divel the coachman, and he hath two whippes: 1. *Libido acquirendi.* 2. *Metus amittendi.*

Most of them, however, are simple similes, like:

> The Dutch which lately stormed the galleys which our ships had first battered, deserve noe more credit than a lackey for pillaging of that dead body which his maister had slayne. (Fol. 59b; putting us in mind of a Falstaff-like courage in battle)

Jokes based on double meaning predominate.[33] They can pun on names, as Barker's puns on dogs (fol. 57, 91) and Rook's on birds (fol. 46); or, as in the clever verse Payne wrote after he had been unjustly expelled from New College in Oxford by Dr. Colpeper: "Paena potest demi, Culpa perennis erit" (fol. 81b),[34] and of course in simple wordplay, like "Dunne is Undonne" (fol. 75b). This type of wordplay is also used in jokes like Rudyerd's on fol. 35b ("fa"-"soule"). Often witty changes are effected by switches from metaphorical to literal use, as in this example: "One said the Recorder was the mouth of the cytie; then the city hath a black mouth, said

Harwell, for he is a verry blacke man" (fol. 54); or by the application
of ideologies in the wrong place, as in:

> One Merredith, a notable coward, when he was in [the] field, and de-
> maunded why he did not fight and strive to kill his enemies, he, good
> man, told them, he could not finde in his heart to kill them whom he
> never sawe before, nor had ever any quarrell with them. (Fol. 78b; again
> it may be wondered whether Manningham would have seen subtle anar-
> chism in Falstaff)

This type of joke mainly depends on unexpected applications and
displacement.[35]

Antimetabole can be found in the jokes on fols. 26b, 102, 116,
119; and in two mock epitaphs on fol. 2, in one of which Spenser
is called "Then God of the Poets, nowe Poet of the Gods." A slight
modification occurs on fol. 99, "Non sic fuit ab antiquo"—"non sic
fuit ab initio." There are relatively few jokes on condensation
proper. The "double enemies" of "Cousin she" on fol. 10b, coined
from "double anemonies," is an example; another, already border-
ing on wordplay, is the wit of More, quoted on fol. 29, on "memento
morieris," which is broken up into "memento Mori aeris."

As with the sermons, Manningham is not very explicit about his
motives for writing down the jokes and their explanations. The
above-quoted example of note-taking on fol. 119, from Horace, explained that taking notes could be done for the purpose of preserving a noteworthy event, but the example mentioned there
serves also as a specimen of a joke on multiple use of material
which, when distorted, gets an opposite meaning. This kind of play
may also be applied to translations, such as the translation of *na-
tura brevium* as "the nature of the Pigmies" (fol. 119), or ironies
(euphemisms), like coney-catchers calling themselves "gentlemen
at dice." Yet one may also suspect jokes to have had a social
function:

> One told a jest and added that all good wittes applauded it; a way to
> bring one to a dilemma, either of arrogance in arriding, as though he
> had a good witt too, or of ignoraunce, as thoughe he could not conceive
> of it as well as others. (Fol. 39b)

This example (another one is on fol. 58) indicates that to be witty
is to gain social esteem. There are examples in the diary which
show that in practice wit functioned to assert one's power; one
needed wit to get one's way.[36] A very blunt witticism is that of Lord

Manwood, who tried to escape being committed for abuse of a goldsmith with the verse "*Malas causas habentes, semper fugiunt potentes. Ubi non valet veritas, prevalet authoritas. Curat Lex, Vivat Rex,* and soe fare you well, my Lordes; but he was committ" (fol. 70). Numerous examples of witty repartee in the courtrooms indicate that witticisms, particularly those based on double meaning and multiple use, could serve to redress the balance in a law case. Here is one:

> A gent[leman] whose father rose by the lawe, sitting at the benche while a lawyer was arguyng in a case against the gen[leman], touching land which his father purchased, the gent]leman], more collerick then wise, sayd the lawyer would prate, and lye, and speake anie thing for his fee. "Well," said the lawyer, "yf your father had not spoken for a fee, I should have noe cause to speake in this cause today." (Fol. 31b)

In the Middle Temple wit became particularly considered as an index of a man's force both in terms of physical strength and of sexual potency. The Revels of the Prince of Love (Middle Temple, 1597–98) introduced the theme of love by establishing the relationship between wit and strength:

> And as the vertuous, though laborious walks of Love have been thus unfrequented; so the wonted Feats of Arms now a long while have been unpractised. There's not one that is now swarty with the heat and dust of the School, by managing his weapons from morning to night: But who, in matter of difference, relieth more on hi[s] Manly courage, than on witty evasions to shift off a quarrel, he is now esteemed unexpert and Fool-hardy; Nay, so far hath proceeded this making War by Wit and writing, as men wretchlesly abandoning the auncient and unassaultable Fort of the Buckler (I think because the expence of Swords was too great) that the merciless troops of Catchpoles dare now make Inrodes to the very gates of our Cities, where the *Aquaducts in Platea Fletesi* hath wont to be the uttermost border of their approach.[37]

Not only are wit and strength related, but the social consequences of that relationship are firmly established as well: the Templars are warned that due to their reliance on linguistic force, they lose their territory to neighboring groups. These warnings may be taken in the sense of (youth) groups struggling for predominance, which— as the text as a whole also indicates—is a struggle for sexual dominance over the women in that area as well.

The revels of 1597–98 give more than one indication of the direct relationship between wit and sexual potency (probably as a replacement for the overtly phallic display of sword fighting). Inability in verbal wit was related to sexual incompetence. This connection appears in the jokes on pp. 22 ("to stand" connected with "to urge reason"), 31 (to court with apt witticism and not with political news), 43 (the Knights should "once in three dayes speak with some spice of wit, and to the purpose twice every night if it be possible") 60 (impotence connected with "willful babling"), and 61 (the lover unable to speak for himself is an "impaired fool"). Manningham's reproof of a joke of Danvers's (fol. 57) also parallels wit and the sexual act. Wit and spirit can pun on the phallus.[38] Spending of spirit or wit, termed "life-blood," can also mean losing semen. The Revels of the Prince of Love abound in jokes that focus on or imply male failure (see the Lord Admiral's duties, pp. 26–30). Jokes of such a type can often be found in the comedies related to the Middle Temple. Marston's *The Fawn* (1604–6, directly borrowing from the revels of 1597–98) and Sharpham's comedies are crammed with them. Both authors were probably participants in the revels of 1597–98. In comical satires (unlike the revels) homosexual elements are overt, particularly in Jonson's, Marston's, and Chapman's comedies. These also abound in verse satire, possibly even alluding to Richard Martin as the Prince of Love.[39]

Twelfth Night took particular interest in the Revels of the Prince of Love, and its erotic devices and may well have been devised for the Middle Temple performance in 1602.[40] Manningham probably did not participate in the revels of 1597–98, but he was admitted some weeks later (16 March 1598). He was acquainted with the chief revelers and it may be asked therefore how his erotic views relate to Temple revels' humor, and particularly to the erotic ambiguity of *Twelfth Night*. Manningham describes one of the plot lines mainly in terms of a love story. Can his ideas of love and friendship be deduced from the diary's notes and be used to throw light upon both form and content of his account of *Twelfth Night*?[41]

Manningham's information about the formation of and motivation for relationships are mainly restricted to the wealth of the female partner. Thus he thinks "[Mr. Vane's] possibility of living by his wife verry much." In Sir Moyle Finch's case the daughter and heir of Sir Francis Hastinges is said to be "worth to him £ 3,000 per annum," but the lady in question does not seem to have had a name (fol. 10). The preacher Mr. Layfield, criticized on fol. 126, also married "a rich wife, worth above 1,000£"; there is no mention of a name of any information about motives and affection, although in this case we are dealing with criticism on the different claims of Word and Flesh. Yet a certain kind of "love" seems to have been deemed necessary by Manningham. Noticing that young Lord North received through marriage £ 800, he remarked: "Shee is not yong nor well favoured, noe marvaile yf he love hir not" (fol. 37b). This "love" is related quite casually to physical appeal, not to any spiritual or emotional attraction. Such an impersonal view of women appears in Manningham's description of Jane, the second wife of his "father in Love," Richard Manningham, as "cousin she" (fol. 10b, 13b). Their marriage had just started at the beginning of the notebook. Both partners had been married before and it was apparently Jane's third marriage. "Cousin She" frequently emerges in the diary. She was not the type of woman to be ruled easily, as becomes clear from her decision not to return to her first husband after he had failed to notice that she had slipped from her horse (fol. 10b, and see below).

The diarist's callous outlook on marriage was perhaps influenced by the rather negative attitude towards its blessings, which—insofar as may be deduced from the diary—was the prevailing view in his milieu. He cracks a joke against marriage: "Vita coelibis, bis celestis, considering the crosses of marriage and the advise of the apostle" (fol. 96). Two similar statements directly concern the academic milieu. In a sermon, Mr. Hemming of Trinity College Cambridge estimated the chances of a healthy marriage at one in a thousand, "for women are like a coule full of snakes amongst which there is one eele, a thousand to one yf a man happen upon the eele, and yet if he gett it in his hand, all that he hath gotten is but a wett eele by the tayle" (fol. 133b). Manningham took this joke from Mr. Osborne, a fellow student. In itself it is an elaboration on the proverb "to have a woman is to have but an eel by the tail." Dr. Parry is quoted on fol. 38 for his wisdom that there can be no greater fool than the man willing to leave university to marry a wife. Dislike of married life, still connected with approval of celibacy, seemed to have been strong in an age in which "holy matrimony" was on its way to conquer our Western culture, particularly in Protestant ideology. The survival of the old ideal may have had to do with the poor chances of marriage in the intellectual milieus.[42] About children Manningham has nothing special to say (remarks on fols. 9b, 58, and 58b).

Although Manningham more than once—and certainly in relation to the sermons—exhibits a severe sexual morality, particularly regarding marriage, he writes about incest without being shocked at the phenomenon itself. Thus, on fol. 33b he discussed the remarkable marriage of one Mr. Sappcottes, who married his own bastard daughter. Manningham says he "had never anie issue by hir; after his death shee was with child, would not discover the father. Sappcottes left her worth some 400£ yearely, yet none will marry hir." The problem may even be turned into a kind of joke (not much of a compliment to the joke's victim), but even then, his denunciation is inspired by Sappcottes's Catholicism rather than by Manningham's misgivings about incest. A Catholic whom the authorities thought to catch at Mass was caught indeed "At it," but with his daughter (fol. 97b). That Laetus kept his sister as a whore (fol. 26b) could be a rhyme from the Temple revels, as Laetus figured as a character in the *Prince of Love*.[43]

For Manningham, too, submissiveness was an excellent thing in woman. When "cousin she"'s behavior towards her husband ended in "a strange hott contradiction," it was she who afterwards "fell a kissing his hand at table with an extreme kinde of flattery." This in itself is indicative of a negative value judgment, but Manningham's judgment becomes even more explicit when he calls his cousin "moved (and not without cause)," and finds fault that she "never confest shee was too violently opposite" (fol. 38b). She was a woman from whose mouth he took, "to furnish a shipp requireth much trouble, but to furnish a woman the charges are double," (fol. 9b), in her case probably decidedly ironic. Direct disapproval of "women on top" can be found on fol. 15: "I had rather be a whore maister, then maistered by a whore as thou art" comes from his cousin's mouth. Indirect concern for males with a view to their position towards women will be discussed below. Typically male notions of things "women really like" are on fols. 118 and 54: the joke of a maid who did not call for help when she was raped because she liked it, and a man rebuking his wife for her constantly scolding about the thing she ran after fastest.

The impression of insensitivity is only strengthened when we look at Manningham's remarks on women. Here, too, we can distinguish between real jokes and more or less "earnest" anecdotes, "true stories." The tendency is towards derision. Mrs. T has indeed tried to accuse her brother of theft, because he opposed her affection for "hir man" (servant) H., but this affection, without further ado, is described as "lascivious love," and the statement closes with the following moral: "soe violent and unnaturall a womans malice.

Hir owne daughter knowes hir luxurie (*quam incaute, quam inepte, quam indigne*)" (fol. 59). On the borderline of joke and earnest observation we find the remarks about a woman's right to free a man from the gallows by marrying him (fol. 77). Obviously a man would rather die than be saved in such a manner. Manningham's discussion of the burning of widows in Gao shows the same tendency (fol. 34b). These women were "exceedingly given to the synn of Lechery" and were trained by this custom to take good care of their husbands, instead of poisoning them, which had been their joy before. The misogyny of the joke even prevents logical thought on the joys of marriage. More significant is the social aspect of a joke on fol. 70: "women, because they cannot have their Wills when they dye, they will have their will while they live." Here a sexual joke is coined from women's social inferiority; Manningham himself described a typical result of such inferiority on fol. 118b: Mr. Marrow did not even leave his wife her own clothes. Shortly after the deplorable death of Queen Elizabeth, Manningham writes that, in future, women shall no longer be worshipped (fol. 119), a remark which, joking on religion, derives its social sting from the succession.

Five remarks on women reflect Manningham's vulgar, negative sexual approach: fol. 2 (Luce's body and its chastity); fol. 24b (the outward appearance of Mrs. Fouler); fol. 57 (Nel Frengtham's [57] kissing habits); fol. 59b (a drunken cunt has no porter); and fol. 9b (about the best sport). Rather insipid negative jokes can also be found on fols. 60 and 113. The lines on the skull are explained as the result of women's being shut out from reason. All in all, we can notice a constant opposition between men as reasonable beings and women as untrustworthy, passionate beings, objects of lust and scorn, or sources of wealth. These very negative remarks about women are complemented by remarks concerning the physical side of sexuality. They incorporate a strong phallic-centred bias.

In Manningham's humor close relationships and their results concentrate particularly on the male contribution—even though the woman may be the initiator. Two jokes center on the clever way men get "their game" by outwitting others: those concerning Bodley (fol. 46) and Shakespeare (fol. 29b). The joke by Sergeant Ylverton (fol. 29b), in which a woman at least shows the wit to decide herself when she wants to make love, also tries to keep the focus on male prestige: Heale is accused of sexual failure because of his having intercourse only once a year. In the explanation the polarity of "round summe" and "driblets" plays with feat and failure.

The diary repeats a particular type of joke which we will analyze in closer detail, as it proves to be important in connection with the account of *Twelfth Night.*

> One told Sergeant Harrys howe many there were newe prickt ser-geantes. "Would I were neweprickt to," q[uoth] he; "it would be the better for my wife then." (Hoskins). (Fol. 98)

Approached by means of Freud's formal analysis it is a joke on displacement, the word "prick," meaning "to appoint," and "to have or get a (new) phallus." The displacement, then, involves a shift from the legal to the sexual meaning. In itself, the joke, both to its narrator and to its listener, contains the common idea of "smut," in which Hoskyns presents the woman as a desirable object to Manningham. But the focus is not actually on her, but on failing masculinity, castration, or rather, self-castration, which is the more interesting because a father-like figure of authority is involved. As such it has an oedipal aspect, but the comic nature of the joke allows Manningham and Hoskyns to avert fear of castration: "He has no prick for a wife—we do, don't we?"

> Where is your husband?" said Mr. Reeves to a girl. "He is a building," said shee. "The worse luck for you," q[uo]t[h] hee; a building in Wiltsh. signifies a male with one stone. (Ch.Da.) (Fol. 24b)

Here, too, the joke is one of displacement, the "double" word being "building." The displacement is from the world of construction to the world of sexuality. The idea of smut is more direct. Reeves draws attention to his sexual potency as being greater than her husband's, thus trying to tickle her fancy to have sex with him. Ch. Daver's communication of the joke to Manningham is also meant to tickle sexual feelings towards a woman. Again, however, what is averted at the same time is fear of castration and failure. The superiority of the three jokers involved inspires them to make fun of one inferior being, the husband. He has only one stone—we don't, do we? A certain obsessiveness with castration and/or failure as a men-ace to manhood is more apparent in this joke than in Harris's one. Even as pure wordplay, the displacement from building/construc-tion to building/sexual is rather forced in comparison with the

Harris joke. His "newe-prickt" keeps its meaning in the aforementioned sense until he himself indicates displacement, whereas
Reeves immediately extracts a sexual meaning from a word, a compulsion indicated by the occurance of an explanation in addition
to the joke itself. Anyone unacquainted with the word building's
sexual sense cannot understand the joke as a pun on sex. Reeves's
reaction follows the woman's claim that her husband is a building.
Humor defends Reeves against the possible fear that she herself
might have done it. The mechanism of defense even rules out the
possibility that, with the husband away and the sexually potent
Reeves around, things might have proved "best luck" for the
woman.

> A wenching gent[leman], desyrous to put an opinion on some that he
> spent his tyme well, told them he laid close and did nothing but looke
> on his booke. One told him that his booke was a fair volume, but it had
> but two leaves (legs) to open, and he was a bad scholler—could doe
> nothing without his fescue (i.[e.], his p'). (Fol. 70b)

The joke is based on the use of double meaning, which has to be
explained by Manningham to be understood by the recipient, and
is thus not primarily generated through customary meaning of the
words themselves. Here, too, fear of failure is the underlying notion.
Without his fescue the gentleman does not do anything. But the
joke becomes more complicated, because it implies that a "good
scholler" apparently does not need his "p" in such studies.

> A whore is noe worse then a Catt for she plays with her tayle, and a cat
> does no more. (One in the tillbuow as I came from Lond.). (Fol. 103b)

The joke focuses on the female role in sex, developed from a common expression. But "tail" has also a phallic connotation. Then
the cat plays with "her" tail (the male phallus) as if it were her
prey, and the joke suggests the dangerous qualities of the cat/whore
as a plaything and castrating beast of prey. The joke on fol. 10b,
"you cannot put down my middle finger," also reflects this sense
of danger which always seems present; for "it is a great thing must
stop a feme covert," said Justice Fennar (fol. 39), but a man's "thing"
may always be too small.

The description of the Malvolio plot line on fol. 12b corroborates
this type of joking in which men laugh at the expense of the sexual
failure of another man. Malvolio cannot fulfill his sexual fantasy

towards Olivia, aroused by Toby, Andrew and Maria, and is made a scapegoat. Yet Andrew (among the aggressive men) is himself a failure towards women, which appears clearly in 1.3 and 3.3, and he is connected in more than one way with the kind of revelers the Templars were themselves. Andrew fails in what Templars considered to be their standard of behavior (learning, dancing, music, courtship, courage). In this way, laughing (with Andrew) at Malvolio's failure provides the same assertion of manhood as supplied by the jokes on triangle situations.

The dangers threatening men are of a rather fundamental nature: in the common Renaissance view on the physiology of sex, the male is the weaker part. This idea also emerges in the diary. The comparison on fol. 109b shows that old men and male wolves die when they have sexual intercourse. Clapham, on fol. 119b, points out the loss of semen weakens men. Less important remarks can be found on fol. 10b: "rootes"; fol. 59: "to sting a wench," followed by the menacing joke "they have lockt us up with delays"; fol. 44: "to inward with her"; fol. 31: "to have and to hole"; and fol. 39b: "the hole needs not the physician," which must be related to the same idea, although the remark has a Biblical origin—they are the words of Christ.

The jokes (listed in note 41) have been divided into six categories:

1. Social reality and relationships, including financial matters,
2. Man and woman in their several relationships,
3. Judgment of women,
4. Children,
5. Physical aspects of sex,
6. Phallic elements.

Category:	counts:	
1	6 remarks	2 negative
2	34 remarks	25 negative
3	47 remarks	30 negative, 2 or 3 positive
4	4 remarks	2 negative
5	2 remarks	both menacing to men
6	16 remarks	8 menacing to men

There are sixty-one remarks taken into account of which fifteen are "earnest," six half-jocular, half-serious, and forty are jokes. One jest can have been put into more than one category.

Of course this calculation has no statistical value, and is only meant to indicate the use of the materials and the way in which they are appreciated, so that conclusions might not prove resistant to falsification. The categorizing of remarks and jokes does form an indication of the way in which Manningham responded to remarks and jokes on women and men. In defining the remarks as either positive or negative the extent to which these remarks are aggressive or contemptuous was examined; defining them as menacing takes into account the extent to which they are indicative of a disfunctioning of male sexuality. As most of the jokes stem from Manningham's social equals, both in London and Kent, and as there is no significant difference in types of jokes between these groups, they are treated as part of the structure of one social group.

Contempt for women and phallicentricity therefore, can be found along with male uncertainty regarding their own symbol of power and the knowledge that, physiologically, women are sexually unconquerable. This can be explained both in terms the psychology of humors—the man is losing whilst the woman is gaining (especially as semen was considered to be blood)—and by the dichotomy which is so fundamental in Renaissance thinking, that of reason versus passion, the latter always threatening the former. To relate contempt for women to fear does not seem to go too far in an overall interpretation. But the phallicentricity also indicates a narcissist tendency, and the type of joke intended to "strengthen one another at the expense of a third party" can indicate the need of a constant affirmation of (a masculine) self, which is normally related to narcissism. Manningham's way of looking at sex and relations with women is, to say the least, autoerotic. In concentrating on his own "I" (the male input), it shows the homoerotic element contained in narcissism, certainly where men need each other to allay dangers, and threaten each other to assert their own proper functioning. This aspect, quite interestingly, crops up in relation to the menacing qualities of women in the statement concerning the wolves (fol. 109b).

The obsession with cuckoldry can be related to it as well. In Renaissance literature the use of imagery of castrated or female animals related to cuckolds is fairly normal.[44] Manningham's statements on cuckoldry are few in number. He notes that upper-class males are generally a menace because of their power (fol. 10b), but more interestingly, he also relates the case in which a man came to prove himself a cuckold in such manner that "it" was something one could better not say aloud (fol. 43b, and compare Coke's embarrasment, fol. 90b). The same mixture of rivalry and suppressed homoeroticism can be found in the joke on fol. 98:

> I offered Mr. Kedgewin as being myne ammiral in the house to cutt before me; he refused with this phrase: "Nay I regard not men as women doe, for their standing."

It shows the Freudian mechanism of "I do not appreciate men for their standing, they do," transferring a desire of one's own to another, with Kedgwin projecting his own regard for the phallus onto the female mind. The joke shows that homosexuality is being prevented from rising to the surface. It raises the question of Manningham's notions on friendship and homosexuality. This question is of interest regarding *Twelfth Night*, with its ambivalent erotic patterns.

Nothing much can be said. The anagram "Martyne: myne art" (fol. 70) was considered worth cutting by the Camden editor, Bruce, which shows he read it in an erotic sense.[45] The erotic/preventive remark by Kedgwin quoted above may be compared to an interesting note on fol. 118: "Two were going to washe them selves; one spied the others preputian discovered: 'I pray you be covered,' q[uoth] he." The joke conceals two actions. The first involves the fact that the first man "spied" the other—a process of active watching. The second action is the discovery that the thing looked for is more seductive than normal. A reaction of defense follows: the stone of offense must be removed/covered, as happened to the informant's name, which in the MS is heavily canceled (showing the joke was risky somehow). Curiosity and repression of seduction here are indicated both by Manningham's taking the situation as a joke, as with the one on "standing" (the object to be averted is first called to attention before being rejected), and by the fact that he reported it.

He reported it from an interesting occasion. Fol. 118 is filled with two long jokes from Mr. Nicholas Hare, with whom Manningham spent some time in the King's Head, as he reports earlier on the same folio. It is likely that the two jokes between the remark on the King's Head and the two jokes of Mr. Hare's, the quotation from Donne's *The Storm* and the joke on the bathing men, also stem from this same occasion. It would make Nicholas Hare the obvious narrator of the joke on the bathing men. Manningham calls Nicholas Hare "A gallant yong gent, like to be heir to much land; he is of a sweet behaviour, a good spirit, and a pleasing witty discourse." Manningham's friendly affection cannot be called "ingling" but combines his preference for wit and the materialistic outlook so often found in the diary. Yet it is one of the very few remarks in which personal affection is shown at all; strikingly, it is in combination with one of the very few remarks on the need to avert inter-male eroticism. Thus the canceling of the name could be interpreted as an act of covering inter-male eroticism itself.[46]

Clear references to homosexuality in the diary are rare. A Latin epigram on fol. 54 clearly depicts it as a normal practice of the Jesuits, which is also implied in the double meaning of the joke on condensation, transferring seminaries into semmimaries (fol. 125b; playing on *semimas, semivir* was an old Latin word for homosexual and on semen). For Manningham homosexuality had the same association as it had in some of the verse satires. Marston, for instance, called it a vice introduced from the colleges of Douai (*The Scourge of Villany*, sat. 2). The common practice in verse satire and comical satire—to consider young men from court or the Inns of Court and their page boys to be prone to homosexual behavior—is absent in the diary. The few examples of particularly scatological humor in the diary are not of any specific interest.

Manningham, then, appears to have been in line with the prescribed views of his time. Politically, as well as in religious matters, he is on the side of law and order. Patriarchal attitudes, scarce affection, and repressed libido make his diary an ideal source to support Stone's thesis that the attitudes in this period were dominated by the "restricted patriarchal family." (Stone never mentions Manningham.) The more remarkable is Manningham's active interest in sexual joking, which becomes particularly evident in his response to *When Gossips Meet* (fol. 45, and compare his comments on a joke on fol. 57). Here, interest in double entendre is displayed to the point of quoting out of context, thereby making the lines even more bawdy. The fragments Manningham notices contain all aspects we have discussed already in the other types of witticism and bawdiness which appeared to have interested him, and need no further discussion. They serve to support the idea that his response to literary fiction focused on pleasure, on simple bawdy wit. The only type of hidden meaning to be found in it is double entendre, the only theme arousing interest is the male sexual organ.

Manningham probably distinguished between those kinds of literature and the sermon texts in terms of a difference between pastime and training, passion and reason. As such he may have conformed to some general ideas in his environment. Note-taking of sermons was considered a worthy undertaking, while note-taking on plays was not.[47] Even the Revels of the Prince of Love jokingly criticize the lover "that he learn no speeches out of Playes to entertain the time" (p. 45).

Moreover, Manningham had a certain prejudice against players and musicians. On fol. 11b he quotes one Leydall speaking against spending Sunday afternoons "either idly or about temporall affayres"; he uses the terms treason and profanation. Without any signs of disapproval he quotes remarks against fiddlers on fol. 55b from a sermon delivered by Clapham, and from Davers: "rogues as they were" (fol. 90b). The literal applications from the sermon of 12 December 1602 (fol. 76; Abraham traveled, thus traveling is lawful) contain the statement that "the trade of stageplayers [was] unlawful," which Manningham reports without further comment. He denounces fencers because he thinks their activity unchristian (fol. 98). John Chamberlain reported on the same accident. Curiously, Chamberlain's comment is legalistic; he wonders whether lawyers will take it as murder or manslaughter, whereas the lawyer's, Manningham's, is exclusively moralistic.[48] As an apparently noteworthy detail, Manningham writes on fol. 98 that "the towne of Manitre in Essex holdes by stage playes." This, and the virtual absence of anything theatrical, could reflect his lack of interest in the profundities proclaimed on stage.

The contrast between play and work remained conspicuous for a long time and even as late as 1639 Robert Chamberlain observed in his conceits:

> One asked another what Shakespeare's works were worth, all being bound together. He answered, not a farthing. Not worth a farthing! Said he; why so? He answered that his plays were worth a great deale of money, but he never heard, that his works were worth any thing at all.[49]

Manningham's account of *Twelfth Night* in performance conformed to prescribed standards of treating plays. Attending plays was not work in the sense that attending sermons was work, or in the sense that writing sown verbal wit was work, because thes were useful in practice. To have dived into the depths of drama would in Manningham's view probably have been a waste of his time, a defilement of his reason, and an unworthy activity. Here, too, a dichotomy between reason and passion might have been operative.

IV

Reading Rowland's poem as a bawdy joke, and relating bawdiness to the kind of jokes on sex mentioned elsewhere, will put us in a better position to reflect once more on the account of *Twelfth Night*. Manningham was not interested in the play's verbal witticisms, which he could have related to the verbal wit displayed in the diary elsewhere. The Malvolio plot line, which he describes in some detail, did not appeal to him because of the problems related to treatment of texts and Puritanism; the account focuses on love matters, and here shows the same structure as his bawdy jokes analyzed above. Here, too, we are dealing with a triangular situation in which one man is made the laughingstock because of his sexual failure.

Two circumstantial arguments can help to explain why the Malvolio plot line took the shape of a sexual joke in Manningham's mind. In the first place, we must be careful not to expect a detailed interpretation of thematic or texual matters. Manningham only watched the play, and that during a party. The circumstances were probably rather unfavorable, considering the open fire in the hall and the huge cupboard in the middle (which may have proved an obstacle, as discussed both by Sorlien and Wiesen)—let alone the "festive (including intoxicated) disposition" of the spectators, whose unquiet behavior probably influenced their response, too.[50] Secondly, there is the tradition of the Temple revels. Especially the Middle Temple's *Prince of Love* focused on sexual matters. It had the same type of boasting, phallicentric heterosexual jokes, accompanied by expressions of fear of menacing women, we noticed in the diary. The response to the Malvolio plot, therefore, could have taken form and content as a result of the revels' tradition.

But what about the Orsino plot? It cannot be denied to be a plot line concerning love. Possibly it raised erotic tensions which in the verse satires were more overtly criticised: boy-man relationships. Why did not Manningham say anything about its action? He probably did say something about it. Manningham's report includes a short dividing line, indicating—as it does elsewhere in the diary— that he is actually discussing two topics. The reference to the three other plays in the first statement can hardly have been included to indicate something other than the twins. They do not have anything like a Malvolio plot line, and treat the topic of madness in too different a manner to make it the likely center of the comparison.

It would be rash to conclude that Manningham referred to these other plays as sources for *Twelfth Night.* There is nothing to suggest that he made the comparison for that specific reason. Moreover, he separates the Italian play from *The Comedy of Errors* and *Menechmi* by "but," placing them in some sort of opposition. It is also important to stress the fact that throughout the diary Manningham notices things which are remarkable, strange, and uncommon, and the tradition of twins-and-error-plays was already too well-known to be even remotely amazing or worthy of special comment. The mentioning of these titles must have been the result of some special interest on Manningham's part. Finally, Manningham only remarks that the performance of *Twelfth Night* resembled the others. What needs be discussed is this aspect of the performance, as opposed to the literary text. The first sentence should probably be read as a comparison between performances, not between literary texts.

The account of *Twelfth Night* does not even come close to being a description of the text; it is a representation of what he saw, rather than of what he heard, of what characters did and looked like rather than of what they said or were. Manningham writes "we had a play." The word play here certainly means "performance" or "pastime," and certainly does not refer to a text. As part of the play Manningham describes a "practise." He uses the word "practise" again when Malvolio comes to perform "his Lady widdowes prescriptions." "He comes to practise," in this case, means "to perform," "to act." The word evidently describes the play as action.[51] The "lady widdowe" also indicates a visual mistake. The play's text clearly states that Olivia mourns for a brother (1.1, 1,.2, 1.3), and as remarked above, the mistake more likely originated from the kind of dress than from "widow-lore."

Manningham's account in its second statement clearly refers to a play in performance and uses the word "play" in the first statement. How does that fit in with the assumption that he could compare the stage performance with the details of written texts of other plays? *The Comedy of Errors* is mentioned first and considered to be "much like" *Twelfth Night.* It may even be that he thought of Plautus's play only, giving it two names, as he did with *Twelfth Night.* This possibility is unlikely, however, because of the lack of proof that Plautus' *Menechmi* was known in English as *The Comedy of Errors*, while there is proof in the *Gesta Grayorum* that Templars could distinguish between the plays, even though they could also see their similarity.[52]

The punctuation also indicates that Manningham had two different plays in mind. "*Menechmi* in Plautus" could mean that he was thinking of an edition of this play because of the word "in" ("Plautus" meaning "the works of Plautus"). If he thought of two plays and knew *Menechmi* from a textbook of Plautus (or possibly the 1595 translation), how could Manningham know the text of *The Comedy of Errors*, as the play, like *Twelfth Night*, did not appear in print before the Folio of 1623? It may go without saying that he knew the play from a performance. That he knew it from personal experience follows from the fact that he makes no mention of any informant in his account. Normally he gives his source.

Although *Twelfth Night* was "much like" *The Comedy of Errors*, it was "most like and neere" another play, "that in Italian called *Inganni*." Many critics have taken it for granted that Manningham meant *Gl'Ingannati*, misquoting the title. Could he have known the Italian plays? Could he have read them in the Italian language, as texts available in London? It is possible, but unconfirmed. It would mean he established a close connection between a performance and a literary text, a text, moreover, which was written in another language. Of course he could have been simply referring quite roughly to the plot. But is the plot he indicates, *Gl'Inganni*, sufficiently similar to *Twelfth Night* to be described as "most like and neere?" Yet, since his account must be accepted as a description of what he experienced, there must have seemed something familiar about "*Inganni*."

To illuminate the problem, the question may be put why he is so awkward with his information here. Manningham is not providing information for a third party; he is writing a note for his own reference. He just wrote down the names of plays and performances known to him. Why does not he simply write: "most like and neere *Inganni*?" For if he knew the play, and wrote for himself rather than for a reader, this would have been perfectly sensible. The line he wrote is not clear in another respect either: What are we supposed to read?

1) most like and neere to that in Italian—called *Inganni* (meaning the title of an Italian play)? or:

2) most like and neere to that—in Italian called *Inganni* (meaning the title of a play which in Italian probably would have
been called so)?

In the text's otherwise transparent punctuation, a comma is badly
needed.[53]

The problem might be solved if we assume that Manningham
compared several performances and not performances with texts.
When seeing *Twelfth Night*, the visual experience impressed him
most, and must have been on his mind when comparing *Twelfth
Night* with *The Comedy of Errors*. Would the "most like and neere"
element in this performance have been something he knew only
from a text of which even the very title we must doubt? If we
compare the three plays mentioned on one and the same level,
as we probably should because of the structure of the statement
(*Menechmi* standing apart for reasons discussed above), it may be
argued that Manningham in this third case, too, is referring to a
play in performance. Which performance? Obviously not an Italian
one.

A possible answer, then, is that he was thinking of a performance
he saw in Cambridge in March 1595 as a student at Magdalene
College. At the time, the Latin *Laelia*, an adaptation of *Gl'Ingannati*,
was performed at Corpus Christi College before a notable audience,
including the earl of Essex. It was of such high quality that it was
still referred to, years after the event had taken place, by Weever in
his *Epigrammes* (1598). Would not the occasion have drawn the
Magdalene student to Corpus Christi College? We can imagine
Manningham wanting to write "most like and neere to *Laelia*," but
having forgotten the name of that performance, he only remembered it was an Italian adaptation. He coined a title, which he got by
translating a word which had been on his mind recently, "errors" or
"deceits" (in Italian: "inganni"). Thus *Laelia* was the play on fol.
12b remembered as the play "in Italian called *Inganni*." This hypothesis at least gives Manningham's account a coherent structure
as a comparison between performances.[54]

There is another problem to discuss: the response to the twins
in *Twelfth Night*. The fact that *The Comedy of Errors* had not been
printed yet and that *Twelfth Night* is decribed as a performance,
combined with the strong probability that Manningham mentions
them together because of the twins, leads to the hypothesis that he
thought them "much like" each other because he primarily saw the

twins in *Twelfth Night* as males, like those in *The Comedy of Errors*. Only in the course of the action was Manningham able to see that the plot differed from *The Comedy of Errors*. Yet he happened to know another play that looked like what he saw. The note, then, presents a chronological account of his experiences. Another example of such chronological presentation of a sequence of actions in comedy, also related to disguise, can be found in Jonson's *The New Inne* (ed. 1631). The Persons of the Play says:

> as Latimer fall's enamour'd of Prudence, so doth Beaufort on the boy, the Host's sonne, set up for Laetitia, the yonger sister, which shee prooves to be indeed. (Lines 44–46)

Here the male character Frank (Laetitia in disguise, disguised as Laetitia) is also described in terms of his supposed female sex, until the recognition takes place.

This would corroborate other elements of Manningham's account. He did not only take the boy player acting Olivia for a woman, but for a widow as well; he did not even give her a name but just a description of her apparel: a widow's dress. Would not he have seen the boy player acting Viola disguised as Cesario in the same manner, that is, in terms of the latter's apparel: a page's suit? This might well cause him to think Cesario was indeed a brother of Sebastian, in the way the Antipholi and Menechmi had been brothers.

This might explain one feature of Manningham's account that distinguishes it from other direct evidence related to performances, i.e., its mentioning of other titles. E. Gombrich discussed similar problems from the point of view of the psychology of perception. One tries to come to grips with the unfamiliar through the familiar. Something unfamiliar resembles A but is even more like B. Normally, one changes an object one does not know into something familiar when one has to make a drawing of it. Of even more interest for the present analysis is Gombrich's observation that one leaves out the things one cannot, or will not, deal with.[55] Manningham's opening lines may be illustrative of a need to relate something strange (*Twelfth Night* as it was performed) to familiar objects (the other plays as performed).

The problem of looking at a sexual disguise which is not immediately perspicuous may be compared to the "gestalt-switch" of the rabbit and the duck. Gombrich says of it, "we can switch from one reading to another with increasing rapidity; we will also 'remember' the rabbit while seeing the duck, but the more closely we watch ourselves, the more certainly will we discover that we cannot experience alternative readings at the same time."[56]

If Manningham at once saw through the sexual disguise in *Twelfth Night*, the comparison with *The Comedy of Errors* in performance would be incomprehensible. Manningham may have given precisely the process of switching from duck to rabbit, just as he accurately reported: "making him believe they took him to be mad." Both plays which came to his mind were like the play he saw; both were separate experiences (the account separates them by "but"), yet one of them turned out to prevail, leading to "much like" as distinguished from "most like". His account of the Orsino plot line, then, indicates that, at first, he was fooled. That must have made the Orsino-Cesario relationship very ambiguous (not to speak of the Antonio-Sebastian relationship.) As suggested, this ambivalence would have contradicted the admiration of plainness Manningham showed. The ambiguity would moreover have actualized Manningham's tension between a negative response to romanticism and women, and his rejection of ambivalent eroticism and homosexuality.

The fantasy raised by the play need not have been totally unrelated to Manningham's social situation. The interchangeable twin fantasies, particularly in the case of interchangeable brother-and sister twins (biologically doubtful, as uniovular twins are always of the same sex), play with the split of the self, even with the self as a person of the other sex. In a play like *Twelfth Night* this fantasy is related to another one, also displayed in *As You Like It* and rather satirically in Marston's *What You Will*: that of the depraved male's ambiguous (Orpheus-like) withdrawal from females to feminine boys. In the former play, the boy proves to be the very woman desired and thus saves the hero from being considered morally blameworthy, but in the latter play the desired woman proves to be a boy: Simplicius Faber who is sexually attracted to Pippo, wishes to marry Pippo in female disguise and is gulled. At the basis of such actions are fantasies about male behavior as regards each other in situations of (relative) deprivation or unavailability of females.

Manningham may not have been completely free from such tensions, for what were Manningham's motives for marrying his roommate's sister? This unsolvable question actually brings us to the crucial question about the relationship between facts of life and fictions about, life, between life as it was lived and as it was imagined—with the possible result of reflecting back on reality. We may, indeed, shrug our shoulders at the mere coincience (and likewise at Hoskyns's marrying the widow of his best friend), as Anne Curle was probably simply both within Manningham's reach and to his liking. Yet the coincidence might have been influenced by precisely the emotional backgrounds, conscious or not, resulting from the organization of the lives of the educated classes. Manningham for ten years (1602–12), shared the room of the man whose sister he married in 1605. He was sharing part of his mind, too, including such erotically complex jokes (from a psychoanalytical point of view) as the idea of sharing a woman (fol. 98), and two more triangle jokes (fols. 74 and 101). Until his death in 1621, Edward Curle remained a resident in the Temple, apparently a bachelor—a rather common demographic feature in his peer group, which called seminaries semimaries. It does place Manningham in a rather prosaic way in the position of Orsino, for whom the (supposed) sister of his intimate male companion became his fancy's queen, or even in that of Olivia, for whom the marriage with a sister turned out to be that with a brother. There may be a link between the tensions raised in fictions of split selves and sex changes and the tensions raised by actual social situations of room- and bedfellowship and intermarriage. These fictional switches may have originated from the structure of the social round of the elite audiences, and may have helped to regulate their affective life (both as "right rule" and as wish fulfilment). The problem is that we lack tangible evidence here.

It may be conjectured that Manningham did not write about the Orsino plot line because it was already familiar to him, but, on the contrary, because it was unfamiliar and, in the way he experienced it, almost unacceptable to him: Orsino's wavering between being in love with his page and with a lady needed to be connected with familiar, acceptable plots. The implications of the erotic tension raised by the Orsino plot line may have been covered by selective attention on the other plot line, thus leaving out what was both unacceptable and unfamiliar. His account merely contains a comparative statement about the ambivalent plot line, which almost drew him into areas which needed to be covered as soon as they were spied, as in the joke on the bathing gentlemen, and which were out of tune with his penchant for bluntness in wit and clear borderlines between the sexes. Instead, he focused on the other side of the play, which is also about male failure, but of a type he liked better, as his jokes on the triangle of rivalry show.

Van Emde Boas's hypothesis regarding the farcical plot line in *Twelfth Night's* that it was purposely made a necessarily dominating factor in order to prevent the disguise plot line from generating mechanisms of defense, particularly aggression, because of its erotic ambivalence.[57] Although we can hardly claim this hypothesis to have been tested, Manningham's account could actually fit in. As the diary shows, Manningham's mentality invited him to reject the romantic plot line of life.

Notes

1. For a definition of theatre focussing on interaction, see: A. Paul, "Theaterwissenschaft als Lehre des Theatralischen Handelns," *Kölner Zeitschrift für Soziologie und Sozialpsychologie* 22 (1971): Heft 1, pp. 55–77; A. Paul, "Theater als Kommunikationsprozess," *Diskurs: Zeitschrift für Theater und Fernsehen* 2 (1972): pp. 33–58; For a theory on history of reception, stressing external evidence, see: Grimm, *Receptionsgeschichte* (München, Fink, 1977).

2. S. Freud, *Jokes and their Relation to the Unconscious,* ed. A. Richards (Harmondsworth, Penguin Books, 1976). A psychoanalytic approach to the joke was chosen, because eventually we want to form an impression of what may have been on a person's mind when watching *Twelfth Night.* Psychoanalytic theory is a consistent hermeneutic theory which claims to interpret mentality through verbal expressions. Even if rejected, it may help to understand the frame of the conclusions drawn in this essay.

3. R. Parker Sorlien: *The Diary of John Manningham of the Middle Temple, 1602–1603* (Hanover, University Press of New England, 1976), pp. 251–79. Manningham's father died in 1588 when he was about thirteen years of age. His mother apparently administered her husband's estates. The specific date of her death is unknown, and the diary never mentions her. John started his studies at Cambridge University in 1592 at the rather isolated and Puritan Magdalene College. The diary bears no witness to any feeling of sympathy towards Puritanism. The years immediately following John's graduation (1596–98), form a gap in his biography; on 16 March 1598 he starts his studies at the Middle Temple. Accordingly, he was about twenty-six years of age when he watched the performance of *Twelfth Night.* He was still unmarried at the time, sharing his room with Edward Curle, whose sister he married on 16 July 1605. As far as we know, their first child was born in 1608. Five out of their eight children survived childhood.

4. L. Stone: *The Family, Sex and Marriage in England 1500–1800* (London, Weidenfeld and Nicolson, 1977), chapter 2.

5. Sorlien, pp. 275–76.

6. *John Marston of the Middle Temple* (Cambridge, Mass., Harvard U.P., 1969), pp. 45ff., 261ff.

7. The fact that a love affair is crossed out may relate to the danger of prosecution because of slander, since J. S. Cockburn argues that it was the most likely way to get one in legal trouble. J. S. Cockburn, "Early Modern Assize Records as Historical Evidence," *Journal of the Society of Archivists* vol. 5, no. 4 (1975): pp.

215–31. In the area of politics the diary notices sometimes rather revolutionary ideas, such as were put forward by cousin Cranmer:

> That which men doe naturally they doe more justly; subjectes naturally desire liberty, for all thinges tend to their naturall first state. And all were naturally free without subjection. Therefore the subject may more justly seeke liberty then the prince incroach upon his liberty. (Fol. 66)

This seems a dangerous statement in the late 16th century. Manningham himself should not be regarded as a political or social revolutionary. However, the political side of the diary will not be considered here.

    8. Digges's verses to the edition of Shakespeare's poems of 1640, probably meant for the Folio of 1623, mention Malvolio; the Lord Chamberlain's accounts of 2 Feb. 1623 call the play *Malvolio* (those of 6 April 1618 mention the play as *Twelfth Night*); Charles I noted down "Malvolio" on the list of characters in his copy of the second folio of 1632. See E. K. Chambers, *William Shakespeare: A Study of Facts and Problems* (Oxford, Clarendon Press, 1930), II, pp. 233, 346.

    9. *Coryat's Crudities* (London, 1611), p. 247, thinks Italian actresses as good as London boy players; F. Boas, *University Drama in the Tudor Age* (London, 1914), p. 103, discusses the impact of the Oxford Aemilia (1566); J. Rainoldes, *The Overthrow of Stage Plaies* (Middelburg, 1599), pp. 45, 102, discusses the quality of female impersonation in Oxford in 1592; G. Tillotson, "Othello and *The Alchemist* at Oxford in 1610," *TLS*, 20 July 1933, p. 494, quotes the account on the effect of Desdemona; P. Sidney, *The Defence of Poetry*, ed. J. van Dorsten (Oxford, Oxford University Press, 1978), p. 65, sees "women" in the improbable stage romances; Forman refers to female characters as women, including Imogen (Chambers, *Shakespeare*, II, 327–41).

    10. Salingar's analysis that above all Manningham recognized the pattern of *Menechmi* in *Twelfth Night* is not supported by Manningham's text. See L. G. Salingar, "The Design of *Twelfth Night*," *Shakespeare Quarterly* 9 (1958): 117–39. The idea of the predominance of *Menechmi* is left out of his *Shakespeare and the Traditions of Comedy* (Cambridge, Cambridge U.P., 1974), though the idea of Manningham indicating sources remains intact, p. 241.

    11. In Beaumont and Fletcher's *The Coxcomb* (ca. 1608), in *The Dramatic Works in the Beaumont and Fletcher Canon*, gen. ed. F. Bowers (Cambridge, Cambridge U.P., 1966–), vol. 1, there are allusions to *Twelfth Night* through names of characters. Among intertextual links, Pedro's comment on Viola that "'tis a good loving little foole that dares venture her selfe upon a coast she never knew yet; but these women, when they are once thirteene, good speede the plough" (1.2.3ff.) may harken back to *Twelfth Night* (1.2.1–2, 5.1.243). The hour of Viola's eloping is "twelve night" (3.1.18). It may be that Shakespeare's comedy was considered another midnight revel, like *A Midsummer Night's Dream*. At court the play was acted on 6 April 1618, "On Easter Monday Twelfte night the play soe called" (Chambers, *Shakespeare*, II, p. 346), which suggests that the performance was at midnight and the play's title interpreted as meaning midnight as well.

    12. J. Ramsey: "The Importance of Maningham's Diary," *Shakespeare Studies* 10 (1974): 327–43, cites fol. 54b–55 (p. 332).

    13. *Every Man Out of his Humour*, eds. C. H. Herford, P. Simpson, and E. Simpson, *The Works of Ben Jonson* (Oxford, Clarendon Press, 1925–52), vol. 3, 2.6.171.

    14. W. Frazer Mitchell, *English Pulpit Oratory from Andrewes to Tillotson* (New York, 162), p. 36; Sorlien, p. 13; Ramsey, pp. 331–34. As neither Sorlien nor Ramsey gives arguments from the diary itself, a short discussion on textual signs may be useful.

At first sight reports in the third person suggest writing from memory. Many of those are very short statements (e.g., fols. 28b, 54b, 66b, 119b, 120b, 126). Notes like those on fol. 119b, from a sermon preached at night, easily suggest memory notes. On the other hand, Manningham heads his reports with "notes" (fol. 5; compare fols. 6, 107b, 108b), which would be in line with the use of a notebook.

Normally two types of reports occur: short, unconnected notes and longer reports giving the narration in brisk paragraphs. Manningham's longest report, the sermon of King, fol. 46ff., differs from other reports in that it does not show as many dividing lines. Moreover, it is written fluently. This may suggest foul papers for its sources. The opening paragraph ("the length .. etc.") could refer to what King said beforehand, or to what Manningham concluded finally, and thus does not make clear whether a kind of edited account is given of a report from memory, containing Manningham's addition that it was not too difficult to divide King's text.

The long reports on Clapham's sermons refer to the third person, but when Clapham tells his audience about the suicide rumors (fol. 97), his account is followed by "he told another report," which is cancelled after the first sentence. Did Manningham decide not to write it down from notes or from memory? When reporting Spenser's sermon (fols. 40ff.) Manningham writes "I pray God . . . ," as if he is directly taking notes (or—which is comparable—transcribing foul papers). The latter also may have been the case in the report on Barker's sermon, including the hyperbolic comparison of the ministers to stars. The notes break off, while apparently another point should be discussed and a blank leaf follows fol. 25b. A not-too-unreasonable explanation is either direct note-taking and a breaking off because of the irritating comparison, while more space had been reserved for the notes, or a breaking off while transcribing foul papers either with a continuation in view (blank leaf) or not. Memory notes cannot, I think, fully explain these two instances. Why "remember" all such sidetracks at all?

Sentences between short lines like "he would not speake against the good use of riches" (fol. 104b) or the very long-winded introductions, like that on fol. 86, are not easily explained by reports from memory, even though they show the third person. Why on earth remember? Why would the sentence in the short note "men were a feard to commit synn" (fol. 28b) have a superscribed correction ("shamed" above "feard") if it was a report from memory? It looks like a correction of a badly written note.

Manningham also preserves the specific idiom of the diverse ministers. Memory reports would probably have shown more of his own style than of theirs, or memory reports would possibly have altered the brisk syntax and faulty grammar in the short paragraphs.

We could force the matter and explain away all objections to either *sola memoria* or *sola scriptura*. Ramsey and Sorlien, therefore, to me appear to have walked the safest way in concluding that diverse methods of report have been used. I also agree with Ramsey that we cannot compare the memory of Manningham's cousin, who narrated two books of Virgil by heart (fol. 107), with memory note-taking of sermons (p. 334). Behind his cousin's feat lies the practice of traumatic learning, glorified in Renaissance education (learning Latin by the yard).

15. Compare, for instance, the descriptions of looks and habits of ministers (fols. 55b, 65, 76, 79, 99b), with that of Mr. Beckingham (fol. 45b), and the literary pieces of character writing (fols. 2, 39b).

16. Still followed by Sorlien in his note on fol. 12b, but it would distort the analogy of two dead brothers, Olivia's and (as it seems) Viola's, and the relation

between this kind of mourning and its possible explanation through the myth of Narcissus.

17. Fols. 76b–77, Egerton's sermon. The same can be found in Layfield's sermon fol. 73. See, for other structural schemes: fols. 67, 71, 99b, 104, 113, 121b.

18. Guilpin's (?) reply to "the whipper" of satirists argues along these lines. Among the examples: a man who ran out of a sermon because satirists had made him so sensible against vices that he could no longer stand the minister's elaborations on sins. *The Whipper of the Satyrist his Penance* (London, 1601).

19. References are to *Hamlet*, ed. H. Jenkins (London, Methuen, 1982), *Coriolanus*, ed. P. Brockbank (London, Methuen, 1976), *Twelfth Night*, eds. J. M. Lothian and T. W. Craik (London, Methuen 1975).

20. P. Sidney, *Defence*, the second examination, pp. 28–42 discusses the relations between poetry, history and philosophy in terms of abstract rule and example.

21. N. K. Hayles, "Sexual Disguise in *As You Like It* and *Twelfth Night*," *Shakespeare Survey* 32 (1979): 63–73.

22. See, for instance, fol. 86, where Manningham wrote down a very elaborate (theoretical) introduction to a sermon.

23. R. J. Schoeck: "Rhetoric and Law in Sixteenth-Century England," *Studies in Philology* 50 (1953): 110–27, criticized by D. S. Bland; "Rhetoric and the Law Student in Sixteenth-Century England," *Studies in Philology* 54 (1954): 498–508.

24. Fols. 5–5b; 18–19b; 19b–20; 21b–24; 28b; 46b–52b; 72–74; 108b–109; all sermons from 110 onwards to 120b, because of their preoccupation with the succession; 121b–125, to mention only the most obvious examples.

25. If "last Christmass" is the end of December indeed, Manningham himself was absent, as he was staying with his cousin in Kent until the beginning of January.

26. As Herford and Simpson show, the tale had been known in English at least since Hoby's translation of Castiglione (1561), but possibly the term "sordid" is a reference to the farmer in Jonson's play. He certainly influenced the "legend," in John Taylor's version of 1640. (*Ben Jonson*, vol. 9, pp. 455–57).

27. *The Picture of the Perfect Common Wealth*, fol. 6b; *News from Ostend*, fol. 11; *Quodlibets . . . against the Jesuits*, fols. 151–52; notes of Howard's dedication to the queen, of the instructions of Charles V to Philip II, fols. 32–33; *An Politici Horum Temporum* of Stapleton, fol. 61–63b; *The Tragicall History of Mary Queen of Scotts*, fol. 91b–94b; *Some Partes out of John Hawards [Hayward] Answere to Dolmans Booke of Succession*, fol. 128b–132b.

28. Manningham was a conformist when it came to the matter of James's succession. His diary does not show any sign of awareness of the queen's fatal illness until the eve of his death. The relationship between politics and pulpit was enforced by Parry's sermon on oaths, a sermon attended by the entire court (Manningham mentions several of the most prominent dignitaries), while the Queen was about to die within a few hours. Only after her death did he use his contacts with Dr. Parry to remain informed, and attended sermons at court.

29. Sorlien's note, pp. 48–49.

30. Freud, *Jokes*, pp. 76–78.

31. Richard Levin, "The Relation of External Evidence to the Allegorical and Thematic Interpretation of Shakespeare's Plays," *Shakespeare Studies* 13 (1980): 1–29, and "The Contemporary Reception of *Tamburlaine*," *Medieval and Renaissance Drama in England* 1 (1984): 51–70, discusses the lack of proof for allegorical and thematic response, although he is too extreme in rejecting them.

32. Fols. 8, 10b, 11b, 12, 29b, 39b, 44, 59b 2x, 70b, 98, 99, 113.

33. Fols. 27; 29; 35b 3x; 54; 58b 2x; 59b; 70b; 78b; 102; 103b; 117; 117b; 118;

particularly on names on fols. 12; 26b; 57; 75b; 81b; 91 2x; 97b 2x. The jokes involving relationships will be discussed below. The examples in the text are taken from these folios. Other variants will be summed up in the notes below.

34. This joke recurs in the *Banquet of Jests* (London, 1639), vol. I, no. 44, pp. 31–30 [sic]. Here it is told as a jest, with no clear signs of historicity. The line *Poena perire potest, culpa perennis erit* is said to be "Ovid's prophecy."

35. As on the fols. 11 3x; 26b 2x; 45b; 59 2x; 66b; 90b and a slightly different kind on the fols. 12 3x; 12b; 64b.

36. Examples can be found on fols. 24b; 29b; 31b; 39b; 46; 54; 58; 58b; 66b; 91; 102; 127b.

37. *Le Prince d'Amour, or the Prince of Love. With a Collection of Several Ingenious Poems and Songs by the Wits of the Age* (London, 1660), p. 7.

38. Stephen Booth, *Sonnets* (New Haven, Yale U.P., 1977), pp. 176ff., 441ff.

39. Third satire, lines 81–110, E. Guilpin, *Skialetheia*, ed. D. Allen Carroll (Chapel Hill, 1974), which is crammed with homosexual allusions; see also pp. 185–87. I doubt a personal allusion to Lodge through Del Phrygio (Lodge had by then left England), or an innocent reference to the romance hero, for jokes on homosexuality can be framed from all Phrygic things because they allude to Ganymede. The content of all jokes and their relationships with social groups cannot, of course, be discussed here. My impression from a comparison of Temple Revels and the so-called jestbooks is that the sexual jokes in the Middle Temple were of a particular kind, stressing fear of castration.

40. See the author's "*Twelfth Night, Every Man Out of his Humour*, and the Middle Temple Revels of 1597–98," *Modern Language Review.* 84:3 (1989): pp. 545–64.

41. The materials taken to shed light upon the connections between Manningham's "mentality" and his response to *Twelfth Night* are from the following folios: 2, 9b 2x, 10 2x, 10b 6x, 12b, 13b, 15, 15b, 24b 2x, 26b, 29b 2x, 31 2x, 34b, 37b, 38b 2x, 39, 39b, 44, 44b, 46, 54, 57 2x, 58, 58b, 59 2x, 59b, 60 2x, 70b, 74b, 75b, 77, 77b, 90b, 97b 2x, 98, 102, 103b, 109b, 113, 113b, 118, 118b, 119, 119b, 126, 133b. I have left out the sermon materials, although the ministers used most of the contemptuous references to women found in the literature of the time. Manningham's favorite, Clapham, particularly boasted of his being free from any affection for women (fol. 80). Under the heading "of love," he is quoted as saying: "They [women] will be at your commandment, but you may doe it your selfe. You shall command and goe without."

42. Stone, *The Family*, chapter 1. John Hoskyns, with whom Manningham entered a bond on the latter's admittance in the Middle Temple, and who is quoted more than once in the diary, spoke against married men taking up residence with their wives and families in colleges, cathedral churches, and the universities of Oxford and Cambridge. He stated that virginity is a virtue, and that marriage is not a necessity. Characteristically, an opponent exclaimed: "And yet this ientleman saieth he is not popish!" Hoskyns himself, at thirty-five, married the widow of his close friend Francis Bourne, a lady of twenty-six. *The Life, Letters, and Writings of John Hoskyns*, edited with an introduction by L. Brown Osborn (New Haven, Yale U.P., 1937), pp. 24–25 and p. 22.

43. Sorlien, p. 324.

44. C. Kahn, "This Savage Joke," in *Masculine Identity in Shakespeare* (Berkeley, University of California Press, 1981); D. Cohen, "Law, Society, and Homosexuality in Classical Athens," *Past & Present* 117 (1987): 3–22.

45. There is one joke containing the traditional inversion of warriors into a married couple on fol. 11, and some neutral remarks implying inversion on fols. 70 and 118b.

46. Regarding the social frame of this type of joke, it may be connected with the custom of mutual masturbation during bathing noticed by Louis XIII's master of the robes as an English "remedy" (O. Ranum, *History of Childhood Quarterly* 2 (1974): 181, 185–86; Middleton has a character in *More Dissemblers Besides Women* (1616?) complain about a page (a disguised woman) that he will not swim and have sex with him (*Works*, ed. A. Bullen [London, 1885–86], VI, 3.1.91ff.). It might cause confusion about the borderline between accepted sexual practice and sodomy (see also A. Bray, *Homosexuality in Renaissance England* [London, Gay Men's Press, 1982], chapter 1).

47. Remarks from Simonds D'Ewes and Lady Hoby are quoted in Ramsey, note 11.

48. John Chamberlain, *Letters*, ed. N. E. McClure (Philadelphia, 1939), vol. 1, pp. 184–85.

49. J. Munro et al., eds., *A Shakespere Allusion Book*, ed. E. K. Chambers (Oxford, 1932), I, p. 438.

50. Sorlien, p. 313; see also P. Wiesen, *Twelfth Night: A Stage History* (Ph.D. diss., University of Wisconsin, 1962), pp. 32–39.

51. "Performance" is the first meaning listed in the OED ("practice," 1). Manningham uses the term "practice" in the same sense of "activity" on fol. 10b ("she practised some wit upon my cosen she") and on fol. 13, where Mr. Copping "is a notable practiser."

52. Ed. W. W. Greg, Malone Society reprints, 1914; pp. 20–24.

53. Of course, in the second reading "in Italian" should have taken a different position, but the syntax is very poor elsewhere in this account. Other instances from the diary indicate that he used "called" to express "named," as in: "whereof the one called Frances was married" (fol. 16b); "by whome one daughter called Frances" (fol. 16b—same account); "the cupboard, which one called St. Albanes" (fol. 26b). But the first reading, too, raises some problems. Why "in," if he might as well have written "that Italian play called *Inganni*," or something still clearer and more economical?

54. That Manningham, then, could have pointed to an important direct source for *Twelfth Night* is a casual consequence. Shakespeare might have known of the performance of *Laelia* both through his future son-in-law John Hall and through Weever (with whom he must have had some personal connections, as Honigmann points out). The case of *Laelia* as the *Ingannati*-like source for *Twelfth Night* has been neglected, but—because of two persons who may have been Shakespeare's informants—appears stronger than the Italian comedies, echoes from which are all very remote. Moreover, the echoes are mostly derived from English translations of those comedies. On John Hall, see M. Mahood, *Twelfth Night* (Harmondsworth, Penguin Books, 1968), pp. 27–28; on Weever, see Honigmann, *Shakespeare: The "Lost Years"* (Manchester, Manchester University Press, 1985), pp. 50–59. Salingar, *Traditions*, quotes Weever's lines on *Laelia*, pp. 238–39, suggesting that *Laelia* might have drawn Shakespeare's attention to the type of plot. See Lothian and Craik, *Twelfth Night*, p. 1, for a concise statement about the Italian sources.

55. E. H. Gombrich: *Art and Illusion*, 5th ed. (London, Phaidon Press, 1977), pp. 64–73.

56. Ibid., pp. 4–5.

57. C. van Emde Boas: *Shakespeare's Sonnetten en hun verband met de travesti-double spelen* (Amsterdam/Antwerpen, Wereld bibliotheek, 1951), pp. 486–88. For a remarkable piece of stage criticism in line with van Emde Boas' view, see the anonymous *Sunday Telegraph* commentary on the all-male *As You Like It* (National Theatre, 1967) in: *"Much Ado About Nothing" and "As You Like It": A Casebook*, ed. J. R. Brown (London, 1979), pp. 239–40.

Making Places at Belmont: "You Are Welcome Notwithstanding"

NANCY ELIZABETH HODGE

IN *The Crisis of the Aristocracy*, Lawrence Stone states:

> Power takes many forms: it may be composed in varying degrees of physical force, economic pre-eminence, and social or personal prestige; it may express itself in coercion, authority, or manipulation.[1]

Commentators have more recently complicated any articulation of the sources or expressions of power, warning that oversimplified notions, reductive and prescriptive, fail to take into account its complexity. With this caveat in mind, I propose to explore some of the manifestations of power ascribed to the gentility in *The Merchant of Venice*. To interrogate power in this instance, I subscribe to its analysis as implicitly and inherently social, a force which cannot be divorced from, or exist in a vacuum unconnected to, the persons who struggle to achieve or maintain it.[2] And that amorphous label "gentility" may obscure rather than enlighten unless we register awareness that "the system of social evaluation and the complex constructions to which [the period] gave rise [can]not be reduced to a single, consistent, yardstick."[3] For present purposes, I will consider *The Merchant of Venice*, addressing the "alternate" site, Belmont, as an aristocratic retreat from a mercantile center—a specific cultural manifestation common to both Venice and England in the sixteenth century which is demonstrated in contemporary accounts of class relocations and redefinitions in the Venetian territories and in England. Further, I propose that the concept of Belmont as a "court" allows an exploration of power ". . . directly linked, as always, to wealth, status, and the monopoly of violence, but also thought of as something quite independent, a possession to be wrestled from another, an object of intellectual interest, a consummate manifestation of human energy."[4]

When considering Belmont as a site of at least physical withdrawal from a mercantile center, one may ask whether such an oasis was exceptional for Venetians during the sixteenth century. Alberto Tenenti, for instance, notes that patterns of colonization were changing in the quattrocento. At the same time the Venetians were losing their monopoly on Mediterranean shipping,[5] many of the patriciate took part in the move "to consolidate acquisitions on the *terraferma*."[6] Besides Trevigiano, the Venetians added Padua, Vicenza, Friuli, Brescia, and Bergamo to their territories, though not without contest. And, in a change from previous colonial practice, they transplanted themselves among the citizens of the regions. Whether Venice pursued this two-century expansion (or retrenching) in the optimism that such territories would be necessary to maintain a vigorous position in a changing commercial climate, or whether the *Signoria* anticipated the inevitable and rushed to secure holdings which could support a more circumscribed Venetian economy, we do not know. What can be established, however, is a general shift, both in the wealthy Venetians' attitude toward direct involvement in trade and in their estimation of merchant venturing.

During the first quarter of the sixteenth century, Girolamo Priuli recorded a lament in one of the many volumes of his diaries. Having spent a portion of his youth in London as a merchant, he returned to Venice to find a transition in his compatriots' occupations, habitations, and perspectives.

> Before these forefathers of ours had the *terraferma*, they devoted themselves to voyages and navigation to the great advantage and emolument of the city, and they earned much money each year, and yet they were not renowned throughout the world and were regarded as fishermen. Whereas, having conquered the *stato* of the mainland, they have gained great reputation and name on that account and are much esteemed and appreciated and honoured by the signori of the world and respected by all.[7]

Priuli's assertion of the honor accorded landholding Venetians remains problematic at best. We can conclude, however, that by the sixteenth century the Venetian nobility, who, it must be remembered, had achieved entry into that limited stratum primarily by centuries of successful trading, seemed to grow embarrassed; as "fishermen," no matter how rich or how successful they might be, they derived their wealth not from land but from trade. Evidently, the Venetian patriciate felt uncertain of their eminence.

Although Venetian nobles had owned mainland estates from as early as the fourteenth century, the War of the League of Cambrai [1509] seems to mark the beginning of their increased acquisition of such holdings. Economic historians are still debating the reasons for the shift of interests, but the causes do not appear to be entirely or perhaps even primarily economic. . . .[8]

Many Venetians appeared to begin registering a type of international class consciousness which had not surfaced in their previous centuries of mercantile renown.

The tranquil charms of landed possession . . . were converting an ever-more conspicuous number not only of Patricians but also of *Cittadini* and even simple *popolani*. The *terraferma* was progressively seducing the Venetians, a people still without cultural myths in spite of the prestige of maritime tradition and the evidently greater profits to be derived from overseas trade.[9]

Ugo Tucci agrees that the "cinquecento . . . saw the progressive detachment of the nobility from trade; though certainly not a new phenomenon, this was the period in which it became most pronounced."[10]

Oliver Logan speaks of the appearance of a new entity in the *terraferma* landscape as a result of the migration in progress from island city to mainland estate.

At the beginning of the sixteenth century, Venice chose a somewhat idiosyncratic and isolated culture, but as the century progressed it showed the fruits of an increasing intimacy between the *Citta dominante* and the mainland. At the same time, testimony of Venetian penetration into the *terraferma* was provided by a new art-form: the country villa.[11]

Ugo Tucci's description of "the tranquil charms of landed possession" for these Venetians bears marked resemblance to the Belmont we witness in Shakespeare: "The palaces and seignorial villas, made for celebrations, entertainments and the carefree but decorous parties which passed the time with storytelling and discussion, remained for the most part shut off from problems connected with working in the fields"[12]—or working at all, one might add. S. J. Woolf concurs in this judgment, noting that these places of resort provided no additional source of income and were not expected to.[13] Instead they imparted a kind of instant legitimacy, something trade could no longer do:

It is clearly characteristic of the desire of so many mercantile oligar-
chies (such as that of Florence in an earlier period) to transform themselves into landed proprietors, while providing one more example of
the predominant attraction of land for the society of pre-Revolutionary
Europe.[14]

And as large numbers of Venetian aristocrats were ferrying their
belongings to the mainland, many of their English counterparts
were trundling at least portions of theirs to London—willingly,
even eagerly. The sixteenth-century English with inherited wealth,
while not exchanging their landed prerogative with the rising merchant class, flocked to enjoy the profits and pleasures of an increasingly international capital; the privileged Venetians, while not
abandoning their legislative and governmental responsibilities, re-
treated to their own static paradises, removed from the embarrass-
ment of commerce.

Did Shakespeare know of the Venetian retreat to the mainland,
know of the Venetian aristocrats' hesitation at appearing more than
simply to dabble in trade, know of the nonagricultural atmosphere
of a mainland country villa? Did casual conversations at the
Bankside's The Oliphant, gossip with the loquacious John Florio, or
nostalgic reminiscences by the numerous Venetian Bassanos who
supplied music at Elizabeth's court[15] provide Shakespeare with an
inkling of the social shift Venice experienced at this time? Possibly.
Does the text of *The Merchant of Venice* reflect these Venetian
cultural phenomena? Perhaps. Yet such hypotheses, regardless of
their appeal, must finally be labeled hopeful speculation, wishful
thinking. A line of inquiry more likely to reward the reader rests
instead in this query: Does this Belmont, like the Venice of Shakespeare's merchant, embody particular characteristics of social and
economic movements current in late sixteenth-century England?
To this question I believe one may answer yes. In the universe of
The Merchant of Venice, we can see such characteristics expressed—tangible acknowledgment of "the dynamic, unstable, and
reciprocal relationship between the literary and the social."[16]

Critics of *The Merchant of Venice* have long devised responses
to the play which confront its reliance on a social hierarchy vividly
aware of "them" and "us," most often ascribed to the virulent hatred between Christian and Jew. Yet I question whether this play
presents a plot in which we can with ease delineate the lines between "them" and "us"—or, further, place characters firmly and
permanently in either camp. Rather, a portion of the play's atten-

tion to societal placement confronts the conundrum inherent in featuring a merchant as one hinge of this plot. Does the text picture as an aristocrat a rich Venetian trader, equal or superior to all whom he encounters? Struggling with an additional four centuries of accumulated and evolved conflicts over rank, how can we decide? At the very least we should refrain from imposing both our own and early modern definitions on the structures we believe we witness; instead we should attempt to analyze without preconception the dynamics of the social relations presented.

The recent work of Keith Wrightson grapples with the problems of accepting Shakespeare's contemporaries' analyses of social standing. We may fail to acknowledge that these perspectives are articulated most frequently by those individuals who rest (as they may hope to convey) somewhere nearer Fortune's cap than elsewhere. Wrightson shrewdly reminds us that the criteria so glibly listed to facilitate assignment of categories of rank or status are themselves confused.[17] Further, the divisions enumerated vary from commentator to commentator, obscuring rather than clarifying the vision of Renaissance English society. Wrightson cautions that we go too far if we suppose these observers indulge in willful obfuscation. Instead, he contends, "helpful" illuminations of social structure in William Harrison's *Description of England* and Thomas Wilson's *The State of England Anno Dom. 1600* reveal that at this juncture in England's history we witness a "peculiarly ambiguous situation. . . . For the key to the distinctive social experience of early modern England may lie in the developing ambiguity of its social relations, the very lack of an easily predictable pattern."[18] Wrightson further posits that this very ambiguity of rank underlines a pervading societal consciousness of strata.[19] Wealth remained central to any lasting affiliation with the upper reaches of society, yet that wealth's source, not merely its display or its use, remained ineradicable. Those who read *The Merchant of Venice* as an affirmation of mercantile status among the elite, at or near the apogee of this society's set network of obligation, either fail to perceive the switches in allegiance and dependence the play reveals or else facilely label those shifts as simply the transfer of love from friend to spouse. Wrightson urges those who attempt an encounter with Renaissance English social structures to face the "contradictory yet coexisting variations in social alignment: deference and resistance; cooperation and conflict; and countless local variations on the contrapuntal themes of differentiation and identification."[20]

More than the court, according to the analysis of Lawrence and Jeanne Stone, the grand country seats of England's landed elite, often the source of much of a family's income and central to its dynastic identity, proved the strongest bastion of exclusivity in the face of attempted incursions by commercial men. It was not an impenetrable barrier, since by ". . . the late sixteenth and early seventeenth centuries, newcomers to the landed classes had begun to include a handful of men like Sir Arthur Ingram, who had succeeded entirely through trade and who had no claim, or at best a very remote one, to gentle birth." But as the Stones add, "the extent to which the landed elite were willing to accept the gentleman merchant on an equal footing remains doubtful."[21] I would contend that in Belmont we do not visit simply a local habitation embodying untold wealth as a reward for the intrepid. Nor do I agree with Walter Cohen that Belmont represents an "aristocratic fantasy," one which in the ". . . concluding tripartite unity of Antonio, Bassanio, and Portia enacts . . . interclass harmony between aristocratic landed wealth and mercantile capital, with the former dominant."[22] Instead, to explore the tension inherent in Antonio's introduction to Belmont, I suggest we first consider Belmont as an aristocrat's country seat, omitting much of the emphasis on fantasy.

Earl Rosenthal concludes that after 1550, English "seignorial residences" increasingly exhibited an awareness of Renaissance Italian style, most frequently in the "Italians' accommodation of the classical orders to the pavilion-and-corridor format common to both the French and English traditions."[23] Like the enclaves of Venetian aristocrats who sought the delights of the terraferma in secluded and tasteful remove from both the grit of an international market town and the grime of working estates, English country homes had come increasingly to serve as Italianate retreats, where time was spent in the pursuit of pleasure, in games, music, and dalliance. At Belmont, we witness some of the aspects of the new English country house which were shared with their parallels, Venetian mainland villas.

In Belmont, Shakespeare also creates for his venturers a fit port, outfitted with risk, rank, romance, reward—all the elements of a climate sure to draw Jasons. Quite possibly we have in Belmont a metaphoric version of the treasures glimpsed at journey's end by the Elizabethan aristocratic voyager. Those who sailed from Southampton or Plymouth or London did not do so in search of "richly left" ladies, but some hoped to gain the favor of a lady "richly left" behind, that is, the queen. Raleigh, Essex, and Drake all pursued the pecuniary benefits and royal favor which accrued to the hearty (and successful) voyager, whether his journeys took him to Virginia, Cadiz, or around the world in an attempt to conquer or allegedly simply to explore.

At the outset Bassanio frames his newest enterprise in glorious terms for Antonio; Portia's worth is no secret to the world:

> For the four winds blow in from every coast
> Renowned suitors, and her sunny locks
> Hang on her temples like a golden fleece,
> Which makes her seat of Belmont Colchos' strond
> And many Jasons come in quest of her. (1.1.168–72)[24]

And herein we find a difference between Antonio and Bassanio. If an aristocratic adventurer like Bassanio needs to enlist cash support, he couches his descriptions of the enterprise with an eye toward the heroic, noble experience it promises. Antonio himself does not talk about his ventures; others talk of them to him (as we discover in act 1, scene 1, in Salerio and Solanio's vivid and picturesque portrait of Antonio's mercantile drama of risk and reward).[25] He hazards his wealth on a number of voyages, but shows no compulsion to urge their glamor upon his hearers. His modesty about his cargoes and their destinations reconfirms his great concern to be taken for a man of gravity, of solidity, a "good" man.[26] Yet, were he comfortably an aristocratic venturer, he would be likely to portray himself as a man of glory. The cargoes, "silks and spices," and their points of disembarkation—Tripoli, Mexico, England, Lisbon, Barbary, and India—smack of adventure, but again it is not Antonio from whom we learn of either goods or destination.

We cannot see in Antonio an English aristocratic venturer; in Bassanio we can. Glory and profit (inextricably tied and likely so ordered) instigated the elite to set sail. Those (like merchants) who were toiling up the social ladder had not the luxury of seeking out such glory, however it might beckon, clad in promised riches. They perspicaciously pursued less evanescent rewards, and they took care to present a public face which stressed their dependability.

It is clear that nearly all Elizabethan maritime ventures sprang from the initiative and financial backing of two very restricted social groups: the great merchants of London and the West Country, and the peers and leading courtiers. The relative importance of the two groups varied widely, but systematic study of the evidence would suggest that the riskier the venture, the more important was the role of the court and peerage. For example, George Beste exclaimed that Frobisher "perceyving hardly was he hearkened unto of the merchants, which never regarde venture without sure certayne and present gaynes, he rapayred to the courte," where he was taken up by the Earl of Warwick.[27]

Yet regardless of the actual importance of the money promised by a venture (and it could be very important), the privileged preferred to associate their venturing, at least rhetorically, with glory first, with profit only second. And sometimes that glory was of paramount importance. Sir Francis Drake, for example, launched his disastrous last voyage not only because of his desperate need for money but also because of his poignant hope to fulfill his image as England's Jason—to legitimize his reentry into England, he needed gold.[28]

Giannetto, the Bassanio figure in *Il Pecorone*, a source of *The Merchant of Venice*, embarks on a trade venture only to veer off course to Belmonte, a bustling seaport. Bassanio too embarks on a trade venture, but he knows at the outset that the destination is Belmont, an estate, site of the prize cargo, a rich wife, certainly, but much more. In addition to embodying a "Colchos' strond," this Belmont represents the graciousness which, contemporaries grieved, no longer characterized the great majority of English country establishments. As fit preserve for aristocratic pastimes, Belmont is permeated by the music to which Jessica's exposure must have been limited ("Let not the sounds of shallow fopp'ry enter / My sober house" [2.5.35–61]). Yet Belmont, however lavish in its entertainments, does not seem a complete return to the self-sufficient agrarian great house of an earlier age. In no way locked to the land, Belmont seems almost suspended, approached on foot, visible for a great distance, equipped with musicians and a host of servants, furnished with carriages at the gate, surrounded by terraces from which to view the night. In fact, although physically disparate from the waterlogged republic, Belmont, like Venice, is severed from dusty courtyards replete with domestic livestock. Like Venice, Belmont has no vigorous country flavor,[29] and like the new English country retreats, Belmont evinces little concern with cornfields or sheep shearing.

As mentioned previously, Belmont may present an "aristocratic fantasy"; no one works there, Portia's wealth has no apparent source, and "all comers are welcome to a communism of consumption."[30] This last contention does not stand examination, however. The welcome a Shylock would encounter, indeed fails to encounter, precludes such a blanket assumption. Burton Hatlen chooses another socioeconomic label, agreeing to Belmont's communal atmosphere, but noting its resemblance to an outdated social order, reliant on a feudal hierarchy, with Portia as gracious mistress of an estate organized along medieval lines.[31] Frank Whigham, less enamored of Portia and her motives, concurs with Cohen that Belmont seems the quintessence of aristocratic life—but not in its charm nor in its freedom from sordid monetary concerns; instead, our first (and lasting) impression cannot be divorced from the heavy "boredom of country-house life, where the only activity of interest for a daughter is speculation regarding marriage."[32] W. H. Auden too reflects that the society at Belmont does little to justify its existence; his indictment includes references to the labors or machinations necessary to perpetuate such a society while at the same time those who toil are excluded from its benefits: ". . . Bassanio, Gratiano, Lorenzo and Jessica, for all their beauty and charm, appear as frivolous members of a leisure class, whose carefree life is parasitic upon the labours of others, including usurers."[33] And, in agreement with Auden, M. M. Mahood concludes: "Behind the romanticizing of Belmont, we sense from time to time the admission that the rich are indeed different from us: they have more money."[34] But money alone cannot assure a place in this society. Neither can a place in this society be perceived in the static terms which each of these critics seems to advance.

In act 3, when Portia awaits Bassanio's choice, her words emphasize a context that departs from that of an aristocratic retreat or country house. We witness the self-conscious protestations of a woman who, though "curb'd by the will of a dead father" (2.1.24), seems still very much the center and the head of a court. She calls for music, which will sound "Even as the flourish, when true subjects bow / To a new-crowned monarch / . . . " (3.2.49–50)—if Bassanio wins. Allusion to a "new-crowned monarch" implies the self-reflexive; she herself has till now held this post. Upon Bassanio's success at the casket test, she acknowledges her new allegiance. No longer sovereign of her own court, she commits herself to the loving will of her lord, renouncing her former precedence and autonomy:

> But now I was the lord
> Of this fair mansion, master of my servants,
> Queen o'er myself: and even now, but now,

> This house, these servants, and this same myself
> Are yours,—my lord's! (3.2.167–71)

Here Portia also indulges in the explicitly gendered rhetoric of Elizabeth. Portia as "master" and as "lord" echoes those titles at once appropriate and inappropriate—an uneasy tension exploited by a canny monarch in her efforts to articulate an empowered female self within a patriarchal society, a society, moreover, which seems paradoxically to have accommodated as well as necessitated such rhetorical formulations.[35] Bassanio pleads that his success leaves him too confused to speak, although of course, he does, echoing the dual-gendered labels of his prize:

> Madam, you have bereft me of all words,
> Only my blood speaks to you in my veins,
> And there is such confusion in my powers,
> As from some oration fairly spoke
> By a beloved prince, there doth appear
> Among the buzzing pleased multitude,
> Where every something being blent together,
> Turns to a wild of nothing, save of joy
> Express'd and not express'd. (3.2.176–84)

Portia's oration confuses and pleases, eliciting inchoate expressions of joy and devotion. Certainly Bassanio evokes Petrarchan tradition here, but I think we witness something more than an observance of courtship ritual. Portia submits momentarily to Bassanio, but he himself acknowledges her primacy. She stands again the "beloved prince" of this court (or this court-ship).[36]

After the trial scene, Bassanio experiences the contrary pull of a friend's love;[37] the priority of his obligations suffers confusion because of Antonio's urgings to compensate Balthazar.

> My Lord Bassanio, let him have the ring,
> Let his deservings and my love withal
> Be valued 'gainst your wife's commandment. (4.1.445–47)

Here Bassanio makes his last concession in deference to Antonio, as their relationship shifts into its final pattern. No longer the feckless though noble young gallant, dependent on a merchant for his venture capital, obligated to a paternal figure who offers advice as well as money, Bassanio directs their plans for Belmont, after one last

Venetian night under Antonio's roof. And at Belmont, Portia prepares us for the reaffirmation of allegiance to be finalized here:
"A substitute shines brightly as a king / Until a king be by . . ."
(5.1.94–95).

If we consider the Antonio/Bassanio/Portia triangle in terms of
"patronage and clientage, paternalism and deference,"[38] we may
begin to address the fluidity of obligation and of deference apparent
in this tripartite arrangement. Antonio defers to Bassanio even
though he secures the gift of the ring to Balthazar. In fact, Antonio's
humility may underscore his right to request that final favor, begged
as recompense for "[his] love" (4.1.446). At the same time we witness his relationship and affectionate leverage with his former
debtor shift. Bassanio becomes "Lord Bassanio" (4.1.445) to Antonio in his effort to see Balthazar compensated; he remains "Lord
Bassanio" (5.1.256) to Antonio in his only other direct address
thereafter, while performing as intermediary in the ring ceremony
Portia engineers. Interestingly, during her exposure of the ill-con-
sidered gift, Antonio maintains silence long after he might have
explained his part in the loss of the ring—perhaps evidence that
rather than risk a gaffe, he prefers to remain invisible. He has been-
mocked by non-merchants for his self-presentation before
(1.1.73–76, 79–102). We must notice, too, that here his identity is
that of "friend,— / . . . the man . . . Antonio, / To whom I am so
infinitely bound" (5.1.133–35). Reduced in means, no longer is he
"royal merchant." And Portia's gracious welcome does little to
abate the strain underlying Antonio's introduction to Belmont. As
Bassanio's bride, she greets him:

> Sir, you are very welcome to our house:
> It must appear in other ways than words,
> Therefore I scant this breathing courtesy. (5.1.139–41)

In the midst of the ring wrangle, after Antonio's second speech, "I
am th' unhappy subject of these quarrels" (5.1.238), she again asserts, "Sir, grieve not you,—you are welcome *notwithstanding*"
(5.1.239; italics mine). Denials of worth or claims of being at fault
often elicit reciprocal demurs—"no, you are not to blame."[39]

Here, however, Portia offers Antonio no such amelioration. He is
welcome to Belmont, notwithstanding the fact that he represents
the problem remaining to be solved, the cause of misalignment in
this particular court.[40] Antonio's silence during this exchange may

also be ascribed to a discomfort in acknowledging his part in this abrogation of obligation between husband and wife (or suitor and patron). Rather than explain it was he who "enforc'd" (5.1.216) Bassanio to send the ring to Balthazar, who insisted until Bassanio was "beset with shame and courtesy" (217), who "enforced" (240) the wrong, he interposes himself as conciliator. Portia, however, takes from Antonio this precedence by once more reminding him of his position as collateral and creditor: "you shall be his surety . . ." (5.1.254).

And finally, after revealing her role as deliverer and just before she informs Antonio of the miraculous return of three of his argosies, Portia says again, "Antonio, you are welcome" (5.1.273). This repetition, however courteous (or labored), indicates Portia's acute consciousness (and serves perhaps as a reminder) that Antonio is not a creature of Belmont, is not a participant in the repartee which the Belmontians toss about. Now in the home of "Lord Bassanio" and the "lady richly left," his special link with Bassanio has been superseded. He has been repaid bountifully by a woman who welcomes him and at the same time provides the news that "three of your argosies / Are richly come to harbor suddenly" (5.1.276–77). Her announcement insures both his departure and his reinstatement in a mercantile world.

In Belmont, Portia's legendary wealth simply exists. It is not the profits of carefully calculated shipping, not the embarrassing excrescence accompanying a usurer's sharp practices, not (as it is for the lady of Belmonte in *Il Pecorone*) the booty she has gained by outsmarting the lusty youths whose abortive attempts to bed her require the forfeit of their goods. Portia's resources seem unlimited and so her liberality, unlike Antonio's, unlike Bassanio's, appears to have no uncomfortable conditionals. She does not need to borrow to supply a borrower. She does not need to affect a wealthy pose to win a spouse. Although upon successful completion of the casket trial she acknowledges Bassanio as her master and the master of all he surveys, we sense in act 5 (as in act 3) that Portia will always remain the true director of events—the stage manager, the mistress of ceremonies, the dispenser of rewards. The endless beneficence of Portia (and her *pro forma* abdication) should not make us forget the very distinctly casted society of which she is a part. In wealth and in love and in status, she has the power to offer most. But how does she reiterate and affirm that power at Belmont?

In response to this question, it is interesting to reexamine Portia's revelation of the return of Antonio's argosies. Antonio receives the announcement as if she has made him a gift; his response is perhaps evidence of that social structure implicit at Belmont, with Portia in the ascendant. A woman, bound by a dead father's will, committed to a marriage determined by a task not of her own improvising, submissive to "Lord Bassanio" yet immediately setting in motion a test which proves the frailty of love and necessitates its reaffirmation in the presence of the one whose claims subvert her power, she stands at the center of a court in which infractions of love and loyalty may repeatedly occur. Through the infinite capacity she demonstrates as stage manager and as actress, she resumes or reasserts her dominance over events. In the return of Antonio's ships we may witness as well a similitude with the experience of many at the charitable hands of Elizabeth—the courtier's unique opportunity to receive from a sovereign what was in fact already rightfully his own. Antonio greets the "news" with so much gratitude we are left with the mysterious sense that it is through Portia's good offices these ships and their goods have miraculously reappeared—as might title to land, pay for military and political duties rendered, even interest on loans for which the crown had undertaken responsibility.[41] Whether an embodiment of the Venetian retreat to the mainland (with tainted merchant money) or a nod to Queen Elizabeth, whose beneficence owed as much to the power of her persona as to that of her purse, Portia's strength must not be perceived as either perpetual or unquestioned. In the last act of *The Merchant of Venice*, we witness a "queen's ability at once to fashion her identity and to manipulate the identities of her followers."[42]

As for Antonio, his identity is too closely tied to goods and ships to achieve or maintain primacy at Belmont. When he leaves Venice, he leaves behind the actions and the appurtenances which identify him as "royal merchant," the only character with a livelihood directly resulting from shipping and receiving. Shylock's role as usurer is not confused by any assertion that he trades in other than gold and silver. Bassanio, Gratiano, Lorenzo, even Salerio and Solanio, give the impression that they spend their time hanging about on canal corners, interestingly insulated from the toil and the responsibility of Venice's trade. Their status seems derived from their genteel lack of occupation. As Stephen Greenblattt has recently hypothesized, "property may be closer to the wellsprings of the Shakespearean conception of identity than we imagine," dependent upon the community's acknowledgment of an individual's rights "to a name and place in an increasingly mobile social world."[43] And the means of securing and increasing that property signify much. Called "friend" and "man" by Bassanio in his introduction to Belmont, Antonio is deprived of that identity as merchant which paradoxically empowers him yet limits his access to a court of the kind where a Portia presides.

When Jessica and Lorenzo learn of Shylock's enforced provision for them ("manna in the way / Of starved people" [5.1.294–95]), the audience has no impulse to conjecture that, upon Shylock's death, Lorenzo will return to Venice with the stake and turn his hand to trade. Instead, he and Jessica consider this promised wealth celestial spoils indeed, not the means by which to fabricate more manna. Antonio receives word of his miracle in different part, reaffirming his status as a being at some remove from Belmont life, where gracious consumption, not anxious production, reigns.[44] For Antonio the news that his vessels survive promises not only sure sustenance but also the means for attaining continued sustenance by trade. Again he is surely apart from his fellows.[45]

During Arragon's pompous posturings in front of the caskets, we are invited to chuckle at his complaints about the increasing number of undesirables among the rightful elite:

> —Let none presume
> To wear an undeserved dignity:
> Oh that estates, degrees, and offices,
> Were not deriv'd corruptly, and that clear honour
> Were purchas'd by the merit of the wearer!—
> How many then should cover that stand bare!
> How many be commanded that command!
> How much low peasantry would then be gleaned
> From the true seed of honour! (2.9.39–47)

Jessica, through conversion and a Christian husband (and because she gilds herself with ducats), can escape an ignominious heritage, can achieve "honour," that is, a recognizably gentile, gentle life, even though her acceptance might raise the price of pork. The noble but impecunious Bassanio through marriage with Portia assures his continued place among the elite, although in an anomalous position—both ruler and subject in his household. Even Launcelot, through changing masters, gains status as the servant of a Christian rather than of a Jew. Yet the Jew cannot change his identity, nor can he expect to be acknowledged as an equal by those who mercifully convert him. And Antonio possesses definite employment, yet lacks title, "house," and landed estate; he lacks the offspring Shylock once had, and which Bassanio and Gratiano intend to have. Either informally or formally he has played or will play the role of guardian—to Bassanio and to Jessica and Lorenzo. Yet these relationships finally define themselves in terms of monetary bonds. Though earnest and openhanded, Antonio cannot affect the ease, the *sprezzatura*, displayed by the rest of Belmont's celebrants. He does not know how to play their games.[46] Unlike these revelers he cannot traverse the twenty miles between Venice and Belmont and remain within his element.

Wrightson's caution remains central for any response to "making places" in *The Merchant of Venice*:

> Patronage and clientage, paternalism and deference, should never be abtracted from the essential context of the realities of power in society. Given those realities, the deference accorded to superiors might be little more than a form of demeanor, a recognition of the imperatives of the particular social situation, and a willingness to adopt a conventional posture of subordination in return for assistance, favour, or protection. It did not necessarily involve, as is so often assumed, a full and unconditional subscription to a moral order which endorsed and legitimized the social and material subordination of the inferior.[47]

The choices each member of this play's mobile society makes to acquiesce or antagonize, to engage in subversive complicity or forthright contradiction, may remind us of the first appearance of Antonio, who "hold[s] the world but as . . . / A stage where every man must play a part, / And [his] a sad one" (1.1.77–79).

Antonio's isolation, his life's difference from that of his companions, achieves highest relief at Belmont. There, without "life and living" until the announcement of his ships' survival, he resumes his role as merchant once again. There, thrice-welcomed, he nonetheless receives impetus for departure, a return to Venice and to business, to a world in which his identity as merchant bestows some power. At Belmont, without prospect of propagating his own line, he hears the jovial joking which confirms a future for the "houses" of Bassanio and Gratiano, whether the bedding proceeds at once or waits until the next night. So, regardless of the director's ingenuity, there stands Antonio alone amid the hymeneal festivities of landed wealth. He may be drawn in, but being thus included only underlines his separateness. In their country retreat from the world Antonio represents, Belmont's privileged denizens maintain the same relation with trade which they and those like them appear always to have sustained—"what news among the merchants?" (3.1.21). We are left to ponder Antonio's position and the movements he has undertaken with regard to both Bassanio and Portia:

> Whatever its ideological legitimation, deference was ultimately a social bond based upon the dual foundations of interest and dependence, and deriving its strength therefrom. At best, it might seem a fair exchange on the part of the client in return for tangible benefits. At worst, it was a necessary acceptance of the realities of social power.[48]

Whether withdrawing to *terraferma* villas or Hertfordshire estates, the privileged among the Venetians and the English exhibited clear awareness of the exclusive nature of those retreats, of the social power they implied. Although not proof against the intrusion of quotidian monetary concerns, at least a portion of these dwellings served primarily as sites for aristocratic amusements and conspicuous consumption. In England, they might also serve as destination or waystation during the summer peregrinations of the monarch, when these households became courts in every sense, reigned over by the virile prince/virginal mother Elizabeth, herself a master of fostering interest and dependence. Here are grounds for a culture's "shaping fantasies," indeed.

After considering this amalgam of contemporary and current texts, what may we conclude about the shifts of power demonstrated in the social relations at Belmont? Perhaps that the privilege enjoyed by one nation or one individual may be superseded by that attained by another; that identity derives from occupation or lack of it; that social skills and self-presentation color an individual's perceptions of himself and others' perceptions of him as well; and, finally, that patronage and clientage (or largesse and obligation) continually inspire and provoke changes in allegiance. To rephrase another queen, sometimes no amount of running allows one to remain in quite the same place.

Notes

This article, accepted by *Studies* in 1988, could not be updated in the time allowed the author for the publication of this volume.

1. Lawrence Stone, *The Crisis of the Aristocracy, 1558–1641* (Oxford: Clarendon Press, 1965), p. 199.

2. See, for example, the work of Louis Montrose on the dynamics of power in the Elizabethan pastoral in "'Eliza, Queene of Shepheardes' and the Pastoral of Power," reprinted in Arthur F. Kinney and Dan S. Collins, eds., *Renaissance Historicism: Selections from English Literary Renaissance* (Amherst: University of Massachusetts Press, 1987), pp. 34–63. Montrose acknowledges his debt to Abner Cohen, *Two-Dimensional Man: An Essay on the Anthropology of Power and Symbolism in Complex Societies* (1974; rpt. Berkeley, 1976), *passim*, in developing his analysis of power.

3. Keith Wrightson, "The Social Order of Early Modern England: Three Approaches," in Lloyd Bonfield, Richard M. Smith, and Keith Wrightson, eds., *The World We Have Gained: Histories of Population and Social Structure: Essays presented to Peter Laslett on his Seventieth Birthday* (Oxford: Basil Blackwell, 1986), p. 181. See also Kate Mertes, *The English Noble Household, 1250–1600: Good Governance and Politic Rule* (Oxford: Basil Blackwell, 1988) for the indeterminacy inherent in the label of "gentleman," itself without "legal definition," p. 26.

4. Stephen Greenblatt, *Renaissance Self-fashioning: From More to Shakespeare* (Chicago: The University of Chicago Press, 1980), p. 180. See also Greenblatt's work, "The Circulation of Social Energy," in *Shakespearean Negotiations* (Oxford: Clarendon Press, 1988). He reflects on the "social energy" in transmissions of and negotiations for works of art in their own times and in the present. His reflections on the "dynamic exchange" (11) inherent in these negotiations can inform an analysis of the negotiations implicit in any social exchange, complete with the anxieties, misapprehensions, and misalignments such exchanges presuppose and invite.

5. See Nancy Hodge, "The Merchant and His Venice: Setting Antonio to Scale in His Proper World," Ph.D. diss., Vanderbilt University, 1984, esp. chapters 2–4.

6. Alberto Tenenti, "The Sense of Space and Time in the Venetian World of the Fifteenth and Sixteenth Centuries," in *Renaissance Venice*, ed. John Rigby Hale (London: Faber & Faber, 1973), p. 19.

7. Diaries from the first quarter of the sixteenth century, quoted in Tenenti, pp. 21–22.

8. Edwin Muir, "Images of Power: Art and Pageantry in Renaissance Venice," *The American Historical Review* 84 (1979): p. 32.

9. Tenenti, p. 21.

10. Ugo Tucci, "The Psychology of the Venetian Merchant in the Sixteenth Century," in Hale, p. 346. See Tucci as well for discussion of Venetians' estimates of what enabled or precluded one's inclusion among the *cinquecento* elite, pp. 350–60.

11. Oliver Logan, *Culture and Society in Venice, 1470–1790* (New York: Charles Scribner's Sons, 1972), p. 36.

12. Tucci, p. 350.

13. S. J. Woolf, "Venice and the Terraferma: Problems of the Change from Commercial to Landed Activities," in *Crisis and Change in the Venetian Economy in the Sixteenth and Seventeenth Centuries*, ed. Brian Pullan (London: Methuen, 1968), p. 189.

14. Woolf, p. 176. See also Muir (p. 33), who particularizes the image of the newly landed Venetian gentry and their struggle to present a liberal front, not unlike their anxious English contemporaries with or without land:

... patricians whose forefathers, including Marco Polo, had molded their renowned prosperity as capitalist adventurers now avoided risks, occupied spring days strolling their estates instead of rigging ships, and fed silk worms during the summer months their fathers had spent haggling in the bazaars of the Levant.

Besides living on great estates, nobles were supposed to be generous and open-handed, as the saying went, *spendere largamente*. As if in almost desperate compensation for their mercantile heritage and despite engrained habits of personal frugality, many patricians in the middle and late sixteenth centuries spent reckless sums on building tombs, entertainments, and other ostentatious items.

15. S. Schoenbaum, *William Shakespeare: A Compact Documentary Life* (New York: Oxford University Press, 1977), pp. 169–70.

16. Louis Adrian Montrose, "The Elizabethan Subject and the Spenserian Text," in Patricia Parker and David Quint, eds., *Literary Theory/Renaissance Texts* (Baltimore: Johns Hopkins University Press, 1986), p. 305.

17. See Wrightson, pp. 188, 191; this confusion exists both in the number of occupations impossible to fit neatly into any criteria and in the evolution of rankings from the terminology of "degrees" to that of "sorts."

18. Wrightson, p. 201.

19. Keith Wrightson, *English Society, 1580–1680* (London: Hutchinson, 1982), p. 22.

20. Wrightson, "Social Order," p. 201.

21. Lawrence Stone and Jeanne C. Fawtier Stone, *An Open Elite? England 1540–1880* (Oxford: Clarendon Press, 1984), pp. 399, 288. Although generalizing from extensive research on the landed elite of Hertfordshire, Northamptonshire, and Northumberland, the Stones' conclusions regarding the possibilities of the successful assimilation into this elite set by an individual labeled "merchant" support the position that such inclusion, or further, integration, remained at best tentative.

22. Walter Cohen, "*The Merchant of Venice* and the Possibilities of Historical Criticism," *Essays in Literary History* 49, no. 4 (1982): 772.

23. Earl Rosenthal, "The Diffusion of Italian Renaissance Style in Western European Art," *Sixteenth Century Journal* 9, no. 4 (1979): 37–38.

24. The text used is *The Merchant of Venice*, New Arden Shakespeare, ed. John Russell Brown (1955; rpt. London: Methuen, 1977).

25. Frank Whigham, *Ambition and Privilege: The Social Tropes of Elizabethan Courtesy Theory* (Berkeley: University of California Press, 1984), p. 104. Whigham finds this reticence a mark of Antonio's superiority; I find it rather a mark of the actual trader, who must appear solvent for a general audience. See also John McVeagh, *Tradefull Merchants: The Portrayal of the Capitalist in Literature* (London: Routledge & Kegan Paul, 1981), p. 19:

A reason why Solanio and Salerio are present in the play is to add to the documentation of the busy mercantile Venetian life which is its background, but, without subtracting from this effect, Shakespeare makes them talk of argosies, ramps, and searoads instead of dockyards and cargoes, and gives commercial Venice a romantic slant rather than a physical trading realization.

I agree with McVeagh's assessment, but assert that this "romantic" slant reflects the ideas and the actual language used by those not identified as merchants.

26. Shylock's emphasis on Antonio's status as "a good man" (1.3.11) may involve, beyond a mocking nod to Antonio's virtuous reputation and commercial stability, a fleeting reference to Antonio as "good man" or goodman, hardly a title accorded one among the elite.

27. Lawrence Stone, "The Nobility in Business, 1540–1640," *Explorations in Entrepreneurial History* 10, no. 2 (Dec. 1957): 59.

28. Theodore K. Rabb, *Enterprise & Empire: Merchant and Gentry Investment in the Expansion of England, 1575–1630* (Cambridge: Harvard University Press, 1967), pp. 36, 38.

29. See Burton Hatlen, "Feudal and Bourgeois Concepts of Value in *The Merchant of Venice,*" *Bucknell Review* 25, no. 1 (1980). Hatlen disagrees, noting that Belmont represents "the agrarian mode of life of the landed aristocracy, which stands in contrast to the urban milieu of the Venetian bourgeoisie," 95.

30. Walter Cohen, 777.

31. Hatlen, 95.

32. Frank Whigham, "Ideology and Class Conduct in *The Merchant of Venice,*" *Renaissance Drama* 10 (1979): 97.

33. W. H. Auden, "Brothers and Others," in *Shakespeare: The Merchant of Venice, A Casebook,* ed. John Wilders (London, 1968; rpt. Nashville: Aurora Publishers, 1970), p. 239.

34. M. M. Mahood, "Golden Lads and Girls," *The Aligarh Journal of English Studies* 4 (1979): 120.

35. Montrose, "Elizabethan Subject," pp. 309–10.

36. Both Lisa Jardine, ("Cultural Confusion and Shakespeare's Learned Heroines: 'These are old paradoxes,'" *Shakespeare Quarterly* 38 (1987): 1–18) and Karen Newman ("Portia's Ring: Unruly Women and Structures of Exchange in *The Merchant of Venice,*" *Shakespeare Quarterly* 38 (1987): 19–33) deal at length with Portia's power. Their valuable readings confront Portia's anomalous position as educated woman, lawyer "lord" of her home, or gift-giver. Each critic cites Portia's speech (3.2.149–71) to build her case, yet neither associates the speech's imagery of monarchy—nor Bassanio's subsequent acquiescence in the face of the awesome portion Portia represents, both in her goods and in her self—with Elizabeth herself, a primary presence in any "shaping fantasy" of gender and power in England. See Louis Montrose's work on the subject in "'Shaping Fantasies': Figurations of Gender and Power in Elizabethan Culture," in *Representing the English Renaissance,* ed. Stephen Greenblatt (Berkeley: University of California Press, 1988), pp. 31–65.

37. See Wrightson, *English Society,* p. 46, on the terminology for extended kin: "'kinsman', 'cousin', even 'friend', being commonly employed without further specification of the exact nature of the relationship." See also Lawrence Stone, *Family and Fortune: Studies in Aristocratic Finance in the Sixteenth and Seventeenth Centuries* (Oxford: Clarendon Press, 1973), p. 270, on aristocratic borrowing and the label debtors applied (at least face to face) to their creditors; Thomas Howard, later earl of Suffolk, under heavy need for ready money in the 1590s, borrowed "from all the leading moneylenders of London, including the greatest of all, Sir John Spencer, and especially from Thomas Sutton, the latter of whom he was careful to address as 'my loving and assured good friend'."

38. Wrightson, *Social Order,* p. 193.

39. Whigham, *Ambition and Privilege,* pp. 49, 66.

40. Adjusting to and moderating such discomforts of faction were some of Elizabeth's greatest achievements. By exhibiting in high relief the discomfiture one courtier caused another, she did not draw displeasure on herself, but rather diffused the intensity any such connection (or alliance) might once have possessed.

41. See Greenblatt, *Renaissance Self-fashioning,* pp. 165–66, for the story of Sir Robert Carey's reimbursement for services rendered, "no longer civil servant demanding his pay, but a lover at the feet of his mistress. He had been absorbed into Petrarchan politics." See Newman (p. 20) for consideration of gift-giving in

NANCY ELIZABETH HODGE

this context; her theoretical premises are derived from Marcel Mauss and Levi-Strauss.

42. Greenblatt, p. 169.

43. Stephen Greenblatt, "Psychoanalysis and Renaissance Culture," in Parker and Quint, *Literary Theory/Renaissance Texts*, pp. 220–21.

44. Antonio, however, when given half of Shylock's estate to deliver to Jessica and Lorenzo upon Shylock's death, immediately announces his plans to put the money "in use" (4.1.379). See Brown, p. 119, for a discussion of what this term may be meant to convey—ranging from Antonio's total disinterestedness to a possibility he will thrive quite nicely on the interest from this sum.

45. Here too, in an uncomfortable echo noted by many commentators, Antonio closely parallels Shylock: "You have given me life and living" (5.1.286), he tells Portia. Shylock, when it seems he will be stripped of all his wealth, underscores the futility of life without the resources to practice his particular trade:

> Nay, take my life and all, pardon not that,
> You do take my house when you do take the prop
> That doth sustain my house: you take my life
> When you do take the means whereby I live. (4.1.370–73)

46. The proliferation of Renaissance courtesy literature confirms these uneasy social dynamics:

> . . . courtesy theory was precisely a tool for "making places" in the social order and was used for this purpose by Elizabethans on both sides of the struggle. First promulgated by the elite in a gesture of exclusion, the theory was then read, rewritten, and reemployed by mobile base readers to serve their own social aggressions. Both purposes are decisively Elizabethan.

See Whigham, *Ambition and Privilege*, pp. 5–6; see also his discussion of Castiglione's *sprezzatura*, an effortless display "designed to imply the natural or given status of one's social identity and to deny any earned character, any labor or arrival from a social elsewhere," p. 33.

47. Wrightson, *English Society*, pp. 193–94.

48. Wrightson, *English Society*, p. 61.

Shakespeare's Purge of Jonson:
The Literary Context of
Troilus and Cressida

JAMES P. BEDNARZ

IN HIS *History of the Worthies of England* (1662), Thomas Fuller concluded a series of biographical notes on Shakespeare with a now famous passage contrasting the dramatist with Ben Jonson. Fuller's rendition of their rivalry is elaborated in terms of a vivid literary daydream that has become a cornerstone in the legend of Shakespeare's association with his talented compeer:

> Many were the *wit-combates* betwixt him and *Ben Johnson,* which two I behold like a *Spanish great Gallion,* and an *English man of War;* Master *Johnson* (like the former) was built far higher in Learning; *Solid,* but *Slow,* in his performances. Shakespear with the *English-man of War,* lesser in *bulk,* but lighter in *sailing,* could turn with all tides, tack about and take advantage of all winds, by the quickness of his Wit and Invention.[1]

Fuller cleverly suggests that Shakespeare and Jonson had reenacted the sea battle of the Armada—with predictable results. It remained for William Gifford, however, writing about a century-and-a-half later, to provide Fuller's fantasy with a local habitation and a name. Gifford in his biographical introduction to *The Works of Ben Jonson* (1816) asserts that Sir Walter Raleigh "had instituted a meeting of *beaux esprits,* including Shakespeare, Donne, and Jonson, "at the Mermaid, a celebrated tavern in Friday-street." It was here, he continues, that "in the full flow and confidence of friendship, the lively and interesting 'wit-combats' took place."[2] This unsubstantiated biographical context, showing Shakespeare and Jonson as witty tavern companions, was generally accepted as historical fact until I. A. Shapiro's rigorous study of "The Mermaid Club" revealed that

Gifford had fictionalized Fuller's account in order to celebrate a utopian moment in English literary history—a gathering that "combined more talent and genius, perhaps, than ever met together before or since."[3]

Once we have honed away Gifford's elaborations, however, we are still left with the question of the extent to which Fuller's characterization of Shakespeare and Jonson as mighty opposites was merely the visualization of a Restoration literary commonplace that balanced Jonson's rich neoclassical learning against Shakespeare's superior inventiveness. There is at present a general consensus, reflected in the work of S. Schoenbaum, that Fuller's characterization of Shakespeare was based solely on "lines laid down by Jonson," upon which he wildly elaborated. The very idea of their "wit-combates," Schoenbaum writes, illustrates "the imagination of the biographer operating upon tradition"; it is a myth that lives on, among the legion of "old ghosts" that "haunt biography and criticism."[4] But I am convinced that Fuller's allusion contains a grain of truth and that a thorough examination of Shakespeare's role in the *Poetomachia* or Poet's War at the end of the sixteenth century provides a historical base for Fuller's narration as well as furnishing us with the primary dichotomy of learned, slow Jonson and inspired, quick Shakespeare that shapes its perspective.

I

During a scene in the second part of the *Return from Parnassus*, an anonymous student play produced at St. John's College, Cambridge, for the Christmas season of 1601/2, the actors impersonating Will Kempe and Richard Burbage discuss a recent literary flyting between rival dramatists. "Kempe" not only suggests that Shakespeare actually engaged in this skirmish of wits but that he also managed to overcome all other combatants in the process:

> Why heres our fellow *Shakespeare* puts them all downe, I and *Ben Jonson* too. O that *Ben Jonson* is a pestilent fellow, he brought up *Horace* giving the Poets a pill, but our fellow *Shakespeare* hath given him a purge that made him beray his credit.[5]

The struggle for literary preeminence mentioned in this scene specifically refers to a theatrical controversy that Dekker first called the "Poetomachia" in his preface to *Satiromastix*, registered for publication on 11 November 1601. This was primarily a contest between Jonson and Marston, to which they both contributed three plays in succession, lampooning each other with varying degrees of sarcasm. In pointed allusions Marston attacked Jonson in *Histriomastix* (1599), *Jack Drum's Entertainment* (1600), and *What You Will* (1601), after which he assisted Dekker on *Satiromastix* (1601). Jonson countered each of these thrusts with parodies of Marston in *Every Man Out of His Humour* (1599), *Cynthia's Revels* (1600), and *Poetaster* (1601). When the anonymous author of *2 Return from Parnassus* informs us that Jonson "brought up *Horace* giving the Poets a pill," he is directly recalling Jonson's longest and most explicit denunciation of Marston and Dekker in act 5, scene 3, of *Poetaster*, in which the poets Crispinus and Demetrius, thinly veiled parodies of these two poets, are arraigned for slandering Horace, Jonson's autobiographical persona of enlightened authority. At the climax of this play, Horace does indeed feed emetic "pills" to Crispinus, who vomits up choice tidbits of Marston's eccentric poetic diction.

But though critics have unanimously accepted the observation that the "pill" mentioned in *2 Return from Parnassus* was administered by Jonson in *Poetaster*, they have been at odds over the meaning of the "purge" that Shakespeare is said to have given Jonson. One influential interpretation, first posited by Josiah Penniman and then popularized by J. B. Leishman, in his edition of *The Parnassus Plays*, claims that the "purge" is actually *Satiromastix*, which had been associated with Shakespeare simply because he was a member of the Lord Chamberlain's Men, the company that produced it. In *Satiromastix* Horace/Jonson is not literally purged, but he is "untrussed," whipped and crowned with nettles by Crispinus and Demetrius, who convict him of arrogance and self-love. "It may well be," Leishman writes, "that for the majority of Elizabethan playgoers and play-readers, the Globe and the Chamberlain's Men were as much 'Shakespeare's theatre' and 'Shakespeare's Company' as for us of to-day." It is important to remember, however, that Penniman, in proposing this very theory, had initially admitted, with unusual candor, that it was a "possible, but rather unsatisfactory solution of the difficulty."[6]

This rather desperate theory remains unconvincing for three main reasons. First, it disregards the overt meaning of a passage that twice cites Shakespeare as being directly involved in the Poets'

War. The players are in fact specifically celebrating their "fellow" Shakespeare's revenge on their most consistent detractor. Second, since there is no record of any Elizabethan who spoke of the Globe and the Chamberlain's Men as "Shakespeare's," this notion is entirely anachronistic. And third, Leishman doesn't do justice to the deliberate wordplay upon which the wit of the passage in 2 Return from Parnassus depends. Before accepting Satiromastix as the "purge" of Jonson, we should first explore the plays that Shakespeare wrote during this period to see if a credible antecedent can be found. In particular, scholars have not examined the full network of external and internal evidence that links the patterns of topical allusion in Troilus and Cressida to their theatrical context. Shakespeare's "purge" of Jonson will only become intelligible after we have established the nature of the quarrel he is reacting to and have examined his motive for participation.

II

Jonson abruptly terminated the Poets' War late in 1601, when he penned "an apologeticall Dialogue" claiming that in Poetaster he had done no more than defend himself reluctantly against his persecutors. Here a character called simply the "Author" assures that audience that

> three yeeres,
> They did provoke me with their petulant stiles
> On every stage: And I at last, unwilling,
> But weary, I confesse, of so much trouble,
> Thought, I would try if shame could winne upon 'hem.
> (lines 96–100)

More than a decade later, however, Jonson was more explicit about the prime source of his irritation; he confided to Drummond that the satire of Marston in Poetaster was in retaliation for the latter's unflattering dramatic impersonation of him: "he had many quarrels with Marston beat him & took his Pistol from him, wrote his Poetaster on him[;] the beginning of y^m were that Marston represented him in the stage" (I, 140). F. G. Fleay in his Biographical Chronicle of the English Drama (1891) was the first post-Renaissance critic to discover that the source of Jonson's anger was a roman à clef in Histriomastix that referred to him as the poetic sage Chrisoganus.[7]

In the "apologeticall Dialogue" appended to *Poetaster*, Jonson states that he was drawn into the controversy in only that one play, after tolerating three years of caustic allusions. *Poetaster* does show a fury not evident in earlier works, but he had first responded to *Histriomastix* in *Every Man Out of His Humour*, through a set of interpolated passages that he added to its script when it was originally being produced at the Globe. In these brief passages, two characters, Clove and Orange (parodies of the bitter Marston and his companion, the simpleton Dekker) are present for two short scenes merely to be practised upon by Jonson's rapier wit (3.1 with Chorus to line 35 and 4.6–40). The high point of the parody comes when Clove launches into a disquisition of pompous gibberish, using sixteen words strung together from Marston's eccentric diction, climaxing with the title of his recent play *Histriomastix*. Jonson resented having been made to mouth the stilted jargon of Chrisoganus, and he couldn't resist turning Marston's strained diction against him, exposing him in the process as a fraudulent scholar, who, through the facade of language, merely pretended to be learned.

The first recorded criticism of Shakespeare by Jonson also appears in *Every Man Out*, and the critical attitude that he formulated at this time was to be subsequently reiterated throughout his career. In particular, Jonson faults Shakespeare personally for the common arrogance of players who aspire to gentility, and he chides him, in a literary context, for the twin flaws of absurd diction and the violation of verisimilitude in the plotting of his drama.

Thus, Shakespeare's newly acquired coat of arms that bore the "word" *Non sanz droict* (Not without right), is travestied when it is suggested that the clown Sogliardo adopt the heraldic motto, "*Not without mustard*" (3.4.86).[8] Jonson supplements this playfully aggressive posture toward Shakespeare with criticism of two recent plays, *Julius Caesar* and *Henry V* (alongside allusions to *1 Henry IV* and *Two Gentleman of Verona*), which are coordinated with the critique of gentility. Jonson's selection of *Julius Caesar* and *Henry V* for attack is conditioned by a neoclassical perspective, as he focuses on the purported failure of diction in the former and the unreasonable chorus, violating the laws of writ, in the latter. Consequently, a passage from *Julius Caesar* that Jonson found to be inherently absurd—"O judgment! thou [art] fled to brutish beasts, / And men have lost their reason" (3.2.104–5)—is quoted by the indiscriminate Clove: "*Reason long since is fled to animals, you know*"

(3.4.33). It is from this same spirit of mockery that Fastidious Brisk disappears from the drama with a facetious lament, "Et tu Brute!" (5.6.79), a phrase for which Shakespeare had no classical validation. The Chorus of *Henry V* that asks the audience's acquiescence in violating the unities of time and place, allowing Henry to travel from Calais to London between scenes, is another of Jonson's targets. Shakespeare had "humbly" asked his auditors, in the king's name, to "let him land, / And solemnly see him set on to London," in their mind's eye, since "So swift a pace hath thought that even now / You may imagine him upon Blackheath" (5. Pro. 13–16). Jonson restages this request when his commentator asks the audience to

> let your imagination be swifter than a paire of oares: and by this, suppose PUNTARVOLO, BRISKE, FUNGOSO, and the dogge arriv'd at the court gate, and going up to the great chamber, MACILENTE and SOGLIARDO, we'le leave them on the water, till possibilitie and naturall meanes may land 'hem. (4.8.175–81)

This critique is underscored in the induction, where Mitis asks Cordatus, "how comes it then, that in some one Play we see so many seas, countries, and kingdomes, past over with such admirable dexteritie?" and he ironically responds, "O, that but shewes how well the Authors can travaile in their vocation, and out-run the apprehension of their auditorie" (lines 281–86). *Henry V* is the only play by Shakespeare that follows the classical tradition of having choruses between *each* act, and Jonson seems to be indicating that when Shakespeare uses ancient forms, he botches the job, violating a prime classical premise—the unity of place—in attempting to be "classical." Part of the humor of Jonson's joke comes from the fact that he "excuses" Shakespeare's violation of the unity of place with the same words Falstaff uses to defend theft in *1 Henry IV*—"'Tis no sin for a man to labor in his vocation" (1.2.104–5). That Jonson is here measuring his own poetic powers against those of Shakespeare is evident in the final words of *Every Man Out*, where Asper solicits the audience for applause with the reminder that if they come to accept this new play, they "may (in time) make leane MACILENTE as fat, as Sir JOHN FAL-STAFFE" (5.11.86–87). The gleeful aggression that Jonson brings to this deconstruction of Shakespearean *topoi* is perfectly represented by the treatment of Puntarvolo and his dog, whom the Chorus describes as having been transported to the court. "It seems doubtful," writes

Anne Barton, "that Puntarvolo . . . would have been accompanied by so palpably engaging and omnipresent a dog had Jonson not been remembering Launce and his friend Crab in *Two Gentlemen of Verona*."⁹ The seemingly gratuitous poisoning of Puntarvolo's dog by Macilente at the conclusion of the play represents, in this context, a symbolic act of iconoclasm, set forth as a triumph, wherein Jonson violently reinscribes Shakespeare's romantic comedy within the domain of comical satire.

Jonson's reservations about *Julius Caesar* and *Henry V*, recent plays probably still on the boards, represent the first recorded instance of his dissatisfaction with Shakespeare's work, an obsessive theme to which he returns throughout his career in his comedies, the conversations with Drummond, and the notes of *Timber, or Discoveries*.¹⁰ The prologue to the 1616 folio edition of *Every Man In* repeats his disparagement of the Chorus that "wafts you ore the seas" (line 15), again distinguishing his own superior technique in his other early play for the Chamberlain's Men. Asked to contribute commedatory verse to the First Folio of 1623, Jonson praised Shakespeare as the culminating genius of literary history, but still had to work in one qualification, remembering, for the sake of honesty, Shakespeare's "small Latin and lesse Greeke." This reservation was surely Jonson's way of vindicating himself in a manner that he had first established during the *Poetomachia*. And when Heminges and Condell in their epistle "To the Great Variety of Readers," prefacing the First Folio, praised Shakespeare for having "never blotted out line" Jonson characteristically replied, "would he had blotted a thousand"—not in malice, he argued, but merely because Shakespeare's wit "flowed with that facility, that sometime it was necessary he should be stop'd" (VIII, 583–84). The consistency of this settled judgment is revealed when he cites a second line of *Julius Caesar* in *Discoveries* to illustrate the absurd diction that he attributes to Shakespeare's copiousness. "His wit was in his owne power," Jonson writes; "would the rule of it had beene so too. Many times hee fell into those things, could not escape laughter: As when he said in the person of *Caesar*, one speaking to him; *Caesar, thou dost me wrong*. Hee replyed: *Caesar did never wrong, but with just cause*: and such like, which were ridiculous" (XIII, 584). Jonson recalled this line again, a decade after Shakespeare's death, still relishing its humor in the induction to *A Staple of News* (1626) (line 32). Since the passage in *Julius Caesar* now reads, "Know Caesar doth not wrong, nor without cause / Will he be satisfied," it is likely that the original line was altered in deference to Jonson's critique, either by Shakespeare or a subsequent editor, who left a half-line indicating the revision.[11]

It is thus evident that the basic literary distinction between learned Jonson, the scholar, and imaginative Shakespeare, fancy's child, fundamental to Fuller's history and to Restoration and Romantic criticism generally, finds its origin in the topical allusions of *Every Man Out*. Jonson felt that to be honest was to be critical, and although he was lavishly to praise Shakespeare's dramaturgy on other occasions, admitting that there "was ever more in him to be praised than to be pardoned," he nevertheless maintained that single but multifaceted critique which he later summed up in three short words: "Shaksperr wanted Arte" (I, 133).

Despite Jonson's polemics against Shakespeare, however, it was Marston who remained Jonson's principal antagonist, and who indeed set the stage for Shakespeare's involvement in the Poets' War by continuing to aim satiric barbs at Jonson in his comic plots. As O. J. Campbell has shown, Asper, Jonson's spokesman in *Every Man Out*, constitutes his first attempt to invent a figure to perform in drama the function assumed by the author in formal satire.[12] Even before the play has officially begun, Asper steps forward to justify comical satire by asking: "Who is so patient of this impious word / That he can checke his spirit, or reine his tongue?" (*"After the second sounding,"* lines 4–5) In *Jack Drum's Entertainment*, produced by the Children of Paul's, Marston subsequently lampooned Jonson's new strategy of self-assertion, through which he clearly divided his dramatic world between one clever satirist and a society of conceited dupes. Morse Allen outlines the strategic plot parody of *Jack Drum* when he notes that the character of Brabant Senior "is aimed at this aspect of Jonson's plays. Brabant Senior is made as foolish as his dupes, and Marston takes their side against him, making him fall into the pit he digged for others."[13] Once Brabant, by playing a trick on his wife, has accidently made himself into a cuckold, Marston's interlocutor Planet crowns him with a "Coronet of Cuckolds" and numbers him among the fools: "Now you Censurer, be the ridiculous subject of our mirth" (3.240). Jonson replied to Marston in *Cynthia's Revels* by demonstrating how Criticus, favored by Arete, Mercury, and Cynthia—a representation of Queen Elizabeth—ultimately triumphs over his detractors. Foremost among his foes we find Hedon, a "voluptuous reveller," and his friend Ananides, an "arrogating puff," characters that Marston and Dekker perceived to be directed at them. When Criticus walks by, Hedon encourages his companion to laugh at him and the malicious Anaides mocks his scholarly diligence: "Fough, he smels all lamp-oyle, with studying by candle-light" (3.2.11). Later Anaides impudently derides Criticus's learning to Hedon and boasts: "Death, what talke you of his learning? he understands no more than a schoole-boy; I have put him down myself a thousand times (by this air) and yet I never talkt with him but twice in my life" (4.5.40–44).

Yet Marston was not interested in denying Jonson's reputation as a scholar, but only in classifying his dedication to learning as a form of excess—a humor. Lampatho Doria, the next Jonsonian scapegoat in *What You Will*, an answer to *Cynthia's Revels*, exhibits the predictable symptoms of pedantic arrogance already touched on in *Histriomastix*. Quadratus, an open-minded skeptic, mocks Lampatho for being "a fuskie caske / Devote to mouldy customes of hoary eld," who in reciting a sample of his own writing, "spittes, / And sayes faith 'tis good" (2.246). This last phrase echoes Jonson's boast in the closing words of the epilogue to *Cynthia's Revels*, "By God 'tis good, and if you like't, you may" (line 20). Lampatho delights in the "ridiculous humour" of others (2.247), and, when crossed, threatens an opponent with the wrath of satiric verse. Jonson's stand-in fawns on prospective patrons until he is suddenly convinced by Quadratus that nothing is "more vile, accursed, reprobate to blisse, / Then man, and mong men a scholler most" (2.257). Scorned for having pored over "old print / Of titled words," as he "wasted lamp-oil" and "bated" his "flesh," he admits his program's failure and his final conversion to the doctrine of Socratic ignorance: "I fell a-railing, but now ... I know I know naught but I naught do know" (2.257–58). Marston again uses the parodic technique of submitting his Jonsonian impersonation to the indignities of Jonson's conventional plotting. Lampatho is forced to embrace the "phantasticall" nature of existence (2.250), a quality that the erring courtiers of *Cynthia's Revels* had been compelled to renounce when they bid farewell to all "phantastique humours" (palinode, line 5), and he is betrothed to Meletza in the final scene of *What You Will* in a parody of the couplings over which Criticus presides in Jonson's play.

The pattern of topical allusion that we have been following so far, however, seems restrained when we consider the full-scale warfare that erupted in 1601, once Jonson decided to launch a frontal assault on both Marston and Dekker in *Poetaster*. Against a back-drop of Augustan Rome, Jonson returned to the drama of self-justi-fication with a vengeance, identifying himself with the ideal poet Horace and transforming Marston and Dekker into Rufus Laberius Crispinus and Demetrius Fannius, respectively, partners in malice. Jonson explains Dekker's involvement in this last phase of the quarrel when he relates how Histrio, leader of an unscrupulous acting company, had hired Demetrius, "a dresser of plaies about the towne here . . . to abuse HORACE, and bring him in, in a play" (3.4.322–24). Jonson had apparently discovered that the Chamberlain's Men had commissioned Dekker to rebuke him in *Satiromastix, or the Un-trussing of the Humorous Poet*, and he raced to complete his work before Dekker, with Marston's assistance, had an opportunity to stage their production. *Poetaster* is of course the play in which Jonson "brought up *Horace* giving the Poets a pill" (in the memorable phrasing of *2 Return from Parnassus*). Crispinus and Demetrius are tried for slander and are convicted by a literary tribunal. Crispinus/Marston is, furthermore, singled out for special ridicule, as Horace/Jonson feeds him emetic pills, forcing him to vomit up specimens of Marston's exotic vocabulary. This protracted scene contains thirty examples of Marston's vocabulary, from *The Scourge of Villainie* and *Jack Drum*, as well as *Antonio and Mellida* and its sequel *Antonio's Revenge*. Jonson, who championed "language such as men do use" throughout his career, ends *Poetaster* with Virgil's patient explanation that it is pointless to hunt for "wild, outlandish terms / To stuff out a peculiar dialect" (5.3.498–99).

When Dekker in *Satiromastix* brought Horace on stage for a second time, after his initial appearance in *Poetaster*, the character had undergone a damaging metamorphosis, as Dekker naturally took the side of Crispinus and Demetrius against him. Although we possess only this one play by Dekker in the Poets' War, he shows knowledge of all three works that Jonson contributed, since his character Captain Tucca (borrowed from *Poetaster*) rebuffs the malicious and impoverished Horace/Jonson with all three of his pseudonyms:

> No you starv'd rascal, thou't bite off mine eares then, you must have three or foure suites of name, when like a lowsie Pediculous vermin th'ast but one suite to thy backe: you must be call'd *Asper*, and *Criticus*, and *Horace*. . . . (1.2.309–14)

Tucca's comment documents the history of Jonsonian self-represen-tation from Asper in *Every Man Out*, through Criticus (changed in the folio to Crites) of *Cynthia's Revels*, to Horace in *Poetaster*. Dekker ends *Satiromastix* by having Horace threatened with being tossed in a blanket and fed his own medicine. It is Crispinus who now wonders:

> should we minister strong pilles to thee:
> What lumpes of hard and indigested stuffe,
> Of bitter *Satirisme*, of *Arrogance*,
> Of *Selfe-love*, of *Detraction*, of a blacke
> And stinking Insolence should we fetch up? (5.2.218–22)

After his conviction for slander, Horace is crowned with nettles (instead of the coveted bays) and "untrussed" in preparation for a whipping. From statements in *Poetaster* and *Satiromastix* it appears that the latter was presented by the Chamberlain's Men as a form of class-action suit against their erstwhile colleague, who, having written his two *Every Man* plays for them, was now allied with their competition, the Children of Queen Elizabeth's Chapel, in producing *Cynthia's Revels* and *Poetaster*. As a playwright for the child actors Jonson used *Poetaster* to pour scorn on the Chamberlain's Men, a troupe that he describes in a joke as being housed on "the other side of Tyber" (3.4.194)—that is, across the Thames, opposite the Blackfriars theater where Jonson's play was performed. Jonson drew a scathing caricature of the adult actors, Histrio and his men, who are denounced as vagabonds, usurers, and pimps, catering to "ribaldry" and "able to helpe to a peece of flesh" (3.4.310). They seek the distinctions of heraldry, but they are already "blazoned" in the "Statute" against rogues, vagabonds, and beggars. The public theaters were "the common retreats for punkes decai'ed i' their practice," and their repertory consisted of "satyres, that girde and fart at the time" (3.4.311; 191). Not at present associated with them, Jonson now linked Marston and Dekker to the adult actors, just as Marston had allied Chrisoganus/Jonson with them in the plot of *Histriomastix*. Chrisoganus's unfortunate bond to Sir Oliver Owlet's Men here becomes Crispinus and Demetrius's sordid patronage by Histrio's company.

That Shakespeare was acutely aware of this final and most inflammatory stage of the Poets' War,—its climax in *Poetaster* and *Satiromastix*,—is revealed in this often-quoted passage from the First Folio edition of *Hamlet* where Rosencrantz anachronistically reports to the prince that the city tragedians are not faring well because they have to compete with a revived theatrical novelty, an "innovation"—plays, particularly of a satiric nature, performed by children who parody them:

> there is, sir, an eyrie of children, little eyases, that cry out on the top of question, and are most tyranically clapped for it. These are now the fashion, and so berattle the common stages—so they call them—that many wearing rapiers are afraid of goose-quills and dare scarce go thither. (2.2.377–42)

Paul's Boys had reopened in the winter of 1599, offering *Histrio-mastix*, and the Children of Queen Elizabeth's Chapel, revived in 1600, would sponsor *Cynthia's Revels* and *Poetaster*. Jonson had referred to the Children of the Chapel as "so manie *wrens*" in *Cynthia's Revels* (induction, line 122), and Shakespeare emphasized their predatory instincts by calling them "little eyases" or young hawks. Jonson in the same play had also twice employed the phrase "common stages" to stigmatize the adult actors (induction, line 182; 4.3.118–19). Hamlet remarks that the children have not only ridiculed their elders but have been forced to "declaim against their own succession" (2.2.349), disinheriting themselves by decrying the very role they will come to enact with time, "if their means are no better." Acknowledging both *Poetaster* (the most recent attack on the Chamberlain's Men) and the company's reply through *Satiromastix*, Rosencrantz comments:

> Faith, there has been much to do on both sides; and the nation holds it no sin to tar them to controversy. There was for a while no money bid for argument unless the poet and the player went to cuffs in the question. (2.2.350–54)

When Hamlet hears of this, he asks in amazement, "Is it possible?" to which Guildenstern knowingly replies, "O, there has been much throwing about of brains." This topical sequence then ends with Rosencrantz's remark that boys have triumphed in the exchange. Indeed, the "late innovation"—this insurrection of the child actors against their spiritual fathers, the Chamberlain's Men—appears to have achieved its end. "They carry it away, Hercules and his ball too," Rosencrantz concludes, implying that, in spite of their diminutive size, the children have borne off *both* Hercules and the world he shoulders, the emblem of the Globe theater.

In *Hamlet*, Shakespeare acknowledges the bitterness engendered by the Poets' War on both sides. But he particularly emphasizes one aspect of the struggle: the attack on the Chamberlain's Men. This topical commentary—a metacritical discourse on recent theatrical history—illustrates Shakespeare's familiarity with this eruption of personal satire, but there are two pieces of contemporary evidence that suggest he elsewhere did more than simply note the controversy in passing. The first of these, as we have seen, is the allusion in *2 Return from Parnassus* to Shakespeare's purge of Jonson. The second indication that Shakespeare participated in the quarrel is present in the "apologeticall Dialogue" of *Poetaster*, where Jonson admits that he did satirize specific individuals in the play, including the adult actors, and laments that some of the more enlightened of their number have retaliated with unexpected severity:

> Now, for the Players, it is true, I taxed 'hem,
> And yet, but some; and them so sparingly,
> As all the rest might have sate still, unquestion'd,
> Had they but the wit, or conscience,
> To think well of themselves. But, impotent they
> Thought each man's vice belon'g to their whole tribe:
> And much good doo't 'hem. . . .
> Onely amongst them, I am sorry for
> Some better natures, by the rest so drawne,
> To run in that vile line. (lines 141–52)

The only candidate who has ever been proposed for Jonson's allusion to "some better natures" is Shakespeare; Jonson's plural reference hides a very singular identification. The person whom Jonson was referring to had to share a dual role as both player and poet for the Chamberlain's Men; he had to be someone who would take offense as an actor and respond as a dramatist. Running "in that vile line" would necessarily mean writing satirical plays against Jonson. Even Leishman, who excludes Shakespeare from the "purge" in *2 Return from Parnassus* admits that: "It is almost certain that among these 'better natures', he [Jonson] had Shakespeare in mind: for what other member of the Chamberlain's company did he ever publicly express admiration or friendship?" Jonson's phrase, "some better natures," anticipates his later praise of Shakespeare in *Discoveries*, with its remembrance that "He was (indeed) honest, and of an open, and free nature" (VIII, 584). And among

Shakespeare's plays, it is in *Troilus and Cressida* that we find the "purge," the dialogue which provides the historical foundation for Fuller's account of a wit-combat between Shakespeare and Jonson.

IV

The claim that *Troilus and Cressida* contains Shakespeare's answer to Jonson depends on three kinds of evidence. First, the text is intelligible in terms of the reference in *2 Return from Parnassus*. Second, it will be seen to function as an extension of the Poets' War, sharing in the set of satirical themes and techniques that appear in the plays of Jonson, Marston, and Dekker. And third, the "purge" may be explained as a logical component of the work in which it is discovered. The contention that *Troilus and Cressida* contains the "purge" has a long tradition which originates in Fleay's often erratic insights. In *A Chronicle History of the Life of William Shakespeare*, Fleay, frequently working with little more than a hunch, guessed that Jonson was Ajax, Dekker was Thersites, Chapman was Achilles, and Shakespeare was Hector. The one substantial coupling that Fleay recorded, that of Ajax with Jonson, was then developed by R. A. Small, who writes that it "is certain that, as Fleay has suggested, the description applies exactly to Jonson and that the character of Ajax is at least in part a personal hit at Jonson." Herford and Simpson, and William Elton have subsequently agreed, and it is only by building on the most plausible of their suggestions that Shakespeare's participation in the Poets' War becomes clarified.[14]

Elton correctly observed that the language of *2 Return from Parnassus* is far more detailed in its connotations than readers had heretofore assumed. He emphasized accordingly the observation that the phrase, "our fellow Shakespeare hath given him a purge that made him beray his credit," uses the word "beray" as a synonym in Elizabethan parlance for "befoul" or "beshit." Elton concluded that "Shakespeare 'purged' Jonson by satirizing him as a witless braggart soldier compounded of humours, and berayed his credit (befouled his reputation) by naming him Ajax, signifying a privy."[15] Shakespeare needed Ajax for the depiction of Trojan history, but he built into the role a reference to Jonson, in order to expose him, by proxy, to the indignities of his comic plotting. Ever since John Harington, in *The Metamorphosis of Ajax* (1596), implicitly encouraged his readers to pronounce the hero's name with a stress on the second syllable (Ajax or a jakes), it increasingly came to trigger a comic response. Harington also incited an anonymous rival, who, soon after, took him to task in *Ulysses Upon Ajax*. Thomas Nashe even boasts that his own pamphlet *Have With You to Saffron-Walden* (1596) will so infuriate Gabriel Harvey that he will have to "beray" himself, upon reading it. In order to emphasize his point, Nashe includes a woodcut caricature (see illustration), entitled "*The picture of Gabriell Harvey, as hee is readie to let fly upon Ajax.*"[16] Shakespeare works this pun into the dialogue of *Troilus and Cressida*. It furnishes the jest behind Thersites' remark that "Ajax goes up and down the field, asking for himself" (3.3.243–44)—that is, the hero, frightened on the battlefield, seeks a privy. Prior to *Troilus and Cressida*, Shakespeare had featured the pun in the name of the melancholy Jaques of *As You Like It* and does so to typify the new breed of formal satirists as unwholesomely noxious "anal" characters.

"In his first two plays for Shakespeare's company," writes Clifford Leech, Jonson "had labelled himself the 'humours' dramatist, and the label stuck."[17] Between 1599 and 1601, however, a witty allusion to Jonson as Ajax possessed an added degree of particularity, since at this time Jonson, in his three comical satires, had insisted that the poet-satirist was a moral physician who purges away the excessive humors of his sick contemporaries. On a superficial level, Shakespeare is branding Jonson with the scatalogical references that typify his work, but, more profoundly, he challenges the very basis of the cathartic theory of comedy that Jonson was currently proposing. Jonson had already employed the language of ancient Greek moral and physical purgation at the end of *Every Man In His Humour*, where Justice Clement laments that "election is now governed altogether by the influence of humour," and that contemporary society "must have store of *Ellebore* given her to purge these grosse obstructions" (5.3.344–49). Horace likewise administers hellebore, an extremely potent purgative, to Crispinus/Marston at the climax of *Poetaster*. If the title of *Every Man In His Humour* suggests that a "humorous" disposition is endemic to mankind, in *Every Man Out* Jonson seeks to alter this condition of bondage by putting the audience "out" of its humor, not in the modern negative sense of being "beside oneself," but rather by being emancipated from absurdity. Jonson attempts to achieve this act of reformation by impressing upon his audience a series of dra-

The picture of Gabriell
Haruey, as hee is readie
to let fly vpon Aiax.

Thomas Nashe, *Have With You to Saffron-Walden* (1596). By permission of the Folger Shakespeare Library.

matic epiphanies in which the play's formerly deluded characters experience the sudden clarification of self-knowledge. Witnessing this spectacle of conversion, Jonson hoped, would force his spectators to undergo a cathartic purge of their own corresponding humors. The metaphor equating literature with a kind of moral medicine was a commonplace of Renaissance humanism, but Jonson's three spokesmen—Asper, Criticus, and Horace—all give it a special prominence in the comical satires.[18] Asper speaks with derision of spectators plagued with misconceptions about both themselves and Jonson's plays. At the conclusion of *Cynthia's Revels* the narcissistic courtiers who have drunk of the fountain of self-love are encouraged to seek the sole remedy for their ailment: *"Now each one drie his weeping eyes, / And to the veil of knowledge haste; / Where purged of your maladies, / You may of sweeter waters taste"* (palinode, lines 35–38). In *Poetaster*, Jonson again returns to this *topos* when Horace volunteers to "purge" the demented Crispinus (5.3.393).

By 1601, having completed his third and final comical satire, Jonson had established for himself a new poetic identity and become known, in the words of *Satiromastix*, as "he, that pennes and purges Humours and diseases" (5.2.307). Shortly before the writing of *Satiromastix*, a pamphlet by a W. I. (probably John Weever) entitled *The Whipping of the Satyre* was being hawked by the booksellers, and it appears to be one of the sources that Dekker consulted in parodying Jonson. In his preface, W. I. personally addresses Jonson as *"Monsieur Humourist"* and argues that the humors which Jonson seeks to purge are only projections of his own moral failings; he is no physician at all, but a murderer of his patients:

> You questionles [would] have made better humours, if it had bene but to better our maners, and not in stead of a morall medicine, to have given them a mortall poyson.[19]

When Shakespeare wove his topical references into *Troilus and Cressida*, therefore, he did so to serve the same purpose that had motivated Marston, Dekker, and W. I. Each had collectively decided to purge the purger, to cure the physician who could not cure himself, and they all used the same bitter medicine that he dispensed to others. When the author of *2 Return from Parnassus* states that Shakespeare "purged" Jonson, he recalls the way in which both the name and character of Ajax in *Troilus and Cressida* possessed a metatheatrical dimension that comprised part of an ongoing critical movement against the "humourous" poet.

References to Jonson through Ajax in *Troilus and Cressida* highlight the main drama and are communicated primarily through the medium of textual parody. Foremost among these passages is Alexander's long description of Ajax to the curious Cressida. Here, Shakespeare's portrait of Ajax mimics the exorbitant praise lavished on Jonson's dramatic surrogate Criticus in *Cynthia's Revels*. Viewing a parade of courtiers walking past, Cupid singles out Criticus and asks his father, "His name, Hermes?" The god of eloquence, responds with a lengthy encomium (quoted from the First Quarto) that Jonson's rivals interpreted as unabashed self-praise:

> CRITICUS. A creature of a most perfect and divine temper; One, in whom the *Humors* and the elements are peaceably met without emulation of precedencie: he is neyther too fantastickly *Melancholy*, too slowly phlegmaticke, too lightly sanguine, or too rashly cholericke; but in all, so composde & order'd; as it is cleare, Nature was about some ful worke, she did more then make a man, when she made him; His discourse is like his behaviour, uncommon, but not unpleasing; hee is prodigall of neither. Hee strives rather to be (that which men call) judicious, then to bee thought so: and is so truly learned that he affects not to shew it: Hee will thinke, and speake his thought, both freely: but as distant from depraving any other mans merit, as proclaiming his own: For his valor, tis such, that he dares as little to offer an Injurie, as receive one. In summe, he hath a most Ingenious and sweet spirit, a sharp and season'd wit, a streight judgment, and strong mind; constant and unshaken: *Fortune* could never breake him, nor make him lesse. He counts it his pleasure to despise pleasures, and is more delighted with good deedes, then Goods. It is a competencie to him that he can be vertuous. He doth neyther covet, or feare: lesse, he hath too much reason to do eyther: and that commends all things to him. (2.3.123–45)

This elegant but tedious character sketch of the ideal man, with its labored Ciceronian balanced clauses, traced without startling turns of phrase for the purpose of developing predictable patterns of thought in the service of self-praise, provided an obvious target for Shakespeare, who uses it as a frame for his criticism of Jonson. Accordingly, when Cressida remarks that Ajax "is a very man *per se*," her servant Alexander expatiates:

> This man, lady, hath robb'd many beasts of their particular additions: he is valiant as the lion, churlish as the bear, slow as the elephant; a man into whom nature hath so crowded humours that his valor is

crush'd into folly, his folly sauc'd with discretion. There is no man hath
a virtue that he hath not a glimpse of, nor any man an attaint but he
carries some stain of it. He is melancholy without cause and merry
against the hair; he hath the joints of everything, but everything so out
of joint that he is a gouty Briareus, many hands and no use, or purblind
Argus, all eyes and no sight. (1.2.19–30)

Shakespeare's passage counters Jonson's evocation of Criticus
through an intricate series of comic deflations. Jonson associates
Criticus with the divine, while Shakespeare derives Ajax from the
bestial. Where "the humours are peaceably met" to form a paragon
of virtue "composed and ordered" by Nature in Criticus, Ajax is
a man into whom Nature has "crowded humours" in a wholly
discordant blend. Instead of the parallel syntax of redolent praise
found in *Cynthia's Revels*, the wit of *Troilus and Cressida* depends
on counterpoint and antithesis, as the auspicious beginning of each
phrase is canceled by its conclusion. He is valiant as the lion, but
churlish as the bear and slow as the elephant. He may have valor,
as Jonson claims for Criticus, but it is tainted by folly. He has the
virtues of all men, as well as their vices. Indeed, each of his virtues
is either inappropriate or hampered by vice and debility. His natural abilities are as a result completely useless: he is like a multi-
armed giant with gout or a blind hundred-eyed monster.

Jonson is consequently the unwilling sponsor of the satire generated against him in *Troilus and Cressida*, since not only the content
of this passage but also its literary form bears the stamp of his
influence. One of the revolutionary subgenres that Jonson developed in the comical satires was the character sketch—a literary
type that he formally introduced into English literature in the first
edition of *Every Man Out*, where he prefaced the play with a list
of characterizations of its main protagonists.[20] Jonson first incorporated these lengthy portraits within the action of *Cynthia's Revels*
(as we have just seen in the case of Criticus) and repeated this
procedure in *Poetaster*. Not confining himself entirely to a
Theophrastan model, Jonson felt free to create both idealized and
satiric character sketches, and he systematically contrasts the virtues of one good man (Asper, Criticus, or Horace) with the vices
of his humorous antagonists. Shakespeare, however, returned the
character sketch to its Theophrastan base by negating Jonson's distinction, rewriting Criticus as Ajax, in the generically formalized
criticism of Jonson inscribed in the text of *Troilus and Cressida*. In
doing so, he created a specific literary kind—the anti-Jonsonian

character sketch—that was to have a tenacious lifespan. When Jonson's contemporaries focused on the immense gulf of characterization that divided the description of Criticus, on the one hand, from Clove and Orange, on the other, they could not help but consider the lack of intellectual generosity this strategy exhibited and seek out faults in Jonson to balance his mode of self-representation. Even his Scottish host, William Drummond, was prompted to include a character sketch of Jonson at the end of his *Conversations* (including a phrase lifted from the induction to *Every Man Out*, lines 359–60). Only at the conclusion does Drummond modulate his derogatory tone into qualified compliment:

> He is a great lover and praiser of himself, a contemner and Scorner of others, given rather to losse a friend, than a Jest, jealous of every word and action of those about him (especiallie after drink) which is one of the Elements in which he liveth, a dissembler of ill parts which raigne in him, a bragger of some good that he wanteth, thinketh nothing well bot what either he himself, or some of his friends and Countrymen hath said or done. . . . he is passionately kynde and angry, carelesse either to gain or keep, Vindictive, but if he be well answered, at himself.
> (I, 151)

Jonson had taught those with whom he associated to regard criticism as an indication of honesty, and, all too often, his independent and harsh judgment of others, as well as the literary vehicles he devised to project his opinions, returned to plague him.

Why in *Troilus and Cressida* did Shakespeare then ignore the figure of Horace, in the most recent comical satire, and base his satiric sketch of Ajax on Criticus, a character in a work that was almost a year old? The answer to this question is actually quite amusing: in praising himself in the figure of Criticus, Jonson had borrowed phrasing from the conclusion of *Julius Caesar*, the very play whose diction he had ridiculed in *Every Man Out*. Jonson's evocation of Criticus as "A creature of a most perfect and divine temper . . . in whom . . . the elements are peaceably met . . . as it is cleare, Nature . . . did more then make a man, when she made him," echoes Antony's praise of the dead Brutus: "His life was gentle, and the elements / So mix'd in him that Nature might stand up / And say to all the world 'This was a man'" (5.5.73–75).[21] But in converting Antony's elegy into the stuff of self-praise, Jonson adds a further touch of hyperbole. While Nature might say of Brutus, "This was a man," she is said to have created "more then . . .

a man" in fashioning the singular Criticus. Shakespeare's parody of Criticus as Ajax, the "very man, *per se,*" thus springs from an understanding of the inherent contradiction in Jonson's own attitude toward himself—from Jonson's readiness to emulate language from the same play whose diction he had previously mocked. By appropriating Jonson's medium of comical satire in *Troilus and Cressida,* Shakespeare likewise reclaimed his own language and turned Jonson's self-flattering rhetoric against him. He therefore also wittily inverted the same technique that Jonson had formerly used to expose Shakespeare's purported deficiencies in the textual parody of *Every Man Out.*

Readers who fail to examine the strategic pattern of imitation that underlies Shakespeare's parody of Criticus/Jonson are consequently blinded to the principal function of Alexander's speech in *Troilus and Cressida.* Without an understanding of its theatrical context, critics have been compelled to agree with E. K. Chambers that the description of Ajax is both "unnecessarily elaborate for its place" and "has not much relation to the character of Ajax as depicted in the play." Kenneth Muir, for instance, repeats this observation in his introduction to the recent Oxford edition of *Troilus and Cressida,* in which he writes that "the portrait bears little or no resemblance to the character when he appears later" and conjectures that "the discrepancies" we notice "may have been due to a change of plan during the composition of the play."[22]

If one hesitates to concur with Muir's assumption that the bard was napping during the revision of his work, a far more convincing contextual explanation for the linguistic peculiarities of this passage is immediately apparent. Shakespeare's parody of Criticus/Jonson creates a slight disjunction in *Troilus and Cressida* between two sets of meanings, one self-contained within the opaque plot and another superimposed on it, as a semi-autonomous lode of literary allusion. A similar kind of disjunction is more widely recognized in Shakespeare's permitting a discussion of *Poetaster* and *Satiromastix* to go forward between Hamlet and his former friends in twelfth-century Denmark. These two passages are explicable only in terms of their theatrical context, in relation to the Poets' War, and were originally devised for an audience that had at their disposal intimate knowledge of the cultural scene for which these metatheatrical commentaries were generated. A contemporary audience of theatergoers and fellow professionals could be counted on to supplement their understanding of *Hamlet* and *Troilus and*

Cressida with a specific kind of social information that twentieth-century scholarship can only roughly approximate.

In parodying the description of Criticus, Shakespeare was faulting Jonson for the same excesses of arrogance and vindictiveness for which Jonson had been lampooned on the stage for the previous two years. This can be illustrated by the animal analogies that Shakespeare applies to Ajax/Jonson, who is compared in turn to the valiant lion, the churlish bear, and the slow elephant. The lion is mentioned in a positive light, even though the beast was proverbially a symbol of arrogance. So Ajax himself notes of Achilles, when he pronounces him sick: "Yes lion-sick—sick of proud heart" (2.3.89). That Jonson possessed the aggressive, brutal surliness of a bear had previously been pointed out by Captain Tucca in *Satiromastix*, who called him "that Beare-whelp" (5.2.185) and named him the "great Hunkes" (1.2.319), after the famous animal baited at Paris Garden, where Jonson had formerly acted. The comparison was probably furthered by Jonson's broad shoulders and large head, as well as by the fact that the playwrights involved in the Poets' War viewed their verbal combat against the ursine Jonson as the literary equivalent of bearbaiting.

The third animal analogy that Shakespeare devises in reference to Jonson—the claim that Ajax is as "slow as the elephant"—is even more telling. Of all the qualities attributed to Ajax, this charge of slothfulness is the one that causes Muir the most difficulty, since, he writes (in his note to 2.1.30) it is in "apparent conflict with one's impression of Ajax's character." Muir is correct insofar as Ajax always seems eager to come to blows. He is more than ready to beat Thersites and seeks out the challenge to single combat with Hector as a special privilege. Yet Shakespeare has Thersites call him "the elephant Ajax" (2.3.2) and remind him that "when thou art forth in the incursions, thou strikest as slow as another" (2.1.30). And even Nestor contributes to this theme when he plays on the animal metaphor initially established by Alexander and bids "the snail-paced Ajax arm for shame" (5.5.18). Shakespeare describes Ajax as being "slow" in *Troilus and Cressida* in order to link his description of the Trojan hero to his topical parody of Jonson's theory of literature.

Contrary to what the modern reader might expect, however, when Shakespeare writes that Ajax is "slow as the elephant," he is not alluding to his rival's physical size. Jonson had not yet acquired the "mountain belly" that adorned him a decade later when he wrote "My Picture Left in Scotland." In fact, he was thin enough to be contrasted with the original Horace in *Satiromastix.* "Horace," explains Tucca, "was a goodly Corpulent Gentleman, and not so leane a hollow-cheekt Scrag as thou art" (5.2.261–63). Elsewhere in *Troilus and Cressida* the elephant, which was thought to have inflexible front legs, is regarded as a creature of pride by Ulysses, who remarks that "the elephant hath joints, but none for courtesy" (2.3.108). But the main connotation in Shakespeare's allusion is primarily literary, referring simultaneously to: (a) Jonson's "slow" or labored style; (b) the relatively "slow" pace of his dramatic production during the years 1599 to 1601; and, finally, (c) the slow-wittedness indicated by a dull style and a retarded output. Following the genesis and transmission of this particular epithet permits us to see how Shakespeare's contribution to the *Poetomachia* became transformed into the legendary wit-combats waged by the quick bard and his "slow" contemporary.

Marston in *What You Will* had depicted his Jonsonian alazon, Lampatho Doria, as a waster of "lamp-oil," who slaved over his work well into the night while more sensible writers slept. But by the time that Jonson had come to write *Poetaster,* he was eager to ward off this accusation of laboriousness and consequently named his Marstonian surrogate "Crispinus," after the idiotic poetaster who had challenged Horace to a literary race in order to determine which of them could write verses more quickly. Jonson also boasted in the same play that he had composed it in only fifteen weeks, well ahead of his antagonists, whose attack-in-progress, *Satiromastix,* had not yet reached the stage. Jonson, as a result, had it both ways: he followed a precedent established by Horace that art should consist of extended concentration, effort, and revision, even as he beat his competition to the punch in completing his masterpiece early. Nevertheless, in *Satiromastix,* for the first time, Jonson's obsessive work habits are explicitly attributed to a fundamental lack of inspiration that leads to a cumbersome straining for poetic effect. This imputation must have seemed quite appropriate coming from Dekker, whose literary output had been phenomenal, especially since he had been described by Jonson as a mere "dresser" of plays, a hack who approached writing as a trade and not as a sacred vocation.

From the opening of *Satiromastix,* we encounter the figure of Horace/Jonson suffering from perpetual writer's block. He is hard at work on a poem that includes lines from "An Ode to James,

Earl of Desmond" (later published in "Underwood") and seeking inspiration from the reluctant Muses. Horace is shown agonizing over his verse and exulting about his own "rich and labor'd conceipts" (1.2.85–86). "Oh the end shall be admirable," he predicts. When Crispinus and Demetrius visit his chamber, they are met by Asinius Bubo, who explains with adulation that "Horace is always in labour when / I come, the nine Muses be his midwives" (1.2.22–23). Horace with customary arrogance then greets his guests by commending his own poetry. "Dam me ift be not the best that ever came from me," he boasts, as he hastens to explain that "my braines have given assault to it but this morning," in order to produce "the best and most ingenious peece that ever I swet for" (1.2.36–38; 101) With this Asinius, unaware of the scatalogical implications of his own language, concurs: "'tis the best stuffe that ever dropt from thee" (1.2.88–89). "I wey / Each sillable I write or speake," Horace concludes, "because / Mine enemies with sharpe and searching eyes / Look through and through me, carving my poor labours / Like an Anatomy" (2.1.194–98). Captain Tucca, assigned the role of hounding Horace, is nevertheless astounded by the writer's paucity of wit, especially the claim that *Poetaster* was written in what was for Jonson record time:

> What will he bee fifteene weekes about this Cockatrice's egge too?. . . .
> His wittes are somewhat hard bound: the Puncke his Muse has sore labour ere the whoore bee delivered.
>
> (1.2.362–67)

Tucca repeats this complaint, with reference to *Cynthia's Revels* and *Poetaster*, in again reprimanding Horace: "you Nastie Tortois, you and your Itchy Poetry break out like Christmas, but once a yeare, and then you must keepe a Revelling, and Araigning, and a Scratching of mens faces" (5.2.201–4).

Although Jonson had already been taken to task in *What You Will* and *Satiromastix* for the relentless drudgery entailed in his method of composition, it is in *Troilus and Cressida* that the specific epithet "slow" is first applied to Jonson as a term of derision. Marston and Dekker had implied as much, but they had never used this particular multifaceted word, which was to haunt Jonson's reputation throughout the seventeenth century. That Jonson was cognizant of this negative characterization by Shakespeare is apparent in the same "apologeticall Dialogue" to *Poetaster* where he regrets that "some better natures" have maligned him. Listing the "particular imputations" voiced against the Author, his friend Polyposus confides, "they say you are slow, / And scarce bring forth a play a year" (lines 191–92), to which the poet replies with contempt:

> 'Tis true.
> I would, they could not say that I did that.
> There's all the joy I take i' their trade. (lines 194–96)

Only stoic self-sufficiency saves him from the threat of despair, when the ignorant multitude condemn his "long-watch'd labours" (line 211). But Jonson, despite this justification, was unable to suppress the use of the word "slow" to stigmatize his whole poetic project. If Jonson had pointed to Shakespeare's artlessness, Shakespeare had in turn diagnosed Jonson's antithetical literary failing—a studied tediousness lacking inspiration. The myth of Shakespeare and Jonson as paradigms of nature and art begins with this personal exchange. Shakespeare's quip that Jonson was as "slow as the elephant" took root at once in contemporary criticism, and the author of *2 Return from Parnassus*, who mentioned Shakespeare's "purge" of Jonson, is the first person to play upon it, when Ingenioso criticizes Jonson for being "so slow an Inventor, that he were better betake himselfe to his old trade of Bricklaying."[23] The word soon found wide dissemination in both defenses of and attacks on Jonson. John Davies of Hereford, for instance, in his poem "To my learnedly witty friend, Mr. Benjamin Johnson," written in 1617, claims that the sheer fecundity of Jonson's wit made it difficult for him to compose:

> that plenty makes thee scarce,
> Which makes thee slow, as sure in prose or verse,
> As say thy worst detractors, then if thou
> For all eternity, writ'st sure and slowe,
> Thy Wits, as they come thronging out of dore,
> Do sticke awhile, to spread their praise the more.

For Davies the perceived liability of Jonson's slowness turns out, upon reflection, to be an asset, a guarantee that his thoughts will endure. An opposing appraisal, however, is evident in John Milton's first published English poem, "On Shakespeare," featured in the Second Folio of 1630, where he notices how "to the shame of slow-endeavouring art" Shakespeare's "easy numbers flow." During the

course of the seventeenth century, this contrast between Shakespeare and Jonson, which both poets certainly shaped during the
Poets' War, became a commonplace of literary criticism.[24] The *topos* that Fuller and Dryden popularized, and passed on to Coleridge for further Romantic elaboration, was thus derived from late
Elizabethan criticism and not invented during the Restoration.

V

As I have indicated, Shakespeare embeds his literary criticism of
Jonson's poetics in *Troilus and Cressida* within a dramatic structure in which it constitutes a secondary semiotic system of contextual reference. Long before Ajax is introduced, Shakespeare alerts
his audience to the polemical relation his play bears to the humanist program of didactic dramaturgy that Jonson had set forth in
his comical satires. Jonson begins *Poetaster* by bringing an "armed
Prologue" before the audience to slay the allegorical monster Envy
and to justify his own militancy:

> If any muse why I salute the stage,
> An armed Prologue; know, 'tis a dangerous age:
> Wherein, who writes, had need present his *Scenes*
> Fortie-fold proofe against the conjuring meanes
> Of base detractors, and illiterate apes,
> That fill up roomes in faire and formall shapes.
> > (Prologue, lines 5–10)

Jonson's beleaguered spokesman was on guard particularly against
"that common spawn of ignorance, / Our fry of writers," who were
ready to "beslime" his fame. Once the Prologue has slain Envy,
Jonson explains the meaning of his dramatic tableau by stating that
he will fearlessly confront his rivals in a similar manner:

> the allegorie and the hidden sense
> Is, that a well erected confidence
> Can fright their pride, and laugh their folly hence.
> > (lines 12–14)

In *Troilus and Cressida*, Shakespeare directly echoes these lines
by having the Prologue similarly "Enter . . . in armour." But he
subverts Jonson's "well erected confidence" by representing his
Prologue as a figure of tentativeness and indeterminancy:

> And hither am I come,
> A Prologue arm'd, but not in confidence
> Of author's pen or actor's voice, but suited
> In like conditions as our argument. (lines 22–25)[25]

The Prologue of *Troilus and Cressida* is eminently "suited" to the play he introduces. Where Jonson's Prologue predicts the triumph of reason over malice, Shakespeare's heralds in a world where this kind of "confidence" is entirely misplaced. Shakespeare's Prologue expects no standard of reason from spectators, and thus invokes them to "Like or find fault; do as your pleasures are: / Now good or bad, 'tis but the chance of war" (lines 30–31). This assertion, linking judgment to pleasure or appetite rather than certainty, epitomizes the pervasive skepticism voiced throughout the play, which counters the intellectual arrogance of the comical satires, where Jonson projects a purportedly unassailable set of fixed moral and literary values. In inserting his most detailed commentary on the Poets' War into *Troilus and Cressida*, Shakespeare visualizes the competition not as a legal proceeding, in the style of *Poetaster* and *Satiromastix*, but as part of the archetypical war in Western literature.

The echoes of *Poetaster* in the prologue and those of *Cynthia's Revels* in 1.3.19–30 of *Troilus and Cressida* bear an important structural relation to each other. In asking his auditors to be cognizant of the Jonsonian source for the Prologue's language, Shakespeare was preparing them for the "purge" that he delivered to him as Ajax. Trapped within a dramatic context, Ajax/Jonson is subjected to the same minute scrutiny that he himself had applied to his literary victims. While Shakespeare inherited much of the love story of his play from Chaucer, the Ajax material which he elaborates within it exhibits an immediate theatrical concern. Shakespeare' wide-ranging critique of Jonson has three main plot coordinates: (1) the abusive quarrel of Ajax with Thersites, which comes to represent the meaningless wrangling of the Poets' War; (2), the gulling of Ajax by the Greek generals, which undermines the principle of self-confidence championed in the comical satires; and (3) Ulysses' discussion with Achilles on the impossibility of achieving any knowledge of the self that is not socially mediated, during which Ajax is cited as an example of a man who mistakes his own value.

The pairing of Ajax and Thersites as combatants locked in irreconcilable antagonism recapitulates Jonson's struggle against Marston during the Poets' War. With his taunting language of sexual perversion, disease, and the bestial—all enlisted for the sake of railing—Thersites mirrors the worst side of Marston's satiric impulse. When Thersites is described as having "mastic jaws" (1.3.73), the phrase resonates with significance. The word "mastic" refers to a sticky substance which is repugnant. But it also might play on the word "mastix" or "scourge," in an allusion to Marston, who called himself "Theriomastix" (the scourge of beasts) in *The Scourge of Villanie* and wrote *Histriomastix* (the scourge of players). Like Marston's dramatic agents, Thersites similarly chastises Ajax for the arrogant sluggishness exhibited by previous Jonson straw men, such as Lampatho Doria:

> Why, 'a walks up and down like a peacock—a stride and a stand; ruminates like a hostess that hath no arithmetic but her own brain to set down her reckoning; bites his lip with a politic regard, as who should say there were wit in this head and 'twould come out—and so there is; but it lies coldly in him as fire in a flint, which will not show without knocking.
>
> (3.3.251–57)

The often virulent *ad hominem* abuse that Jonson and Marston exchanged from 1599 to 1601 is perfectly set off at the beginning of the second act, where Ajax, having failed to gain Thersites' attention, resorts to a mixture of invective and violence:

> AJAX. Thou bitch-wolf's son, canst thou not hear?
> Feel then.   [*Strikes him.*]
> THERSITES. The plague of Greece upon thee, thou mongrel beef-witted lord!
> AJAX. Speak then, thou whinid'st leaven, speak; I will beat thee into handsomeness.
> THERSITES. I shall sooner rail thee into wit and holiness, but I think thy horse will sooner con an oration without book than thou learn a prayer without book. Thou canst strike, canst thou? A red murrain o' thy jade's tricks! (2.1.10–20)

On the basis of style alone, Harbage, who usually avoids any hint of a connection between Shakespeare's characters and his contemporaries, was nevertheless prepared to acknowledge that the audience of *Troilus and Cressida* would view Thersites as Marston:

> of all the hypothetical identification of characters in Shakespeare's plays, that of Thersites with Marston has the most to recommend it. . . .

The voice of Thersites is remarkably like the voice of John Marston. He is at once enraged and exhilarated by the sexuality and other abuses against which he inveighs: his railing is uncouth and filled with the imagery of disease. A kind of gleeful morbidity links the pair, and would have made the association inevitable in the minds of contemporaries.[26]

But this analogue is not only offered in the play's language: it is woven into a series of reinforcing topical allusions. When Thersites scoffs at Ajax that "thy horse will sooner con an oration . . . than thou learn a prayer without book," Shakespeare explicitly refers to a personal and embarrassing event in Jonson's recent past. Jonson prided himself on his physical prowess, viewing himself as a soldier. He boasted to Drummond of having killed two men, the first during his service in the Low Countries and the second in 1598, when in a duel he murdered Gabriel Spenser, one of Henslowe's actors. Jonson was convicted of this second murder but was not executed, because he proved in court that he could read a verse from the Bible in Latin. Since a law allowing one to plead "benefit of clergy" by reading the "neck-verse" was still extant, Jonson only had his goods confiscated and was branded on the thumb.[27] It is this incident that lurks behind Thersites' rebuke. Jonson had previously mentioned the practice of benefit of clergy in *Cynthia's Revels*, certainly remembering his own experience, when the child actor of the induction announces the name of this work, which was probably posted on a sign near the stage: "the title of his play is 'Cynthia's Revels,' as any man, that hoped to be saved by his book, can witness" (lines 35–36). In *Satiromastix* Tucca had taunted Horace: "Art not famous enough yet, my mad *Horastratus*, for killing a Player, but thou must eate men alive? thy friends?" (4.2.61–62), adding later that his "best verse . . . was his white necke-verse" (4.3.105–6). Earlier in the same play Bubo had observed to Horace that "for thy wit thou mayst answer any Justice of peace in *England* I warrant; thou writ'st in a most goodly hand . . . and readst as leageably as some that have bin sav'd by their necke-verse" (1.2.114–17).

Ajax's trouncing of Thersites during this same scene recreates on the stage the physical violence into which the Poets' War escalated when Jonson (in his own words to Drummond) "beat Marston & took his Pistol from him." Indeed, Drummond mentions this incident twice in separate contexts (I, 136; 140), and Jonson even commemorated his triumph in Epigram 60, "On Playwright," where he savors his rival's overthrow:

> Playwright convict of public wrongs to men,
> Takes private beatings, and begins again.
> Two kinds of valour he doth show, at once;
> Active in's brains, and passive in his bones.

The plot of *Troilus and Cressida* fictionalizes Jonson's assault in multiple stage directions concerning Thersites, as Ajax "*Strikes him*," "*Beats him*" again, and then "*offers to strike him*," through seventy-eight lines of dialogue. Thersites is left with only one bit of consolation from this strife with his violent antagonist: "I have bobbed his brain more than he has beat my bones" (2.1.69), he confides. The antagonistic symbiosis of Ajax and Thersites locks them together in a pointless combat of invective from which neither can emerge as a victor. This, Shakespeare implies, is the pattern of conflict elicited by the Poets' War, a skirmish of wits in which both Jonson and Marston exposed each other's flaws.

Jonson's shortcomings, detailed in *Troilus and Cressida*, are not completely literary, however, since they reflect a problem grounded in the man himself. What makes Ajax intolerable is his overweening pride, his unshakable certainty in his own merit, despite his patent folly. In order to emphasize this quality of Ajax/Jonson, Shakespeare imitates one of the central plot characteristics of Jonsonian comedy in his depiction of Ulysses' plan to undermine Achilles' reputation by gulling Ajax into thinking himself superior to even the greatest of the Greek warriors. David Bevington has observed that this key feature of Jonson's satiric method consists of "an exposure plot manipulated by witty persons against a socially ambitious hypocrite who prepares his own trap, is laughed at scornfully by the audience, and is subjected to a ridiculous form of punishment befitting the nature of his offense."[28] We have already seen how Marston and Dekker used this very technique to torture their Jonsonian alazons during the Poets' War. Shakespeare employs this same device when the Greek generals, under the influence of Ulysses, act as a band of gull-gropers in bringing out the essential humor of their dupe Ajax, inflating his conceit for the audience's derision. Agamemnon's caveat can be read as the prime theme of Shakespeare's parody, with its warning against the pitfalls of self-justification:

He that is proud eats up himself: pride is his own glass, his own trumpet, his own chronicle; and whatever praises itself, but in the deed, devours the deed in the praise.

(2.3.154–57)

After Ajax has been stroked with false praise, coupled with a denigration of his rival Achilles, he earnestly tells Nestor, "I do hate a proud man as I do hate the engendering of toads," at which point the elderly statesman offers an amused rejoinder, "And yet he loves himself: is't not strange?" (2.3.160–62). The ensuing dialogue draws Ajax out, to the very limits of arrogance and jealousy, when in attacking Achilles he actually defines his own defects.

AJAX.   A paltry, insolent fellow!
NESTOR.   [*Aside*] How he describes himself!
AJAX.   Can he not be sociable?
ULYSSES.   [*Aside*] The raven chides blackness.
AJAX.   I'll let his humours blood.
AGAMEMNON.   [*Aside*] He will be the physician that should be the patient.

(2.3.208–14)

In the surface plot of *Troilus and Cressida*, Ulysses' strategy fails to achieve the desired effect, and his objective, like so much of the play's action, never reaches fruition. Achilles is not prodded into combat by the temporary inflation of Ajax's honor. But as part of the covert plot, the theatrical inside story, the episode successfully performs its function of "letting" Jonson's "humours blood" and giving the self-styled doctor of letters a taste of his own medicine. Ulysses' final encomium in this scene flatters Ajax for his learning: "Famed be thy tutor, and thy parts of nature / Thrice fam'd beyond, [beyond] all erudition" (2.3.242–43). These words, as Honigmann observes, "have little to do with Ajax's pretensions, but connect with Jonson's."[29] At Westminster, Jonson had studied with William Camden, one of Elizabethan England's leading schoolmasters, whom he would describe (in Epigram 14, 1–2) as a mentor "to whom I owe / All that I am in arts, all that I know." What is more, a unique feature of the Huntington Library's copy of the first edition of *Cynthia's Revels* is a dedication to Camden (inserted between A1 and A2), in which Jonson describes himself as "Alumnus olim, aeternum Amicus" ("a student once, always a friend"). In *Twelfth Night* Shakespeare had used the exposure plot to ridicule the upstart Malvolio, but in *Troilus and Cressida* he gave it a self-reflexive twist in an effort to stigmatize Jonson, who had staked much of his dramatic reputation on this plot strategy as the basic structure of his comedy.

The most important contribution that *Troilus and Cressida* makes to the final phase of the Poets' War is its delineation of how the satiric impulse had turned against itself in a self-subverting struggle for poetic mastery. In *Troilus and Cressida* the logic of self-justification central to Jonson's humanist program of moral instruction was, as we have seen, immediately contested in reactive fashion by Marston and Dekker, and precipitated a general crisis of legitimation in English drama. Although Jonson had claimed for himself a pivotal position in culture as the arbiter of judgment, Shakespeare negated the first principles on which Jonson had grounded his perspective—the self-confident conviction that he was capable of obtaining a knowledge of truth. The confutation of Jonson's dogmatism is most forcefully broached when Ulysses, discussing Ajax's fame with Achilles, agrees with the unnamed author whose book he reads that

> no man is the lord of anything,
> Though in and of him there be much consisting,
> Till he communicate his parts to others;
> Nor doth he of himself know them for aught,
> Till he behold them formed in the applause
> Where th' are extended; who like an arch reverb'rate
> The voice again, or like a gate of steel
> Fronting the sun, receives and renders back
> His figures and his heat. I was much rapt in this,
> And apprehended here immediately
> Th' unknown Ajax.
> Heavens, what a man is there! A very horse,
> That has he knows not what. (3.3.115–26)

Rather than positing an inner voice of conscience as the sole arbiter of identity, Ulysses states that man is capable of knowing himself only by understanding what others think of him. Where Jonson had taken upon himself the mantle of poetic authority, through spokesmen such as Asper, Criticus, and Horace, affirming his right to judge himself and others, Shakespeare through Ulysses stresses the dependence of the individual on the "applause" of spectators who determine his significance. Shakespeare uses this theatrical metaphor to reveal the distinction that obtains between the actor, on the one hand, and the source of dramatic validation, the audience's judgment, on the other. The consequence of this theory of the social determination of value is an effective invalidation of the aggressive self-assertiveness which gave rise to the Poets' War, since each antagonist would judge his success, according to this radically decentered perspective, not by what he thought of himself but by what his critics conceived him to be. It was, consequently, Shakespeare's paradoxical destiny both to participate in the Poets' War and to confute the fundamental assumptions that brought it into existence.

VI

The unflattering references to Jonson found in his fictional cognate Ajax and the critique of comical satire that are textured into the plot of *Troilus and Cressida* have a personal and a literary component. The Poets' War was a witty game of covert allusions that combined a strange mixture of playfulness and aggression. The quarrel was at times capable of engendering a considerable degree of malice, especially between Jonson, on the one hand, and Marston and Dekker, on the other. But this did not prevent Jonson from subsequently collaborating with Marston on *Eastward Ho!* and with Dekker on an entertainment for James I in 1604, nor did it hinder Marston from dedicating *The Malcontent* to his "friend" Ben Jonson in the same year.[30]

At the end of 1601, when Shakespeare wrote *Troilus and Cressida*, he had two personal reasons for attacking Jonson. Jonson had not only parodied Shakespeare's coat-of-arms and several of his plays in *Every Man Out*, but he had also travestied the Chamberlain's Men in a far more vicious manner in *Poetaster*. That *Satiromastix*, the play originally commissioned to refute *Poetaster*, was considered to be highly unsuccessful is apparent in Shakespeare's statement in *Hamlet* that the Children of the Chapel were able to "carry it away, Hercules and his ball too." It is very likely that Shakespeare therefore set about to redress this unfortunate state of affairs by "purging" Jonson in a far more sophisticated manner. Unlike Dekker in *Satiromastix*, Shakespeare in *Troilus and Cressida* refused to sanction the authority of reason upon which Jonson had grounded his poetics, and instead of fighting Jonson on his own ground, he sought to undercut the most critical aspect of his rival's defense. It was consequently this strategic interaction between Shakespeare and Jonson during the Poets' War that became, after the Restoration, the basis for Fuller's commentary.

Fuller's account thus contains an element of historical truth that during the nineteenth century was transformed into an unalloyed literary myth, once Gifford had severed the events of the *Poetomachia* from their theatrical origins and inserted them into the pseudobiographical context of the Mermaid Tavern. Fuller's concept of *"wit-combates"* between Shakespeare and Jonson is thus a transitional stage in this process of fictionalization, inasmuch as it still contains vestigial recollections of Dekker's contemporary description of the *Poetomachia*. His evocation of a *"Slow"* Jonson reiterates Shakespeare's first application of the word in the topical allusions of *Troilus and Cressida*. But by the time that Fuller utilized this epithet, it had already become a literary cliché, part of the popular mythology surrounding Jonson and Shakespeare. Fuller had already lost contact with the Poets' War that rattled the stages more than a half-century earlier, but he was nonetheless still close enough to the controversy to preserve in his language the terms of the original theatrical debate that reached its climax at the turn of the seventeenth century.

The writing of this paper was made possible by grants from the Huntington Library and the Research Committee of C. W. Post College.

Notes

1. Thomas Fuller, *The History of the Worthies of England* (London: Printed by J. G. W. L. and W. C.), 126.

2. William Gifford, introduction to *The Works of Jonson*, vol. 1 (London: G. and W. Nichol, etc., 1816), lxv–lxvi.

3. I. A. Shapiro, "The Mermaid Club," *Modern Language Review* 45 (1950): 6–17. See also S. Schoenbaum, "Gifford and the Mermaid Club," *Shakespeare's Lives* (Oxford: Clarendon Press, 1970), 294–96.

4. Schoenbaum, *Shakespeare's Lives*, 95, and "Shakespeare and Jonson: Fact and Myth," *The Elizabethan Theatre*, vol. 2., ed. David Galloway (New York: Macmillan, 1970), 5. M. C. Bradbrook, *Shakespeare, The Poet in His World* (New York: Columbia University Press, 1978), 148–49, similarly writes that "The nature of . . . [Jonson's] exchanges with Shakespeare must remain part of the legend only." Anne Barton, *Ben Jonson, Dramatist* (Cambridge: Cambridge University Press, 1984), 89, gives a more tentative response, however, when she admits that Shakespeare might have "purged" Jonson, but concludes that if "he was at last impelled, uncharacteristically, to give Jonson a taste of his own medicine, the rebuke cannot now be traced."

5. Anonymous, *2 Return from Parnassus*, lines 1769–73, in *The Parnassus Plays (1598–1601)*, ed. J. B. Leishman (London: Ivor Nicholson & Watson, 1949), 337. All citations from this play are to this edition. Furthermore, quotations from Jonson's writings as well as the "Conversations with Drummond" are derived from *Ben Jonson*, ed. C. H. Herford and Percy Simpson, 11 vols. (Oxford: Clarendon Press, 1925–52). Quotations from Marston's dramas are from *The Plays of John Marston*, ed. H. Harvey Wood, 3 vols. (London: Oliver and Boyd, 1934–39). Since this edition does not assign line numbers, references to this edition will be by volume and page. Material from his satires is quoted from the *Poems of John Marston*, ed. Arnold Davenport (Liverpool: Liverpool University Press, 1961). I have quoted *Satiromastix* from the first volume of *The Dramatic Works of Thomas Dekker*, ed. Fredson Bowers, 4 vols. (Cambridge: Cambridge University Press, 1953–61). Passages from Shakespeare's plays are quoted from *The Riverside Shakespeare*, ed. G. Blakemore Evans (Boston: Houghton Mifflin Company, 1974). All citations from these works will hereafter be included in the text.

6. Leishman, *The Parnassus Plays*, 370, presents this argument in his appendix on "The Purge." The position was first formulated by Josiah H. Penniman in *The War of the Theatres* (Boston: Ginn & Company, 1897), 149, who writes that *Satiromastix* "was by Shakespeare's company at Shakespeare's theatre, and therein may have consisted the giving of the 'purge' to Jonson by Shakespeare." Leishman's reiteration, however, gave the theory wide credence and is usually reproduced without further substantiation by those who credit it.

7. For further analysis of this issue, see James P. Bednarz, "Representing Jonson: *Histriomastix* and the Origin of the Poets' War," *The Huntington Library Quarterly* 54 (1991): 1–30.

8. E. K. Chambers points out in *William Shakespeare*, vol. 2 (Oxford: Clarendon Press, 1930), 23, that the grant of this coat-of-arms was made in 1596, and that such devices usually bore "the Invention or Conceit of the Bearer," so that the "word" was probably of Shakespeare's own devising.

9. "Shakespeare and Jonson" in *Shakespeare, Man of the Theater; Proceedings of the Second Congress of the International Shakespeare Association, 1981*, ed. Kenneth Muir, Jay Halio, and D. J. Palmer (Newark: University of Delaware Press, 1983), 161. Barton also identifies another point of rivalry in the scene where Jonson "allows one of his characters [Fungoso] to describe another as 'a kinsman to Justice Silence,' in full consciousness of the very different comic kingdom that reference will conjure up" (160).

10. One intriguing passage in *Every Man Out* (3.6.chorus.195–201) has been mistakenly taken as a parody of *Twelfth Night*. Although A. J. Honigmann, *Shakespeare's Impact on His Contemporaries* (Totowa, N.J.: Barnes & Noble Books, 1982), 100–2, reads this as an allusion to Shakespeare's play. *Every Man Out* was registered in April of 1600, long before *Twelfth Night* had been completed some time after January of 1601. It is more likely that Shakespeare was implicitly defying Jonson in setting out the cross-wooing of his next comedy *Twelfth Night*, and that he saw this passage as a challenge.

11. This revision is mentioned in passing by Schoenbaum, "Shakespeare and Jonson," 4, who suggests that perhaps "Shakespeare heeded his friend's advice and deleted—not an absurdity, surely—but a penetrating paradox." See also J. Dover Wilson, "Ben Jonson and *Julius Caesar*," *Shakespeare Survey 2*, ed. Allardyce Nicoll (Cambridge: Cambridge University Press, 1949), 36–43. For a vindication of the witty paradox of Shakespeare's imputed original line, see G. A. Starr, "Caesar's Just Cause," *Shakespeare Quarterly* 17 (1966): 77–79.

12. See Campbell, *Comicall Satyre and Shakespeare's "Troilus and Cressida"* (San Marino, Calif: The Huntington Library, 1938), 54, and *Shakespeare's Satire*

(Oxford: Oxford University Press, 1943), 56–64, as well as Alvin Kernan, *The Cankered Muse* (New Haven: Yale University Press, 1959), 137–64.

13. Morse Allen, *The Satire of John Marston* (Columbus, Ohio: The F. J. Heer Printing Company, 1920), 36.

14. The contention that the character Ajax functions as part of the "purge" mentioned in *2 Return from Parnassus* has a long history, during which the case has never been adequately presented with the full weight of available evidence. In *A Chronicle History of the Life of William Shakespeare, Player, Poet, and Playmaker* (London: John C. Nimmo, 1886), 36, Fleay claims that Ajax is Jonson and Dekker is Thersites. Later he adds the groundless assumption that Chapman is Achilles and Shakespeare, Hector (221). However, in *A Biographical Chronicle of the English Drama, 1599–1642* (London: Reeves and Turner, 1891), I, 366, he again speculates that Ajax is Jonson, but now declares that Thersites is Marston, not Dekker. But in the second volume of this study, published in the same year, he once more changes his mind. Thersites is still Marston (as in the first part), but now Ajax is Dekker and Achilles has become Jonson (189). Small subsequently picked up the identification of Ajax with Jonson, writing that it "is certain that, as Fleay has suggested, the description applies exactly to Jonson" (170). After which, Herford and Simpson (I, 28n) concurred that "it seems probable, on the whole, that the 'purge' was given in *Troilus and Cressida*."

15. "Shakespeare's Portrait of Ajax in *Troilus and Cressida*," *PMLA* 63 (1948), 745.

16. *The Works of Thomas Nashe*, ed. Ronald McKerrow (London: A. H. Bullen, 1905), III, 38 and III, 11. Nashe depicts Harvey, "with his gowne cast off, untrussing, and readie to beray himselfe." He had previously discussed "*Monsier Ajaxes* of excremental conceipts and stinking kennel-rakt up invention."

17. Clifford Leech, "The Incredibility of Jonsonian Comedy," in *A Celebration of Ben Jonson*, ed. William Blisset, Julian Patrick, and R. W. Van Fossen (Toronto: University of Toronto Press, 1973), 5.

18. For a general treatment of this topic, see Mary Claire Randolph, "The Medical Concept in English Renaissance Satire," *Studies in Philology* 38 (1941): 125–57. A specific application to Jonson is outlined in John Thatcher French, "Ben Jonson: His Aesthetic of Relief," *TSLL* 10 (1968): 161–75.

19. Preface to *The Whipping of the Satyre*, in *The Whipper Pamphlets*, ed. Arnold Davenport (Liverpool: Liverpool University Press, 1951), 6–7.

20. See Edward C. Baldwin, "Ben Jonson's Indebtedness to the Greek Character Sketch," *MLN* 16 (1901), 193–98. John Enck, "The Peace of the Poetomachia," *PMLA* 77 (1962), 389, notes that by "appropriating another classical model for English Jonson consolidated his formulae for portraiture." Campbell, *Comicall Satyre and Shakespeare's "Troilus and Cressida*," 89–90, states that this technique is an "economical way of launching characters upon the action of the play" but admits that "the crowding of eight long sketches" in the single act of *Cynthia's Revels*, where Criticus first appears, "clogs it with material essentially undramatic and places a heavy restraint upon the forward movement of the action." This burden of exposition certainly contributes to the judgment that Jonson's writing is "slow."

21. J. Dover Wilson, "Ben Jonson and *Julius Caesar*," 36, writes that, although it expresses a "commonplace of the age," nevertheless "the wording of the eulogy on Crites is so similar to that of Antony's on Brutus, that an echo can hardly be questioned." Wilson further adds that Drayton combined *both* Shakespeare and Jonson's wording in praising Mortimer in the 1603 edition of *The Baron's War*:

He was a man, then boldly dare to say,
In whose rich soul the virtues well did suit,
In whom, so mixed, the elements all lay
That none to one could soveraignty impute,
As all did govern, yet all did obey,
He of a temper was so absolute
As that it seemed, when Nature him began,
She meant to show all that might be in man.

Here, Wilson concludes, lines four and five derive from Jonson's "without emulation of precedency," while "so mixed, the elements," a formulation that Jonson does not use, recalls Shakespeare's phrasing. These lines are not in Drayton's original *Mortimeriades* (1596), so that he added them sometime between its original and its revised publication. Wilson, however, overlooks the fact that Shakespeare in *Troilus and Cressida* commented on Jonson's imitation of *Julius Caesar*. Drayton consequently represents a contemporary reader, who, like Shakespeare in *Troilus and Cressida*, associated the praise of Criticus in *Cynthia's Revels* with that bestowed on Brutus in *Julius Caesar*.

22. Chambers, *William Shakespeare* (Oxford: Clarendon Press, 1930), I, 72; Muir, *Troilus and Cressida* (Oxford: Clarendon Press, 1982), 6. Enck agrees that it is outlined "gratuitously, for the scene itself and his later traits" (391).

23. Ingenioso's complete statement reads: "A meere Empyrick, one that getts what he hath by observation, and makes onely nature privy to what he endites; so slow an Inventor, that he were better betake himselfe to his old trade of Bricklaying; a bould whorson, as confident now in making of a booke, as he was in times past in laying of a brick" (lines 294–99). This passage is replete with echoes of *Satiromastix*, *Poetaster*, and *Cynthia's Revels*. From the induction of *Cynthia's Revels* comes the criticism of Jonson's method by a speaker who regrets that poets, "so penuriously gleane wit, from everie laundresse, or hackney-man, or derive their best grace (with servile imitation) from common stages, or observation of the companie they converse with; as if their invention liv'd wholly upon another mans trencher" (lines 180–84). Sir Vaughan, the Welshman, in *Satiromastix*, refers to Jonson's apprenticeship as a bricklayer, when he asks Horace, "how chance it passes, that you bid God boygh to an honest trade of building Symneys, and laying Brickes, for a worse handicraftnes, to make nothing but railes" (4.3.156–59). The opinion that Jonson is "confident" comes from the prologue to *Poetaster*. The phrase "so slow an Inventor" finds its source in *Troilus and Cressida* ("slow as an elephant") and Jonson's response in the "apologeticall Dialogue."

24. The metaphoric elephant that Shakespeare evokes was recalled much later, as Herford and Simpson point out (I, 186), in Jasper Mayne's tribute "To the Memory of Ben Johnson" in *Jonsonus Virbius* (1638): "Scorne then their censures, who gav't out, *thy Witt* / As long upon a *Comoedie* did sit / As *Elephants* bring forth."

25. "Confidence" was a key attribute of Jonson's spokesmen, and although Shakespeare approaches it in relation to the prologue of *Poetaster*, he probably recalled other examples of this *topos* as well. In *Every Man Out*, Asper vows to "stand as confident as *Hercules*," and when Cordatus asks the timid Mitis how he likes Asper's mood, the latter replies, "I should like it much better, if he were lesse confident" (induction, line 223). In *Cynthia's Revels*, Hedon complains of Criticus's bearing: "How confident he went by us, and carelessly! never moov'd! nor stirr'd at any thing! did you observe him?" (3.2.13–15). Lupus, when confronting Horace with purported evidence of his treason in *Poetaster*, sneers, "Doe but marke, how confident he is" (5.3.59). Virgil then vindicates Horace from the accu-

sations of those who think "his portion is as small" as theirs: "For they, from their own guilt, assure their soules, / If they should confidently praise their works, / In them it would appear inflation" (5.3.359–61).

26. *Shakespeare and the Rival Traditions* (Bloomington: Indiana University Press, 1952), 116 and 118.

27. For details of this incident, see Herford and Simpson, I, 18–19. A letter from Philip Henslowe to Edward Alleyn on 26 September 1598 notes with obvious derision, "I have loste one of my company . . . slayen . . . by the hands of benge<-men> Jonson bricklayer" (*Henslowe's Diary*, ed. R. A. Foakes and R. T. Rickert [Cambridge: Cambridge University Press, 1961], 286). Spencer, who had been imprisoned with Jonson during the *Isle of Dogs* fiasco, had previously killed one Feeke in an altercation on 3 December 1596.

28. "Shakespeare vs. Jonson on Satire," in *Shakespeare and His Contemporaries: Proceedings of the World Shakespeare Congress, Vancouver, August, 1971*, ed. Clifford Leech and J. M. R. Margeson (Toronto: University of Toronto Press, 1972), 120.

29. *Shakespeare's Impact on His Contemporaries*, 103.

30. For a study of the lesser-known of these collaborations, see David Bergeron's article "Harrison, Jonson, and Dekker: The Magnificent Entertainment for King James," *JWCI* 31 (1968), 445–48. Marston dedicates the first quarto of the *Malcontent* to "Benjamini Jonsonio, Poetae Elegantissimo Gravissimo, Amico, Suo Candido et Cordato" (I, 138).

The Subversive Metaphysics of *Macbeth*

James L. O'Rourke

THE PERSISTENCE OF THE providential reading of *Macbeth* may be the best evidence for the continuing influence of A. C. Bradley on Shakespeare studies. Based on the introductions to *Macbeth* in standard classroom editions,[1] Bradley's blend of metaphysical idealism and psychological realism which presents *Macbeth* as a drama about the purgation of the evil embodied in the figure of a murderer and the consequent restoration of a political and providential order is still the most common reading of the play presented to American students. This echoing of a Bradleyan line in *Macbeth* criticism would seem to have bypassed Harry Levin's attack, thirty years ago, on Bradley's approach to the tragedies. At that time, Levin characterized Bradley's metaphysical framework as an amalgam of Hegel and Aristotle,[2] in which Bradley's usual description of a Shakespearean tragedy as a process leading from the temporary disruption of cosmic order to its restoration displaced the idea of catharsis from an account of the experience of a playgoer to a description of the world of the play. In this interpretation of Aristotle, the *Poetics* has become, as Stephen Booth puts it, "a sign of the covenant between literature and the ultimate values of the universe."[2]

Interpretations of *Macbeth* which have departed from Bradleyan beliefs about the "ultimate values of the universe" have nonetheless generally remained faithful to Bradley's emphasis on character and action as the primary vehicles of the conceptual framework of the play. Bernard McElroy and E. A. J. Honigmann focus on the character of Macbeth and stress his capacity for conscience and his consequent suffering; Wilbur Sanders and Harry Berger, Jr. go past the level of individual characters to describe Duncan's Scotland as a troubled society; and Karl F. Zender seems to offer a challenge to

213

at least the more extreme views that *Macbeth* offers "an optimistic view of life" when he contends that Young Siward's death represents a shift from an ameliorative to a pessimistic conception of the significance of human struggle."[4] But Zender reinscribes Young Siward's death within a Bradleyan universe when he frames it thus: "His death reminds us, in the midst of the triumph of natural and providential order, of its limitations" (425). This is consistent with Bradley's principle that tragedy depends upon a sense of "waste" within the structure of a cosmic order.[5] Berger's and Sanders' critiques of Scottish society as depicted in *Macbeth* are not really, despite Berger's use of the word, "structuralist"; Berger has done more than what he calls "smok[ing] the edges of this structuralist approach with an existentialist emphasis" when he describes *Macbeth* as expressing the "realistic view that history is largely the work and burden of man" (Berger 3), a conclusion that is far more traditionally humanist than it is structuralist.

There is not much about the witches in character and action criticism which seeks to assess the depth of Macbeth's character or his responsibility for his fate. A more truly structuralist analysis of the play that concentrates on the image of the witches in *Macbeth* is Peter Stallybrass's "*Macbeth* and Witchcraft," in which Stallybrass argues, I think justifiably, that the Weird Sisters of *Macbeth* embody all that stands in opposition to the political order not only of medieval Scotland but of Jacobean England. I agree entirely with Stallybrass that a reader should see as a "manoeuvre of power"[6] the creation of a symbolic order which demonizes witches in order to justify a patriarchal polis, but I do not agree with Stallybrass that to see this is to disagree with Shakespeare. Stallybrass seems to believe that Shakespeare actually wrote the play that Bradley et al. describe, but that a modern reader should dissent from Shakespeare's conservatism. I would argue that in *Macbeth* Shakespeare wrote a play that is profoundly subversive of the Christian metaphysics that structured the symbolic order of his society. The subversion is in the poetry of *Macbeth*, and the pattern, as Paul de Man said of the structural intentionality of Derrida's reading of Rousseau, is too interesting not to be deliberate.[7]

A shift from critical analysis of character and action to a concentration on the language of the play can bring about a markedly different view of the determining forces of *Macbeth*. At one level, the problem is put very well by L. C. Knights, who, although he advocated a providential reading of the play, showed exactly what has to be ignored to come to that conclusion when he said of the "sound and fury" speech that "the poetry is so fine that we are almost bullied into accepting an essential ambiguity in the final statement of the play."[8] It seems an odd conception of poetic value to believe that "fine poetry" is to be resisted as one would a bully. But poetic language does not only figure as rhetorical persuasiveness in *Macbeth;* a poststructuralist conception of metaphor as the constitutive principle of metaphysics rather than as an ornament to meaning can demonstrate the close-knit integrity of the language of *Macbeth,* and can open up a reading of the play that goes beyond the quasi-naturalism of the Bradleyan universe of tragedy which, as Levin so succinctly put it, "presupposed that man is both the master of his fate and an object of supervision on the part of the gods, to a much greater extent than either science or theodicy would encourage us to believe."[9] The deconstruction of this providential view of *Macbeth's* metaphysics has taken several forms in recent studies of the play. D. H. Fawkner, while avowing a Derridean approach to *Macbeth,* has simply flipped the metaphysical coin and discovered that the witches create a "hyperontological zone" in which "vanishing" is "structurally 'stronger' than presence"; Stephen Booth and Marjorie Garber have found reasons to celebrate the play's undecidability; and Malcolm Evans has adopted the Derridean principle of supplementarity to insist that "if 'nothing' is identifiable with sin and chaos, it is also the ground of all creation."[10] But I would argue that all of these readings underestimate the centrality of the weird sisters to *Macbeth.* What the witches represent is precisely the opposite of undecidability; they are more than a simple principle of absence, and are even more than a supplement to the Creator of the Christian tradition. When Booth's especially close reading of the effects of iteration and wordplay in *Macbeth* leads him to the conclusion that "cause and effect do not work in *Macbeth,*"[11] he puts his finger on the metaphysic embodied by the weird sisters. If Stallybrass's observation that the weird sisters represent a challenge to the entire symbolic order of a traditional Western political system is pursued, then the stakes of Booth's observation become clear: the action of *Macbeth* is determined either by the Christian God who guarantees a traditional symbolic order and the Bradleyan/Aristotelian covenant, or by the weird sisters who replace that Creator in the position of omniscience and represent an acausal determinism.

Macbeth clearly has much to say about Christian metaphysics,

and specifically with the central paradox of a metaphysic which
asserts both the omniscience of a divinity possessed of a simultaneous vision of all eternity and the free will of mortal beings who
exist within that vision. In the economy of *Macbeth*'s metaphysical
speculations, the "sound and fury" speech subverts both halves of
that Christian paradox, and comes to be far more than an eloquent
expression of Macbeth's despair. The imagery of the speech draws
together many of the themes of the play's own subversive metaphysics, and the speech itself functions as an anagnorisis in which
Macbeth crystallizes the terms of the conditions he addresses as
"fate" or "time" in his asides and soliloquies throughout the play.
A trope that anchors the metaphysics of the speech and of the
play occurs in Macbeth's imagining of days stretching to "the last
syllable of recorded time." The notion that time should end on a
"syllable" supplants the Christian notion of the Last Judgment, as
this "syllable" recalls, and provides a tightly logical completion to,
the opening of the Gospel according to John which says that "In
the beginning was the Worde."[12] This wordplay about language
completes a tropism which replaces the metaphysical governance
of the word *(logos)* that gives order and purpose to the whole of
creation with the prophecies of the witches, the "weyard sisters"
who represent the blind determinism of Wyrd.

The subversive pun by which Wyrd supplants Worde anchors a
metaphysics of linguistic determinacy that, in *Macbeth*, is a metaphysic devoid of allegorical reach—it "signifies nothing." The
seemingly curious word choices which occur in the "sound and
fury" speech are precise expressions of Macbeth's realization of the
structure of this closed and meaningless determinism. When he
responds to the news of Lady Macbeth's death by saying, "There
would have been a time for such a word" (5.5.18),[13] "word" does
not mean only "message," and one underestimates the degree of
Macbeth's fatalism if the line is paraphrased to mean that there
would have been a better time for such news.[14] There is an old
English proverb about the operation of Wyrd which says "After
word comes weird"—as the OED glosses it, "The mention of a thing
is followed by its occurrence."[15] When Macbeth refers to his wife's
death as a "word" he collapses the distinction between "word" and
"weird," the saying of a thing and the thing itself. The irony here
is that Macbeth has, for most of the play, attempted to live under
the naturalistic assumption that he could race against time. Elimi-
nating the space between imagining and doing seemed to him the

necessary means of his own success; he had sought to "trammel up" consequences and overtake time by making the "firstlings of [his] heart . . . The firstlings of [his] hand" (4.1.147–48). As he contemplates attacking Macduff's castle he says "be it thought and done" (149), but he echoes himself in a way that subverts his attempt to impose his own form of closure on history. His promise that "This deed I'll do" (154) unintentionally parodies his earlier assertion that "I have done the deed" (2.2.14), where the emphatic past participle expressed the wish that the murder of Duncan "Might be the be-all and the end-all—here" (1.7.5). When "I have done the deed" turns into "This deed I'll do," the iteration suggests an endlessly reopening chain of consequence.

In the "sound and fury" speech, time jeopardizes Macbeth not in its naturalistic speed but in its metaphysical scope; it "creeps in this petty pace," but comes relentlessly to the be-alls and end-alls of death and last syllable which end life and history. As Macbeth no longer sees any possibility of outracing time, the depth of his fatalism can be measured in the contrast between the flatness of the lines, "She should have died hereafter: / There would have been a time for such a word," and the eagerness which had informed his plans and desires to bring "Strange things . . . in head . . . to hand, / Which must be acted, ere they may be scann'd" (3.4.138–39), and "To crown my thoughts with acts, be it thought and done . . . This deed I'll do, before the purpose cool" (4.1.149–54). By the time of the "sound and fury" speech, Macbeth is not inclined to think that there would have been a better time for Lady Macbeth to have died; he says, rather, that it doesn't really matter when an inevitability happens to occur. His collapse of "tomorrows" into "yesterdays" grounds his fatalism in a denial of the reality of "time" itself as it is seen within a mortal perspective, and his detachment depends upon his approximation to a perspective which is superior to temporality and is inhabited, in *Macbeth*, by the "weyard sisters." Lady Macbeth had defined the power of this perspective early in the play when she said that Macbeth's letters had transported her "beyond / This ignorant present" (1.5.56–57) until she felt "The future in the instant" (58). Seeing the "future" as the present is, in a Christian metaphysic, an attribute of God, who sees all time as simultaneous. The subversive metaphysics of *Macbeth* depersonifies this perspective which sees all time, all tomorrows and yesterdays, as simultaneous—that is, it removes the figure of "God," or the *logos*, from that position—but it does so without restoring freedom to human action. Even after replacing the figure of God with a trio of exaggeratedly fantastic figures that cannot inspire literal belief, Shakespeare binds all of the action of *Macbeth* to the vision of these figures. They do not cause events to occur, but neither can the action of the play be explained without reference to their prophecies. The most seemingly commonsense interpretive questions, such as whether the witches are autonomous and cause Macbeth to murder Duncan, or if they are simply manifestations of Macbeth's unconscious, are made unanswerable by a play that does not operate within the assumptions about causality and temporality implicit in the questions. Such questions do not capture the mode of the "existence" of the Weyard Sisters, because these figures do not exist within the assumptions of a language which presumes causality. As Wyrd replaces Worde, the witches embody a literally nonexistent condition; what they represent defies the language, because it escapes the foundational categories of metaphysics of presence; "Wyrd," as Derrida says of "différance," is neither active nor passive, present nor absent, sensible nor intelligible.[16]

Macbeth thus engages the central problem of a Christian metaphysic, the conflict between divine omniscience and human free will, and emerges with the gloomiest of verdicts, as neither Divine Providence nor human volition can account for the action of the play. The idea of free will is dissipated in the failure of naturalistic questions to produce a causal chain that runs from motivation to action to consequence. The inadequacy of such questions shows through the prose of the foremost of Shakespeare's character-and-action interpreters when Bradley describes Macbeth's feelings at the murder of Duncan: "The deed is done in horror and without the faintest desire or sense of glory—done, one may almost say, as if it were an appalling duty; and, the instant it is finished, its futility is revealed to Macbeth as clearly as its vileness had been revealed beforehand."[17] It was, however, the futility of the act which Macbeth had noted well before it took place. He wished that "th' assassination could trammel up the consequence," and "be the be-all and end-all here" (1.7.2–5), but he finally came to acknowledge the inevitability of retribution, saying:

> in these cases
> We still have judgment here; that we but teach
> Bloody instructions, which, being taught, return

To plague th'inventor: this even-handed justice
Commends th'ingredients of our poisoned chalice
To our own lips.

(1.7.7–11)

Macbeth says that he has no desire to kill Duncan ("I have no spur /
To prick the sides of my intent," [1.7.25–26]). He sees that the
prophecies mean that there is no necessity for him to do anything
in order to become king; when he says "If Chance will have me
King, why, Chance may crown me, / Without my stir" just after
the meeting with the Witches [1.3.143–44], this suggests that the
prophecies, rather than inciting Macbeth towards the killing of
Duncan, should have led him to view Malcolm's nomination as the
royal heir with an equanimity born of the certainty of his own
eventual accession. And he shows no sense of accomplishment
even immediately after he has performed the murder: "Wake Duncan with thy knocking: I would thou couldst" (2.2.73) he says, only
minutes afterwards.

    Why, then, does Macbeth kill Duncan? Bradley's description of
Macbeth's motivation toward the murder is that it is "as if . . . an
appalling duty." It is, Bradley sees, more accurately described as a
compulsion than as a decision, and Bradley's attempt at a quantifi-
cation of what drives Macbeth to the act of regicide, that "neither
his ambition nor yet the prophecy of the Witches would ever without the aid of Lady Macbeth have overcome . . . [Macbeth's] resistance"[18] to the idea of killing Duncan will, to a modern ear, too
easily recall "The woman gave me of the tree, and I did eat," to
sound like a balanced assessment of blame. Macbeth's action is not
entirely explicable in psychological terms, and the terms of any
explanation are greatly complicated by the means of representation,
in structure and language, of the murder itself. A significant feature
of the representation of Duncan's murder is that it takes place offstage. This is a departure from the Shakespearean norm, and even
from the norm in *Macbeth*, where Banquo, Macduff's son and
Young Siward are murdered onstage, and Macduff exhibits the severed head of Macbeth. When this unseen murder is placed between
Macbeth's wish that "I go, and it is done" (not "and I do it") and
his emphatic assertion just after the killing that "I have done the
deed," where the rhetorical finality expresses his desire to send the
deed to a safely completed, "trammelled up" past, the psychological dimension of the dramatic absence of the murder becomes

220   James L. O'Rourke

clear; the play is representing Macbeth's avoidance of any thought
of the act.

A thoroughly naturalistic vocabulary would offer, then, "repression" as the explanation for why Macbeth never discloses an adequate motivation for the killing of Duncan. One would say that
Macbeth never allows himself to acknowledge that he has, of his
own free will, committed this murder. But the imagery of the play
suggests that there is something other than a personal unconscious
below the level of autonomous will, and it uses the vehicle of
dreams as the means of access to that world. When Macbeth contemplates the assassination of Duncan, he says "Stars, hide your
fires! / Let not light see my black and deep desires" (1.4.50–51).
This image of extinguished stars is recalled and given a domestic
cast which counterpoints the impending horror of the murder
when Banquo says to Fleance, "There's husbandry in heaven; /
Their candles are all out" (2.7.4–5), but the imagery takes on a
more ominous tone as Banquo goes on to say

> A heavy summons lies like lead upon me,
> And yet I would not sleep: merciful Powers,
> Restrain in me the cursed thoughts that nature
> Gives way to in repose!
>
> (2.1.6–9)

He gives definition to these "cursed thoughts" moments later when
he meets Macbeth and says, "I dreamt last night of the three weird
sisters" (2.1.20). Macbeth, on his way to murder the sleeping Duncan, then sees the bloody dagger and draws the conclusion that

> Now o'er the one half-world
> Nature seems dead, and wicked dreams abuse
> The curtain'd sleep; witchcraft celebrates
> Pale Hecate's off'rings . . .
>
> (2.1.49–52)

This surreal "dream" world finally swallows Lady Macbeth; she
had sought to live entirely on a naturalistic plane, only borrowing
from the witches the expediency of a "fair is foul" morality. She
ends, however, in a madness which cannot distinguish a "real"
world from one of sleep and dreams. Macbeth's image of life as a
player is a transformation of this experience of irreality. As he lives
with the consequences of a murder which he consciously disa-
vowed and then performed as if *in absentia*, his guilt is like that

experienced in dreams: retribution is relentless and its means exceed the scale of realism (as Birnam wood comes to Dunsinane) but the actual transgression which inspires this retribution has only a shadowy, ambiguous existence. In Macbeth's metaphor, he is playing the role of the regicide, coping with the consequences of that "even-handed justice" which returns his "bloody instructions" upon himself, but he is no more responsible for the action of this world than the self in a dream, or an actor for the drama in which he exists.

The larger context, the unknown which is not comprehended by the individual "player," is a metaphysical order rather than a personal unconscious in *Macbeth*. In the "sound and fury" speech, Macbeth surrenders the naturalistic assumptions that had constituted his belief that time's challenge resided in its fleetness, and that his own success would depend upon overtaking events. He speaks of the two natural divisions in time as they appear to a mortal consciousness—a day and a life—and he imagines the larger frame of history, or "recorded time." Just as he sees that tomorrows end by becoming yesterdays, he describes life and history from their endpoints of "dusty death" and "last syllable." But any perception which is limited to temporal terms, even one running from first Worde to last syllable, is only ignorance in relation to the perspective of the weyard sisters, who see that "tale" which tells all of history at the border where it meets the "nothing" that is an eternity beyond that last syllable. They themselves are only a literary device, a personification of such a perspective, and when Macbeth describes this perspective without personifying it, the place occupied by God in a Christian metaphysic is left empty. But the very possibility of an atemporal vision to which all time would be simultaneous abrogates causality and choice, and binds all human action to a single story.

Much of *Macbeth* is designed to give an audience the experience of living through such a predetermined tale. Macbeth's repeated professions of confidence in his own security "till Birnam wood come to Dunsinane" have the effect of assuring an audience that this realistically unlikely event will occur. The irony is intensified by the rapid alternation, in the later part of the play, of short scenes of Macbeth in Dunsinane with those of the forces attacking the castle; from both sides the references to Birnam and Dunsinane are so regular as to become almost incantatory. Angus, with the rebellious Scots, says of the English forces, "Near Birnam wood /

Shall we well meet them" (5.2.5–6); Caithness informs him that "Great Dunsinane he [Macbeth] strongly fortifies" (12), and Lennox closes the scene by saying "Make we our march towards Birnam" (31). Macbeth then opens the following scene by saying

> Bring me no more reports; let them fly all:
> Till Birnam wood remove to Dunsinane
> I cannot taint with fear
>
> (5.3.2–3)

and closes it with "I will not be afraid of death and bane, / Till Birnam forest come to Dunsinane" (59–60). When Siward then asks at the outset of scene 4 "What wood is this before us?", the answer is entirely predictable: "The wood of Birnam" (3). The realistic rationale behind Malcolm's order to "Let every soldier hew him down a bough / And bear't before him" (5.4.4–5)—that this will disguise their numbers—has already been dispensed with; Macbeth has just been warned that there are ten thousand soldiers in the English force moving toward the castle (5.3.15.) The fact that Birnam wood will move toward Dunsinane is locked into place by the witches' prophecies, but its explanation in realistic terms is, dramatically, an afterthought.

Macbeth's expressions of confidence in his own security create a dramatic irony that Bradley refers to as a "Sophoclean irony," in which, as Bradley puts it, "a speaker is made to use words bearing to the audience, in addition to his own meaning, a further and ominous sense, hidden from himself and, usually, from the other persons on the stage."[19] While broad structures of foreshadowing such as that employed with Birnam wood make this kind of irony available to an audience seeing the play for the first time, a more detailed sense of such irony increases with an audience's familiarity with the story. Lady Macbeth's statement that "A little water clears us of this deed" takes its resonance, for a knowledgeable audience, from her later obsessive hand washing. The exchange between Macbeth and Banquo in which Macbeth urges him to "Fail not our feast" and Banquo promises "My Lord, I will not" (3.1.27–28) is grimly amusing to those who know that Banquo will keep this promise despite the impediment of having been slain in the meantime. The better an audience knows the story, the more capable they become of escaping the illusion of suspense in an "ignorant present" and approximating the perspective of the witches. The ability to see the playing out of a tale from which there is no possibility of deviation erodes any sense of morality; if there is no choice, there is no responsibility, and if there is no responsibility, there is no point to moral distinctions. As the sense of irony increases, partiality declines, and the foreshadowing of Banquo's death, although he is a "good" character, is more a source of black humor than of terror.

The play seems to begin and end happily, in each case with the victory of the "good" army, and its conclusion has encouraged traditional interpreters to overlook suggestions of cyclicity and to describe *Macbeth* as embodying a traditionally Christian story of the "temporary triumph of evil" but the ultimate restoration of "virtue and justice."[20] But the characteristic wordplay of pun and echo in the play's final scene subverts the optimistic interpretation of its events, and reinscribes the story of the dominion of Wyrd, in which, as the witches say, "Fair is foul, and foul is fair." To their unearthly perspective, at the border where the entire tale of history drops into "nothing," all of history is a zero-sum game. This informs the detachment behind their initial plan to meet again "when the battle's lost and won" (1.1.4). To them, since the entire story is zero-sum, so are the individual events, or "words," and the play's language does much to reinforce this perspective. As we enter one of the camps to which it does matter who wins the battle, the supposedly "good" camp, moral distinctions seem nonetheless slippery. The first report of the battle is balanced, as the sergeant compares the two armies to "two spent swimmers, that do cling together / And choke their art" (1.2.8–9). The first character to be distinguished is "the merciless Macdonwald" (9), and this sounds like a condemnation, but then he is called "worthy to be a rebel" (10), and the usually positive connotation of "worthy" suggests for a moment that the sergeant may be praising Macdonwald for his valor. But then we find that "worthy" does not here mean "commendable" but only "appropriate," for, the sergeant says, "to that [name of 'rebel'] / The multiplying villainies of nature / Do swarm upon him" (10–12). His opposite is then named as "brave Macbeth (well he deserves that name)" (16), but so was Macdonwald worthy of his name, and the distinction between "brave" and "merciless" is difficult to maintain throughout the description of Macbeth's conduct on the battlefield:

> Disdaining Fortune, with his brandish'd steel,
> Which smok'd with bloody execution,

> Like Valour's minion, carv'd out his passage,
> Till he fac'd the slave;
> which ne'er shook hands, nor bade farewell to him,
> Till he unseam'd him from the nave to th' chops
> And fix'd his head upon our battlements.
>
>   (1.2.17–23)

Duncan complicates the matter even further when he uses that ambiguous word just applied to Macdonwald in praise of Macbeth, saying, "O valiant cousin! worthy gentleman!" (24). These words echo again in the often-noted irony in which Duncan says of the executed traitor Cawdor, "There's no art / To find the mind's construction in the face: / He was a gentleman on whom I built / An absolute trust" (1.4.11–14), and then turns to greet Macbeth; his words of greeting are "O worthiest cousin!" (14).

The ironic perspective invites us to compare Macbeth with a rebel, and, in this case, one who has just been praised for the manner in which he faces death: first, because he repents his crimes ("frankly he confess'd his treasons, / Implor'd your Highness' pardon, and set forth / A deep repentance" [1.4.5–7]), and secondly because of his bravery, manifested in his ability to "throw away the dearest thing he ow'd / As 'twere a careless trifle" (10–11). When Macbeth comes to face his own death in the play's final scene, he expresses, first, remorse, and then courage; he is at first reluctant to fight with Macduff because of having already shed too much of Macduff's blood; he says "get thee back, my soul is too much charg'd / With blood of thine already" (5.7.5–6), and then, after he learns of Macduff's unnatural birth and recognizes him as the inevitable agent of his own death, he rejects the terms of surrender and accepts that inevitable death, saying:

>   I will not yield,
> To kiss the ground before young Malcolm's feet,
> And to be baited with the rabble's curse.
> Though Birnam wood be come to Dunsinane,
> And thou oppos'd, being of no woman born,
> Yet I will try the last: before my body
> I throw my warlike shield: lay on, Macduff;
> And damn'd be him that first cries, "Hold, enough!"
>
>   (5.8.27–34)

The subsequent valorization of Young Siward's courage in the play's closing scene serves further to blur the distinction between the forces of good and those of evil. The "good" characters attempt to enforce this distinction as they repeatedly refer to Macbeth in demonic terms just before his death. When young Siward confronts Macbeth, he says that he will not be afraid to hear his opponent's name "though thou call'st thyself a hotter name / Than any is in hell" (5.7.6–7). Then, when told that he faces Macbeth, he says, "The devil himself could not pronounce a title / More hateful to mine ear" (8–9). Macduff calls Macbeth "Hell-hound" (5.8.3) and bids him relinquish "the angel"— meaning a fallen angel, a devil—"whom thou still hast serv'd" (14). While Macduff is dueling with Macbeth offstage, the onstage action consists of young Siward's death being reported; the proof given that "like a man he died" (5.5.9) is that he "Had . . . his hurts before" (12). This is obviously the way in which Macbeth is dying even as they speak, and if the contrast between "Hell-hound" and "man" isn't pointed enough, Siward says that his son's wounds, gotten "on the front" (13) in battle prove him to be "God's soldier" (13) and that there could not be a "fairer death" (15).

The echo of "fair" in this phrase is the subtlest and most ominous reminder of the spirits to whom "fair is foul and foul is fair"; Siward's belief, that there could be "none fairer" than his son's death, recalls Macbeth's early line "So fair and foul a day I have not seen." Other jogs to the memory at the play's close are the "Hails" with which Malcolm is greeted, recalling the witches' greeting of Macbeth, and Malcolm's reiteration of his father's metaphor of planting, last used when Duncan thought that, having suppressed a rebellion, he had ushered in a era of peace and stability. These verbal repetitions are a device used in the early scenes of the play, where the characters repeat the witches' words (as, "When the battle's lost and won" comes back as "What he has lost, noble Macbeth has won," and "Fair is foul and foul is fair" returns as Macbeth's "So fair and foul a day I have not seen") and represent a determinism without temporal development or causality. The absurdity of a world governed by Wyrd, as is the dramatic universe of *Macbeth*, does not depend upon the degradation of reality into unassimilable pieces; when Macbeth finds his experience to be surreal, it is because it seems too much like the experience of an actor playing a part in a prescribed story, where the pieces fit together so perfectly that they form a matrix of absolute, and unalterable, interdependence. This sense of internal coherence is given substantive, auditory presence through the device of iteration, while the failure of the play to provide fully formed psychological or philosophical answers to the questions it generates about its

own nature makes it impossible to explain the whole through contexts of signification which exist beyond its borders. In Macbeth's
words, this world "signifies nothing" beyond itself.

The explanations that reside within the play's own verbal context
do not depend on causality; the witches do not "cause" the characters
to repeat their words, and neither do they "cause" Macbeth to think
of killing Duncan or cause any of the later action of the play. The determinism of "after word comes weird" operates without causality,
because its agent does not really exist; the weyard sisters remain a
hypothetical, rather than a reified, personification of the perspective
which transcends time and sees past, present and future as simultaneous. As the play's conclusion, the time is not truly free, though it
may look so from within the "ignorant present." In truth, the concluding action of the play remains within the ironic command of the
representatives of Wyrd. They had provided two prophecies, one that
told of the accession of a tyrant and a second that seemed, since it
told of his displacement, to promise a liberation. But interpreters
who have agreed with Macduff that at the conclusion of the play "the
time is free" have underestimated the ability of the weyard sisters to
speak in a double sense. The witches have told a literal truth, but
through it they have inspired in interpreters, as in Macbeth, a false
hope. The fact that they foretold Macbeth's inability to perpetuate his
line places even the final action of the play within their vision, and
makes the victory of Malcolm's forces just another word in the playing out of the story that the Weyard Sisters, if they really existed,
would know comes in the long run to nothing.

Notes

1. Frank Kermode, in the introduction to *Macbeth* in *The Riverside Shakespeare*, ed. Evans et al. (Boston: Houghton Mifflin, 1974); Sylvan Barnet, ed., *Macbeth* (New York: New American Library, 1963) and Kenneth Muir, ed., *The New
Arden Shakespeare: Macbeth* (London: Methuen, 1951) all give the play a fairly
uncomplicated providential reading. There is an interesting change in emphasis
away from the providential reading in the introduction to *Macbeth* in the *The
Complete Works of Shakespeare*, edited by David Bevington (New York: Harper
Collins Publishers, 1992; formerly published by Scott, Foresman and Co., 3d edition 1980), possibly due to the addition of Jean E. Howard to the editorial advisory
board for this play.

2. Harry Levin, "The Tragic Ethos" in *The Question of "Hamlet"* (New York:
Viking Press, 1961), p. 134.

3. Stephen Booth, *"King Lear," "Macbeth," Indefinition, and Tragedy* (New
Haven: Yale University Press, 1983), p. 83.

4. Bernard McElroy, "Macbeth: The Torture of His Mind" in *Shakespeare's Mature Tragedies* (Princeton: Princeton University Press, 1973), pp. 206–37; E. A. J. Honigmann, "Macbeth: The Murderer as Victim," in *Shakespeare: Seven Tragedies: The Dramatist's Manipulation of Response* (New York: Harper & Row, 1976), pp. 126–49; Wilbur Sanders, "Macbeth: What's Done, Is Done" in Wilbur Sanders and Howard Jacobson, *Shakespeare's Magnanimity: Four Tragic Heroes, Their Friends and Families* (New York: Oxford University Press, 1978), pp. 57–94; Harry Berger, Jr., "The Early Scenes of *Macbeth*: A Preface To a New Interpretation," *ELH* 47 (1980), pp. 1–31 and "Text Against Performance in Shakespeare: The Example of *Macbeth*," *Genre* 15 (1982): 49–79; Karl F. Zender, "The Death of Young Siward: Providential Order and Tragic Loss in *Macbeth*," *Texas Studies in Language and Literature* 17 (1975), pp. 415–25.

5. A. C. Bradley, *Shakespearean Tragedy* (1904; New York: Fawcett World Library, 1966), pp. 40–41.

6. Peter Stallybrass, "*Macbeth* and Witchcraft," in John Russell Brown, ed., *Focus on "Macbeth"* (London: Routledge & Kegan Paul, 1982), pp. 189–210. Some recent un-Bradleyan studies of the symbolism of witchcraft in *Macbeth* are those of Dennis Biggins, "Sexuality, Witchcraft, and Violence in *Macbeth, Shakespeare Studies* 8 (1975), pp. 255–77; Luisa Guj, "*Macbeth* and the Seeds of Time," *Shakespeare Studies* 18 (1986), pp. 175–89, and Harry Berger, Jr.'s "Text Against Performance in *Macbeth*." While Biggins and Guj never seriously challenge the assumed Christian framework of the play, Berger sees a critique of a Christian ideology that valorizes *machismo* as it demonizes women. While I find Berger's essay acute at the level of social critique, I do not see why it is necessary, as Berger argues, to dissociate that critique from Shakespeare or from the dramatic structure of the play. Even Berger seems to have accepted, at least implicitly, Bradley's contention that Shakespeare was uninterested in or incapable of thinking in metaphysical terms.

7. Paul de Man, "The Rhetoric of Blindness," in *Blindness and Insight*, 2d ed. (Minneapolis: University of Minnesota Press, 1983), p. 140.

8. L. C. Knights, *Explorations* (London: Chatto & Windus, 1951), p. 36.

9. Levin, "The Tragic Ethos," pp. 133–34.

10. D. H. Fawkner, *Deconstructing "Macbeth"* (London: Associated University Presses, 1990), p. 123; Booth, *"King Lear," "Macbeth,"* Indefintion and Tragedy, pp. 114–15; Marjorie Garber, *Shakespeare's Ghost Writers* (New York: Methuen, 1987), p. 118; and Malcolm Evans, *Signifying Nothing* (Sussex: Harvester Press, 1986), p. 117.

11. Booth, *"King Lear," "Macbeth,"* p. 94.

12. "In the beginning was the Worde, and the Worde was with God, and that Worde was God" (John 1:1, Geneva Bible, 1560).

13. Quotations from the play are from *The New Arden Shakespeare: Macbeth*, ed. Kenneth Muir (New York: Random House, 1962).

14. I am presuming that "should" in this case means "would." This is a common locution in Shakespeare, which occurs at least eleven other times in *Macbeth* (2.3.2; 3.1.4; 3.1.5; 3.1.20; 3.6.19; 3.6.20; 4.2.61; 4.3.79; 4.3.82; 4.3.97; 5.3.62).

15. Under "weird," this is meaning 4a in the *Oxford English Dictionary*, vol. 12, p. 273.

16. Jacques Derrida, "Différance," in *Margins of Philosophy*, tr. Alan Bass (Chicago: University of Chicago Press, 1982), pp. 1–27.

17. Bradley, *Shakespearean Tragedy*, p. 297.

18. Ibid.

19. Ibid., p. 281.

20. Kermode, introduction to *Macbeth*, p. 1307.

The Winter's Tale and the Language of Union, 1604–1610

Donna B. Hamilton

I

IN 1604, the first year of debate over King James's proposal to unify England and Scotland, the anonymous *Rapta Tatio*,[1] a tract written to argue for the Union, urged a politics of expediency attentive to the special situation of a new king's accession: "The use of all things is all . . . and offices perfourme their functions, not always as order leads, but sometimes as occasion serves . . . Can any perswade you . . . how unlike so ever this dayes garments are to yesterdayes roabes?" ([D4ᵛ]); and "Now is this union on foote; much hath beene said therein; much written thereupon; Our Kinges affection is setled thereto. All these will do hurt, if this now do not good" (F3).

The directness in this writing about a topic of contemporary concern differs markedly from the methods of many literary texts, in which indirection, opacity, and multivocality often conceal ideology and context. Such surely is the case for the Shakespeare plays that have resisted efforts to define their relation to culture. In those plays, "universal" dimensions tend still to remain more available for attention than features that suggest context-dependence. *The Winter's Tale* is such a play. Cherished for its depiction of the recreative potential of the human spirit and of "union" understood in broad relational terms, the play can seem far removed from political or historical realities. Nevertheless, it is possible to find that *The Winter's Tale* too is deeply implicated in political discourse, and, like *Rapta Tatio*, especially in that of the Union controversy;[2] to find that many of the details of the lexicon and structure that distinguish Shakespeare's play from Robert Greene's *Pandosto*, or *The Triumph of Time* derive from this highly conceptual and oppositional language of public discourse on the Union;[3] and indeed to find that Shakespeare's appropriation of political discourse belongs to the same traditions of political writing that characterize so much early modern literature, including the traditions of using pastoral for political commentary which Louis Adrian Montrose and Annabel Patterson have described.[4]

The rhetoric of the Union—one of the most significant controversies in the first decade of the reign of James[5]—was a mystified language that represented many of the issues of the Union metaphorically. Although the forms these metaphors took were specific to the controversy, they can appear to later readers as entirely nonspecific. As is often the case with political discourse, language that functions for a time and an occasion in quite specific and even compelling ways gradually loses its referentiality and takes on or resumes the appearance of having only universal and undistinguished (even sentimental or trite) valencies. The ability of later readers to access some of the more particular aspects of a text depends on their refamiliarizing themselves with the contexts in which the writing was embedded.[6] For The Winter's Tale, that task includes learning the language of the Union controversy by reading such documents as the speeches of King James, the Union pamphlets, the parliamentary debates, and various diaries and letters, including the papers of Francis Bacon.

As is apparent from these documents, the controversy was organized around disputes about how the Union would affect commerce, citizenship, and hostile and Border laws, arguments that were constituents of the larger question as to whether either nation would benefit from the Union and—perhaps the biggest worry for some English—whether Scotland might benefit more than England. When James and Parliament discussed these matters, much of what they said was in the languages of trade and law, as they debated how English merchants might lose to the Scots, or what legal precedents there were for or against naturalization. Thus, like other discourses, the Union discourse comprised the component parts of other languages that existed before it did and that would continue to exist separate from it, even as it developed. Also central to the Union discourse were the languages of family relations and of nature, both of which have an especially universalized and metaphorical cast. Those in favor of the Union explained that the Union was like a brother helping a brother or like two branches of a vine being grafted together, while those opposed explained that the Scots were

like thieves and rogues. Those in favor explained that the opposition was consumed with an irrational jealousy; those opposed explained that the king's bounty toward Scotland was a betrayal.

The Winter's Tale replicates the language of the Union controversy and critiques its central issues; it also grapples with the more
general issue of English unity with James. The oppositions that
structure the play, the chief of which are Sicily-Bohemia and
Leontes-Polixenes, stand in homologous relationship to the English-Scottish oppositions of 1604–10. Within these oppositional
fields, the pivotal figures are Hermione and James. Situated between the claims of her husband and those of her guest from another country, Hermione occupies a place in The Winter's Tale
similar to that which James occupied, situated as he was between
the claims of England and Scotland.[7] Both arouse in their respective "dramas" great suspicion, and both hold fast to the notion that
their double loyalties are legitimate, natural, and necessary. Like
Hermione, James sought to harmonize those commitments. But despite his eloquence on the matter in his 1604 speech on the
Union—"What God hath conjoyned then, let no man separate. I am
the Husband, and all the whole Isle is my lawfull Wife; I am the
Head, and it is my Body . . . I hope therefore no man will be so
unreasonable as to thinke that I that am a Christian King under the
Gospel, should be a Polygamist and husband to two wives; that I
being the Head, should have a divided and monstrous Body"[8]—he
appeared to many English (as to many Scottish)[9] as someone whose
situation was irreducibly conflicted.

A further rhetorical complication was that the English opponents
of the Union obfuscated James's rhetoric of oneness and equality
by defining the Scots as aliens and strangers, as thieves and rogues,
and, in general, as a hopelessly backward people. By implication,
such rhetoric cast the king himself (in so far as he was Scottish and
a supporter of the Union) as the Other. Thus the source of all authority and all mystification was simultaneously constructed as the
excluded and marginalized. Such is also the situation of Hermione,
who defines herself in terms of absolute values, but whom Leontes,
her opposition and accuser, constructs as an outcast: "O thou thing
. . . She's an adulteress . . . More, she's a traitor" (2.1.82, 88, 89).[10]

In so reworking the Union rhetoric, The Winter's Tale critiques
the situations that were making the Union impossible and union
of other kinds difficult, defends the project of naturalization, and
finally, in a gesture of mediation, refigures the rhetoric in a form

that represents not necessarily an idea of *the* Union, but at least an idea of union. The task of locating the language of this controversy in *The Winter's Tale* and then of considering the implications of its presence promotes new readings of the play that are important to current interest in historicizing Shakespeare and in rewriting the Shakespearean narrative.[11]

II

The Winter's Tale is usually dated 1610–11; Simon Forman recorded having seen the play at the Globe on 15 May 1611, the Revels Accounts show a performance at court on the sixth anniversary of the Gunpowder Plot, 5 November 1612, and the play was performed again in 1613 for the wedding festivities of Princess Elizabeth.[12] This performance record attests to the play's capacity to function for a variety of occasions on which an idea of national or even international peace and union would have been not only appropriate but virtually required. The play's staying power does not, however, diminish the potency of its distinguishing lexicon; to the contrary, that lexicon, which developed over the specific issue of the Union, became an important resource for articulating the implications of successful or failed resolution of political disharmonies.

The controversy over the Union became an issue as soon as James succeeded to the throne. Featured in his first speech to Parliament in 1604, the Union was also immediately the focus of several tracts, including *Rapta Tatio*.[13] James appointed his commission on the Union also in 1604; Henry Wriothesley, earl of Southampton, and William Herbert, earl of Pembroke—important to this discussion because of Shakespeare's connections to them—were both members of this commission.[14] The most important parliamentary debates on the Union took place during the 1606–7 session (which ran from 18 November 1606 to 5 July 1607), when, as shown in the *Commons Journals*, the Commons spent some time nearly every day, and often a very long time, debating this matter. During this session, James spoke to Parliament on the Union on 31 March and 2 May 1607. On 1 June he sent a letter to the Commons, which is recorded in the *Journals* as having been "read twice over, by the Direction of the House (377)."[15] (This means, incidentally, that when *King Lear* was first played at court on 26 December 1606, it was presented during the Christmas recess—18 December to 2

February—of this most important parliamentary session.)[16] In
1608, Francis Bacon, who had been from the start one of the
Union's most able defenders and who had spoken frequently on
behalf of the Union during the 1606–7 session of Parliament, argued in court the landmark Case of the Post-Nati (Calvin's Case), a
case for the naturalization of the infant Robert Calvin.[17] Because
the agenda which James set for the parliament of 1610 was not the
Union but his financial needs, the Union was not debated directly
during this next session, and because it never again became, during
the reign of James, the focus of a campaign, it has been possible for
historians to conclude that the Union was, in effect, dead by the
close of the 1606–7 session of Parliament.[18]

Nevertheless, it is also clear that King James was disappointed
that the Union had not succeeded, that he used his prerogative to
move the two nations toward de facto union,[19] and that he retained
the hope that somehow it could be revived. One record of that
continuing hope is a 18 September 1608 letter of the Venetian ambassador which explained that James would not call Parliament
into session again until he could be sure that the Union would
pass: "The meeting of Parliament is being delayed on this account,
as it does not suit him to convene it without certainty of success."[20]
In 1609, Jams issued in Scotland an "Act against Scandalous
speeches and Libellis," in which, asserting "that there is nathing
sa necessair for the perpetuall weill and quietnes of all his subjectis
of this monarchie As the furtherance and accompleshment of the
union of his twa famous and maist ancient kingdomes of Scotland
and England," he forbade the Scots from speaking or writing anything "In their meetingis at tavernis ailhouses and playis . . .
whereby they slander maligne and revile the poeple estait and
countrey of England." Such behavior, he emphasized, could
"hinder the intendit unioun."[21]

Another record of James's enduring hopes for the Union is the
advice that Salisbury gave James when he wrote, during the parliament of 1610, that a careful response from the king to the Commons's objections to his fiscal policies might provide "one step to
the Union gained by the Union of hearts."[22] Recalling how criticism
of royal expenditures on the Scots had earlier plagued the passage
of the Union, Salisbury argued that this issue was still inhibiting
progress in fiscal reform: "For whoso sees not that the harsh effects
and ill order of your Majesty's gifts heretofore hath troubled the
passage of this desired Union, and certainly would have much en-

dangered the success, were not law and nature fully resolved to bring forth and nourish that beloved child [the Union], which must be the life and strength of this island" (310). As this passage also illustrates, reference to the Scots had, by 1610, become a standard way to articulate apprehension about James.[23]

Fully operative during the 1606–7 parliament, this common means of criticizing the king remained current during the 1610 parliament and was particularly in evidence in December 1610, when Parliament was virtually at every moment in danger of being prorogued by a king grown increasingly impatient with its inability to settle his supply. The French ambassador Boderie reported "that parliament wished '*mal de mort*' to the Scots." John More remarked that Parliament believed "that his Majesty's largess to the Scots' prodigality would . . . cause a continual and remediless leak" to the treasury.[24] And John Hoskyns mused suggestively that "some kind of people were much to blame that begged so much of the King . . . but where he should lay it, he knew not. The Irishmen, he said, certainly were not to blame for this . . . The Dutchmen could not be accused . . . And the English, he said, he could quit of this offense. But a fault there was and therefore he wished that we might . . . examine what hath been the cause of [the King's] wants . . . For without doubt . . . the royal cistern had a leak."[25] On the brink of adjourning Parliament, James wrote to Salisbury about these exchanges, reporting as well the most recent insult: "ye had intelligence that if the lower House had met again, one had made a motion for a petition to be made unto me that I would be pleased to send home the Scots, if I looked for any supply from them."[26]

As these examples suggest, during the early years of James's reign, anyone who talked about the Union or used the idioms that had come to be associated with the Union was apt also to be in the broader semiotic territory of concerns about whether this Scotsman could rule the English nation, whether James was favoring his Scottish countrymen, and what was at stake if king and Parliament did not find a way to work together. The language of the Union debate thus constituted the linguistic territory within which some of the central issues of 1604–10 were formulated and articulated. And the topic of the Union did indeed become also an issue of union, not in a universal sense, but in regard to how and whether this English nation and its Scottish king could come to live in peace and harmony with each other.

III

The language and structure of *The Winter's Tale* encompass four interrelated issues of the Union debates, all of which remained issues for the parliament of 1610: the value of U/union, the fear that the poorer Scots would get a greater share of English wealth than they deserved (an issue that touched everything from the policies for trade to the financing of the king's Scottish bedchamber),[27] the problem of what the formal relationship between the two peoples ought to be now that England and Scotland had one king (another issue that took different forms, but included the need to settle the matter of the naturalization of citizens), and the problem of the relationship between king and Parliament.[28] In the following discussion, supporting documentation from 1604–10 will illustrate the distinguishing features of the discourse on English-Scottish relations as well as the continuity of this discourse.[29]

The first speech of the play expresses the oppositional structures which organize it—"you shall see . . . great difference twixt our Bohemia and your Sicilia"—an articulation that yields almost immediately to the contrasting declaration that difference is no hindrance to union. Polixenes of Bohemia has come to Sicilia to visit his friend Leontes; because these men were raised together— "trained together in their childhood"—the assumption is that their "rooted . . . affection . . . cannot choose but branch now."[30] An emphasis on the naturalness of the friendship, together with the metaphor of the branch (which can also suggest a disunity) is also present in John Thornborough's *The Joieful and Blessed Reuniting the two mighty & famous kingdomes, England and Scotland*. Describing England and Scotland as two branches of one vine,[31] Thornborough proposed that England and Scotland were "to grow up and agree togither: seeing nature hath made them all of one kinde, forme, complexion, habit, and language" (A3). Just as it is assumed that the reuniting of Leontes and Polixenes is right and natural, so had it been argued that the Union was a natural condition for England and Scotland, two nations that had been one at birth even though they had long been separate.

Similar expressions of the oneness of England and Scotland are available in the *Commons Journals*. On 19 February 1607, Thomas Hedley argued that the Union was "a Question between Two Brothers . . . Both Son to one Father . . . We are not now to make an Union: It is made already. We are to seek, how to maintain Unity."

Lawrence Hyde agreed: "Entertain Scotland . . . as lovingly, as any younger Brothers" (1017). In his March 1607 speech, James transformed this sibling metaphor into a twin metaphor to express his expectation that his succession to the English throne and the Union of the two countries should "as two Twinnes . . . have growne up together" (291). In *The Winter's Tale,* a similar relationship is attributed to Polixenes and Leontes; in the second act, Polixenes describes his childhood with Leontes as that of "twinn'd lambs that did frisk i' th' sun" (1.2.67). Later, there will be a grafting image when Perdita reflects with Polixenes on how the union of flowers through crossbreeding and grafting lets art assist nature's creation (4.4.86–97).

The idea that it is natural for two things to be one, or to be made one, sits alongside reminders that forces exist that keep two from becoming one. The union of Leontes and Polixenes is disrupted first by geographical distance and then by Leontes' suspicion of Hermione. In the case of England and Scotland, each nation's sense of its own value as a separate nation was always the chief obstacle to the Union, and one which was exacerbated by the fear that James, having united the two countries in his crown, would not treat each country as it deserved.

IV

When supporters of the Union defended their position by arguing the essential oneness of England and Scotland, they were countering the accusation that, because Scotland was the poorer nation, Scotland would benefit from the Union more than England. The English were afraid, said Bacon, speaking in 1608 in defense of naturalization, that the Union would mean "a diminution of the fortunes and conditions of those that are native subjects of this realm" (310). This fear about material benefit expressed the prejudice that the English had always held about the Scots, and also the suspicion that James would give the Scots preferential treatment. As Sir John Holles would say of the Scots during the parliament of 1610, "they should not seem to be the children of the family and we the servants."[32] No anxieties—in 1604 or 1610—got more emphasis than the worries that the Scots were being promoted and that they were costing the English money.

In *The Winter's Tale,* where one nation is also poorer than another, Shakespeare reversed the geography of *Pandosto* so that now it is Leontes who comes from Sicily and Polixenes who comes from Bohemia, the poorer and more rural of the two countries. In the first scene, where the love between the old friends provides the introduction to the story, Archidamus (from Bohemia) refers to the fact that the Bohemians cannot afford to entertain the Sicilians as well as Leontes has entertained them, a shortcoming which, he explains, is compensated for by how much love the Bohemians can offer Sicily: "Wherein our entertainment shall shame us: we will be justified in our loves" (1.1.8–9; cf. 1.1.13–16). The rejoinder to this remark is that, given the great love that exists, not only is Bohemia's poverty not an issue, but neither is the amount of money that Sicilia spends on Bohemia: "Sicilia cannot show himself over-kind to Bohemia." Thus, even as anxieties about money focused the debates about the Union, the underlying anxiety in this first scene of the play has to do with the fear of being found wanting, and hence, a fear of experiencing prejudice. It is expressed first by way of Archidamus's reference to the inadequacy or "shame" (line 8) of Bohemia's entertainment, and shortly thereafter, by his reference to the "malice" (line 33) which he is sure does not exist.

In *The Winter's Tale*, as in the debates on the Union, hope that old love will branch and grow into new love and new union is not fulfilled. The second scene opens with Leontes and Hermione encouraging Polixenes to extend his stay, but shortly Leontes becomes suspicious and jealous as he considers what Hermione's hospitality toward Polixenes may imply. In no time at all, he is convinced that Hermione is making him a cuckold, that Polixenes is stealing his wife. This sudden jealousy, an adaptation of the jealousy that comes upon Greene's Pandosto only gradually, has always been seen as a special feature of this play, and as suggestive of the relationship between Leontes and Polixenes as of the threat that Hermione is to Leontes.[33]

In the years 1604–10, accusations of jealousy, envy, or suspicion were common idioms for explanations for English opposition to the Union.[34] Pondering the inexplicability of anyone opposing it, Hayward concluded that the opposition was "carried . . . by fear, the underminer of all determinations, or by envie, the rebell to all reason."[35] Similarly, Bacon, arguing the Case of the Post-Nati of Scotland, explained that only "envious estates" (665) do not receive people for naturalization. And Thornborough speculated that everything would be all right as soon as the two peoples became better acquainted: "there be a kinde of jealousie . . . among men, until they better grow in knowledge one of the other (I3ᵛ–[I4])."

The English desire to prevent the Scots from sharing in their wealth and status also provoked James, in March 1607, to speculate that the problem was of "some jealousie of me the Propounder" (291). Like characters in *The Winter's Tale* who understand Leontes' jealousy and suspicions to be groundless and of a "diseas'd opinion" (1.2.297), so James declared that English accusations of the Scots were irrational: "It is alleadged, that the Scots are a populous Nation, they shall be harboured in our nests, they shall be planted and flourish in our good Soile, they shall eate our commons bare, and make us leane: These are foolish and idle surmises" (298). In his 2 June letter to Parliament, he said that the parliamentarians had exhibited "a Mark of Jealousy" (378), a "Suspicion" of "our Sincerity" (377). Similarly, in a letter of 20 February 1609, the Venetian ambassador, discussing the court decision on naturalization, declared "The King . . . who supports the Scottish to the jealousy of the English, is determined to uphold it."³⁶

Thus in the question of whether Leontes was wrong to be angry with Polixenes, as in the question of whether the English were justified in their denunciations of the Scots, situations that arouse some people to suspicion and jealousy may seem to others as appropriate expressions of hospitality, friendship, and love. Consumed with his fears of betrayal, rejection, and unworthiness, Leontes fumes about the man whose "pond [is] fish'd by his next neighbor" (1.2.195). Meanwhile, Hermione declares herself to be Polixenes' "kind hostess" (1.2.60). Decontextualized, these attitudes function easily and coherently within more than one metaphorical, psychological, even political narrative. Historicized, they constitute a homology that finds completion in the idioms which were used to discuss English-Scottish relations and to consider the policies of James. As the author of *Rapta Tatio* would have it, it is only proper that the English should extend hospitality to the Scots—even as the Scots "have reason to follow, where their King is; wee cause to imbrace them, who come with him" (B3ᵛ; cf. G3ᵛ). Or as Salisbury stated it, in his 1610 treatise to James, "who could expect to have a king to be gracious to us, to whom we were unknown, if he could so far degenerate from all generosity as to leave them that had nourished him and spent their fortunes under him, to such a privation?" (309). But clearly not everyone—in Sicily and in England—saw the same truth or even meant only one thing when they defended the value of hospitality. For even as Salisbury asked James the question just cited, he was negotiating a way to explain to James the need to "take the object of distaste away" (310), "to forbear all extraordinary gifts to private men" (302)—and especially during the period in which the king was seeking a solution from the Commons on the matter of supply.

The most politically and economically sensitive way to broach the issue of hospitality was to cast it as an issue of the bounty of the king, the "guarantor of justice and giver of favor,"[37] the source from which all social and political goodness was to flow. James had elaborated that function in *Basilikon Doron* by instructing his son to "Use true liberality in rewarding the good and bestowing frankly for your honor and weal."[38] By 1610, a point at which overexpenditure and favoritism had tainted James's image as a figure of bounty, James sought (unsuccessfully) to decontaminate that image by issuing his Book of Bounty, in which he professed a policy of fiscal and legal responsibility in regard to monopolies, rents, customs, impositions, and tenures, all of which were at issue when it came to practicing "the Princely offices of Favour and Protection."[39]

The Winter's Tale suppresses the contamination of the ideal of bounty known in the real world of Jacobean politics. Displaced to a domestic narrative, the idea of bounty is here reconstituted in Hermione, an impeccably noble wife, hostess, and mother. So domesticated and purified, bounty and union are mystified as the values that create and sustain society, and thus are represented as the values around which even a divided and heterogeneous group may find agreement and unity. But however representative Hermione may be of absolute value, she is not a figure who has any real power, and hence she is powerless to reverse the effects of her husband's exclusionist rhetoric. All she can do is deliver an eloquent verbal defense of herself, after which she falls silent.

By way of the reversal that represents authority and bounty in a queen rather than in a king, *The Winter's Tale* evaluates the compromised and conflicted situation of King James. England's figure of bounty and, as he would have it, of absolute power, James himself was being contained by angry and jealous subjects, a reversal compatible with feminized representations of authority.[40] At the same time, having a woman as its central character also gives the play an opportunity to represent the importance of naturalization and thus to validate the king's position on the central issue of the Union debates.

V

Naturalization raised the question of the rights the Scots would have in England now that their king was also England's king. Even as it seemed obvious to some that two nations who had the same king ought to be one nation, so did it seem obvious that at least the citizens of either nation born after James's accession (that is, all post-nati) were now by law naturalized citizens of both. The relationship between the two people was not that of foreigners.

As the Union debates wore on, those who opposed naturalization argued that there was not room enough in England for the Scots, and that naturalization would give them "rights and privileges" of the English without necessarily requiring that they obey all English laws (*CJ* 314). Bacon countered that actually few Scots had come to England, that there was room for more (311–12), and that naturalization should in fact be the first step of the movement toward the Union, for naturalization prior to both countries being brought under the same laws would in itself erase the alien status: "Naturalization doth take out the marks of a foreigner . . . Naturalization taketh away separation" (314). And, as he argued in Calvin's Case (1608), which was decided in favor of naturalization, the plaintiff (in this instance an infant born after James's accession) was "*ipso jure* by the law of England a natural born subject to purchase freehold, and to bring real actions within England" (642).

This language of naturalization recurs in *The Winter's Tale* in the scenes that treat the fate of the infant Perdita, the child born to Hermione but rejected by Leontes. Convinced that Leontes will come to love the child he now considers a bastard if he will but look on it, Paulina describes Perdita's situation and in the same language in which Bacon and others had spoken in defense of the naturalization of the post-nati:

> This child was prisoner to the womb, and is
> By law and process of great Nature thence
> Freed and enfranchis'd, not a party to
> The anger of the King, nor guilty of
> (If any be) the trespass of the Queen. (2.2.57–61)

Law and nature establish the child's rights; no person, faction, or cause can take those rights away.

In the next scene, Paulina confronts Leontes and hears his disclaimer: "This brat is none of mine,/ It is the issue of Polixenes"

(2.3.93–94)—an argument she answers by calling attention to how much the child is like Leontes: "It is yours . . . So like you." Refusing to listen, Leontes arranges for Antigonus to "bear it / To some remote and desert place quite out / Of our dominions," and, after hearing more protestation from Antigonus, finally declares, "I'll not rear / Another's issue" (2.3.192–93). In 1604–10, the child of Scottish parents was in much the same position. Dubbed post-nati, such a child looked like an English child, had the same language, the same religion, even the same king—and yet was regarded by those who opposed naturalization and the Union as one who did not belong, as "another's issue." In *The Winter's Tale*, the unrecognized child Perdita becomes an object onto which Leontes can project his several fears—including his fear of, and denial that, he might himself be deeply similar to the designated Other—and thereby construct a validation of the extreme position he has taken. Ironically, in her exile among the Bohemians, Perdita easily becomes one with these other people, even as her special nobility remains apparent—a combination of sameness and otherness that ultimately leads to a resolution of distrust and unacceptance.

VI

These scenes that give the account of the infant Perdita frame the scene where Hermione stands trial. Hermione's defense of herself, expanded far beyond that which the falsely accused wife in *Pandosto* has to say, occurs in three speeches of approximately twenty lines each. The language of these speeches is generally identifiable as a language of the unjustly accused, that is, of the law court. More specifically, many elements of her rhetoric are available in the Union speeches that James gave to Parliament, the highest court of the land. Especially in his speech of March 1607 (which was also printed in 1607), James adopted the stance of someone defending a worthy cause to a body that had, it appeared, already passed judgment against him.

Lamenting that too many false complaints had been made against the Union, James asked the Commons to "judge rightly . . . be the more upright Judges . . . There is a conceipt intertained, and a double jealousie possesseth many, wherein I am misjudged" (294). This speech is also the one in which James, as even in the lines just cited, identified the problem as one of jealousy and then later argued that the fears that the Scots would benefit exorbitantly from the Union were "idle surmises." In the trial scene of the play, Hermione also defines her situation as one of "false accusation" (3.2.32) and describes herself as a victim of jealousy and surmise: "if I shall be condemn'd / Upon surmises (all proofs sleeping else / But what your jealousies awake), I tell you / 'Tis rigor and not law" (3.2.111–14).

These speeches of James and Hermione also contain references to the issue of generosity. James explained why the bounty that he had shown to the Scots during the past three years was fully necessary. He had, after all, been their king in Scotland; he would not have wanted them to think that he had forgotten them:

> should I have bene oversparing to them? they might have thought Joseph had forgotten his brethren . . . if I had not in some measure dealt bountifully with them that so long had served me, so farre adventured themselves with me, and beene so faithful to mee. (295)

In Hermione's first two longer speeches, she assumes an analogous position, as she reminds Leontes first that "I was in your grace, / How merited to be so" (3.2.47–48), and next that it was necessary that she extend to Polixenes the love that she did: "I lov'd him as in honor he requir'd . . . / Which not to have done had been in me / Both disobedience and ingratitude" (3.2.63–68).

Another idiom shared by both texts is that of "commodity," a word James used when he addressed the issue of the "Commodities that would come by the Union of these Kingdoms." The word "commodity," which recurs at various points in his speech and regularly in many other Union texts,[41] entered the discussion on the Union because there was dispute over whether only the Scots would benefit from the increased trade of "commodities" between the two countries. Finally, some members of the Commons, irritated with this anxiety over material gain, turned the standard meaning of commodity against itself. Thus it was said in the Commons that "No Commodity [was] to be expected" from the Union; for the Union would be "Profitable not in Merchandize . . . but in common Service, Love, Strength" (1027). This is the point that James was also addressing when he continued his thought about commodities in this way: "as for Commodities that come by the Union of the kingdoms, they are great and evident: Peace, Plentie, Love, free Intercourse and common Societie of two great Nations" (297).

In the trial of Hermione, the word "commodity" has just such a nonmaterial meaning when, near the beginning of Hermione's third major speech, she explains how Leontes' actions have stripped her life of all value: "To me can life be no commodity" (3.2.93). In this section of her defense, she enumerates all that she has lost. First, she says to Leontes, "your favor, / I do give lost, for I do feel it gone, / But know not how it went." Then she refers to the loss of joy and comfort in having both Mamillius and her new baby taken from her. In addition, she says that she has suffered the humiliation of having been "Proclaim'd a strumpet," has been denied "The child-bed privilege," and has been "hurried / Here to this place."

Although Hermione's story in itself is not the story of James or of the Union, it is a story about how a show of hospitality has led not to more opportunity for service and nurture but to separation and loss of society. Unable to defend herself effectively, Hermione finds herself cut off from her kin and subjected to public humiliation, circumstances that are quite beyond anything she could have imagined possible. Interestingly, modern historians speak similarly of the implications for James of having two of his projects—the Union and fiscal reform—fail in the early years of his reign. As Bruce R. Galloway has written, the Union was "the first occasion on which a major Stuart proposal openly backed by the king met defeat in and by the English House of Commons."[42] In his speech of 1607, James assessed his predicament as follows: "what will the neighbour Princes judge, whose eyes are all fixed upon the conclusion of this Action, but that the King is refused in his desire . . . the King disgraced?" (293–94).

VII

In the fourth act, the action of The Winter's Tale moves to Bohemia, the land of Polixenes, Leontes' nemesis. It is the land, thus, of "aliens, strangers,"[43] the land of the Other. Written in pastoral form and narrating a story about determined young lovers, this section of the play presents yet another mystified model within which to consider ideas of Union.[44] And here too the language participates in the idioms of the Union discourse. This scene is the one that contains Perdita's speech about grafting. With yet another appeal to the authority of nature, she defends Florizel against the anger of Polixenes, who objects that his son has fallen in love with someone who appears to be poorer and less sophisticated than he is. Like Thornborough, who had argued that the Union was natural because the same sun shone on both Scotland and England (C^v-C2), Perdita declares, "I was about to speak, and tell him plainly / The self-same sun that shines upon his court / Hides not his visage from our cottage, but / Looks on alike" (4.4.443–46).

The germ of this story about lovers whose fathers harbor an old enmity is present in *Pandosto*. New in *The Winter's Tale* is the episode just mentioned, the moment when the father confronts and thus comes between the two who desire union. This structure mirrors Leontes' earlier disruption of the harmony between Hermione and Polixenes. Obviously, Leontes is not the only one who can cause dissension between Sicily and Bohemia.

Similarly, in 1604–10, it was apparent that some Scots were as opposed to the Union as were some English, a situation of which the Commons made a great deal during the debates of 1606–7, and which the Scottish made well-known to James all during the 1604–10 period we are considering.[45] Exasperated over the attention the Commons had been giving to this issue, James asked, in his March 1607 speech, if it were not contradictory for the Commons to claim, on the one hand, that the problem with the Union was that the Scots were greedy for it and, on the other, that the Scots did not want it: "For how can they . . . be beggers and backwards, in one and the selfe same thing, at the same time?" (300).

For James to refer to the Scots as "beggers" was to appropriate the English deprecatory idioms for the Scots, idioms that had been in particular prominence during the 1606–7 parliament. On 14 February 1607, Nicholas Fuller made the soon-to-be-famous charge about letting in the Scots: "Pull down the Hedge, the Cattle in one will come into another" (1013). Two days later, Sir Christopher Piggott cautioned, "Let us not join Murderers, Thieves, and the roguish Scotts, with the well-deserving Scotts," a speech for which the Commons voted to send Piggott to the tower and to "dismiss . . . his place in the house" (1014). In Dudley Carleton's letter of 18 December 1606 to John Chamberlain, Carleton reported, "honest Nick Fuller was somewhat too forward, saying that the Scots in other countries were more like peddlars than merchants."[46] The existence of such a rhetoric of exclusion makes all the more interesting a proclamation that James issued in Scotland, on 10 May 1611, declaring that masters of ships were not to "transporte or cary in thair schippis . . . to England" any "ydill rascallis and poore miserable bodyis," lest such persons cause disgrace and slander to Scotland.⁴⁷ And we recall as well that in 1610 it was Salisbury, among others, who spoke to James about the perception that the Scots were greedy, that there were those who would "repair hither out of Scotland to your Majesty's court . . . for your service and for their own particular comfort" (305). Apparently just as it was possible for any number of Scots (merchants, courtiers, landholders) to give the impression that they were greedy, so was it preferable to contain actions that might corroborate that the Scots were backward beggars.

In *The Winter's Tale*, when the rhetoric of the Other is associated with Hermione, it tends to function ironically. In act 4, where the Other is represented partly by way of a geographical location, that rhetoric is deflated. The poor and rustic country of Bohemia is depicted not as backward, but only as pastoral. And its material interests are focussed in a clown, Autolycus—who plays the "bagpipe" (4.4.185). Clownish but also somewhat reprehensible, he is, we might say, a mere caricature of a villain. Pretending to be a victim ("I am a poor fellow"), Autolycus is actually a cheat ("What a fool Honesty is") who intends to further his own interests at the expense of others: "I have sold all my trumpery," he brags; "I picked and cut most of their festival purses" (4.4.606, 625).

Depicted as a rogue, pedlar, and thief,⁴⁸ Autolycus next travels by ship to the more sophisticated Sicilia. Previously described as having more "points . . . than all the lawyers in Bohemia can learnedly handle" (4.4.207–8), Autolycus now has his most fortuitous moment as he and Florizel exchange clothes. As Camillo puts it to Autolycus, "Change clothes with this gentleman." If this cross-dressing across the borders of class and nation makes Florizel safer, it allows Autolycus to get something for nothing: "I see this is the time that the unjust man doth thrive . . . What a boot is here, with this exchange" (4.4.673–76). His new identity put on, Autolycus turns on the Shepherd and the Clown, calls his former friends mere "rustics" and, in language that recalls the rustic appearance of the hairy Saltiers, denounces them for their crudity ("you are rough and hairy"). Of himself he merely says, "Whether it like me or no, I am a courtier. Seest thou not the air of the court in these enfoldings?" The Bohemian Autolycus is not a Scot exactly, but he is a refiguration and an acknowledgment of a social and political phenomenon in which the Scottish people were implicated and one that was threatening the English system of legitimation.⁴⁹

VIII

The Winter's Tale concludes with the lovers returning to Sicilia and with three successive scenes of reunion, all done differently and, taken together, providing a veritable flood tide of peace, plenty, love, and common society. In these utopian moments, Leontes, fully repentant for his misplaced jealousy, has exchanged his rhetoric of suspicion and irrationality for one of generosity and forgiveness. Welcoming his visitors, he sees Florizel as so like Polixenes that he wants to call this foreigner "brother."

The central attraction of act 5, however, is the presentation of Hermione, first as a statue and then later as a statue that comes to life. Whatever anyone who considers the play in any context other than that of political discourse makes of this moment, writers like Hayward and Thornborough, whose tracts on the Union included consideration of the Union in its philosophical and mystical aspects, were the kinds of readers and writers who could have found the statue a repetition or representation of their own rhetoric. Like Hayward, who spoke of the Union as "the very image of God" and as "the beginning and end of all things" (B), Thornborough spent three pages on the notion that "divine is the mistery of union" (A3; A3-[A4]).[50] Thinking how variously such an idea could be represented "in lively colours," he imagined that it would be possible to "expresse the image of this union" by showing her as "a Goddes, faire, and beautiful, & sitting in a Chaire of State, with al good fortunes, vertues and graces attending her" (C2).

To a writer like Thornborough, the miracle of the Union lay not only in the idea of the One but also in the conviction that the Union—and the accession of James, which was the enabling historical event—offered an opportunity to restore Britain to its original condition.[51] As Thornborough himself stated it, "now the first and Ancient common weale of great Brittaine is again conformed to his prime estate" ([E4v]). The Union is then both a joining and also a restoring. As Thornborough noted, "King James, and his Royal issue doe gather togither that, which was lost . . . even by this meanes, uniting al in one name of Brittaine" ([D4v–E). And later, in an apostrophe to the Union, Thornborough declared, "Thou wert lost, and art found,[52] bond, and art free, Eclipsed, and art glorious, dead, and art alive ([E4]).

Like Thornborough's Union, Hermione, though aged, is restored to her original condition in a moment of reunion. And like

Thornborough's Union, the statue that comes to life is a miracle that refers to a realm of mystery and Idea. More important, however, is that this ending achieves a union of value and power, the ideas which Hermione could not, at an earlier moment in the play, represent in herself at one and the same time. Here the two ideas merge, as the figure of bounty and union reappears in an action that represents her first as triumphant over death itself, and next as more powerful than art, as she steps beyond the pose of a statue and takes her place among her family and friends. If this moment reaffirms her importance and worth, it nevertheless cannot occur until the re-creation and renewal of other characters—and especially of Leontes and Polixenes—is complete. The correction of the entire social order is, then, both preliminary to and constitutive of reconciliation and union around a single figure in whom all can locate meaning and relationship.

The ideal represented in this ending was also an ideal that James and the English people wanted for themselves. Ironically, it was over issues of political union that many of the terms of dissension in the early years of James's reign came to be formulated. *The Winter's Tale* does not tell what actually was occurring in history. But it does record and refigure the divisiveness that threatened the social order and the struggle in which the society—at court and at the Globe—was involved as it sought to constitute and legitimate itself.

Notes

I am grateful to Jean Howard, Linda Levy Peck, Theodore Leinwand, Hank Dobin, Jackson Barry, Gary Hamilton, and S. Schoenbaum for comments on this paper.

1. *Rapta Tatio: The Mirrour of his Majesties present Government tending to the Union of his whole Iland of Brittonie* (London, 1604).

2. Glynne Wickham, "Romance and Emblem: A Study in the Dramatic Structure of *The Winter's Tale*," in *The Elizabethan Theatre 3*, ed. David Galloway (New York: Archon, 1973), 82–99, argues that WT is a Union play, but focuses on the coincidence that the plot features a king who is first separated from and then reunited with his wife, an action which, to Wickham, represents the disunion of the kingdom under Brutus and the reunification under James. Murray M. Schwartz, "Leontes' Jealousy in *The Winter's Tale*," *American Imago* 30 (1973): 250–73 and "*The Winter's Tale*: Loss and Transformation," *American Imago* (32 (1975): 145–99, considers union and separation from a psychoanalytic point of view. Leah S. Marcus, *Puzzling Shakespeare: Local Readings and Its Discontents* (Berkeley: University of California Press, 1988) argues that *Cymbeline* also is concerned with the Union; I have offered a different reading of *Cymbeline* in *Shake-*

speare and the Politics of Protestant England (London: Harvester-Wheatsheaf, 1992; Lexington: University Press of Kentucky, 1992), 128–62.

3. For the text of Pandosto, see Geoffrey Bullough, Narrative and Dramatic Sources of Shakespeare, vol. 8 (New York: Columbia University Press, 1975). On the popularity of Greene's Pandosto, which prior to 1610 was printed in 1588, 1591, 1595, and 1607, see Stanley Wells, "Shakespeare and Romance," Later Shakespeare, Stratford-Upon Avon Studies 8 (London: Edward Arnold Ltd., 1966), 64.

4. See Louis Adrian Montrose, "Celebration and Insinuation: Sir Philip Sidney and the Motives of Elizabethan Courtship," Renaissance Drama n.s. 8 (1977): 3–35; Montrose, "'Eliza, Queene of shepheardes,' and the Pastoral of Power," English Literary Renaissance 10 (1980): 153–82; and Annabel Patterson, Censorship and Interpretation: The Conditions of Writing and Reading in Early Modern England (Madison: University of Wisconsin Press, 1984) 24–43; and Patterson, Pastoral and Ideology: Virgil to Valéry (Berkeley: University of California Press, 1987).

5. See Bruce Galloway, The Union of England and Scotland 1603–1608 (Edinburgh: John Donald Publishers Ltd., 1986); Brian P. Levack, The Formation of the British State: England, Scotland, and the Union 1603–1707 (Oxford: Clarendon Press, 1987); Neil Cuddy, "The Revival of the Entourage: The Bedchamber of James I, 1603–1625," in David Starkey et. al., The English Court: From the Wars of the Roses to the Civil War (London: Longman, 1987), 202; Wallace Notestein, The House of Commons 1604–1610 (New Haven: Yale University Press, 1971); Linda Levy Peck, Northampton: Patronage and Policy at the Court of James I (London: George Allen and Unwin, 1982) 186–92; David Harris Willson, ed., The Parliamentary Diary of Robert Bowyer 1606–1607 (Minneapolis: University of Minnesota Press, 1931); Francis Bacon, Works, ed. James Spedding (London: Longmans, Green, Reader, and Dyer, 1868) 10: chap. 8 and chap. 7: 641–79. For a succinct summary of the issues, see J. R. Tanner, Constitutional Documents of the Reign of James I (Cambridge: Cambridge University Press, 1930), 23–24.

6. See especially J. G. A. Pocock, Virtue, Commerce and History: Essays on Political Thought and History, Chiefly in the Eighteenth Century (Cambridge: Cambridge University Press, 1985); J. G. A. Pocock, "Texts as Events: Reflections on the History of Political Thought," in Politics of Discourse: The Literature and History of Seventeenth-Century England (Berkeley: University of California Press, 1987) 21–33; Dominick LaCapra, Rethinking Intellectual History (Ithaca: Cornell University Press, 1983); and John E. Toews, "Intellectual History after the Linguistic Turn: The Autonomy of Meaning and the Irreducibility of Experience," American Historical Review 92 (1987): 879–907. For discussion of how texts provide the means for their own decoding, see Michael Riffaterre, Text Production (New York: Columbia University Press, 1983). On a society's use of Metaphor to characterize social and political realities, see Victor Turner, Dramas, Fields, and Metaphors: Symbolic action in Human Society (Ithaca: Cornell University Press, 1974), 23–31. On the dialogic effect of an author's using reported speech, see V. N. Voloshinov, Marxism and the Philosophy of Language, trans. L. Matejka and I. R. Titunik (New York: Seminar Press, 1973) 116–17; and Mikhail Bakhtin, The Dialogic Imagination, ed. Michael Holquist, tr. Caryl Emerson and Michael Holquist (Austin: University of Texas Press, 1981).

7. In some eighteenth-century treatments of the Union, the relationship of the monarch to the two nations was similarly represented. See Torsten Dahl, Conflicting Comments on the Union of England and Scotland (Aarhus: Universitetsforlaget, 1940), 38–39. In "Angelicus and Fergusia: A Tale," the Steward (James) resides with the jealous Angelicus (England), while the neighbor Fergusia (Scotland) lives in apprehension. In The Comical History of the Marriage-Union Betwixt Fergusia

and *Heptarchus* (1706), it is related that in the days of Pacifico (James), who moves his residence away from Fergusia (Scotland) to the home of Heptarchus (England), Heptarchus and Fergusia try but fail to agree on terms of marriage.

8. C. H. McIwain, ed., *Political Works of James I* (Cambridge: Harvard University Press, 1918), 272.

9. On the strength of Scottish opposition to the Union, see especially Levack, *The Formation of the British State*.

10. All references to *WT* are to *The Riverside Shakespeare*, ed. Herschel Baker (Boston: Houghton Mifflin Company, 1974).

11. See Andrew Gurr, *Playgoing in Shakespeare's London* (Cambridge: Cambridge University Press, 1987); Annabel Patterson, *Shakespeare and the Popular Voice* (Oxford: Basil Blackwood, 1989); Leeds Barroll, *Politics, Plague, and Shakespeare's Theater* (Ithaca: Cornell University Press, 1992); Margot Heinemann, "Rebel Lords, Playwrights, and Political Culture: Notes on the Jacobean Patronage of the Earl of Southampton," in *Yearbook of English Studies: Politics, Patronage and Literature in England, 1558–1658* 21 (1991): 63–86; and Hamilton, *Shakespeare and the Politics of Protestant England*, preface.

12. See E. K. Chambers, *William Shakespeare*, vol. 2 (Oxford: Clarendon Press, 1930), 340, 342, 343; Barroll, *Plague*, 204; Hamilton, *Shakespeare and the Politics of Protestant England*, 130.

13. On the characteristics of the Union tracts, see especially Galloway, *The Union of England and Scotland 1603–1608*, 30–57; and Bruce R. Galloway and Brian P. Levack, eds., *The Jacobean Union: Six Tracts of 1604* (Edinburgh: Clark Constable for the Scottish History Society, 1985).

14. See Brian O'Farrell, "Politician, Patron, Poet: William Herbert, Third Earl of Pembroke, 1580–1630" (Ph.D. diss., University of California at Los Angeles, 1966), 135.

15. The speeches of 1604 and 31 March 1607 are reprinted in McIlwain, ed., *The Political Works of James I*; that of 2 May 1607, and the letter of 2 June 1607, in *The Journals of the House of Commons*, vol. 1. All references are in the text.

16. For this point, see also Marie Axton, *The Queen's Two Bodies: Drama and the Elizabethan Succession* (London: Royal Historical Society, 1977), 135; and Patterson, *Censorship and Interpretation*, 70.

17. See Spedding, ed., *Works of Francis Bacon* 10: 90–99; and *Works* 7: 641–79. All references to Bacon's works in the text are to vol. 10, except references to the Case of the Post-Nati, which are to vol. 7.

18. See Notestein, *The House of Commons 1604–1710*, 254.

19. Levack, *The Formation of the British State*, 8–9, comments, "Not to be discouraged, James decided to pursue his unionist objectives through nonparliamentary means."

20. *Calendar of State Papers, Venetian 1607–1610* 328 (p. 172); see also 360 (p. 187).

21. *Acts of the Parliaments of Scotland*, ed. T. Thomson and C. Innes (Edinburgh, 1814–44) 4: 436.

22. Pauline Croft, ed., "A Collection of Several Speeches and Treatises of the Late Lord Treasurer Cecil and of Several Observations of the Lords of the Council given to King James Concerning his Estate and Revenue in the Years 1608, 1609, and 1610," in *Camden Miscellany: Vol. 29*, Camden Fourth Series (London: Royal Historical Society, 1987), 34: 310.

23. See Jenny Wormald, "James VI and I: Two Kings or One?" *History* 68 (1983): 187–209; and Jenny Wormald, "Gunpowder, Treason, and Scots," *Journal of British Studies* 24 (1985): 141–68.

24. Elizabeth Read Foster, ed., *Proceedings in Parliament 1610* (New Haven:

Yale University Press, 1966) 2: 345n. For other uses of the "leak" metaphor, see Cuddy, "The Revival of the Entourage: The Bedchamber of James I, 1603–1625," 203–5.

25. Foster, ed., *Proceedings in Parliament 1610* 2: 344.

26. Foster, ed., *Proceedings in Parliament 1610* 2: 346.

27. On the king's bedchamber, see Cuddy, "The Revival of the Entourage."

28. For a summary of major issues that includes a discussion of the issue of "opposition" in Parliament (as that issue has been complicated by the revisionists), see Galloway, *The Union of England and Scotland 1603–1608*, 161–69. Cuddy, "The Revival of the Entourage," 202, writes, "First, whatever the 'revisionists' may argue, there *was* opposition . . . and it was focused explicitly on the two key issues of government policy: Union . . . and fiscal reform."

29. On the continuity of this discourse, see Galloway, *The Union of England and Scotland, 1603–1608*, 30–32. Galloway and Levack, eds., *The Jacobean Union* xliv, remark, "The tracts and treatises of 1603–5 stand therefore not only as products of a particular political and intellectual milieu but as documents that defined the terms of a debate which lasted more than one hundred years."

30. On the centrality of this metaphor in the play, see especially Schwartz, "Leontes' Jealousy in *The Winter's Tale*," 255–56.

31. John Thornborough, *The Joiefull and Blessed Reuniting the two mighty & famous kingdomes, England & Scotland into their ancient name of great Brittaine* (Oxford, 1604), sig. A2.

32. Quoted by Linda Levy Peck, "'For a King not to be bountiful were a fault': Perspectives on Court Patronage in Early Stuart England," *Journal of British Studies* 25 (1986): 46.

33. See Schwartz, "Leontes' Jealousy in *The Winter's Tale*"; and "*The Winter's Tale*: Loss and Transformation."

34. For the recurrence of these idioms during eighteenth-century discussion of the Union, see Dahl, *Conflicting Comments on the Union of England and Scotland*, 38. Daniel Defoe wrote copiously about the Union, on occasion replying to Jonathan Swift. For bibliography, see John Robert Moore, *A Checklist of the Writings of Daniel Defoe* (Bloomington: Indiana University Press, 1960); and W. R. McLeod and V. B. McLeod, *Anglo-Scottish Tracts, 1701–1714: A Descriptive Checklist* (Lawrence: University of Kansas Libraries, 1979).

35. John Hayward, *A Treatise of Union of The two Realmes of England and Scotland* (London, 1604), sig. [B4].

36. *Calendar of State Papers, Venetian, 1607–1610*, 444 (p. 234).

37. Peck, "'For a King not to be bountiful were a fault': Perspectives on Court Patronage in Early Stuart England," 31.

38. *Basilikon Doron*, in McIlwain, ed., *The Political Works of James I*, 52.

39. *A Declaration of His Majesties Royall pleasure, in what sort He thinketh fit to enlarge, Or reserve Himselfe in matter of Bountie* (London, 1610), sig. A4. According to Croft, "A Collection of Several Speeches," 249, the Book of Bounty, "not published until 1610 . . . was drafted in 1608 by Salisbury and Sir Julius Caesar." The Book of Bounty is also printed in *Commons Debates 1621*, ed. W. Notestein, F. H. Relf and H. Simpson (New Haven: Yale University Press, 1935) 7: 491–96.

40. On the representation of James as both father and maternal nurse, thus "sui generis, self-contained as a hermaphrodite," see Jonathan Goldberg, *James I and the Politics of Literature* (Baltimore: Johns Hopkins University Press, 1983), 230. On homosexuality and WT, see Schwartz, "Leontes' Jealousy in *The Winter's Tale*."

41. For example, see Galloway and Levack, *The Jacobean Union*.

42. Galloway, *The Union of England and Scotland 1603–1608*, 163.

43. Sir Henry Spelman, "Of the Union," in Galloway and Levack, eds., *The Jacobean Union*, 174.

44. Abner Cohen, *Two-Dimensional Man: An Essay on the Anthropology of Power and Symbolism in Complex Society* (1974; rpt. Berkeley: University of California Press, 1976), 32, comments, "The degree of 'mystification', and of the potency of the dominant symbols that are employed to create it, mounts as the conflict, contradiction, or inequality between people who should identify in communion increases." And see Louis Adrian Montrose, "'Eliza, Queene of shepheardes,' and the Pastoral of Power," *English Literary Renaissance* 10 (1980): 179, who also cites Cohen.

45. See Levack, *The Formation of the British State*, and Galloway, *The Union of England and Scotland*. Also, Maurice Lee, Jr., "Scotland and the 'General Crisis' of the Seventeenth Century," *Scottish Historical Society* 63 (1984): 146, quotes a letter from the Scottish secretary of state Balmerino to Robert Cecil, in which Balmerino explains why some Scots oppose the Union: "Most of us could be rather content to continue in our wonted condition" than "to match with so unequal a party, strengthened by the continual presence of our Prince, to whom time and subsequent ages will make us strangers." In *Dudley Carleton to John Chamberlain 1603–1642, Jacobean Letters*, ed. Maurice Lee, Jr. (New Brunswick, N.J.: Rutgers University Press, 1972), 100, Carleton writes to Chamberlain on 16 September 1607, that members of the parliament in Scotland "are no more fond of the union than we here." There is also the anonymous letter from "a Scotchman" to James, dated 3 March 1607, in *Calendar of State Papers, Domestic, 1603–1610*, ed. M. A. E. Green (London: Longman, Brown, Green, Longmans, and Roberts, 1857), that "Begs the King to give up the Union, employ the subjects of both kingdoms alike, and reside in each in turn." (An aside: the reference here to residing in each country "in turn" should be of interest for the study of *Lear*. Cf. James's speech to Parliament, 2 May 1607, *CJ* 1: 367, where he says that, if it will help the Union cause, "I will keep my Seat *alternatim*, in the several Countries; I will stay One Year in Scotland, and another here.") In *Calendar of State Papers, Venetian, 1607–1610* 719 (p. 390), the ambassador's report for 26 Nov. 1609 stated, "The Scotch are very unwilling to accept English law or to unite with this Kingdom."

46. *Dudley Carleton to John Chamberlain*, 94.

47. *The Register of the Privy Council of Scotland*, ed. David Masson (Edinburgh: H. M. General Register House, 1889) 9: 173–74.

48. In the Folio, "The Names of the Actors" refers to Autolycus as "a Rogue." At 4.4.181, 214, 312, 321, etc., Shakespeare refers to him as a "pedlar," at 4.3.28, 120, as a "cheat," and at 4.4.251–53, as a "cozener."

49. See Cohen, *Two-Dimensional Man*, 37 (quoting Berger and Luckman), "*All* social reality is precarious. *All* societies are constructions in the face of chaos. The constant possibility of anomic terror is actualized whenever the legitimations that obscure the precariousness are threatened or collapse."

50. Cf. D. J. Gordon, "Hymenaei: Ben Jonon's Masque of Union," *Journal of the Warburg and Courtauld Institute* 9 (1945); reprinted in *The Renaissance Imagination*, ed. Stephen Orgel (Berkeley: University of California Press, 1980), 157–84.

51. The same idea that led Wickham, "Romance and Emblem: A Study in the Dramatic Structure of *The Winter's Tale*," to argue that *WT* is a Union play.

52. Although the words "lost, and art found" would seem to echo Shakespeare's *WT* oracle ("if that which is lost be not found"), all we have here is (for Shakespeare) a convenient coincidence. The oracle in *Pandosto* also reads, "If that which is lost be not founde" (169). No doubt the common source is the parable of the prodigal son: "he was lost, and is found" (Luke 15:31).

REVIEWS

Shakespeare's Playhouses by Herbert Berry

Reviewer: Remington P. Patterson

Shakespeare's Playhouses collects six essays by Herbert Berry written over the past twenty-five years on four theatres that have Shakespearean associations: the Theatre, the Blackfriars, and the first and second Globe. The essays derive from research in the Public Record Office chiefly, introducing documents from Chancery, Exchequer, King's (Queen's) Bench, Star Chamber, the Court of Requests, Common Pleas, and so on through State Papers and the more recently transferred class of Canterbury Wills. Drawings by C. Walter Hodges illustrate each chapter, among which is a view of "The Round Room at the Public Record Office c. 1920." As rendered, the Round Room suggests the interior of a theatre, complete with gallery and spectators, and this reminds us that we are looking at theatre history from Chancery Lane.

How compelling the need is for just this collection of essays is hard to say, unlike the example of the author's earlier essays that evolved into *The Boar's Head Playhouse* (1986). Three of the six chapters in *Shakespeare's Playhouses* are reprinted from chapters in books published in the past dozen years (two of the three being from the same work, *The First Public Playhouse* [1979]), edited by Berry himself; the other from *The Third Globe* [1981]). Two of the remaining chapters reprint journal articles of 1966 and 1984, the earlier (and more important) of which is extensively revised, however. The sixth, last, and longest chapter, "A New Lawsuit about the Globe," is new, though the major evidence on which it draws was announced and discussed by Berry in an article in *Shakespeare Quarterly* in 1981; and Berry's article followed an earlier announcement and brief summary at the end of the article printed in the *Globe* volume (which is reprinted now without the sum-

AMS Press, 1987, pp. x + 260.

mary). The essays are solid and informative, to be sure—basic and expert archival research—but one can't help asking whether their collection and printing issues from the needs of Elizabethan stage history or reflects, rather, the current trend to recycle the same article.

One must wonder, too, whether the title *Shakespeare's Playhouses* doesn't imply more focus and unity than the contents actually deliver. Two of the essays concern the Theatre in Shoreditch, one concerns the Blackfirars, one the first Globe, and two the second Globe. It is of course true, as Berry tells us, that these are the four playhouses in which Shakespeare "was (or became) a shareholder." It is true, too, that the four playhouses "are important because they embrace and virtually define the whole of the most remarkable period in English theatrical history." But neither as shareholder nor playwright does Shakespeare represent a controlling or even connecting presence in Berry's book. His name occurs no more than half a dozen times, except in its adjectival form, and the only mention of his works is a single reference to two plays and the *Poems*. The play that is the focus of the chapter containing "an account of what happened at the Globe one afternoon in August, 1634," is *The Late Lancashire Witches* by Thomas Heywood and Richard Brome. We don't know what play was being performed at the Blackfriars in the winter season of 1631–32 when a quarrel broke out in the boxes, which is the subject of another chapter.

In fact, the emphasis of *Shakespeare's Playhouses* falls well into the last years of the period, the 1630s and 40s, as in the Blackfriars episode of 1631–32 (chapter 3); the survey of map views of London from Hollar's of 1647 to the end of the seventeenth century, which is the first part of chapter 4; the Globe performance of 1634 (chapter 5); and especially the new essay (chapter 6), which introduces a lawsuit in the Court of Requests involving the King's Men from 1632 to 1637. It is not just quibbling to question the accuracy of "Shakespearean" when, for example, Berry acknowledges in the Blackfriars essay that the document he is introducing refers "to a relatively late time, the winter season of 1631–32," yet adds: "But the main inferences about the stage are quite clear, and it seems that Blackfriars was not seriously altered from its expensive rebuilding by the Burbages in 1596, and its occupancy by Shakespeare's company, the King's men, some twelve or thirteen years later, to its closing in 1642." Perhaps so, but the history of almost every other theatre we know anything about—including those

Berry discusses here and elsewhere—does not suggest that a play-house would have stood unaltered for forty-six years.

Granting without further consideration here the interest and use-fulness of the previously published and unrevised essays on the Theatre and the first Globe, and leaving aside for the moment the new essay, one may suggest that the Blackfriars essay—"The Stage and Boxes at Blackfriars"—is in many ways the most stimulating chapter of the book, even though the main argument is substantially what it was more than twenty-five years ago, despite considerable revision and some additional findings. The basic source and center is a brief comment in a newsletter dated 4 February 1632, pre-served among the class of Masters' Exhibits in the Court of Chan-cery. It tells of recent cases in Star Chamber, including one in which the lords of the court required Lord Thurles of Ireland to give satis-faction to Captain Charles Essex for having drawn his sword and run at him in a quarrel over Thurles's having obstructed the view of the captain and his noble companion (and stepmother, as Berry omits to say), the countess of Essex. They, it is said, were "in a boxe in the playhouse at the blackfryers" when Thurles, "coming upon the stage, stood before them and hindred their sight." From this, Berry argues that gallants sometimes stood on the stage at Blackfri-ars ("at least in 1632"); that the select seats at the Blackfriars were in boxes at stage level (not in the gallery above the stage); and that these boxes were at the back of the stage, not on the sides. In both the original and revised essays, Berry acknowledges that the argu-ments for back rather than side boxes are circumstantial, and he remarks in the revised essay that "neither case can be really proved." But whereas he originally wrote that "it seems much more likely that the boxes were at the back," he now writes, perhaps less confidently, that "the back seems the better choice."

Berry's proposal has not been generally accepted. In retelling the incident in his recent *Playing in Shakespeare's London* (Cam-bridge, 1987), Andrew Gurr simply records that Captain Essex and the countess were "in a box flanking the stage, at stage level." The arguments do not seem stronger now than they did twenty-five years ago, although Berry advances new evidence about the dimensions of the playhouse to "demonstrate why the Burbages might have put their boxes at the back of the stage rather than at the side." Yet if the essay does not persuade, it does, indirectly, point up how little understanding and agreement there is about the location of the best seats in the public and private theatres of Shakespeare's time—

whether called "boxes," or "lords' room," or "gentlemen's rooms," or "twelvepenny rooms," or "orchestra." The questions are not solved by citing W. J. Lawrence, or J. C. Adams, or Richard Hosley, but neither is the matter settled through the seemingly reasonable yet improbable suggestion of Berry (in both versions) that "In the end, it seems that the most expensive seats were in different places in different theatres." Among other difficulties, by "different theatres" Berry seems to mean public as distinct from private theatres, not simply individual theatres. Moreover, if the best accommodations did vary from theatre to theatre, was there also change within a theatre over the period (as in the "evolution" or "migration" from one location to another that Lawrence and Adams proposed long ago)? In any event, it would be a welcome result if Berry chapter were to renew investigation of select seating and the names by which it was called. (Another question is implicit in Hodges' illustration for the chapter. He shows an agitated captain tapping the shoulder of a feathered lord who has risen from a stool beside him on the stage and is leaning back on his elbows against the railing of the stage box as he watches the actor in front of them. The little play-within-the-play is amusing, but more interesting if perhaps less true to the situation, one wonders, is the representation of the stage boxes as large, partitioned, panelled, and curtained alcoves.)

Much in Berry's last chapter, "A New Lawsuit about the Globe," is interesting, informative, and instructive, if also long. Comprising almost a third of the book, it displays the painstaking manuscript research and careful transcription of public records that we have come to expect from Professor Berry, who has inherited the mantle of C. W. Wallace. (Indeed, his research takes him into the Wallace archives at the Huntington, as we hear in the narrative that leads off Berry's account.) What we have—on the model of Wallace, in fact—is a discussion of the discovered documents that runs to forty-some pages, followed by another forty-odd pages of transcription. First, that is, we have the summary of a lawsuit that was introduced by the King's Men in January 1632 in the Court of Requests against their landlord, Sir Matthew Brend, to extend the Globe lease which was due to expire in 1635 (this was actually an extension of an extension). The action ended in 1637 with the King's Men accepting a court-awarded extension from 1635 down to Christmas 1644 at a rent of £40 per year, increased from the £14 10s. that had been in force since 1598. There follows, then, thirty-three items of documentation from the bill of complaint, answer, replication, interrogatories, and depositions, to various entries in affidavit and order books—the full sequence, in other words, of an action in a popular equity court.

It is not always clear where Berry's investigations begin and Wallace's ended, and the intricacies of the action and the histories of the people involved sometimes obscure the ends in view, but Berry tells us what is new in this "New Lawsuit." This includes evidence that at least the parties in this suit agreed that the original Globe had cost £700 to build in 1599, and that the second Globe had cost £1,400 to build in 1614—twice as much. There is testimony, too, about the materials of the Globe and their cost, which leads Berry to call the building "a great wooden palace." At the same time, we are reminded that the ground plan of this Globe was based on that of the first Globe, and that the ground plan of that was based on James Burbage's Theatre of 1576. "He and his successors, therefore," Berry remarks, "seem to have used the same ground plan from one end of the age to the other." Implicitly, anyhow, this returns us to Berry's first chapter, "Aspects of the Design and Use of the Theatre in Shoreditch," and perhaps justifies his title after all.

"Bad" Shakespeare: Revaluations of the Shakespeare Canon, edited by Maurice Charney

Reviewer: Charles R. Forker

Given the critical fashions of our time—the philosophic and linguistic skepticism of contemporary critical theory, the relentless hunt for "subversive" or "radical" meanings in texts formerly considered benign, the passion for revising or even uprooting traditional literary canons in the wake of Marxist, feminist, anticolonialist, racially conscious, or otherwise politically "contextualized" readings of "power relations" in Renaissance culture, for ex-

Rutherford: Fairleigh Dickinson University Press; London and Toronto: Associated University Presses, 1988.

ample—it was inevitable that a book with such a title as this one should appear. The iconoclastic spirit of the age, one might suppose, could scarcely claim to have established itself as the new orthodoxy until Shakespeare, the primary cultural icon of the English-speaking world, could be properly "demystified," stripped of the royalty in which bardolatry had enrobed him, divested of the "essentialist" or universalist titles awarded him in the past by smug, naive, or sentimental establishmentarians, and reduced to the status of a perenially "interesting" but far from sanctifiable man among men. Paraphrasing *Lear*, the subtext here might appear to read, "Is Shakespeare no more than this? . . . an unaccommodated playwright is no more but such a poor, bare, forked animal as thou art. Off, off, you lendings." This volume (and we can be heartily glad of it) only partly fulfills the deprecatory program suggested by its dark title, severe grey dust jacket, and puritanical black binding. In fact the quotation marks in which the editor has carefully enclosed the word *bad* almost give the game away.

The essays here assembled (they grew out of a seminar at the Montreal meeting of the Shakespeare Association of America in 1986) make up a diverse offering, embracing a refreshingly broad spectrum of ideological and even anti-ideological perspectives; what they have in common, however conservative or revolutionary their critical postures, is agreement on the commonsense proposition that nothing distorts our greatest dramatist so much as the tendency to detach him from his contemporaries, to isolate him from his social and professional milieu, and, by according him a transhistorical uniqueness, to abrogate the rational standards of evaluation that would otherwise apply. The practice of converting every minor Shakespearean blemish, inconsistency, dropped thread, or self-contradiction into yet another stroke of artistic genius at whatever cost to plausibility or interpretive sanity is too well known to require illustration. This book is designed to help us check our instinctive urge to praise Shakespeare against our equally important responsibility to judge and evaluate him. And its intention also is to sharpen our awareness of how our fundamental ambivalence about the proper nature of our responses has functioned historically in the construction of Shakespeare's reputation, how it has conditioned our prejudices—our preference for one genre over another at various times and for one play over another within a genre; how it has affected adaptations, interpolations, cuts, and ideological emphases in theatrical performance; how it has even determined our view of the priority of texts (our designation of "good" and "bad" quartos, for instance).

The collection leads off with four essays that in some sense delimit the margins within which the debate about the nature of Shakespearean "badness" is to be conducted. Richard Levin contributes yet another of his rear-guard attacks on the practitioners of "the thematic or . . . ironic approach" to interpretation (p. 27). Choosing six notorious examples of loose ends or dramatic awkwardnesses from a range of plays (the time discrepancy in *Measure for Measure*, the failure to resolve Antonio's fate in *Twelfth Night*, Prospero's "undramatic" opening narrative in *The Tempest*, the "unfunny" clown scenes in *Othello*, the unaccountable shift of Cassius from cynical hypocrite to noble friend in *Julius Caesar*, the problematically unappetizing character of Bertram in *All's Well*), Levin savages the numerous critics who have attempted to exculpate Shakespeare from artistic failure in such cases. They have customarily done so, he explains, either by invoking some extra-aesthetic cause (commercial necessity, crowd pleasing, exigencies involving theatre personnel, and the like) or by attributing to the dramatist an overarching constructive design that can be used to rationalize stains as beauty spots by taking them as intentionally "ironic" or by absorbing them into a pattern of abstractions through the all-purpose solvent of thematics.

We can certainly applaud the commonsense warning here against interpretive excess, overingenuity, and special pleading, but Levin, in his zeal to crucify the more preposterous abusers of a critical practice that, like any other, requires judgment, tact, and a sense of proportion, sometimes writes as though Shakespearean drama were wholly devoid of thematic coherence and passages of trenchant irony, or at least that such considerations ought to be off limits for critics and readers not soft in the head. This is surely to be guilty of overkill. To take only one of Levin's own instances—the two brief clown scenes in *Othello*: not even the most abandoned bardolator, I think, would wish to claim that these episodes, often cut in performance, rank with Shakespeare's most successful examples of low comedy in tragic contexts (e.g., the Porter scene in *Macbeth*, the gravediggers' badinage in *Hamlet*, the joking of the asp-bringer in *Antony and Cleopatra*); yet it hardly follows that the *Othello* comedy is as contemptible as Levin implies (his adjectives are "not even funny," "irrelevant," and "forgettable" [p. 251]). He dismisses significant analyses of these scenes by Robert Watts, Harold Goddard, and Lawrence Ross without truly engaging their arguments. Yet no one, I believe, can be sensitive to the language of the play without acknowledging the importance of the pervasive harmony-disharmony motif, and the clown, after all, on his first appearance in III.i taunts the musicians (whom Cassio has hired to serenade Desdemona) for their incompetence. The second episode (III.iv) involves a frustrating encounter between Desdemona and the clown over the meaning of the verb "to lie"; to be sure, the wordplay here is hardly subtle, but the double entendre on *lie* (in the senses of verbal deceit and dwelling, with an added suggestion of sexual impropriety) could scarcely be more germane to the tragic matter of the drama. And, in addition, the dialogue lends fresh emphasis to a problem with which Desdemona is elsewhere seriously concerned—the painful and baffling misconstructions to which her words to Othello become increasingly subject. The scene therefore might be said to present (in a farcical way) a vignette of the dangers of verbal naiveté as well as of the evil of willfully perverting innocent intentions. As such it would be far from unplayable in the theatre, nor is it "irrelevant" to the larger concerns of the tragedy. I must add that I find the shrill protest against "thematologists" a little disconcerting in the author of so useful a book as *The Multiple Plot in English Renaissance Drama* (1971), a study that illustrates with admirable perceptivity how dramatists sometimes link contrasting and apparently unrelated actions in the overall structure of their plays by means of shared ideas to which one might reasonably apply the term "thematic." Indeed, in his discussion of the double plot of *The Second Maiden's Tragedy*, Levin very properly points to juxtaposed scenes from the two actions the second of which "matches almost exactly each of the *themes* in the dialogue that precedes it" (*Multiple Plot*, p. 31; emphasis added).

Harriet Hawkins in a delightfully sane and tolerant essay, "From *King Lear* to *King Kong*," explores the synergystic relations between high art and popular culture. Unlike so many contemporary writers on Shakespeare, Hawkins has not forgotten that promoting literary and dramatic enjoyment ought to be among the major justifications of the critical enterprise, and she rightly stresses, without apology, how Shakespeare satisfies our romantic hunger for the mysterious—ghosts, spirits, witches, monsters in human form, and other aspects of the paranormal or unfathomable that lie at the roots of our common but imperfectly understood humanity. Her peroration

makes an eloquent plea to the relentless ideologues, moralists, po-
liticizers, and abstractionists simply to let Shakespeare be Shakespeare. In Hawkins's view the "badness" lies more in the grotesque
distortions that commentators and directors have foisted upon
Shakespeare than in the dramatist himself:

> It is critical and directorial efforts to turn Shakespeare into some kind
> of nonpopular, nonsentimental, nonsensational, antiheroical, antiro-
> mantic moralist or ideologue that have tampered with, to the point of
> destroying, the essential chemistry of the Shakespearian properties
> they are dealing with. By the same token, one could destroy the original
> King Kong, or the werewolf movie, or a song by the Beatles, or practi-
> cally any popular work, if one divested it of the rhythm, the special
> effects, the poetry, the pity, or the terror that made it popular to begin
> with. For, as Yeats reminds us in a poem appropriately entitled "The
> Circus Animals' Desertion," it is a fatal mistake to assume that even the
> most masterful images of art have their origins in, or make their primary
> impact on, "pure mind," or that they can long survive independently
> of their energy sources in, and their power lines leading up from and
> down to the place where all artistic ladders start, in the "foul rag-and-
> bone shop of the heart" (pp. 52–53).

If this be bardolatry, one feels, we need more, not less, of it.

After Levin and Hawkins on the right come Terrence Hawkes
and Anthony B. Dawson on the left. Hawkes's brief position paper
takes Wittgenstein, who opined that Shakespeare's similes were "in
the ordinary sense, bad" (p. 56), as its point of departure. Examining the German philosopher's perception that Shakespeare has
been traditionally praised despite his supposed failure to "match
reality" or present "truth to life" in his works, Hawkes develops
the concept of a nonessentialist, utilitarian, totally relativistic
dramatist—one to be valued only according to the particular uses
to be made of him by individual readers or specific politico-cul-
tural situations. Hawkes sees Shakespeare simply as the raw material out of which a propagandist or polemicist of any stripe or
historical period may make whatever meaning he pleases. There
being no fixed or abiding significances, any age or any interpreter
is free to reconfigure—cannot, indeed, avoid reconfiguring—the
bard in special and nonuniversalist ways. One can make Henry V,
for instance, into a glamorous chivalric nationalist à la Olivier or
alternatively into a cruel Nazi-like warmonger. It all depends on
one's purpose. This is a depressingly bleak statement amounting
to the proposition that Shakespeare remains the hopeless captive of

the infinitely shifting subjectivities of his readers. Why a skeptical German philosopher's view of England's greatest dramatist-poet should be taken more seriously than more sympathetic native voices such as Dryden, Johnson, Coleridge, Keats, Hazlitt, and Bradley, to say nothing of more recent critics such as G. K. Hunter, Alfred Harbage, or Norman Rabkin, Hawkes does not deign to tell us.

Dawson is even more condescending to traditionalists than Hawkes, but he limits himself to a single "most consistently overrated play," *The Tempest* (p. 61). In an irritatingly chatty, irreverent, and journalistic style, he defends Strachey's *fin de siècle* attack on the romances as illustrative of Shakespeare's boredom with life. For Dawson the "real world" means colonial hegemony and enslavement, not "marriage, springtime, harvest, dawn, and rebirth" (p. 65), the values that he despises in "allegorizers" such as G. Wilson Knight and Northop Frye. Dawson is drawn to the "cultural materialists" and eager, with them, to reject the "Oxbridge" tradition of "idealist critics, with their hidden class biases and their supposed commitment to lofty Arnoldian disinterest" (p. 68). It comes as no surprise to learn from this essay that insofar as *The Tempest* has any true relevance for North Americans it would lie in the symbol of Caliban as the focus of tyranical oppression—as a prototypical black, Amer-Indian, or Québecois, say. But Dawson is not entirely happy with the Calibanists of recent revisionist commentary despite the deconstructive revolution they seem to have fueled, for they too argue for an ideology that is just as difficult to stage convincingly as the "pure enchantment" of the romanticists. Dawson has no sympathy with Renaissance artificiality, with the traditions of emblem, masque, or symbolic spectacle that are so vital to Shakespeare's final plays. He seems to care only for "realist" techniques and values—for a Shakespeare stripped of magic and poetry—as though he had hoped to find the Elizabethan counterpart of Theodore Dreiser. More traditional approaches to the play—such as that of Kermode, for instance—he regards as a species of "critical tailoring" that has "dressed up" the play factitiously and paraded it before us as an "elaborate 'con'-text" (p. 72). Dawson's is quite deliberately a minority report—a sort of debunking from left field, as it were; but such provocative exercises have their utility, even if only to help mainstreamers regroup and re-examine their most cherished assumptions.

The two central sections of this collection present "revaluations" of specific plays, one group emphasizing comedy, the other tragedy. In a splendid defense of farce, Russ McDonald takes a fresh look at *The Comedy of Errors*, a play that has often been taken seriously only as a precursor of Shakespeare's more mature style. McDonald sensibly takes the comedy on its own terms—as a structure of imperfect institutions that are designed to facilitate human connection (marriage, systems of law, commerce, language) but that are all too likely to collapse under certain kinds of pressure. Farce exploits the barriers that come between human intention and its crazy effects in a way that is frankly contrived but no less successful and amusing for being so:

> there is no thorough examination of characters, no great variety of tones, no profound treatment of ideas, no deep emotional engagement. But farce gives us what other dramatic forms may lack: the production of ideas through rowdy action, the pleasures of "non-significant" wordplay, freedom from the limits of credibility, mental exercise induced by the rapid tempo of the action, unrestricted laughter—the satisfactions of various kinds of extravagance. Indeed, farce may be considered the most elemental kind of theater, since the audience is encouraged to lose itself in play. This is bad Shakespeare [only] in the sense that the young dramatist was content with an inherently limited mode . . ." (p. 88).

Given the solemnity and implied disparagement of fun that inform so much Shakespearean criticism in our time, this is well said.

Peter Berek in "Text, Gender, and Genre in *The Taming of the Shrew*" asserts that this comedy, if not "Shakespeare's worst play," "surely leads the canon in bad qualities" (p. 91); it is bad in its earliness, in its morality, in its farcical genre (one wishes that Berek had read McDonald with attention), in its "patriarchal chauvinism," and in the "Renaissance commonplaces" (p. 91) out of which its final speech is confected. Berek is primly shocked by Quiller-Couch's tongue-in-cheek remark, "One cannot help thinking a little wistfully that the Petruchian discipline had something to say for itself," as though such an admittedly dubious joke were the equivalent of blasphemy. But he makes a stab at ameliorating "such a deplorable monument" (p. 92) as the early comedy by showing that at least it is better than *The Taming of A Shrew* because "the sexism" of the canonical text "is less automatic, and thus perhaps less offensive, than that in the bad quarto" (p. 96). Berek rejects the "ironic" reading of Kate's final speech as "ahistorical" (p. 98), but he uses comparison of *The Taming* with its cruder counterpart to claim that Shakespeare was at least aware of the humane sympathies that her plight as victim of Petruchio's antifeminism cannot help eliciting. He concludes that the badness of the play consists not so much in its "ineptitude" (p. 102) as in its failure to assimilate its own conflicts satisfyingly. Berek suggests that Shakespeare had to get the badness of sexist farce out of his system before he could move on "toward his astonishing expansion of the possibilities of gender roles, even if within patriarchal bounds, at the end of the decade" (p. 102). Obviously, Berek is as condemnatory of farcical techniques as McDonald is approving of them.

Shirley Nelson Garner also writes on *The Taming*—in a voice of feminist outrage. She accepts Berek's conclusion that Shakespeare may have needed to live through the sexism of his early experiment in order to do better later on, but she is prepared only to grant that the play is "*interesting*," not that it is "*good*." Nothing, according to Garner, can redeem the play from its inherent mysogyny and cruel enjoyment of male domination, from its promotion of values that are essentially "violent," "predatory," and "sadistic" (p. 107): "The male fantasy that the play defends against is the fear that a man will not be able to control his woman" (p. 108). I find Garner's essay not only moralistic but inclining toward the pompous. Her judgment that the play is "humorless," that instead of giving pleasure it makes readers—especially female readers—"sad or angry," will strike many critics, I suspect, as itself singularly lacking in good humor.

Dolora Cunningham analyzes the character of Helena in *All's Well* by contrasting her with earlier comic heroines such as Portia, Rosalind, and Beatrice. The badness of this play, Cunningham contends, lies in a central character who is at first "unusually assertive," then inconsistently "submissive" (p. 125); because the "self-abasement" of the "patient Griselda role" violates "the justifiably realistic expectations of many audiences" (p. 125), "we have to struggle, with the heroine, to achieve even a precarious balance in our response to this play," being left as a result with "opposing elements" that "are simply not reconciled" (p. 127). The unresolved conflict, she finds, results in a "defective aesthetic unity" (p. 127). Cunningham addresses an issue that has long been central to discussion of the "problem comedies," namely the difficult mixture of psychological realism with folkloristic plot elements, but her conclusion that Shakespeare "has paid [too high] a price for the experiment with new materials in old forms" (p. 128) seems tired and unexciting. G. K. Hunter's analysis of Helena's character (which Cunningham cites) is rather more creative than hers if only because Hunter manages to make sense out of the disparate elements and refuses supinely to throw up his hands.

The section devoted to the tragedies and histories takes up various problems in *Romeo and Juliet, Hamlet, King Lear, Timon of Athens,* and *Henry VIII.* Avraham Oz sets up something of a straw man in his insistence that the early romantic tragedy, despite its "vast popularity" (p. 134), is less powerful and profound than the later and greater exemplars of the genre. He finds the world of the youthful lovers insufficiently "alienated" (p. 135) and too unprophetic to give the full tragic effect. By comparison to *Antony and Cleopatra* the play is "naive" and "devoid of any sense of history" (p. 138), although an experimental 1981 production setting the play in the context of "the Israeli-Palestinian conflict in the Middle East" (p. 141) made a futile attempt to lend it political relevance. Oz judges "the poetry of Romeo and Juliet" to be "too harbored in convention to probe profoundly into the world" (p. 139); and since the lovers "are not presented at the outset . . . with any prophetic challenge to get involved in," since they are never given a chance to confront "the historical claims of the world," the play achieves only the status of "a successful melodramatic masterpiece" (p. 142). Oz sets out, in other words, to prove that *Romeo and Juliet* is not *King Lear.* He succeeds, of course, but the argument seems manufactured to suit the theme of "badness" in Shakespeare, and, apart from its unrealistic expectations, is essentially ungenerous. Oz appears insensitive to the actual strengths of the play—its superb formal structure, its soaring lyricism, its strong and varied characterization, its sexual intensity, its control of irony, its impulsive tempo, its fine handling of coincidence, and its thematic and imagistic integrity, for instance. These virtues go unrecognized or at least elicit but grudging praise because *Romeo and Juliet* fails to reflect the philosophically fated universe and the Aristotelian assumptions that Oz considers essential to high tragedy.

The essay on *Hamlet* by Alex Newell is one of the most scholarly of the group and also one of the few that breaks genuinely fresh ground—a not inconsiderable achievement given the immense body of commentary that this tragedy has generated. Newell takes up inconsistencies in the characterization of Horatio—principally the strain we feel, upon reflection, between Horatio's first appearance as a "quasi-officer" (p. 147), a figure throughly familiar with the Danish scene, and his subsequent entrance as Hamlet's "fellow-student just arrived from Wittenberg" (p. 145) who is ignorant of the country's drinking customs. The perception of the contradiction is not itself new, but Newell accounts for it historically by tracing its etiology throughout the various versions of the Hamlet legend, both dramatic and nondramatic, including the Ur-Hamlet, Q_1 and Der Bestrafte Brudermord. He also considers the conception of a scholar-Horatio in the context of the group of students, or sometime students, that the play presents to us (Hamlet himself, of course, in addition to Polonius, Laertes, Rosencrantz, and Guildenstern). The results are illuminating. Although Newell would grant that Shakespeare committed a technical flaw in the "imperfect merging of two distinct conceptions of Horatio—the resident military man [which apparently derives from the Ur-Hamlet] and the visiting university man" (added at a later, more sophisticated stage of the story's development in Q_1 and Q_2 [p. 149]), he nevertheless recognizes that the blurring really causes few problems in the theatre: "The audience, in moving along with the play, simply sheds or modifies its initial assumption, which was based only on Horatio's implicit appearance at the beginning of the play, and accepts the clarification provided by Hamlet's explicit identification of his friend, even though the new Horatio from Wittenberg cannot in fact be fully reconciled with his earlier appearance as a military man who resides at Elsinore" (p. 148). A reasonable statement indeed! And one reflects that an analogous argument might be employed to account for the inconsistent characterization of Cassius discussed less subtly by Levin.

What I find especially fine about Newell's analysis of the inescapable contradiction in logic is his use of it to throw light on the way Shakespeare's mind worked. The dramatist's introduction of the student theme into a story that originally lacked students "helps clarify and enlarge a major universal aspect of the play"—the value of reason in a world consumed by passion and the lust for vengeance. Horatio, "a man of reason," becomes, in Newell's view, "the most important survivor at Elsinore"; and we too "are all sad survivors" with Hamlet's friend, "whom we admire because he is so superbly human" and who represents a potent civilizing force in the complex value structure of the tragedy (p. 154). Thus a small dramaturgical glitch actually pays intellectual, moral, and emotional dividends out of all proportion to its initial deficit. Newell's "bad" Shakespeare becomes, paradoxically, a way of showing how "good" he really is.

John Russell Brown performs a similar function in his discussion of the five cuts (amounting in some cases to nearly a third of the total lines) traditionally made by directors in the last scene of King Lear—"passages . . . considered to be so bad that in the last thirty years I have never seen [the scene] performed as it was written" (p. 158). These passages, several of them involving speeches by Edmund or colloquies among Edmund, Albany, Kent, and Edgar, have been thought to destroy the emotional focus or diffuse dramatic excitement by calling unnecessary attention to offstage events, by "clog[ging] the scene with individual concerns and ineffective assertions" that reduce our concentration on "the heart of the matter, the suffering of Lear" (p. 163). Brown ably defends the full text, suggesting that Shakespeare was willing to "risk a loss of tension in act 5 . . . in order to present all the remaining characters grappling with a changing situation, imperfect understanding, and all the 'long-ingrafted conditions' of their own lives." If an uncut performance were attempted, the "audience might then sense that everything is at risk, even the coherence of the play and the power of fate to draw all to its conclusion." This strategy would undoubtedly result in a play "even more painful to witness, or at least more generally so"; but the cut passages nevertheless "hold clues to reaches of Shakespeare's imagination where directors, actors, and critics have not yet followed" (p. 165). Again the badness is not Shakespeare's but that of directors who are afraid to trust the dramatist.

Ninian Mellamphy, in an essay on Timon of Athens, leads off by justly rebuking the "outrageous liberties" (p. 168) that many modern theatrical directors have taken with Shakespearean texts that don't suit their preconceptions. Such directors make two statements whether directly or implicitly: first, that Shakespeare's plays are "not worth our attention" if they "disagree . . . with our values"; second, that those who refuse to see plays "as ours rather than Shakespeare's" invite justifiable parody or ridicule (p. 168). This formulation might serve as a trenchant summary of the attitude of many critics represented in "Bad" Shakespeare as well as of numerous modern men of the theatre. Having established that too many contemporary productions do horrible violence to Shakespeare, Mellamphy considers a creditable production of Timon, directed by Robin Phillips and performed by the Grand Theatre Company of London, Ontario, with William Hutt in the title role. Despite imaginative direction and good acting, Mellamphy concludes, the production was a failure, not for reasons of imperfect execution, but because the play itself is too seriously deficient: as a character "Timon is the unavailing, resentful defender of an indefensibly romantic thesis that has no close human symbol. We respond more intellectually than feelingly to his predicament: we sympathize, paradoxically, with an abstraction" (p. 173). And in addition, he suggests, the tone of the play is too monotonous for even the most gifted actor to salvage. An excellent, essentially faithful mounting of a flawed play thus provides "evidence that Shakespeare may occasionally nod" (p. 174). Mellamphy's analysis of *Timon* as "bad" Shakespeare possesses the uncommon virtues of sweet reasonableness and respect for cultural assumptions historically different from his own. His essay therefore constitutes one of the more persuasive judgments of artistic failure to appear in this book.

The only treatment of a chronicle play in the volume is that by Iska Alter on *Henry VIII*. Alter thinks that the "badness" of this drama "grows out of the confluence of several troublesome factors" including the fact that it treats relatively recent events, its debatable authorship, the modern shift away from a taste for pageantry, "a problematic definition of the historical process," and "a restrictive generic definition of the form itself" (p. 176). She is much concerned with performance history, especially the way in which sentimentalist ninteenth-century actors and producers tended to exploit and overemphasize the tragic-pathetic roles of Wolsey and Katherine, thus slighting the play's broader and more complex structure of interactions among a larger group of figures (Buckingham, Wolsey, Katherine, Anne Bullen, Cranmer, and the king himself) to all of whom the untruncated text requires us to respond with considerable ambivalence. As she rightly notices, *Henry VIII*, unlike most of the earlier histories, "possesses no clearcut heroes or obvious villains, thereby dispersing dramatic energy throughout the play rather than concentrating attention on singular controlling figures or on a primary dyadic conflict" (p. 177). She quotes numerous negative assessments by such writers as Pepys, Spedding, and Odell to show how their less sophisticated expectations about appropriate content and form have given shape to many of our present-day prejudices against the play. She concludes with the observation that modern awareness of its true "generic design" as well as of its complex relation to the other "last plays" has helped us to understand its "merits" (p. 184) better than we used to do. And as an evidence of this new awareness she cites the commendable BBC television production, which reduced the old-fashioned emphasis on sumptuous spectacle and avoided domination by a pair of theatrical "stars." Alter contends, then, that the "badness" of the play is chiefly the result of "theatrical constructs" rather than inherent, and her essay becomes "a plea for the further exploration of the extent to which theatrical tradition and performance history shape what we have previously assumed to be the instrinsic meanings of a particular play" (p. 184).

The volume ends (Part IV) with an important article by Steven Urkowitz attacking the whole concept and theory of "memorial reconstruction," and hence of the designation "bad quarto." Urkowitz argues (against Greg and others) for a regular process of dramatic revision on Shakespeare's part in which the so-called bad quartos typically represent early drafts while the later quartos and Folio reflect subsequent reworkings. In his attempt to demolish the virtually sacred hypothesis of "reported texts" as a received bibliographical tenet, Urkowitz takes on some big fish—in addition to Greg, for instance, Alfred Hart, Peter Alexander, J. Dover Wilson, Harold Jenkins, Gary Taylor, and Brian Gibbons. He insists that valid objections to the theory of memorial reconstruction (such as those of Brinsley Nicholson) have been systematically ignored or suppressed. He seems to me to score more debating points by exposing tenuousness or dubious logic in the orthodox position than by producing strong positive evidence on the opposing side. Urkowitz, to my mind, does not settle the nagging question of whether or not Shakespeare characteristically revised his plays, and many conservative scholars, I dare say, will continue to believe (with Jenkins, for instance) in the phenomenon of reported texts. But he performs the valuable function of inviting us to reassess the whole complex question, and perhaps even more importantly, he shows that the "bad" quartos are often less bad, or at least that they are worthier of serious study and acting, than has usually been granted. Certainly we can all agree, I think, that the "bad" quartos have been unjustly neglected as theatrically valuable in their own right, that "opportunities for further study of these variant dramatic scripts are unprecedented," and moreover that the "rewards" of such study "promise to be great" (p. 205).

Like most such collections, *"Bad" Shakespeare* is an uneven book. Several of these essays, in the reviewer's opinion, forfeit their right to be considered dispassionately because of their stridency or overheated ideological partisanship. A few of the writers make no attempt to season or modify their negative judgments by acknowledging, for instance, that no Elizabethan audience could be expected to share left-wing twentieth-century attitudes toward gender, race, and religious equality, or to condemn hierarchical social and political relationships on principle. Nevertheless, this is a stimulating volume—one that will probably prove more valuable for the theoretical questions that it raises than for the specific views that it airs.

Shakespeare's Perjured Eye by Joel Fineman

Reviewer: Peter L. Rudnytsky

Like the poems that are its subject, the late Joel Fineman's book comes to its reader already carrying a considerable burden of literary history. Awarded the 1985 James Russell Lowell prize of the Modern Language Association, *Shakespeare's Perjured Eye* awakens curiosity perhaps tinged by skepticism and envy. What is it about this book that generated so much discussion? How can it live up to the expectations aroused by the accolades it has received?

Perhaps the most surprising thing about *Shakespeare's Perjured Eye* is how traditional it is in many ways. To be sure, Fineman sketches out (pp. 44–46) some possible links between his exploration of subjectivity in Shakespeare's sonnets and contemporary philosophical and psychoanalytic thought, but his text is otherwise uncluttered by the litany of names routinely invoked in much recent critical discourse. A theoretically inclined reader will be able to draw the appropriate inferences, but Fineman judiciously allows more conservative scholars an opportunity to assess his account of

University of California Press, 1986, pp. ix + 365.

Shakespeare's sonnets without unnecessary encumbrances. Allied to this exercise of self-restraint is the formidable learning displayed by Fineman in such venerable fields as the history of rhetoric and Renaissance poetry.

These old-fashioned virtues, however, do not account for the impact of *Shakespeare's Perjured Eye*, and may even fail to convey the flavor of the book. For Fineman also advances an original argument concerning the significance of Shakespeare's sonnets. "My reading of the sonnets says that the sonnets do this and not that, whereas a certain kind of literary criticism would sooner say that Shakespeare's sonnets do everything or nothing rather than that they do any one particular thing at all" (p. 220). What the sonnets "do," according to Fineman, is, in the Young Man sequence, to "inaugurate a literature of subjective introspection which is both the consequence of and the epitaph of the death of the epideictic" (p. 217); and, in the Dark Lady sequence, to move fully into a "postidealist" mode that spells "the end of visionary poetics" (p. 287). In brief, Fineman's thesis turns on an elaborate series of analogies or what he would call (following Puttenham) "cross-couplings": the Young Man sonnets stand to the Dark Lady sonnets as a visual poetics stands to a verbal poetics and as the poetry of praise stands to the paradox of praise (i.e., the paradoxical encomium). Most comprehensively, Shakespeare's repudiation of the preceding tradition is figured in the relation of the Dark Lady sonnets to the Young Man sonnets, although "the death of the epideictic" is already inherent in the belatedness of the Young Man sonnets to the tradition it both subverts and perpetuates.

To his credit, Fineman lets the reader know where he stands and does not shrink from propounding a claim about the uniqueness of Shakespeare that is bound to provoke efforts at refutation through counterexample. But Fineman (notwithstanding his use of the "Rainbow" portrait of Elizabeth I on the dust jacket and as a frontispiece) eschews almost completely any effort to situate the sonnets in a political or historical context. His approach, then, is psychological, but it is a specifically formalist—or rhetorical—brand of psychology that he favors. "I want to argue that it is Shakespeare's specifically *literary* insight, his insight into literature rather than his psychological acumen, that makes his psychology effective" (p. 81).

Complementing the rhetorical emphasis of his argument is Fineman's idiosyncratic prose style, which manages to be ornate without unduly sacrificing clarity or lapsing too often into mannerism. Indeed, Fineman moves at a very leisurely pace, frequently pausing to prognosticate or recapitulate. The book as a whole is divided into five untitled chapters, framed by a lengthy introduction and an epilogue, and repetitions are perhaps warranted in a work in which the reader is deprived of the usual structural markers. Fineman is capable of an enigrammatic turn of phrase, as when he terms flattery "the basest form of imitation" (p. 133) or *Will* "a name that dares to speak its love" (p. 27), though the wit of the latter comment does not improve on a second hearing (p. 294); and one might be more prepared to grant that Fineman's insights are "important" if he did not tell us so on a regular basis.

There is much to be learned from this book, both about Shakespeare and about poetry in general. Fineman's fundamental dichotomy between the "double tongue" and the "unifying eye" (p. 15) illuminates not only the relation between the Young Man and the Dark Lady sequences, but also a recurrent tension in modes of literary expression. Fineman's treatment of the theory of epideixis is valuable; his claim that praise poetry is the "ideal kind to which all other kinds aspire to be like" (p. 89) may readily be extended to Ben Jonson and other Renaissance writers. Especially perceptive is the connection Fineman makes between what the Young Man sonnets "themselves characterize as their old-fashioned literary matter and manner" and "the poet's sense of his own senescence" (p. 148). Shakespeare, he notes, presents the opening appeal to procreate "as though it were a Petrarchan commonplace" (p. 256), thereby combining an unprecedented theme with familiar motifs.

Shakespeare's Perjured Eye does not attempt a close reading of very many sonnets, though Fineman's analyses, particularly those of sonnets 44 and 45 (pp. 220ff.), sonnet 20 (pp. 274ff.), and the "Will" sonnets (pp. 289ff.), show even familiar poems in a new and revealing light. Fineman's special gift lies in the ability to expound an argument that does not lose contact with the material at hand while yet managing to open up issues of larger theoretical significance. Thus, when he points out that "because he is the observer of the young man's self-observation, the poet cannot simply identify himself with the young man," but only "with the young man's identification" (pp. 210–11), a subtle insight—whose origins may be traced to the Lacanian concept of the mirror stage—is adroitly imparted. Fineman displays throughout an admirable refusal to simplify the problems he discusses, especially in his repeated insistence (pp. 67, 131, 159, 172) that the contrast he draws between the Young Man and the Dark Lady sonnets is not one of diametric antithesis.

What, then, is one to make of Fineman's central thesis concerning Shakespeare's "invention" of poetic subjectivity? As I have remarked, it invites attempts at refutation by counterexample, as when the claim that Shakespeare marks "the effective beginning of a literature of deep subjective affect" (p. 79) does not pause to consider the precedents of St. Augustine or Chaucer. Similarly, the proposition that Shakespeare's sonnets "made possible for the very first time, an outspoken poetics of erotic desire" (p. 18) is called in doubt by the lyrics of Wyatt, whose revision of the Petrarchan tradition receives scant mention by Fineman. Inevitably, Fineman's insistence on the uniqueness of Shakespeare leads to generalizations concerning his poetic forerunners—from Dante and Petrarch to Spenser and Sidney—that are likely to seem unjust to scholars who have specialized in one or another of these figures. (For a perceptive critique of Fineman in this respect, see the review by Ronald Levao in *Renaissance Quarterly* 40 [1987]: 814–18.)

Ultimately, however, it seems most productive to regard Fineman's theory of literary history not in narrowly positivistic terms, as subject to empirical confirmation or refutation, but as a heuristic construct intended to throw into sharp relief the magnitude of Shakespeare's achievement in the sonnets. As such *Shakespeare's Perjured Eye* is an unqualified success. The footnotes constitute a treatise in themselves, and contain—among much else—Fineman's challenge (p. 333, n. 35) to Norman Rabkin's influential notion of Shakespeare's "complementarity." Even if one wishes to discard one or another portion of his theoretical scaffolding, Joel Fineman has built a house of many mansions. And if, as he has observed, Oscar Wilde's *The Portrait of Mr. W. H.* is "the only genuinely literary criticism that Shakespeare's sonnets have ever received" (p. 28), Fineman's book is as brilliant a work of scholarly criticism as these poems have elicited, and causes one to regret even more deeply the untimely death of its gifted author.

Shakespeare: The Play of History by Graham Holderness, Nick Potter, and John Turner

Reviewer: Grace C. Tiffany

Was Shakespeare a proto-Marxist? That is the question implicitly posed by *Shakespeare: The Play of History,* a three-part work in which Graham Holderness, John Turner, and Nick Potter respectively engage Shakespeare's histories, "tragic romances," and "Venice plays." While explicitly distancing themselves from the new historicists' denial of textual autonomy or pure authorial meaning, these authors share the new historicists' hostility to a centralized and censoring governmental power; they represent Shakespearean theater as an invitation to audiences to consider "how best to resist the supervision of our play by the new alliance between state and capital that was being formed in Elizabethan and Jacobean England" (9). Their Shakespeare is a quasi-visionary with a keen awareness of the losses entailed by the displacement of a feudal world, organized according to social bonds, by a pragmatic, materialistic, and highly individualistic bourgeois society. Analyzing the plays' transgeneric treatment of history, Holderness, Turner, and Potter offer us a Shakespeare committed to reimagining England's past as a progression from a rich, reverent, human world to a crass and mechanistic mercantile state, and to creating in audiences "a hunger . . . for a world yet to be born where these contradictions shall be resolved" (Turner, 154).

Although the nature of this future resolution is left tantalizingly unclear by the authors and, they would argue, by Shakespeare (whose plays look backwards, not forwards), still these essays encourage a view of the plays as deeply dismayed by England's emergent bourgeois culture, while perplexedly aware of the impossibility of a return to feudal roots. Thus, although the plays "appear at last to propose . . . the form of society in which they were produced: commercial, urban, English society as it was under the Tudors," it is "not without regret" that this society is recommended (217).

University of Iowa Press, 1988, pp. x + 240.

This Shakespearean "regret" over a lost "sacred" world (Potter, 157), and over the inhuman mercantile society which has displaced it, is the focus of all three essays in this book. Effectively illuminating Shakespeare's distaste for the cash nexus in human relations, these authors reformulate much that has been said before (for example, what Potter calls "the disappearance of the sacred" in Shakespeare (158) was explored by Alvin B. Kernan twenty years ago).[1] But Holderness, Potter, and Turner also offer intriguing new insights into the ways in which Shakespeare proposes imaginative play as a weapon against cold materialism: a means of sustaining human feeling in an economic world indifferent to its claims.

What is most unusual about this book is its authors' manipulation of genre distinctions to disclose Shakespeare's historical dialectical materialism. All three authors claim histories, tragedies, romances, and problem plays alike as varieties of the history play, as they attempt to demonstrate that Shakespeare's plays consistently "embody . . . an understanding of history that is at once materialist and dialectical" (3). For example, Holderness and Turner discuss the "poetry of feudalism" as it exists in both The Second Tetralogy and what Turner calls the "tragic romances" of King Lear and Macbeth (85). Holderness demonstrates how the language of the histories juxtaposes the competing ideologies of absolutism and feudalism, and Turner traces Shakespeare's continued interest in the feudal world and its discourse in King Lear and Macbeth: here, in Shakespeare's "chosen dramatic form" of "tragic romance . . . we find the poetry of feudalism as it might once have been lived" (85)—a rich verse which re-imagines a world characterized by communal relationships rather than pragmatic power struggles. In the book's third and final section, Potter creates a new genre, the "Venice plays" (157), linking Othello and The Merchant of Venice in a discussion which indicates Venice as the symbolic site for the final triumph of market values over the "sense of the 'sacred'." In the Venice plays, he says, power "loses its capacity to exalt and becomes the merely pragmatic power of the prince and merchant"; thus these plays take their place in this book's larger argument that "Shakespeare's plays are a reflection on the emergence of the modern, post-feudal, commercial world" (157–59).

Potter's willful interpretation of Othello—a "tragic romance" if anything is—as a "Venice play" rather than a tragedy damages the credibility of the otherwise workable generic distinctions proposed by the book. There is a chilling amorality in Potter's argument that

Othello's imaginative discourse and behavior represent a "richer, more grand, more intense" world than the dominant colorless, "dreary" and "safe" Venetian society which is animated by commercial concerns rather than passions (201–2): Othello may be rich, grand, and intense, but he murders his wife. Potter's disclosure of the cold "'cash payment' nexus" which organizes relationships in *The Merchant of Venice* is a more convincing demonstration of how Shakespeare's Venice anticipates Marx's view of the bourgeois state (164). (Potter calls Bassanio's description of silver as "thou pale and common drudge / 'Tween man and man" [3.2.103–4] "a striking anticipation of Marx's description of the destruction of feudal relations by capitalism in *The Manifesto of the Communist Party* [1848].")

Potter locates the displacement of friendship and love by economic interest in Shylock's Venice in the triumph of the economic metaphor: "Figures whereby human relationships are thought of in terms of money, law or trade are quite frequent in the play" (165). Similarly, Holderness and Turner, in their earlier discussions of histories and tragic romances, present Shakespeare's poetry as the ideological battleground between feudalism and materialism.

Holderness sees the pastoral as the characteristic mode of expression for the absolutist monarch. He illuminates the difference between Richard II's pastoral poetic references to "our kingdom's earth" and "our country's cradle" (*RII* 1.3.125, 132) and the outdated chivalric discourse spoken by Mowbray, Bolingbroke, and the anarchronistic Hotspur, which emphasizes "honour" and the "rites of knighthood" (*RII* 1.1.74–75). Holderness first introduced the concept of *Richard II*'s competing poetries of feudalism and absolutism in his brilliantly persuasive *Shakespeare's History* (1985);[2] the variation he offers here is less convincing than his original argument. In *Shakespeare's History*, Holderness explored Richard's use of the *"sun-king"* metaphor to promote an absolutist fantasy, in defiance of the barons' emphasis on the monarch's feudal ties and responsibilities ("Take Herford's rights away, and take from Time / His charters and his customary rights," argues York [*RII* 2.1.195–96]). In *The Play of History*, Holderness reinterprets Richard's references to the sun as part of the overall pastoral poetic scheme which animates Richard's language and constitutes his imaginative "reclamation of England as the personal property of the king" (36). Holderness's definition of the pastoral is stretched at times; it seems to encompass any reference to nature whatsoever. For example, he

calls Richard's exhortation to "spiders," "heavy-gaited toads," and
a "lurking adder" to impede Bolingbroke's military progress "perverted pastoral" (3.2.14, 15, 20, p. 37). But Holderness's close
analysis of the characteristic speech patterns of absolutism and
chivalry is admirable, as is his demonstration of the ease with
which the modern politician—Henry IV and later Henry V—can
appropriate either language in support of personal power. Holderness demonstrates how Hal's

> elaborate ritual of courtesy exercised towards Hotspur's corpse explic-
> itly dramatizes the temporary appropriation of chivalric values: the
> drama lays bare the device by which the state has not only secured its
> defences against a dangerous enemy, but also seized and appropriated
> that enemy's qualities in a gesture of self-legitimation.

And while his analysis of the Brechtian function of the chorus in
Henry V covers familiar ground,[3] Holderness's argument that it is
Henry's strategic poetic "reconstruction of feudal ideology" in his
St. Crispian's Day speech rather than a "genuine nationalism"
which inspires England's short-lived French victories is original
and intriguing.

Where Holderness focuses on the histories' disclosure of a world
in transition from feudalism to self-serving absolutism, realized
through changes in and manipulation of poetic discourse, Turner
presents *King Lear* and *Macbeth* as explorations of the "might-have-
been of feudalism" (88), and finds in its poetry "a new metaphoric
richness which is Shakespeare's attempt to re-create the totalized
world-view implicit in the concept of the feudal bond." But Turner
reveals how it is this very poetry, emphasizing the bonds of service
between vassal and overlord, which demonstrates the internal contradictions destined to tear feudal society apart. Goneril's and Re-
gan's strategic declarations of love for Lear overlie ambitious self-
interest; they invalidate the courteous expression of love, driving
Kent and Cordelia into silence. Duncan, praising Macbeth's early
military victories, acknowledges the high appropriateness of his
loyal service, yet the qualities of individualistic valor and daring
which have prompted this praise are the same qualities which will
lead Macbeth to break faith with Duncan. Turner strikingly recon-
textualizes these familiar readings of the plays by representing
these tragedies as elegies for a self-destructive and self-destroyed
feudal age. "*King Lear* traces a society where the reciprocal relationship between authority and service has broken down," where

the loyal subject "can no longer say *enough* and flies instead to the limitless extremes of *no less than all*, and where in consequence the vulnerable customs and institutions of that society are destroyed" (116). Similarly, *Macbeth* "traces the collapse of a heroic 'total' civilization before the violence generated in its own contradictions": Duncan depends on and is destroyed by his thanes' energy and "sense of military power" (147).

Despite the stark, inexorable movement from the rich feudal past to the barren commercial present which Holderness, Turner, and Potter see traced by Shakespeare's plays, their book's conclusion insists that the plays offer themselves as healing alternatives to immersion in a materialistic world which provides insufficient nurturance for the human spirit. The rich poetic language of the feudal past discloses "real worlds of the imagination, human possibilities if not political possibilities" (218). In discovering this, the authors succeed in freeing themselves from the limitations of new historicism, as they assert in defiance of "a certain crude materialism" that "the material history of man is a matter not only of the things that have been done but also of the things that have been imagined, desired or regretted" (221).

Notes

1. See Alvin B. Kernan, "The *Henriad*: Shakespeare's Major History Plays," in his *Modern Shakespearean Criticism* (Harcourt, Brace and World, 1970).
2. See Graham Holderness, *Shakespeare's History* (New York: St Martin's Press, 1985).
3. See, for example, Edward Berry's "'True Things and Mock'ries': Epic and History in *Henry V*," *Journal of English and Germanic Philology* 78 (1979): 1–16.

Hamlet: Film, Television, Audio Performance by Bernice W. Kliman

Reviewer: Marvin Rosenberg

The value of film, television and audio recordings as a resource for Shakespeare study is amply demonstrated in Bernice Kliman's

Fairleigh Dickinson University Press, 1988, pp. 344.

book. By viewing over and over important recorded interpretations, she discovers and teaches us to see brilliances in text and performance that we may have missed.

At the same time, Kliman provides valuable insights into the media forms she deals with; she is particularly acute at watching and listening for nuances, at evaluating the use of space in the small and large screens, and at perceiving the "extra-textual" elements that Shakespeare shows as he tells. The focuses come together as she looks at *Hamlet* films, three in particular, beginning with the Olivier, which started her interest. She observes how the film technique stretches the play beyond the limits of theatrical space; but within the expanded form she notes the theatrical styles that are true to Shakespeare.

Kliman is rather forgiving about Olivier's cuts, considering them as fitting his concept of the play. She follows the pattern of his (Hamlet's) life in the expanse of his palace and environs:

> Hamlet descends downward into deep depression then ascends upward into action culminating in a serene compliance with destiny and death.

Kliman has some reservations about Kozintsev's *Hamlet*, though she admires the Russian's poetic film work. She feels Smakhtunowski has a face rich in the subtext of pain and despair, but lacks Hamlet's full complexity, and therefore the play ends as it begins with a kind of anti-Stalinist hopelessness. Yet her sharp eye for visual and dramatic values finds delights:

> The film succeeds on many levels in spite of the pruning of characters forced by the interpretation. We remember the film's demonic use of space—beach, sky, sea, castle; its Hamlet at once desperate and altruistic: its touching vignettes, such as the caging in steel of the mourning Ophelia, her happiness at last when she is mad.

A third *Hamlet* that fascinates Kliman is the 1984 Swedish television version directed by Ragnar Lyth. Her acute ear particularly admires the integrated sound track:

> The eerie whisper and wind noises of the ghost; the rocketing grates of a large wheel associated with the ghost; the sound of the deep bell tones that are related to the ghost's arrival, the contrasting foolish small tinkle of Claudius's scribes' bell; the distant whispering sounds of madness; the outdoor sounds of birds and the sea, the sound of freedom; and the sound of Ophelia's pathetic pipe she plays in her madness.

Kliman is alert to minute details: the intrusion of a stagehand into

the Maurice Evans telecast; the problem of filming the Plummer
Hamlet at the real Elsinore; the presence of Ophelia in the Neville
court scene. She watches Chamberlain's face, and listens to his
voice separately, to detect the true Hamlet; she watches the tight
movements that organize the small screen in the Nicol Williamson;
she is troubled by the repeated closeups of the McKellen soliloquies, so powerful at first, but beginning to pall; she compares the
Jacobi TV *Hamlet* with the actor's earlier stage version.

As Kliman discusses her examples, she instructs us in the background and development of film techniques, as for instance when
she introduces the old Forbes-Robertson movie. Reading this book
is like reexperiencing the films and the audio recordings she discusses, but with more practiced, more understanding eyes and ears.
Thank you, Bernice Kliman.

Hamlet and the Acting of Revenge by Peter Mercer

(The Oxford) *Hamlet*, edited by G. R. Hibbard

(The Critics Debate Series) *Hamlet* by Michael
Hattaway

The Elizabethan Hamlet by Arthur McGee

Reviewer: Maurice Charney

There has been a spate of interest in *Hamlet* recently, which suggests that *Hamlet* may once again be asserting its primacy, against
King Lear, among Shakespeare's tragedies. Certainly, *King Lear* does

University of Iowa Press, 1987, pp. viii + 269; Clarendon Press, 1987, pp. ix + 406;
Humanities Press International, 1987, pp. 112; Yale University Press, 1987, pp.
ix + 211.

not appeal to the young either by its central characters or by its unremittingly bleak outlook. In contrast, *Hamlet* seems vibrant, bold, intellectual, violent, and self-critical, and its questioning of traditional humanistic values as a revenge play may be a point in its favor as a guide to the perplexed. The romantic Hamlet of nineteenth-century matinee idols, resplendent in his black satin doublet with flowing, open, white silk shirt, is fortunately fading from sight. In its place we have a protagonist who is much more contemporary in his thinking, less preoccupied with delay and the puzzlement of the will, who acts decisively and is willing to accept paradoxes in the nature of things.

The most challenging of the books under review is Peter Mercer's *Hamlet and the Acting of Revenge*. Mercer takes *Hamlet* seriously as a revenge play and tries to see it against other revenge plays of its time, especially *The Spanish Tragedy, Antonio's Revenge*, and *The Revenger's Tragedy*. This sets up a pattern of expectations and conventions. Most significant as a model for all revenge plays is Seneca's *Thyestes*, which Mercer discusses brilliantly in his chapter 2, entitled "*Thyestes* and Revenge Structure." The key statement for all revengers is: *Scelera non ulcisceris, nisi vincis* ("Injuries are not revenged except where they are exceeded"), which, in the Elizabethan translation edited by Thomas Newton, reads: "Thou never dost enough revenge the wronge, / Except thou passe." The emphasis on an outrageous excess of emotion heightens the imaginative appeal of *Thyestes*, since its wildness violates both reason and restraint. Revenge is not tepid in any way. In this formulation we have what Mercer calls "the essential dynamic of tragedy, the entangling of human passions and intentions with fate" (p. 28). Revenge is rendered with spectacular and ingenious cruelty; it is a product of the creative imagination of the revenger.

In chapter 2 Mercer lays the basis of his strong argument against an ethical and moral consideration of revenge, which does not occur in a normal world of human concerns and ethical debate. The revenger moves in a world of "savage mania" (p. 29) and gives up all tenderness and compassion in his intense preoccupation with his task. He becomes either subhuman or superhuman in the way he sheds typically human concerns. The revenger is possessed by evil, and to be a revenger means "to wade in blood, to sup full with horrors" (p. 30). The revenge itself is ingenious almost to the point of absurdity, and it is interesting that the climax of revenge plays should border so closely on farce. In his triumph the revenger feels exultation and exaltation, what Mercer aptly calls "savage glee" (p. 35), that is much more melodramatic than tragic. Elizabethan dramatists tried to create a true tragedy of revenge by reversing the polarity of *Thyestes* and preventing the protagonist from also being the villain.

I want to skip over the interesting chapters on *The Spanish Tragedy*, *Antonio's Revenge*, and *The Revenger's Tragedy*, and come to the detailed reading of *Hamlet*, which constitutes a little more than half the book. Mercer's approach is focussed on revenge outside of ethical and moral considerations. He puts strong emphasis on Hamlet's own histrionic sense of a role, a performance. Thus, Hamlet's appearance of persistent grief and the suit of black that he wears are "the sign of his role as a melancholic bitter jester" (p. 142). This is a part that Hamlet has assumed before the ghost appeared to him. It is a pre-revenge attitude meant to shield him from his own emotions. The inadequacy of gesture and language to express feeling remains a problem throughout the play. "At every turn the words that seem the only ones to fit his sworn revenge prove stale, empty, even absurd, their intensity of passion drained off long ago by too much use" (p. 145).

Mercer attributes to Hamlet a degree of self-conscious irony that impedes any straightforward action: "Hamlet not only plays his roles; he plays at playing them: what matters is not only that the King is successfully deceived but that he is played with" (p. 145). This endows *Hamlet* with a subtlety that detracts from the impetuous and even melodramatic action of a revenge play. With the powerful example of Seneca's *Thyestes* in mind (supported by *The Spanish Tragedy*, *Antonio's Revenge*, and *The Revenger's Tragedy*), Mercer wonders whether Hamlet is up to the mark as a revenger, whether he "can ever hope to achieve the terrible simplification of emotion and language, the monstrous concentration of force, that revenge requires" (p. 163). This seems to me an illegitimate question because it depends so heavily on *Hamlet's* relation to its revenge models. There is, after all, no necessary connection except generic, and here too Shakespeare is under no obligation to revenge prototypes.

Mercer has a fascinating discussion of Hamlet and the Ghost, especially the way in which Hamlet assumes the obsessions of his father. Almost everything that happens in the play can be predicated from the encounter with the Ghost in act 1, scene 5. Hamlet's attack on his mother in the closet scene (3.4) is shaped by the imagery of the Ghost, who speaks in violent, horrified, and bestial terms: Gertrude's lust will "prey on garbage" (1.5.57). The hideous and obscene images of old Hamlet's death provide Mercer with a type illustration of the conflict between moral satire and revenge. The Ghost's account of his death resembles the scene in the graveyard at the end of the play, both of which lead to a *memento mori* contemplation rather than to revenge. It is the Ghost who is preoccupied with Gertrude's sexual appetite—a horrible and excitingly forbidden vision that Hamlet can never forget. Again, Mercer seems so intent on making Hamlet a proper revenger that he rejects any of the larger moral satire as counterproductive. I object to Mercer's revenge teleology which wants so rigidly to exclude everything else.

For the *Mousetrap* play, Mercer plays down the idea that it is used to obtain proof of Claudius' guilt. Although Hamlet may talk in these terms, at bottom "what he is hungry for is not discovery but revelation" (p. 197). Hamlet wants the play to be a demonstration of Claudius' guilt, a show presented to the entire court, a spectacle that they will watch "while Hamlet watches the King watching" (p. 197). Mercer seems disappointed with his hero because he doesn't seriously want to murder, as a good revenger should, but to reveal the guilt in the mirror of art both in relation to Claudius and to his mother. "He wants, in essence, not to kill or to torture but to *show*" (p. 197). Mercer is so preoccupied with revenge as the legitimate pursuit of the revenger that he seems to be indignant with Hamlet for failing to come up to the mark in the way of "savage mania" or "savage glee."

At the end, Mercer rejects *Hamlet* as a tragedy or even a proper revenge play. We can see the development of an odd but consistent reasoning in which Mercer seems to be egging Hamlet on to the realization that he is the protagonist of a revenge play, a consideration that Hamlet seems oddly to have forgotten or at least to be distracted from. The thoughts of death in the "To be or not to be" soliloquy, for example, offer Hamlet a diversion from the real issues of the play: "That real issue has to do with his unexpressed and only half-acknowledged reluctance to arouse himself to the condition necessary for the acting of revenge" (p. 204). On the other hand, the "Now could I drink hot blood" soliloquy at the end of the play scene (3.2) appeals to Mercer for odd reasons:

This is the real stuff. Here is the ancient emblem of the feast of flesh, the raging thirst for blood. Now is Hamlet, like Atreus, like Antonio, truly monstrous, inspired by Hell, ready for some consummate cruelty. (p. 213)

But of course Hamlet doesn't follow up his flirtation with "the real stuff" of revenge plays. Mercer has the advantage of being logical and consistent, and he presents a powerful argument that we need ultimately to reject.

If we turn now to George Hibbard's excellent new edition of *Hamlet* in the Oxford Shakespeare series, we are surprised by the fact that the text is based on the Folio version rather than that in Quarto 2, which held indisputable sway until very recently. The many "Passages Peculiar to the Second Quarto" (about 230 lines) have been banished to Appendix A, including the "How all occasions do inform against me" soliloquy of act 4, scene 4. This scene is now reduced to a mere 8 lines from 66 in Quarto 2. It is really invigorating to see Hibbard, following the lead of the Oxford editors, take the bull by the horns and refuse to present the usual conflated edition of *Hamlet* composed of what everyone likes in Quarto 2 and Folio (and Quarto 1 for good measure) put together in a text which never existed in Shakespeare's time and could not possibly exist by itself. At least Hibbard is choosing an authentic and possible version. The alterations in Folio

seem to be parts of a definite policy designed to make the play more accessible to theatre-goers in general by giving it a more direct and unimpeded action, pruning away some of its verbal elaborations, and smoothing out its more abrupt transitions. (p. 126)

But Hibbard goes further and offers an overly elaborate argument to rationalize and justify the Folio changes as improvements over Quarto 2. The "How all occasions do inform against me" soliloquy in act 4, scene 4 is hardly "redundant," though Hibbard says, "it tells us nothing we do not know already, except that the Prince has become unrealistic" (p. 109). If this were used as a criterion throughout the play—"It tells us nothing we do not know already"—most of the soliloquies including "To be or not to be" would have to go. They can hardly be judged on their expository purpose. It seems to me that Hibbard would do better to accept Quarto 2 and Folio as two different and alternative versions of the same play without arguing that one is necessarily better than the other. We all agree that Folio makes for a "better acting version with a wide appeal" (p. 109), but there is no way of determining whether Shakespeare himself revised his own work.

The glosses in Hibbard are admirably lucid and concise without an unnecessarily heavy weight of learning. The theatrical illustrations, however, are inadequately identified. Plates 9, 10, and 11 have no actors' names or other identifying marks. Hibbard's general introduction is disappointing in its generality, often reduced to unnecessary plot review. It is not imaginative and ambitious like the textual introduction. Some of Hibbard's remarks about women seem odd, especially the comment about Hamlet's madness: "Women's sexuality has evidently become an obsession with him; and to this extent he is genuinely mad" (p. 51). If this is true, then we are faced with the odd conclusion that obsession with women's sexuality is one of the leading indicators that Hamlet is really mad. With this criterion, most of the men in the audience would be mad too. The statement immediately following seems excessively moralistic: "It is Ophelia's tragic fate to pay the price in pain and suffering for Gertrude's sins and for the corrosive cynicism those sins have engendered in Hamlet" (p. 51). Gertrude's sins don't seem as clearly evident to me as they do to Hibbard. Hamlet's "corrosive cynicism," if that indeed is what he is suffering from, seems to be engendered by many sources other than Gertrude's sins.

Michael Hattaway's short book on *Hamlet* is part of the Critics Debate series, edited by Michael Scott, and its subtitle, "An Introduction to the Variety of Criticism," shows its academic function. It is designed as an introductory book for students, and it manages to glance at a broad gamut of historical, formal, romantic, psychological, philosophical, and language-based approaches. Hattaway exercises an intelligent, pluralistic approach with a strong foundation in theatrical productions of *Hamlet*. Sometimes the author strays from the play to large theoretical questions that interest him, especially in the area of the semiotics of drama.

I have left for the last Arthur McGee's *The Elizabethan Hamlet* because it seems so bizarre and out of place among the other three books. Published in 1987 by a leading American university press, it is so dubious as a piece of serious criticism that it is worth pausing for a moment to examine its assumptions. In the earlier part of the book, McGee speaks glibly of the Elizabethan audience, Elizabethan attitudes, and Anglicanism as if all of these were a single, unitary, and indisputable entity. McGee's views on revenge are extremely simplified, as if all Elizabethans believed in the official orthodoxy that all revenge is satanic and demonic. An avalanche of quotations is presented—these are the single most attractive feature of the book—but all to support a few elementary propositions that don't need any support. at all. Throughout, McGee's reasoning has the astonishing irrelevance of the crank. Horatio, for example, likens the Ghost to Hamlet's father, because he is "Armed at point exactly, cap-a-pe," or from head to toe. Because Marston uses this familiar expression in *The Malcontent*, McGee concludes that Shakespeare regarded the Ghost as demonic because Marston "uses 'a-cap-a-pe' for Mendoza, who urges Malevole to murder the duke" (p. 57). "Cap-a-pe" is hardly evidence for a demonic ghost in *Hamlet*. Let us look at another example of McGee's sweeping generalizations:

> It is obvious therefore that if the Ghost in Shakespeare's *Hamlet* be good it defied the tradition of the evil revenge ghost which still held the stage at that time, and it also contravened the moral code of the audience, whether Protestant or Catholic. (p. 18)

That the Ghost may not be either good or bad—ambiguous, in other words—is outside McGee's comprehension: he reasons only in simplistic, black-and-white terms.

One could dismiss McGee's book gracefully if it weren't so rabidly anti-Catholic. This deserves comment, since McGee's violent hatred of Catholicism goes beyond the commentary on *Hamlet*. Everything demonic and satanic in the play is identified as Catholic. Some of this is very farfetched, as when the play scene is nailed as Catholic and the Players, as a commedia dell'arte troupe, are of course Italian Catholics clearly identified as Machiavels, "poisoners like the Borgias, libertines like the Venetians" (p. 108). This is wild reasoning, because the players in *Hamlet* are definitely not a commedia dell'arte troupe but rather an adult company that has been displaced by the popularity of the children. Further on, McGee claims that the First Player is obviously dressed to look like Hamlet (p. 118) and the players are revenging themselves against Hamlet because he has antagonized them. Elsewhere, we learn that Claudius kneels before a statue of the Madonna and Child (p. 125) and that Ophelia is an obvious Catholic because she is looking at a prayer book in which there must be a picture of the Annunciation. How does McGee know all this? And what is Yale University Press doing publishing such twaddle?

Shakespeare's Other Language by Ruth Nevo

Reviewer: Jeanne Addison Roberts

Ruth Nevo's latest book, *Shakespeare's Other Language*, is a brave and stimulating work. Bravery and stimulation are closely linked, since what she has undertaken is the formidable task of "psycho-analyzing the text" of Shakespeare's romances and decoding, in Lacanian terms, the "elliptical" (both in the sense of considering gaps and in the sense of creating circuits) interaction between reader and text. Her project is thus to read the "other language" buried beneath the surface of the play. In this process, the reader becomes for her both analysand and analyst and the text serves similar dual functions. Nevo understands the difficulties of her undertaking—such as the problems of distinguishing the conscious from the unconscious, and the overwhelming question of whose unconscious is being analyzed: character's, author's, or reader's—but she nonetheless presses on, concluding, I think correctly, that the chief value of her efforts "will rest in whatever capacity they may have to reilluminate the dramas to which, of which, and through which" (32) her ideas speak.

Her essays do indeed reactivate the texts which they address; and, although many questions remain open, perhaps because questions remain open, this is an exciting book. One feels the strenuous engagement of a mind wrestling with questions at a frontier of critical discourse not yet clearly delineated.

Like her two earlier books, *Comic Transformations in Shakespeare* and *Tragic Form in Shakespeare*, this work addresses a specific group of plays loosely classified generically, this time the romances, *Pericles, Cymbeline, The Winter's Tale,* and *The Tempest.* But unlike the earlier works, her focus here is not on genre—indeed her first chapter is titled "Beyond Genre"—but on finding in these often puzzling plays ways of reading which will defamiliarize them and discover in "rifts at the realist-rational level of plot, character, and diction evidence of unconscious signification, of the language of dream and fantasy" (8).

Simplified to summary, Nevo's psychoanalytic interpretations

Methuen Press, 1987, pp. 170.

may seem banal. Pericles, haunted by incestuous oedipal desires for a mother and by fear of paternal retribution, is driven into passivity and retreat by an enervating death wish. Antiochus, Lysimachus, and possibly Cleon, are Pericles' doubles, born of "the archaic turbulence of ambivalent desire and dread" (59). The play's unsatisfying end may (she concludes the chapter with questions) be simply an unresolved return to its point of origins. The strength of Nevo's interpretation lies in her careful attention to language and to such anomalous details as Pericles' lack of elation at winning his bride, his willingness to give up his daughter after his wife's death, and the sadistic language of the brothel scenes. She demonstrates persuasively that the drama does resemble, as Freud suggested, the "remembering, repeating, and working through" of psychoanalysis (41). She seems to me on less firm ground in insisting that the drama represents elemental and universal fantasy (would a woman's fantasies be the same? a Melanesian's?) and in avoiding the issue of whose unconscious is being analyzed. The implication, based on chapter 1, is that the author's, character's, and reader's unconscious minds operate interactively to achieve a "universal" interpretation of the "dream." The effects of actors, directors, and varying audiences are left unexamined, as is the question of whether the "dreams" of drama can be universal.

The chapter on *Cymbeline* contains some surprises. Confronting the "weirdly replicative" (62) patterns of the play and the flounderings of critics, she offers as key to her reading the premise that there is always in drama "a central ego for a play to be about," and that in this case the ego is Cymbeline's, even though that ego is in abeyance during most of the play (67). She focuses on Posthumus, Cloten, and Iachimo as split parts of Cymbeline's ego, uncovering once again a death wish in a major character—this time Posthumus. By her close reading of the knotted syntax, she also convincingly exposes hostility and resistance to harmonious union on the part of Imogene as well as on that of Posthumus. The surprise comes at the end of the chapter when Nevo returns to Cymbeline, connecting him with Shakespeare himself, newly returned to Stratford after his mother's death and the birth of a daughter to his own favorite daughter. She suggests that in the play splintered segments of the male become proxies for the king, who is, in turn, a proxy, figuring imaginatively the conflicts of "a troubled author" confronting his deeply repressed desire for his daughter.

Provocative as it is, this conclusion is confusing. "Universal" fantasies have now been particularized to the supposed experience of one man, and the text, the unconscious of which we have been analyzing, now becomes the psyche of the author himself. The hypothesis, though certainly suggestive, is unprovable; and we are left to wonder about the position in this circuit of the reader, originally posed as both analyst and analysand. How does uncovering the anxieties of Cymbeline/Shakespeare help us to deal with our own?

Nevo's *Tempest* chapter centers on the consciousness of Prospero rather than the unconscious of the text. The magician's fantasy of omnipotence yields to reality testing. The father's happy fifteen-year idyll with his daughter (Nevo calls it "the loveliest of all fantasies," 133) must come to an end; and Prospero struggles with the drive toward regression (Caliban) and the drive toward sublimation (Ariel). Much in this chapter recapitulates insights of earlier critics (C. L. Barber, Cyrus Hoy, Norman Holland), but the discussion is clearly integrated, concluding with the poignant image of the pain of renunciation and the sorrow of recognizing the human's inevitable destination.

The discussion of *The Winter's Tale* is the most complex and probably the freshest in the volume. Nevo builds on Freud's idea of paired dreams, which produce a two-staged wish fulfillment, the first stage depicting undisguised character with actions only hinted at, and the second stage spelling out the action with disguised character. From this base she develops an analysis of the play as twinned dreams. Her most significant contribution is her explanation of Leontes' "sudden" jealousy, which she sees as not sudden but rather as symptomatic of a marriage troubled by the ambivalence of both husband and wife.

Leontes' problem is that the sight of the pregnant Hermione, closeted first with Polixenes and then with Mamillius, precipitates him back into childhood dread of maternal separation and fears of maternal engulfment. The first part of the play becomes then a reenactment of a childish nightmare, culminating in the death of Mamillius—both sibling rival and surrogate for his father. The key, according to Nevo, is the image of the spider at the bottom of the cup. She says, "psychoanalytic lore informs us [that spiders] unconsciously symbolize devouring mother imagos" (112). At delicate moments of her arguments Nevo frequently resorts to unanswered questions. The technique is not ineffective in highlighting unresolvable problems and hinting at answers, but it is itself often elliptical in the sense of leaving gaps. At the point of supplying the unconscious significance of spiders, she queries "whose unconscious? Leontes'? Shakespeare's? The reader's?" But the questions remain unanswered as she falls back on simply adducing spiders as "test case for the usefulness of the portmanteau notion of a textual unconscious" (112). For me the test is not conclusive. Her case for the eruption of primal oral fantasies as the cause of the initial tragedy is, in fact, considerably stronger than the web of the spider.

In this interpretation, the second half of the play kills off Antigonus, Leontes' "misogynist" double—misogyny is dubiously proven by Antigonus's resolution to "geld" his daughters if Hermione is proven false (118)—reconciles Leontes to the "maternal" Paulina, and recapitulates a benign "childhood" in the pastoral Bohemia. Hunger is legitimated in Paulina's art, which Leontes now declares "lawful as eating." The memory of the trauma of new birth is merely obliquely echoed in the last lines of the play, evocative of the "wide gap of time since first / We were dissevered."

The format of this slim volume is attractive; and the text, though occasionally dense and elliptical in a bad sense, is surprisingly readable and jargon-free. Proofreading should have been better: Barbara Mowat's name is consistently misspelled (62, 65, 164, 168), as are Paulina's (97), Bellarius's (93), and Caesar's (91), as well as several other words; a line is repeated (89–90); and punctuation occasionally confuses long, complicated sentences. The list of references puzzlingly omits those which appear only in footnotes. But these are minor distractions.

There are many places where this book's arguments will invite dissent or at least dialogue; but this is finally a tribute to a text which, like Shakespeare's own, refuses to lie dead on the page and demands a reader's engagement.

Tragedy: Shakespeare and the Greek Example by Adrian Poole

Reviewer: Janel Mueller

This engagingly written and often perceptive study is saddled with an inappropriate title. On either side of the colon, the phraseology misleads in serious ways. As I particularize on this oddity, I will nonetheless be minding what is always a reviewer's chief business—to describe what, in fact, a book is "about" by way of subject, purpose, and method and to give some estimate of its value.

The title *Tragedy* promises comprehensiveness—whether formal or historical or otherwise—even if focus is due to settle on "Shakespeare and the Greek Example." But Poole's is in no systematic or sustained way a study of Greek and Shakespearean tragedy. Brian Vickers's much vaster but more modestly entitled *Towards Greek Tragedy: Drama, Myth, Society* (London: Longman, 1973) answers considerably better to the expectations aroused by Poole's title, especially when the promise of Vickers's own preface is weighed in: "This book is the first of a two-part study called *Comparative Tragedy*. The second part will include discussions of several Greek plays, but will mainly be concerned with tragedy from Shakespeare to the present day" (p. ix).

More particularly, Poole's title *Tragedy* invites expectations of a genre study. For students in the field of Renaissance literature, where generic approaches have been fruitful and become well established, the immediate associations elicited by the term "tragedy" will be formal ones—plot types, resources of staging, and conventions of representing action, speech, and character. A study further specified as *Shakespeare and the Greek Example* is almost certain to arouse further expectations. We anticipate an express engagement with the commanding, if still controversial formulations—reversal and recognition, identification and katharsis—by which Aristotle in the *Poetics* undertook to analyze how tragic enactment and tragic affect conduce to the typically intense involvement of spectators with protagonists in this dramatic genre. Poole, however,

Basil Blackwell, 1988, pp. xii + 265.

disclaims interest in theories of tragedy, Aristotelian or not. But practical criticism always has theoretical presuppositions. His discussions of plays implicitly assume a powerful current of audience identification. At the same time they implicitly repudiate any of the several available understandings of katharsis, since his understanding of the term seems to entail taking art as an anodyne (see pp. 10, 47, 140).

The wording and sequencing of Poole's subtitle also raise expectations that Shakespeare will receive perhaps a priority of concern and at least roughly equal treatment in this study. But this subtitle gestures at both more and less than the eventual truth. More than the truth, for a start, because the six chapters of Poole's study are preponderantly devoted to close readings of selected tragedies by Aeschylus, Sophocles, and Euripides. The distribution of emphasis puts the case clearly. Chapters 3, 5, and 6—a total of 115 pages— contain passing references, but nothing approaching a steady focus, on Shakespeare. Sophocles and Euripides are the subjects of these three chapters. Chapter 3 sensitively compares the portrayals of Heracles in *Women of Trachis* and *The Madness of Heracles*. Chapter 5 suggestively analyzes major Euripidean female protagonists— Alcestis, Medea, and Phaedra—within the framework provided by their male foils and by what can be inferred from dramatic representation about Greek norms for gendered behavior and expression. Chapter 6 offers a provocative brief for interpreting Sophocles' *Philoctetes* as a transformative reworking of his *Antigone*. Only in sections of chapters 2, 4, and 7 does Shakespeare come in for sustained attention. In chapter 2, a twenty-three-page discussion of Aeschylus's *Oresteia* is followed by fifteen pages on *Macbeth*. Chapter 4 allots forty-five pages to *Oedipus the King* and twelve to *Hamlet*. Chapter 7 has eighteen pages on *Oedipus at Colonus* and *The Bacchae* and twelve pages on *King Lear*. All told, just under one-sixth of Poole's study deals expressly with Shakespeare.

Ultimately, however—and this is the first point I wish to stress— the worst disservice done to both author and reader by the undescriptive subtitle lies in its failure even to hint at the finespun, scintillating web of cross-references that Poole casts across his pages. Connections empowered by a well-stocked, ranging, aurally acute literary memory offer much by way of sudden insight to compensate for the expectations of generic or historical scope that the main title elicits but frustrates. If, moreover, Poole's book is far less about Shakespeare than the reader can possibly anticipate, who could even begin to guess from the subtitle at the brilliant instants at which Beckett, Brecht, Freud, and Thucydides are brought into key combination in chapter 2? Or that make Pound, Ibsen, Hegel, Strindberg, and Donne integral to turns of the argument of chapter 3? Every chapter offers arresting collocations of this kind. Not one of them struck me as adventitious.

Allusions to Coleridge and DeQuincey, to Wordsworth and Tennyson, to Emily Brontë and George Eliot, to Charles Kingsley and Richard Wagner, and to Lord De Tabley's dramatic monologue "Philoctetes," reprinted in an appendix, make for a special abundance of insights. Poole commandingly demonstrates how the essayistic mode of T. S. Eliot's studies of Elizabethan and Jacobean drama can be returned from desuetude to currency by a gifted practitioner. While a good deal here must pass for graceful parlaying of received critical wisdom—for example, the sections on the *Oresteia*, *Oedipus at Colonus*, and *The Bacchae* as well as the characterizations of the respective cultural temper of Aeschylus, Sophocles, and Euripides—such discussions may well have utility for the specialist reader of Shakespeare. Overall, the saliency and surprise of the allusions to nineteenth-century writers put Poole's special stamp on this study, for his previous book was *Gissing in Context* (London: Macmillan, 1975).

In my judgment, the rich play of intertextuality reaches its high point when Freud is pressed centrally into the service of Poole's analysis of *Oedipus the King* and *Hamlet* as tragedies of self-questioning. Chapter 4 opens this provocative and frequently original sequence of insights while pursuing what is surely the most substantial connection between "Shakespeare and the Greek Example" to be found anywhere in the book. Poole turns the tables on the master to open up a fresh angle of vision that is sustained and complicated in his subsequent discussion of these two exhaustively discussed plays. Here are portions of the crucial opening gambit of this chapter:

> For Freud, Hamlet was always closely associated with Oedipus. . . . Freud finds a likeness solely in what the two fictional characters suffer from, the desires with which they are supposedly cursed. But Hamlet too has a side to him that Freud ignores. What Hamlet has in common with Oedipus and Freud is that he asks a lot of questions. Freud sees only half of each character, the half that could play the part of patient to his own analyst. And in extricating them from their own dramas and recasting them in his own, Freud seizes the role of analyst for himself,

displacing the Oedipus and the Hamlet who make such courageous efforts to understand the story of their lives in the very act of its composition. The most significant thing that Freud has to say abut Sophocles' Oedipus is to do [sic] with the form and structure of the play rather than its hidden content: 'The action of the play consists in . . . a process of revelation . . . that can be likened to the work of a psychoanalysis'. . . . This suggests that a psychoanalysis is constructed like a tragedy, or at least like this tragedy, and that what a psychoanalysis and a tragedy have in common is something to do [sic] with their work of discovery. In each case we are moved by the products of revelation only in so far as we are moved by the process of revelation. (Pp. 89–90

This quotation coupled with my foregoing remarks will make it clear, I hope, that a more perspicuous subtitle for Poole's study would run "Greek Antecedents, Modern Repercussions." It is indeed symptomatic that a sole footnote cites L. G. Salingar's *Shakespeare and the Traditions of Comedy* (Cambridge: Cambridge University Press, 1974) on "Shakespeare's debts to classical comedy" (p. 249). Despite the shifting parallel drawn between male and female principals in *Agamemnon* and *Macbeth* in chapter 2, and the somewhat more extended parallels in the parent-child relationships of *Oedipus at Colonus*, *The Bacchae*, and *King Lear* registered in chapter 7, Poole is not principally concerned either with the force of any Greek or classical "example" of tragedy in regard to Shakespeare or with comparing Greek and Shakespearian tragedy as species or realizations of tragedy. What does persistently and pervasively concern Poole is "the tragic," and, as the intertextual weave of discussion displays, the tragic may be as readily localized in a poem, a story, a novel, or an essay as in a play. Hence both descriptive accuracy and methodological clarity are at stake in this question of titles.

A much apter main title would have been *What Makes for Tragedy*—or, by extension of the colloquialism that judiciously enlivens these chapters, *On What's Tragic*. From end to end, Poole's book shows itself as a modal rather than a generic study of tragedy. His first chapter, in fact, declares against standard generic concerns with definitions and specifiable repertories and conventions, techniques, and effects. Instead, Poole says, he will pursue an inductive, experiential approach to tragedy. He prides himself on his minimal baggage of categories and generalizations, declining to offer any advance statement of his critical approach or agenda. But his concern with the tragic as a mode quickly asserts itself nonetheless. I borrow from William Arrowsmith's preface to the *Alcestis* he did for the Greek Tragedy in New Translations series (New York and London: Oxford University Press, 1974) to supply general content for the term "modal" that is thoroughly applicable to Poole's study. In Arrowsmith's words,

> the very aim of Greek drama is an account of human fate in a world where any order of "being" is defined by contrast with other modes of existence. Man is modally unique, and his uniqueness is explicitly revealed by informing contrast with the gods (who live forever and know it) and the animals (who are mortal but unware of their mortality). . . . Necessity is the criterion which divides each "species" of existence from the other. . . . Men suffer necessity (anankē) whether as death, political oppression, old age, suffering, sexuality, or slavry; the gods who impose, and often incarnate, human necessities seldom suffer them. . . . The modes of men and gods are defined by their vulnerability to anankē or limits generally. (pp. 4, 5)

Poole's combined psychological and thematic orientation studies the modality of the "human" under the lens of the "tragic." In his discussions, persons tested to their limits by suffering and death disclose their precariousness, their vulnerability, and their potential for greatness. Tragic "diversity," the sole springboard referent permitted in chapter 1, betokens for Poole a varied experience of "dispersal"—"diversity" in the unstringing of outward restraints and inward composure, in the raising of hard, usually unanswerable questions about human nature and human life, and in the engrossing, inexorable going "through" to the limits that actors perform and audiences sustain in reciprocal relation. An inveterate punster in the high Renaissance vein, Poole plays upon the throughness, the thoroughness that he finds intrinsic to tragedy. The sparks struck by the jostling of sound and sense are left to illuminate, as best they may, the subject he sets himself and the method he employs. "If we are to make a true encounter with tragic experience, then the activity of reading will have to involve a 'dynamic passage through'" (p. 5). Although Poole conceives the tragic "passage through" as temporal and active, he associates it almost exclusively with "the activity of reading" texts. Thus his study addresses staging and production only sporadically. By contrast, the "throughness" that he identifies with the tragic modality of living and understanding serves as grounding for the three shaping emphases of his study.

Poole claims first that "the greatness of Greek and Shakespearean tragedy" lies in "the intrinsic resistance to ideology" constituted

by "their ability to represent the unassimilability of pain, and of
the human qualities that survive through extreme suffering" (p. 10).
He claims next that "language is necessarily essential to tragedy
inasmuch as tragedy represents what men and women do to themselves and each other and their world *through* language" (p. 11).
And finally he maintains that tragedy

> *must* be translated, through the imagination. Translation is a strenuous
> activity involving constant comparison. . . . There is peril and difficulty
> concealed in the mild prepositional 'trans-', the sense of passage across
> a border or frontier or gulf that separates one state of being from an-
> other. The word belongs with other words that are essential to the
> substance of tragedy itself, words such as 'transformation', 'transgres-
> sion', 'transience', transmission', 'transition'. What survives such "fear-
> ful passage"? (Pp. 10–11, 14).

This resoundingly rhetorical question will eventually become the
means by which Poole brings his study full circle, for "fearful passage" is the refrain of his seventh and final chapter, "Last Things:
Sophocles, Euripides, Shakespeare."

Together with the play of intertextuality noted earlier, all the
touches of essentialism, universalism, psychologism, and philological acuity in these quotations do accurately indicate the tenor
of Poole's criticism. Where he is not making new vitality course in
Eliot's essayistic vein, Poole can be found on view as a skilled
exponent of a kind of close reading practiced by certain eminent
classicists now writing in English. I associate this kind of close
reading at its best with the Sophoclean and Euripidean scholar,
Bernard Knox, whose name figures in the acknowledgments of
Poole's preface, though Charles Segal and R. P. Winnington-Ingram
must also be mentioned in this connection—and Poole himself
does do so (p. viii). The focal elements of this close reading in
Poole's practice are key words of transliterated Greek, which he
tracks across the spectrum of entries in the magisterial Liddell-
Scott-Jones *Greek-English Lexicon* and through their various ren-
derings by nineteenth- and twentieth century translators. The effect
is bookish and intense, yes, but never bewildering or dull, because
Poole so consistently manages to breathe contemporary life and
spirit into a very recognizable descendant of the traditions of Renaissance humanist scholarship. One passage of illustration must
serve for many, equally characteristic:

Philoctetes' existence is checked by the seemingly incurable wound, and so are the feelings of others towards him. His existence lies at the other extreme from the proud vision of man's resourcefulness at the centre of the famous *Antigone* ode, the vision of man as *pantoporos*, 'all-resourceful' (360). There the chorus think of man as being able to deal with anything, except death. He has learned, they sing, how to save himself from *nosōn amachanōn*, 'incurable illnesses' (362). Philoctetes says that the bow and fire have helped him to manage everything, or in every way *(pant' ekporizei)*, except for his disease (*Phil.* 299). He can never make any gains on nature, for the slender advantages over his physical milieu are surrendered in tax to the insatiable greed of his disease. The images of food and feeding dramatize this vicious balance of power between man and nature. The bow allows him to feed on birds who would otherwise prey on him, but in turn he feeds the wasting disease which eats him away. The voracity of the disease is suggested by a number of adjectives: *diaboros* (97), *adēphagos* (313), *barybrōs* (694). He can never escape from his grim role in this circle of food; he can only hope to hold on to it. As the chorus imagine the nature of his existence, they call him in a memorable phrase *pantōn ammoros en biōi*, 'without a share of everything in life' (182). His life is the embodiment of handicap (pp. 191–92).

Usually Poole's transliterations are meticulous, although here *amachanōn* is a slip for *amēchanōn* in *Antigone* 362. His nuances are always as finely turned as this and always as firmly in the keeping of existential—or, as I am claiming, modal—tragic concerns. Clearly also for Poole, as for any inheritor of the Anglo-American critical practice of close reading that has too rashly been pronounced dead, the very stuff of poetry inheres in imagery and metaphoric texture. Again and again, under his scrutiny, paradoxicality or irony makes language strange, memorable, and newly potent. Here is an instance of Poole's work with Shakespeare from his discussion of *King Lear*:

Cleopatra uses a word close to Kent's "intrinse" when she addresses herself to death and appeals to the asp to ease her passage: "Come thou mortal wretch, / With thy sharp teeth this knot intrinsicate / Of life at once untie" (*Antony and Cleopatra* 5.2.301–3). Tragedy tries to do justice to the intricacy and complication of the knots which bind us to this world, this life. These knots and bonds and cords take many forms and inspire many feelings. They include, to borrow Yeats's image, the revulsion of being "fastened to a dying animal," and the serene, acquiescent wonder of Cleopatra's "knot intrinsicate." It does not need the extreme verge to make us conscious of them. There is a delighted surprise in Juliet's discovery of the "silk thread" which ties Romeo to her, and with which she could tease and torment him if she wished (*Romeo and Juliet* 2.2.181). But no cords are "too intrince to unloose" (assuming that that is what the Folio's "t'intrince" means). Tragedy affirms the ruthless truth that hearts must break, that the cords that bind people to each other and that hold the heart together must all in time fall. Exactly how they fall is our business—whether they are bitten by rats, or untied, or crack, or burst smilingly. (P. 230)

If, on first encounter, such descanting as this seems too beautifully precious and too remote from present-day priorities in Shakespeare criticism to hold attention for long, let me exhort the reader to second thoughts. Poole's dense, resonant textuality has something of value to offer on several fronts, and I will conclude by noting certain of these.

This book should prove a source of invigoration and enhanced insight to Greekless—but nonetheless serious and committed—teachers of courses or course units on tragedy in translation. Poole's discussions and bibliographical notes break a path through the morass of scholarship on Greek tragedy that should beckon many a Shakespearean to enriching collateral acquaintance. His attentiveness to variant translations also provides a surprisingly wide access to linguistic nuances of the originals. Further, although it is a truth we may be prone to forget nowadays, we have long known that close reading lends itself superbly to the classroom situation, especially when it is superbly done—as it is by Poole. He must, I imagine, fill the room where he lectures at Trinity College, Cambridge. I myself, a Renaissance specialist with a reading knowledge of classical Greek, have had more than a decade of experience in teaching classical Greek texts in translation in a core humanities context. Poole's slant on *Philoctetes* as a rewriting of *Antigone*, and on *Oedipus at Colonus* as a rewriting of *The Eumenides*, opened an abundance of fresh angles to consider for my humanities teaching. I had a similar response to his chapter on Sophoclean and Euripidean representations of Heracles, a hero turned divinity who undergoes further important transmutations in classical and Renaissance art and literature—and who, I now think, could be the focus of an interesting interdisciplinary course on either the undergraduate or the graduate level.

If the bilateral engagement of Poole's study alerts us by example to avoid an English-only narrowness in our teaching, we would do well, too, to guard against the effects of programmatic narrowness in our reading of criticism and scholarship. Poole's approach admittedly relies on critical postulates that are unfashionable today, if not discredited outright. One would never surmise the existence, let alone the character, of new historicism and cultural materialism from his pages. Yet feminist work on Shakespeare could stand to learn from work that has been done on gendering and patriarchy in Greek tragedy. Poole goes some way to demonstrate this, not only in the deft syntheses that comprise his accounts of the *Oresteia* and *Antigone*, but also in the advances he scores in discussing the respective suffering of Alcestis and Ophelia. Greek tragedy, moreover, cannot be ignored by anyone with an interest in the history of sexuality and of representations of the body, as Poole's suggestive commentaries on the Heracles plays, *Philoctetes*, *Oedipus at Colonus*, and *King Lear*, will witness.

There is, finally, a question currently under debate among Shakespeareans who profess new historicism and cultural materialism. Is tragedy a radical or a conservative production with respect to its culture? Not surprisingly for a critic who locates the "greatness" of tragedy in its "resistance to ideology" (p. 10), Poole has no truck with such terms as radical or conservative. Yet he inveighs with passion against any proclivity "to idealize the Greek theatre" by treating it as "the example of a theatre which once occupied a central and centering cultural space, a paradigm of the power of representation to hold together the most discrepant needs and motives, instinctual and intellectual, political and psychological" (p. 9). Raising a question at least as old as Ibsen's *Ghosts* or Miller's *Death of a Salesman*, Poole gives an answer that can hold its own against any formulation we presently have from respected newer critics like Catherine Belsey, Jonathan Dollimore, Jean Howard, and Louis Montrose. "To the question 'Can there be such a thing as "modern" tragedy?' the answer," says Poole, "is that *all* tragedy has to be 'modern' if it is to be tragedy at all. It must challenge the conventions which seem to control the needs and manners of the characters and society which it represents, and the means by which they are represented" (p. 12). For all the evident unmodishness of the modal approach taken in *Tragedy: Shakespeare and the Greek Example*, there are live issues on which the yield from Poole's position looks as good as any going. If the acknowledgment embarrasses, well, students of tragedy must learn to cope with unsettling truths.

Shakespeare and the Sense of Performance: Essays in the Tradition of Performance Criticism in Honor of Bernard Beckerman, edited by Marvin Thompson and Ruth Thompson

Reviewer: W. B. Worthen.

Shakespeare and the Sense of Performance honors the late Bernard Beckerman by gathering essays in performance criticism, a tradition he did much extend and elaborate. Bringing together important work by established scholars, a handy list of recommended readings, and a bibliography of Beckerman's publications, the editors have done more than assemble a commemorative volume: they have provided a useful introduction to the field of Shakespeare performance criticism that will be sought after for some time to come. Nonetheless, the diversity of the contributions raises a nagging question: just what *is* the "tradition of performance criticism"? What is its shape as discourse, what does it advance or advocate *as* criticism? What are its characteristic objects, aims, and methods? In all its variety, *Shakespeare and the Sense of Performance* fully represents the disciplinary caprice that currently afflicts "performance criticism," and that makes the sense of a common critical "tradition" somewhat premature.

In their introductory survey, "Performance Criticism From Granville-Barker to Bernard Beckerman and Beyond," the editors define Shakespeare performance criticism as interpretation availing itself of some dimension of stage performance. And in describing how performance criticism differs from exclusively textual or "literary" modes of argument, they offer a convenient overview of the state of performance criticism today. Performance criticism, they say, is

> an approach by which the text of a play is closely related to what can be known or considered about the conditions of the stage; in brief, it is a close and steady relating of the verbal and the visual drawn from both text and stage. . . . an approach that considers a play at its own moment in dramatic history . . . an approach that draws attention to

University of Delaware Press, 1989, pp. 259.

the forward movement of the play as it progresses through time. . . . an
approach that stresses the nonillusory rather than the realistic. . . .
an approach that works toward defining a sense of the authentic.
. . . more nearly capable of self-correction, in that the demands of the text
and stage are considered together. (Pp. 13–15)

In practice, then, performance criticism includes ideal "orchestrations" of possible stage activity (treating the *mise-en-scène* as an illustration of textual meanings), efforts to interpret plays in the light of Renaissance theatrical practices, the analysis of what later stage practice discloses about the text, readings of formal features of the plays in the context of their career in the theater, and possibly a more theoretical investigation of textual and performative signification itself. Although such a disparate catalogue hardly argues for a single "approach," the Thompsons' list nonetheless implies common assumptions informing the practice of performance criticism. For while it valorizes "performance," performance criticism in this collection and elsewhere surprisingly casts the stage as supplemental to the privileged designs of the text. Performance criticism can define a "sense of the authentic" precisely because it regards performance as preserving an authentic text. What is "preserved" in performance and in performance criticism, however, is manifestly not the text—which *as* text is against performance of all kinds, in criticism as well as on the stage—but rather an interpretation, a reading that has been inscribed with the mark of authenticity or fidelity. Performance criticism imitates performance in reifying the text as container, as the origin of meaning rather than as a site traced and transgressed by critical *and* theatrical strategies for producing it. To the degree that it claims for performance the authority of the text, performance criticism becomes blind to its own ideological redundancy, its unacknowledged captivity to preconceived notions of the text, notions usually derived from the textual or "literary" study it repudiates.

Of course, to describe performance criticism in this way begins to undermine its claims as a distinct and privileged "tradition." For although its tendency to mystify the practice and authority of the stage has isolated performance criticism from the insistent controversies driving contemporary criticism at large, its practice suggests that performance criticism occupies a central and visible position on our critical horizon. Regarding the dramatic text as traced by its origin "for" the stage, performance criticism falls squarely across the "humanist" / "historicist" polarities animating Renaissance studies, and literary studies more generally. Is performance a universal technique for presenting a play's authentic shape, intention, and experience? Or is it a richly localized signifying practice, one bound and defined by its relation to other modes of signification, representation, and empowerment informing cultural life? This question runs implicitly through *Shakespeare and the Sense of Performance*, and helps to organize the major lines of inquiry gathered here.

One familiar genre of performance criticism treats the relation between meanings discovered in (or attributed to) the text and their translation into the visual imagery of the stage; it is well-represented by Inga-Stina Ewbank's fine essay "From Narrative to Dramatic Language: *The Winter's Tale* and Its Source." Ewbank traces Shakespeare's alterations of Greene's *Pandosto* in *The Winter's Tale*, suggesting that Shakespeare modifies his narrative source in order to rely on specifically theatrical means to organize the play's thematic development. That Shakespeare relies on theatrical modes of signification is not surprising. But Ewbank ingeniously argues that modern productions of *The Winter's Tale* betray a similar lack of confidence in the verbal design of *their* source—Shakespeare's text—by cutting lines and scenes which, in a given "directorial conception of the play" are simply "not needed: other, nonverbal means are used to establish the play's world and define its themes and meanings" (p. 31). Shakespeare rejects Greene's "fundamental assumptions about language" (p. 39). Similarly, modern productions—Ewbank examines the 1969 and 1976 Royal Shakespeare Company versions of *The Winter's Tale*—develop a complex *mise-en-scène* that competes with or even exceeds the determinations of Shakespeare's text. That is, the stage transforms the text into the discursive structure of performance; the modern stage (*any* stage) modifies the drama in much the manner that Shakespeare modifies Greene, by representing its "source" in a different medium. In recent productions, for example, Leontes' sudden jealousy is staged through reference to behavior, psychology, or other "external means" representative of modern conceptions of character, motivation, and the self—means that necessarily work away from the "specific, self-engendered agony which Shakespeare's language creates" (p. 40). Ewbank disapproves of this recontextualizing of Shakespeare's language by modern psychology, but it's difficult to discover any alternative: is it really possible for us to enact or to interpret "character" in other than our own post-Freudian terms?

Underlying this reading of modern productions is the assumption that a determinate "meaning" can be "authentically" translated from text to performance, rather than being represented (and so altered) by the very different discourses of acting, direction, blocking, the whole form and movement of the *mise-en-scène*. To see performance as a translation of verbal imagery into stage figures, we must attend to how the stage asserts such homologies, given the extraordinary differences between reading and spectating as modes of apprehension. One "approach" to this problem is to ground the relation between staging and textual authority in the conditions of Shakespeare's stage. Reproducing those conditions might lead to a more "authentic" engagement with Shakespeare's stage practice, and so with the plays themselves. In "Stage Space and the Shakespeare Experience," J. L. Styan argues that a "target for performance criticism must be the recreation of the authentic qualities present in the play performed, recapturing its special spirit, its best style, its own mode of working on an audience" (p. 195). By considering how the "neutral" empty space of the Elizabethan thrust stage conditioned the actor's use of the drama to shape their relationship to the surrounding audience, we can assess and perhaps recover the Shakespeare experience in the theater. Styan develops a "principle of imaginative neutrality shared by author, actor, and audience," a principle governing Shakespeare's dramatic and theatrical practice: "By keeping the stage free from the clutter of place and time, we are again the sharers who enable the actors to act" (p. 197). Staging Shakespearean drama in this flexible and unlocalized manner, we are able to rediscover the "spatial relationships between actor and audience" within which the Shakespeare experience—and, presumably, an authentically Shakespearean meaning—transpires (p. 209). This sense that wherever "Shakespeare is played in the Elizabethan way, the medium is the message" (p. 209), is echoed in several essays in which the recovery of Renaissance stage conditions is said to provide a frame for contemporary understanding of the play's performative structures. Derek Peat's provocative essay, "Looking Back to Front: The View from the Lord's Room," explores how the presence of an aristocratic audience in the lords' rooms in the gallery above the stage might have shaped performance practice, forcing actors to direct their attention to the rear of the stage as well as to the front and sides, a factor that would alter movement, pacing, exits and entrances, and ultimately the audience's experience of the play. Peat brings his experience with the New Fortune Theatre in Perth, Australia to bear here, for this theater does in fact have seating that generally conforms to the placement of the lords' room, and Peat suggests some theatrical effects that become possible on a stage combining both the thrust and arena paradigms.

Yet such readings run the risk of disregarding the social functioning of theater and theatricality, the deep and complex ways in which performance is implicated in local conceptions of society, the subject, the self, human identity and action. Certainly it's not simply the presence of an audience to the rear of the stage, but the dynamic class relations that emerge between the lords' room, the performance onstage, and the audience occupying the rest of the house that would have given playing to the lords its particular resonance. Although he is deservedly excited by the theatrical possibilities opened by the New Fortune, and is eager to suggest how such staging exploits overlooked aspects of Shakespeare's dramatic style, Peat is reluctant to claim that his staging recovers the experience of the Globe. As he discreetly reminds us, the relations between actor, character, the lords, and the general audience can't be duplicated in the modern theater, since our sense of the precise social consequences and meaning of actors consorting with aristocrats in the theater is wholly altered. That is, the rhetorical function of the visual lords remains unrealized in a modern mise-en-scène, though a modern production very well might attempt to ascribe an uneven distribution of power to different parts of the house. The signifying structure can be imitated, but the meanings it once generated can no longer be produced through it, precisely because the ideological functioning of Shakespeare's stage is no longer the operation of our own.

Several of the essays train a careful eye on the details of Elizabethan staging, to ask what Shakespeare's stage can tell us about the design of his drama. Alan C. Dessen maps the challenges of such recovery as a mode of performance criticism. Although Shakespeare "crafted his plays for actors and audiences that no longer exist," we must ask "To what 'performance conditions' should we therefore be sensitive or oriented today? To the assumptions and working methods of 'our' theatres, actors, and spectators? Or to the assumptions and stage conditions that informed the original production?" (p. 132). Dessen attempts to "sidestep the reflexes

engendered by naturalism" in order to pursue a "minimalist interpretation" of the staging practice of Shakespeare's theater, using
the tomb scene of *Romeo and Juliet* as an example. He argues that
the text is unclear about the necessity for an actual tomb on the
stage, and that the "conditioned reflexes" that call for such a tomb
may "stand as a barrier between us and the fullness of meaning in
the scene as presented in the original production" (p. 137). Dessen
is surely correct in finding the densely material practices of modern directors and designers to be traced by the inheritance of theatrical naturalism. But to characterize the stage of *Romeo and Juliet*
as "minimalist" (pp. 136, 137) tends to carry the tang of Beckett's
existentially exhausted platform rather than of Shakespeare's
loaded un-locale. In recovering Shakespeare's practice, Dessen silently updates it, rekeys it to our paradigms—as, inevitably, any
"minimalist" production today would have to do.

Yet while Dessen argues that a minimalist stage best realizes
Shakespeare's drama, R. A. Foakes ("Stage Images in *Troilus and
Cressida*") describes a more sumptuous theatricality, rendered
through a host of stage structures and incidental properties. Like
Dessen, Foakes sees these features as redundant translations of the
text's requirements: "There are good reasons for believing that more
than one Greek tent was visually represented on Shakespeare's
stage and for claiming that the meaning of the action is bound up
with the use of tents, torches, groupings, and processions" (p. 160).
The relationship between Renaissance staging practices, those of
our own theaters, and the presumptive authority of the text remains
controversial: Foakes implies that our sense of "authentic" Shakespearean staging, one that resituates the text in its original theatrical environment, is unduly impoverished; Dessen argues that it is
much too rich.

Andrew Gurr argues, however, that the ideal of recovery itself
must remain confined to scholarship, and has only indirect application to performance. In "The 'State' of Shakespeare's Audiences,"
Gurr characterizes behavior—onstage and off, from addressing the
nobility to removing one's hat—as part of the densely particular
context of ideological definition, the collective sense of how individual behavior signifies. Such practices are immediate to a give
culture: "The original performance texts, all that intricate interaction between poet's mind and collective audience mind, mediated
in the familiar structures of the Globe and its players, can never be
reconstructed" (p. 174). Gurr undertakes a telling reading of mod-

ern attempts to imagine the placement of the throne of "state" on
the Elizabethan stage, and persuasively argues that our sense of
such scenes as the deposition scene in *Richard II* is utterly con-
strained by our reliance on habits of attention trained in the proscenium theater, in film, and in perspective painting, and owes little
to the social structure of the display of power known in the Renaissance. While our habits of interpretation locate such thrones at a
focal point upstage center, Gurr demonstrates that in practice the
"state" was more regularly disposed in a central location, among
its audience rather than before it. Like child companies, boy Cleo-
patras, or the lords' room, the placement of the "state" points to a
distant theatrical and social logic, one that binds performers and
audience in terms we can perhaps recover and describe, but are no
longer able to reproduce as theater.

Two essays register the impact of textual criticism on performance criticism; ironically, it's not performance criticism but textual criticism that points up the instabilities lurking in our notions
of textual authority. Philip C. McGuire's "Egeus and the Implications of Silence" considers the problem of Egeus's actions in acts
4 and 5 of *A Midsummer Night's Dream*. Is Egeus present but silent
at the final scene (as the Folio implies), or does he disappear from
the action at the end of the fourth act, as he does in the Quarto?
Egeus's absence from the festivities in the Quarto version tends to
stress his reluctance to accept Hermia's wedding. But though his
presence in act 5 might signal "reconciliation between father and
daughter, it does not mandate it" (p. 109); even Philostrate's lines
(spoken by Egeus in the Folio text) might imply merely a "dutiful
obedience to his duke," since Egeus never speaks directly to Hermia
or Lysander (p. 110). As McGuire argues, then, "The differences in
how the Quarto and the Folio present Egeus in act 5 are radically
imcompatible. There is no way to halve those differences nor to
mediate them away by conflating the two texts. Egeus cannot be
absent as well as present" (p. 111). To decide between such alternatives is to challenge "the limits of the concepts of completeness
and intentionality" as any production must do: "In this instance,
the notion of fidelity to Shakespeare's intentions does not suffice,
and as we try to come to terms with the consequences of that
insufficiency, one of our first priorities must rethink, to reenvision
the relationship between Shakespeare and those who perform what
we reflexively call *his* plays" (p. 113). In a somewhat different vein,
A. R. Braunmuller's "Editing the Staging/Staging the Editing" de-

scribes two kinds of editorial practice: "Either the editor ignores the text as a theatrical script, a guide to performers and for performance, or the editor creates a performance of the play in notes, stage directions, and other commmentary according to the theatrical conventions of the editor's own time, usually in fact the conventions of his or her youth" (p. 139). Yet Braunmuller convincingly argues that a number of textual opacities depend for their resolution on what the editor thinks is happening, both in the dramatic action and in its stage enactment. Through an incisive reading of *King John* 5.2, he demonstrates that both the text of the editors and performance on the stage are, in this sense, *productions;* their designs result more directly from their practices of representing the text than from any recoverable authorial intention.

Several essays in the collection pursue a more direct account of text and performance relations. Glynne Wickham draws on his recent experience directing the plays to develop casting and structural parallels between *Love's Labour's Lost* and *As You Like it*. A group of essays undertakes a reading of the actors'—or, more fairly in this case, the characters'—subtexts. In "Hamlet and the Audience," Ralph Berry considers the actor's use of soliloquy to establish a relationship with the audience, a relationship whose "effective reality" is changed by the disclosure of Hamlet's age in the fifth act, an alteration that Berry suggests is analogous to Hamlet's change from the "alienated individual of the first four acts" to the "public figure of the finale" (p. 28). Maurice Charney ("Asides, Soliloquies, and Offstage Speech in *Hamlet*") finds that the function of soliloquies in dramatic action is not confined to psychological expression. Both of these essays generally conform to Marvin Rosenberg's treatment of subtext in "'Subtext' in Shakespeare," for Rosenberg tends to look for moments in the play that "reveal the motivations of the main characters," as though subtext were in fact latent in the text, rather than produced through the text by actors operating in the experiential and expressive mode of modern realistic acting (p. 90). These essays regard subtextual signification— historically, the discovery of Stanislavsky and the refinement of a stage rhetoric groomed in the modern proscenium theater—as universal to acting and governed by the text, a feature of a stable "character" implicit in the text and awaiting realization on the stage.

Michael Goldman's "Performer and Role in Marlowe and Shakespeare," however, attempts more precisely to pursue the implications of subtextual reading, to define how character as performance may well violate conceptions of a text's or a character's completeness: "In the theatre, characterization is felt, not as a static array of qualities, a set of attributes, but as a process continually flowing between the person on stage and the objects and persons around him, including the audience in the theatre" (p. 91). Goldman develops an original and forthright way of reading the Stanislavskian vocabulary of performance as a means of identifying the actor's production of character in relation to the dramatic text. To actors trained to find them, subtextual objectives signaled by Marlowe's roles differ from those signaled by Shakespeare's, and from this difference arises a marked divergence in characterization and so in the audience's implication in the play: "Marlovian performance requires that the actor constantly *try on* his gestures of self-creation, and make them work in the context of trying them on, rather than hiding behind them. It might be noted for contrast that Shakespearean heroes often begin their plays by refusing this type of revelation, either by rejecting a role that is offered to them—particularly a role which offers an entry into the play's action—or by insisting on a role that muffles them up" (p. 95). For all its attention to the designs of the text, this essay attempts to characterize the relationship between the mode of criticism (regarding "character" as text) and the mode of the theater ("character" as production). Goldman offers a heuristic for conceiving the relationship between performer and role, a way of integrating the text of "character" and the performer's process of characterization.

This essay is complemented by Thomas Clayton's "'Balancing at Work': (R)evoking the Script in Performance and Criticism." Clayton also addresses the text/performance problematic, challenging our notions of "authenticity" as a category of commensurability between text and performance. Taking Michael Bogdanov's controversial 1986 RSC production of *Romeo and Juliet* as a template, Clayton avoids the question of the production's fidelity to the text in order to ask how the *mise-en-scène* establishes claims to fidelity (or, indeed, to exploitation, alienation, and so on) at all. Clayton has a talent for asking the right questions:

1. When is a "production" not a production? In theory an easy one, a riddle, even. Answer: when it's an adaptation, acknowledged or not.
2. What differentiates an "exploitation production" from an

"alienation production?" This question overlaps with the preceding, obviously, owing to the ambiguity of *production* as (a) any stage presentation, a "show"; and (b) a stage-rendition, or performance, of a particular script.
What responsibility have the producers and performers
3. to the playwright and the script?
4. to the particular audience(s) addressed?
5. to make money (for whomever)?
6. to serve the ultimate best interests of society, and/or to promote what they see as ideological imperatives? (p. 234)

Such questions are "of importance for performance *criticism* as well as for stage performance," insofar as a dense network of ideological and representational concerns is encoded by any given production. In raising these questions, Clayton asks one of the basic questions besetting performance criticism (one crucially bypassed in Hugh Richmond's companion essay "Peter Quince Directs *Romeo and Juliet*"). In making the play make sense to us, to what degree are we simply making sense, ignoring, violating, or dismissing what "seems on careful study and reflection to be 'there'" in the text (p. 237)? The question expresses the dialectic that performance criticism has yet to negotiate, namely the degree to which criticism is willing to delegitimate Shakespeare's texts as determining "meaning," in the practice both of criticism and of performance. Clayton's allegiances, in fact, seem largely with the determinable "text": "What fresh, striking, yet congenial means can I use to help the script to speak for itself and to us, our condition, and the resources of our theatre (whatever it might be) at one and the same time?" (p. 237). Yet his keen reading of recent productions of *Coriolanus* demonstrates the unavoidable necessity of reading Shakespeare in the languages of our stage: ". . . there is much to rejoice at in the developments in progress and in prospect, no archaizinng movement or pilgrimage of bardolatry, but a potential revival of major proportions with social value that is cultural not merely with a capital C and swallowed R, as in Cultchah, but in many of the best affective and cognitive modes that verbal dramatic art in action is uniquely capable of achieving" (p. 246). Although my own sense of the possibility of realizing meanings "there" in the text onstage differs from Clayton's, this is among the most scrupulous and cogent pieces of performance criticism currently available.
Finally, two essays undertake such a polemical repudiation of

critical practice that one wonders whether a tradition of performance *criticism* can in fact assimilate them. John Russell Brown's "The Nature of Speech in Shakespeare's Plays" invites us to consider "speech" as a mediating term between text and performance, Speech "identifies an element of Shakespeare's plays that is close to the text and yet also releases a seemingly unfettered theatrical life" (p. 49), a life that is, according to Brown, either ignored or crippled by text-based criticism. Even semiotics, which asks how the words on the page come to signify in the stage events that articulate them, seems to hold little promise. Granted, semiotic studies of theater are often glutted with "specialized jargon, parenthetical references, and exhaustive enumeration" (p. 51), but such paraphernalia is part of a laudable effort to avoid the undisciplined impressionism that afflicts most discussions of theatrical process. Indeed, given the breathtaking difficulty of describing how the theater subjects the actor's (or the spectator's) charismatic immediacy to encoding, we might well find Brown's informal consideration of "what happens when actors assume the personages of the drama, perform their actions and speak their words" to be disappointing as well. "Reading the signs in a text is not enough" (p. 55), but to read acting (or to act oneself) without attending to the signifying practice that determines textual signs *as* behavioral signs seems not to be enough either—at least as far as criticism or pedagogy is concerned. Brown calls for Shakespeare critics and students to "observe actors at work and learn about the nature of acting"; one could hardly disagree (p. 52). We should pause, though, to ask what we are looking at and for when we are observing "the nature of acting." *Is* there a "nature" to acting, one that implies the continuity of human experience, subjectivity, and expression from, say, Shakespeare's era to the present day? Or is the diversity of both dramatic and acting style that's visible in the history of the stage evidence for the continual transformation of such a "nature"? Are dramatic texts haunted by a privileged mode of representation ("the nature of acting"), a means of realizing their immanent textual significance that avoids the complex negations engrained in representation itself? Not knowing exactly "how Elizabethan actors practiced their art" (p. 52) is certainly a problem, but naturalizing acting to the practices of the modern stage is a greater one, a problem that can't be shaken off by saying that "modern actors are responding to qualities inherent in Shakespeare's text; if they did not, they would find acting in his plays a troublesome labor and not a great pleasure" (p. 58). Perhaps this is true, but it's hard to tell whether actors are responding to "qualities inherent in Shakespeare's text," or to the facility of their own technique, which—in a climate of Shakespearean performance preoccupied with "*a sense of the authentic*"—will necessarily develop its own strategies for claiming fidelity to those inherent qualities. Brown clearly demonstrates that the laboratory of the stage can lead us to a richer understanding of Shakespearean drama. Nonetheless, his opposing of criticism to performance prevents us from conceiving performance *as* criticism, as a practice of acting and direction that is precisely responsible for determining how our sense of "the Shakespeare experience" emerges.

Homer Swander's "Shakespeare and Beckett: What the Words Know" takes a similarly exclusive line on the relationship between criticism and stage production. Swander asks how the texts of plays by Beckett and Shakespeare instigate "a necessary and seamless theatrical process" (p. 62) for their own stage production. Many plays certainly contain implied movements, gestures, stage relationships, and so on; but such events are often as likely to be immanent in a given theater's interpretive practice as they are to lie in the text itself. Performance criticism ought to rip such seams open, to reveal how our practices of reading and criticism and acting and directing operate on and through the text. Such criticism would necessarily refuse a privileged status to the stage as a venue for textual realization. The point of performance criticism would be to articulate the systems within which the Shakespearean text is produced, as criticism, as stage performance, but also as a signifier in advertising, as a cultural commodity, as a pedagogical practice, and so on. Swander asks "What do we do with words that were initially conceived and arranged to function only through performance? How do we enter into, get inside, a set of words that from first to last, in *one continuous living process*, exists only for that ultimate moment when—physically, noisily, in front of and with an audience—they play their role in defining space and silence?" (p. 65). Shakespeare's texts are no longer reducible (if they ever were) to Shakespeare's intentions or to their initial functioning in the Globe. Not only is his theater and its culture lost to us, the plays have become part of the text of our world. Unless we can regard our own stage (and critical) practice as historically contingent, we gain insight neither to Shakespeare nor to ourselves. We simply replicate ourselves unthinkingly in the rich, hollow words of our master playwright.

What is the state of performance criticism? To judge by *Shakespeare and the Sense of Performance*, it remains a practical affair, concerned with developing interpretations rather than with a theory of interpretation as such. The rudimentary character of the hermeneutics of text and performance in Shakespeare performance criticism is troubling only because such signal progress has been made in related areas: anthropology, film, performance theory, modern drama and dramatic theory, critical studies of the figuration of the body, and so on, to say nothing of the new historicism's interest in theatrical and cultural representation. In part, this situation may arise from the complexity of ways in which the text of "Shakespeare" (which includes but exceeds Shakespearean drama and theater) operates for us. Oddly enough, the possibility of a tradition of Shakespeare performance criticism suggests a conservative impulse, a desire to preserve Shakespeare's texts from theatrical violation. Although there is performance criticism of, say, Jonson or Congreve or Shaw, the text/performance dialectic seem less pressing with other playwrights, perhaps because their plays are less fully and foundationally encoded in the text of our culture. Only Beckett has attracted a similarly rich and diverse body of performance criticism; I need only mention the fact that before his death Beckett had directed most of his plays to suggest the extent to which questions of textual authority and authorial intention suffuse this work. Of course, it's unfair to ask *Shakespeare and the Sense of Performance* to do what the discipline itself has yet to do—articulate in a more thoroughgoing and substantial way the relationship between the paradigms of criticism and the practices of the stage. As it stands, page after page, essay after essay, are distinguished by energy and reflection, the informed and vigorous exercise of intelligence. Perhaps these qualities best describe the collection, and best commemorate Bernard Beckerman. As Ann Jennalie Cook remarked at the close of the eulogy she delivered at the 1986 Shakespeare Association meetings in Montreal, "Bernie was always so solidly *there* that it is hard to realize he is gone. But he is" (p. 251). *Shakespeare and the Sense of Performance* provides a fitting complement to Beckerman's own wide-ranging work in drama and theater, and in that company provides an elegant and lasting tribute.

Shakespeare's Clown: Actor and Text in the Elizabethan Playhouse by David Wiles

Reviewer: Matthew H. Wikander

"It never was any great ambition in me, to be in this kind voluminously read," Thomas Heywood wrote to the reader of *The English Traveller* (1633). With "either an entire hand, or at least a maine finger" in over two hundred plays, Heywood near the end of his long career felt a need to apologize for his lack of interest in their printed texts. For him, the proper place for the transmission of dramatic texts to their public is the theater, and the proper mechanism, performance. Heywood's attitude by 1633 had been challenged if not displaced by Ben Jonson's aggressive assertion of the dramatist's right to be considered a poet and to present his plays directly to a public, untainted by the distortions of performance, through the medium of the printed book. Lumping Shakespeare together with Heywood and Dekker in "right happy and copious industry," John Webster reveals a rift between playwrights who enjoyed the collaborative give-and-take of the theater and those who preferred their plays to be received as poetic works.

Shakespeare's lack of authorial attention to the plays published in his lifetime (as opposed to his careful preparation of nondramatic poems for the press) testifies that he, if not happy, was at least willing to permit the company he participated in to own and control the texts of his plays, and to rely on actors for their transmission to the public. As Timothy Murray has argued, Ben Jonson looks ahead as he promulgates "allegories of genius" through his printed works. But Shakespeare, David Wiles reminds us in *Shakespeare's Clown*, "was a commercially minded actor-manager rather than a classically trained man of letters, and his art retained its roots in the popular tradition" (ix). When Hamlet complains that clowns should speak no more than is set down for them, he speaks in character, as a university-educated prince, not as a mouthpiece for Shakespeare's own views.

David Wiles's book is both a historical investigation of the clowns

Cambridge University Press, 1987, pp. xiv + 223.

who belonged to Shakespeare's company and an argument that the
clown, as a link back to the older traditions of popular theater, was
an essential part of the theatrical experience of a Shakespearean
play, now lost to us as we read the plays on the page and even
as we see them on our modern stages. Wiles establishes that an
Elizabethan professional acting company would contain a clown
who was usually a star entertainer in his own right. Will Kemp,
Robert Armin and their counterparts in other companies were solo
comic performers; they owed a profound professional debt to Richard Tarlton, who perfected the role of the Elizabethan clown out of
three traditions of medieval entertainer: "the professional minstrel,
the amateur lord of misrule, and the Vice" (p. 19). The third chapter, "Kemp: A Biography," traces what we know of Kemp's career
and of the character he played in his solo turns. Having established
the clown's relative autonomy in the theater company and sketched
out a portrait of Kemp, Wiles is ready at the end of the third chapter
to argue for a view of playwriting in the Elizabethan theater as
collaborative. "Though Kemp had to adapt himself to the demands
of writers," he submits, "it is no less certain that writers had to
adapt themselves to the demands of Kemp" (p. 42).

The heart of the book is devoted to demonstrating that Kemp
regularly had a role in the plays Shakespeare wrote during Kemp's
years with the company and that these roles accommodated the
demands of Kemp's professional status. The testimony of antitheat-
rical propagandists and that of neoclassical elitists agree that Elizabethan plays frequently ended with a jig. Wiles adds the
observation that the Shakespearean comedies in which Kemp
would have appeared end without a marriage for the clown. This
arrangement freed Kemp, he claims, to enact a comic marriage jig
after the play: "the jig purveys anarchy to counterbalance the play's
creation of moral order. . . . The play culminates in the ceremony
of betrothal or marriage, and the jig represents the physical consummation that follows" (p. 56). Kemp's jigs, in effect, helped to
shape the romantic comedies, and when we disregard their presence because they were not written down, we lose the full complexity of Elizabethan dramatic art. "Kemp's departure from the
Chamberlain's men," Wiles continues, "marked a turning point in
Shakespearean dramaturgy" (p. 57).

Documenting the roles that Kemp was known to have played and
extrapolating from them a profile of the "conventions governing
Kemp's scripted roles" (chapter 8), Wiles proposes that the part of

Falstaff "was indeed a part written for Kemp" (p. 116). Kemp's withdrawal from the Lord Chamberlain's Men in the summer of 1599 coincides with the disappearance of Falstaff from *Henry V;* the dancer's false promise at the end of *2 Henry IV,* while it may reflect thematically Rumor's prologue, may also reflect a change in company personnel. "Kemp and Falstaff are one and the same," Wiles argues (p. 120). The traditional elements of Falstaff (his identification with the Vice and the lord of misrule), his skill in improvising and entertaining his mates, and even his bulk are equally characteristic of Kemp in all of his roles. The dancer who speaks the epilogue to *2 Henry IV* is a heavy man, but light on his feet: "with Kemp/Falstaff's dismissal by Hal, and his reappearance in the jig, the conventional structure of comedy is restored" (p. 129). Wiles does not pursue the identification of Falstaff with Rumor (he has, after all, a whole school of tongues in his belly) proposed by the language of the play. The notion that Kemp as Rumor might have introduced the play and that Kemp as dancer might have concluded it, thus framing Kemp as Falstaff within it, would fit nicely with Wiles's analysis of the play's different theatrical styles and worlds. "Hal and Falstaff do not exist as characters within a single fictive universe," for the new aesthetic of the self-contained role governs only Hal's part; thus the rejection scene is made complex as "the pain of Falstaff is simultaneously the mirth of Kemp" (p. 132).

Kemp's departure from the company led not only to the narrated death of Falstaff in *Henry V,* Wiles suggests, but also to the assumption of many aspects of the clown's part by Burbage as Hamlet, Opehlia's "only jig-maker," and a disruptive audience-member at his own play. Robert Armin, who succeeded Kemp with Shakespeare's company, specialized not in jigs and physical comedy but in riddles and singing. "Armin was obsessed with natural fools because he himself, physically though not mentally, *was* a natural fool," Wiles insists, noting the presence of deformity in many of Armin's known roles (p. 148). In addition to parts regularly seen as Armin's (Feste in *Twelfth Night,* the Fool in *Lear*) Wiles discovers Armin's grotesque body in the Thersites of *Troilus and Cressida,* Casca in *Julius Caesar,* and Menenius in *Coriolanus.* Cloten in *Cymbeline,* unsuited for comparison with Posthumus, becomes even more so when played by a stunted fool with a big head. Caliban is Armin as well, contrasted in his natural deformity with Trinculo, the professional fool. Autolycus in *The Winter's Tale,* likened by Simon Forman to a pixie, is Armin again in stature and in calling.

Unlike Kemp, Armin rarely spoke directly to the audience; rather, as Feste demonstrates, he "talks to his own alter ego" (p. 161). The convention has changed: where Kemp dominated the stage and controlled his own subplot, Armin functioned best as member of a group, completing, frequently, "a balanced threesome of fools," pointing up the foolishness of others. A change of dramaturgy reflects a change of personnel, and the change of personnel reflects a larger change, as the theater moves closer to the neoclassical, illusionistic aesthetic of Hamlet and Ben Jonson.

This aesthetic, insistent upon the unity of the text and the authority of the author, has long governed criticism of the Elizabethan drama, despite recent challenges like the canonization of two versions of *King Lear*. Ben Jonson's contention that playwrights, not playhouses, should have custody over plays, however, was exceptional in its time. Wiles proposes, alternatively, the model of Bertolt Brecht. Collaboration with actors, for Brecht, represents a vital component of shaping the dramatic text; performance is the text's primary means of transmission to an audience. The reader of Brecht's drama must turn not only to the script of the play, but to the *Modell-buch* with its photographs and detailed notes of production. Sketching out a series of paradigmatic oppositions in Brechtian fashion ("art" and "philistinism," "plays" and "games") Wiles suggests that "Shakespeare" and "bears foaming at the mouth" are similarly arbitrary opposites (p. 167). William Kemp and Harry Hunks (a celebrated bear) represent not a popular aspect of Elizabethan theater to be deplored, but an essential feature of its integrity and health.

Brecht admired Karl Valentin and Charlie Chaplin; Beckett's clowns owe much to Chaplin and Buster Keaton. The idea that these serious playwrights incorporated the jokes of popular entertainers into their works does not shock or dismay audiences or readers. A modern playwright might incorporate in a script a bit of business improvised by a skillful actor; it is not particularly revolutionary to suggest that Shakespeare might have done so too. Brecht's collective and collaborative schemes of authorship can be marginalized as aspects of his Marxism or his quirky personality. Critical orthodoxy draws the line at seeing Shakespeare's plays as collaborative, although it is willing to place his theater (and Heywood happily in it) at the margins of his culture. The wooden O, equally useful for bearbaiting, is there to be transcended. Brecht ridiculed the idea of transcendence, smoked cigars in theaters, and talked about drama with a boxer named Samson-Körner; next door to Shakespeare's theater a bear named Sampson performed in his pit. Brecht carried over the excitement he found in working with boxers, clowns, and cabaret artists into his discussions of the Elizabethan theater, where the actors and playwrights worked together, engaging like Galileo and Bacon in revolutionary experiments under the open sky.

"A collaborative is a group of people doing what you tell them to," a disgruntled friend of Brecht's is reputed to have complained. David Wiles's book is an attempt to remind us that Shakespeare, too, functioned in an environment where the lines of authority were subject to negotiation. That he could encompass the genius of Will Kemp in the role of Falstaff and digest Armin's songs and riddles into Lear's fool says something about Shakespeare's infinite capacity as a man of the theater. Wiles's book offers a salutary reminder that theater is an art restricted by possibilities and a place inhabited by strong personalities with conflicting ambitions. Attempting to reconstruct what Kemp and Shakespeare generated as they worked together, Wiles has produced a necessarily speculative but intriguing glimpse of one aspect of collaboration in the Elizabethan playhouse.